The Morphosyntax of Gender

OXFORD STUDIES IN THEORETICAL LINGUISTICS

GENERAL EDITORS
David Adger and Hagit Borer, Queen Mary, University of London

ADVISORY EDITORS
Stephen Anderson, Yale University; Daniel Büring, University of California, Los Angeles; Nomi Erteschik-Shir, Ben-Gurion University; Donka Farkas, University of California, Santa Cruz; Angelika Kratzer, University of Massachusetts, Amherst; Andrew Nevins, University College London; Christopher Potts, Stanford University; Barry Schein, University of Southern California; Peter Svenonius, University of Tromsø; Moira Yip, University College London

RECENT TITLES

For a complete list of titles published and in preparation for the series, see pp 287–8.

The Morphosyntax of Gender

RUTH KRAMER

OXFORD
UNIVERSITY PRESS

OXFORD
UNIVERSITY PRESS

Great Clarendon Street, Oxford OX2 6DP
United Kingdom

Oxford University Press is a department of the University of Oxford.
It furthers the University's objective of excellence in research, scholarship,
and education by publishing worldwide. Oxford is a registered trade mark of
Oxford University Press in the UK and in certain other countries

The moral rights of the author have been asserted

First Edition published in 2015

Impression: 1

Published in the United States of America by Oxford University Press
198 Madison Avenue, New York, NY 10016, United States of America

British Library Cataloguing in Publication Data
Data available

Library of Congress Control Number: 2014958986

ISBN 978–0–19–967993–5 (Hbk)
ISBN 978–0–19–967994–2 (Pbk)

Printed and bound by
CPI Group (UK) Ltd, Croydon CR0 4YY

Contents

General preface

The theoretical focus of this series is on the interfaces between subcomponents of the human grammatical system and the closely related area of the interfaces between the different subdisciplines of linguistics. The notion of "interface" has become central in grammatical theory (for instance, in Chomsky's Minimalist Program) and in linguistic practice: work on the interfaces between syntax and semantics, syntax and morphology, phonology and phonetics, etc. has led to a deeper understanding of particular linguistic phenomena and of the architecture of the linguistic component of the mind/brain.

The series covers interfaces between core components of grammar, including syntax/morphology, syntax/semantics, syntax/phonology, syntax/pragmatics, morphology/phonology, phonology/phonetics, phonetics/speech processing, semantics/pragmatics, and intonation/discourse structure, as well as issues in the way that the systems of grammar involving these interface areas are acquired and deployed in use (including language acquisition, language dysfunction, and language processing). It demonstrates, we hope, that proper understandings of particular linguistic phenomena, languages, language groups, or inter-language variations all require reference to interfaces.

The series is open to work by linguists of all theoretical persuasions and schools of thought. A main requirement is that authors should write so as to be understood by colleagues in related subfields of linguistics and by scholars in cognate disciplines.

Gender features stand at the intersection of syntax, semantics, and morphology, and how their role is divided between these three domains has long been a puzzle. In this monograph, Ruth Kramer develops a new theory of the morphosyntax of gender, arguing that gender features appear not on lexical roots or on elements high in the structure of noun phrases, but on the nominalizing head *n*. She defends a particular theory of gender features based on the notions of interpretability and bivalence, and shows how this theory predicts the attested typological variation in gender systems, drawing on fascinating data from a number of lesser studied languages. Overall, the book proposes the first comprehensive theory of gender as a phi-feature in generative linguistics.

David Adger
Hagit Borer

Acknowledgments

This project has been through various stages of development for many years, and it is a challenging task to acknowledge all of the generous people who have assisted along the way. Nevertheless, I will do my best since they all greatly deserve it.

The core of this book originates in my dissertation (Kramer 2009), and I can never thank my committee enough for their help and insights: Sandra Chung, Jorge Hankamer, and James McCloskey. I also thank my peers at Santa Cruz for their feedback and encouragement (especially the members of the Morphology Reading Group): Vera Gribanova, Boris Harizanov, Mark Norris, Kyle Rawlins, Anie Thompson, and Matthew Tucker.

I have presented portions of this book at the University of Pennsylvania, Yale University, the ST@R reading group at Rutgers University, the syntax–semantics reading group at New York University, the University of Delaware, the University of California, Santa Cruz, and George Mason University. I have also presented portions of it at the following conferences/workshops: the 15th International Morphology Meeting, the 30th West Coast Conference on Formal Linguistics, the 43rd and 45th Annual Conferences on African Linguistics, and the workshop on "Allomorphy: Its Logic and Limitations." I thank the audiences at all of these presentations for their invaluable feedback and suggestions, especially Pranav Anand, Karlos Arregi, Mark Baker, Ricardo Bermúdez-Otero, Amy Rose Deal, Marijke de Belder, Rose-Marie Déchaine, David Embick, Jane Grimshaw, Richard Kayne, Jean Lowenstamm, Andrew Nevins, Elizabeth Ritter, Peter Svenonius, Martina Wiltschko, Matt Wolf, and Raffaella Zanuttini.

Portions of Chapters 2 and 3 appear in "Gender in Amharic: a morphosyntactic approach to natural and grammatical gender," *Language Sciences* 43: 102–15. Portions of Chapters 3 and 8 are to appear in "A split analysis of plurality: evidence from Amharic," to be published in *Linguistic Inquiry*. I thank the four anonymous reviewers of these papers for comments and suggestions that have been integrated into this book as well. I also thank the members of the Seminar on Morphosyntax at Georgetown in Spring 2014 for reading "Gender in Amharic" and offering useful feedback: Melanie Ashkar, Colleen Diamond, Ava Irani, Morgan Rood, Brett Sutton, and Katherine Vadella.

I turn next to those who engaged with the book as a manuscript. First credit goes to Mark Norris, for reading almost the entire manuscript with incredible speed and cheer, and for assisting with Icelandic and Estonian data. I am also deeply grateful to the following readers/commenters on portions of the manuscript: Azeb Amha, Peter K. Austin, Joshua Birchall, Héctor Campos, Sandra Chung, Donka Farkas,

Christopher Green, Vera Gribanova, Boris Harizanov, Heidi Harley, Bryce Huebner, Donna Lardiere, Eric Mathieu, Jason Merchant, Francesca Merlan, Doris Payne, Paul Portner, Conor Quinn, James Rupp, Angela Terrill, and Katherine Vadella. None of these people are responsible for errors of fact or interpretation.

I am also profoundly thankful to all the consultants whose insight has shaped this work: Senayit Ghebrehiywet, Girma Demeke, Bekale Seyum, Betselot Teklu, Hileena Eshetu, Harya Tarakegn, Mehret Getachew Tadesse, Meriem Tikue, Azeb Amha, Marta Baffy, Héctor Campos, Angela Donate Velasco, Donka Farkas, Paula Ganga, Nagarajan Selvanathan, and Esther Surenthiraraj.

Additionally, I am grateful for the research support that I have received during the creation of this book. I thank Georgetown University for a Junior Faculty Research Fellowship and Summer Academic Grant that supported several months of writing, and I also thank Carole Sargent and the book club members of Summer 2014 for helping me keep up the momentum. Credit is also due for research assistance to Lindley Winchester, Morgan Rood, Laura Siebecker, and Lauren McGarry.

Finally, this book could never have been completed without the patient support of my family and of Bryce Huebner. This book is dedicated to them.

List of figures and tables

Figures

Tables

List of abbreviations

1	1st person
2	2nd person
3	3rd person
ABS	absolutive
ACC	accusative case
ACT	action particle
ADJ	adjectivalizer
AFFIRM	affirmative
AN(IM)	animate
ANA	anaphoric
ANT	anterior verb suffix
AUX	auxiliary
CAUS	causative
CL	classifier
COLL	collective
COP	copula
D	determiner
DAT	dative
DEF	definite marker
DIM(IN)	diminutive
DIS	distant demonstrative
DM	Distributed Morphology
DUR	durative
EMPH	emphatic particle
ERG	ergative case
F	feminine
F/N	feminine or neuter
FEM	female natural gender
FOC	focus
GC	gender clitic
GEN	genitive case

HAB	habitual
HON	honorific
IMP	imperative
INAN	inanimate
INF	infinitive
INFL	inflection
INT	intensive
LOC	locative case or locative marker
M	masculine
M/F	masculine or feminine
M/N	masculine or neuter
N	neuter
n	'little' n, nominalizing head
NEG	negation
NF	non-feminine
NMLZ	nominalizer
NOM	nominative case
NONFIN	non-finite
.O	object agreement/marker
PAST	past tense
PC	past continuous
PL	plural
POSS	possessive
POSS.ART	possessive article
PP	past punctual
PREP	preposition
PRES	present tense
PROD	product verbalizer
PROP	proprietive case
RED	reduplicant
REFL	reflexive
RF	realis future
RP/P	realis past/present
S	singular
.S	subject agreement/marker

STA	stative
SUP	supine
T	tense
TOP	topic
TV	theme vowel
VBLZ	verbalizer
VICIN	vicinity

1

Introduction

1.1 Major themes

Gender is regularly defined as the sorting of nouns into two or more classes, as reflected in agreement morphology on determiners, adjectives, verbs and other syntactic categories (e.g. Hockett 1958: 231, Fodor 1959: 2, Corbett 1991: 1, Comrie 1999: 457, Matasović 2004: 19–20). Consider the Amharic examples in (1)ab.

(1) a. ya   säw dägg näw   b. yatʃtʃ   set   dägg nat
        that.M man good be.3MS.S   that.F   woman good be.3FS.S
        'That man is good.'   'That woman is good.'   (Leslau 1995: 66, 67)

In (1)a, the demonstrative is *ya* and the copular verb is *näw*, whereas in (1)b, the demonstrative is *yatʃtʃ* and the copular verb is *nat*. Since the demonstrative and the copular verb formally differ depending only on the head noun of the subject, it is clear that *säw* 'man' belongs to one gender (masculine) and *set* 'woman' belongs to another gender (feminine).[1]

Gender has been called "a time-honored subject of linguistics" (Unterbeck and Rissanen 2000: ix), and Matasović (2004: 13) dubs it "the only grammatical category that ever evoked passion." Corbett calls gender the "most puzzling of the grammatical categories" (Corbett 1991: 1). Unsurprisingly then, there are rich and significant literatures on the sociolinguistics of gender (see e.g. Hellinger and Bußmann 2001), the acquisition and processing of gender (see e.g. Franceschina 2005), the typology of gender systems (see e.g. Corbett 1991), and the diachronic development and loss of gender systems (see e.g. Matasović 2004).

However, there has been less research on the morphological and syntactic aspects of gender. There are clear, thorough descriptions of gender assignment in many languages (see e.g. Corbett 1991: chs 2 and 3), but the most basic questions for a morphosyntactic analysis of gender assignment remain controversial: where is gender located in the hierarchical structure? How is gender assignment

---

[1] See Chapter 4 for a refinement of this definition of gender.

The Morphosyntax of Gender. First Edition. Ruth Kramer.
© Ruth Kramer 2015. Published 2015 by Oxford University Press.

morphosyntactically accomplished? Is gender lexically listed on a noun, with relatively little role for the syntax to play? Or is there a gender projection in the syntax that combines with nouns to assign gender? (And if so, what is that projection?)

Additionally, the morphosyntactic literature on gender tends to downplay the relationship between natural gender (gender based on some semantic property, e.g. male/female, animate/inanimate) and (what I will call) arbitrary gender, that is, gender assigned without reference to any semantic property. The arbitrary gender assigned to a noun often varies across languages. For example, the noun 'morning' has a different gender in French (masculine), Hausa (feminine), and Russian (neuter).

(2) a. **French**   b. **Hausa**   c. **Russian**
    matin   sāfiyā   utro
    morning.M   morning.F   morning.N
    'morning'   'morning' (Newman 2000: 204)   'morning'

There is nothing about the meaning of 'morning' that requires it to have a particular gender in any of these languages; its gender is assigned arbitrarily. However, there are other nouns whose meaning does determine their gender in many languages. For example, the word for 'father' is masculine in all three languages, because nouns that refer to male entities are (generally) masculine in all of these languages.

(3) a. **French**   b. **Hausa**   c. **Russian**
    père   ùbā   otec
    father.M   father.M   father.M
    'father'   'father' (Newman 2000: 201)   'father'   (Corbett 1991: 34)

Gender assignment therefore operates in two dimensions: gender is assigned according to some natural/semantic property of the real world, or it is assigned arbitrarily. In many languages, gender is assigned *only* according to some natural property of the noun (e.g. Dieri (Chapter 5), Mangarayi (Chapter 7), Tamil (Arden 1942, Asher 1985)).

Nevertheless, not all morphosyntactic approaches to gender treat natural gender as central to the analysis; many either set natural gender aside, or "convert" it via a rule into the same type of feature as arbitrary gender. This may be because the morphosyntactic relationship between arbitrary gender and natural gender has been explored for only a few related languages which all have gender systems heavily based on arbitrary gender (e.g. Spanish, Italian, Greek). It remains unclear how both types of gender are expressed via the same morphological resources, whether they have the same syntactic location, and even whether they use the same set of features.

This book aims to fill these gaps in the morphosyntactic literature. I develop a theory of gender assignment that specifies the locus of gender features in the syntax as the nominalizing head *n*. A handful of previous analyses have proposed that gender is on *n* (see e.g. Kihm 2005, Ferrari 2005, Lecarme 2002, Lowenstamm 2008, Acquaviva 2009, Kramer 2009), but I significantly expand on these approaches. I adduce evidence for a *n* locus from a detailed case study of Amharic, which furnishes unique evidence for a *n* locus because of its unusual plural system. I argue that gender features are never on Num by studying two cases of gender switch in the plural (Somali and Romanian), and offer further evidence that gender is on *n* by examining the relationship between gender and nominalization, and gender and declension class, cross-linguistically.

None of the previous *n*-analyses systematically address the question of natural versus arbitrary gender, so in this book, I connect the *n*-based analysis explicitly to the two different types of gender: natural gender is an interpretable feature on *n*, whereas arbitrary gender is an uninterpretable version of the same feature on *n*. I develop a theory of gender features on *n*, focusing on how the gender features in the syntax map onto the gender features relevant for morphological exponence. Building on this approach to gender features, I make positive and negative predictions about possible gender systems, and show that they are borne out. Overall, the book provides, within the Chomskyan tradition, the first large-scale, cross-linguistically oriented analysis of the morphosyntax of natural and arbitrary gender.

In the remainder of the Introduction, I first provide some background on the frameworks adopted in the book (Section 1.2). I discuss several topics that the book will not address (and why not) in Section 1.3, and then preview the main claims of the book and the contents of each chapter in Section 1.4.

1.2 Frameworks: Minimalism and Distributed Morphology

1.2.1 Setting the scene

Because this book is an investigation of the morphosyntax of gender, it is necessary to identify the frameworks adopted for syntax and morphology. I take a theoretical approach that is generative and broadly Chomskyan, adopting Minimalist syntax and Distributed Morphology. There are numerous influential approaches to gender both outside of the generative tradition (see e.g. Lakoff 1987) and in non-Chomskyan frameworks (Network Morphology: Corbett and Fraser 2000a, 2000b, Evans et al. 2002; HPSG: Wechsler and Zlatić 2003; Optimality Theory: Rice 2006; and many others). Nevertheless, I take a generative Chomskyan approach for several reasons.

First of all, there is not a universally accepted morphosyntax for gender within the Chomskyan tradition. Consequently, the book aims to develop a benchmark analysis for gender, and to unite (or find reasons to set aside) previous Chomskyan analyses. Since a Chomskyan approach is the mainstream within generative linguistics, the lack of a standard analysis of gender is striking. Moreover, there has been less cross-linguistic work done within the Chomskyan tradition on gender. The main languages investigated have been from the Indo-European and Bantu families, but little attention has been paid to languages like Amharic (Chapters 2 and 3), Dieri (Chapter 5), Wari' (Chapter 7), and Lavukaleve (Chapter 7). This book aims to bring a larger span of data to inform a Chomskyan approach to gender.

Additionally, one of the most fundamental questions in a generative syntactic framework is the relationship between the lexicon and the syntax. Is there a very powerful lexicon containing word-related idiosyncratic information as well as having a generative capacity (lexicalism), or are the capabilities and information associated with the lexicon distributed throughout the grammar (Distributed Morphology)? Gender assignment seems like a quintessentially "lexical" phenomenon, since it can be very arbitrary. However, the analysis developed in this book provides a way to assign gender without a traditional lexicon. As a result, the analysis contributes to the development of linguistic theory in that it provides support for a non-lexical approach to morphology.

A final, more practical motivation for using Minimalism and Distributed Morphology is that they are mutually consistent. Their assumptions do not conflict, and they are capable of being used in tandem without much tension. This is not necessarily true for other theories of morphology, especially lexicalist theories since later Minimalism has moved away from lexicalism (Chomsky 2000, 2001, 2004).

Overall, I do not use this book to argue that a Chomskyan approach to gender is best among all other approaches—it is merely the framework that I assume for the investigation. However, hopefully, the explicit proposals here will serve as a good starting point for cross-framework comparison. In the remainder of this section, I present the details of my theoretical assumptions.

1.2.2 *A little Minimalism, a lot of DM*

On the syntactic side, I assume the conventional Principles and Parameters approach to syntax, adopting the Minimalism of Chomsky (2000, 2001, 2004) in particular. I rely on the phase as a cyclic unit in Chapter 10, and it is largely explained within that chapter. I also occasionally mention the syntactic relation Agree, i.e. a relation between a probe with unvalued features and a goal in its c-command domain with valued features, whereby the probe's features are valued by the goal (Chomsky 2001, Pesetsky and Torrego 2007). However, I do not assume that DP-internal agreement (also called "concord") is necessarily accomplished via Agree (see e.g. Norris 2014 for a non-Agree approach to concord). Accordingly, I often refer to any agreement relation informally as just agreement, not the Agree relation in particular.

In general, I use theory-neutral terminology from Corbett (2006a) to describe the participants in an agreement relationship. The agreement *controller* is the element that determines the agreement; it is born into the derivation already containing the

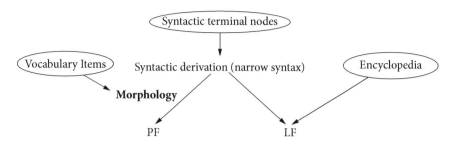

FIGURE 1.1 The DM Model of the grammar (inspired by Harley and Noyer 1999: 3, Embick and Noyer 2007: 22, Kelly 2013: 12)

relevant features. The agreement *target* is the element whose form is determined by agreement; its features are valued or altered through agreement. For example, in (1)b, *set* 'woman' is the agreement controller, and the demonstrative and the copular verbs are agreement targets.

Because it is less well known than Minimalism, and more prominent in the argumentation of the book, I will spend the majority of this section outlining Distributed Morphology (henceforth DM; Halle and Marantz 1993). DM started to be developed as a theory of morphology in the early 1990s. Seminal works include Halle (1990), Halle and Marantz (1993, 1994), Harley and Noyer (1999), Embick and Noyer (2001), Embick and Noyer (2007), and Harley (2014), and many others.

Distributed Morphology maintains that there is no centralized lexicon. Instead, word formation occurs either in the syntax via head movement or at PF via morphology-specific operations. The information contained in the lexicon in other theories (phonological information, semantic information, category, and syntactic features) is 'distributed' throughout the grammar in various lists. Figure 1.1 shows when these lists are accessed, and it also illustrates the DM model of the grammar. The lists are in circles.

Starting at the top, there is a list of syntactic terminal nodes which are manipulated by operations during the syntactic derivation. The terminal nodes are bundles of morphosyntactic features (including category), and these bundles lack any kind of morphophonology in the syntax (this ensures "Phonology-Free Syntax"; cf. Zwicky and Pullum 1986). The feature bundles are often called "morphemes" in DM, and throughout the book, I use the terms "feature bundle" and "morpheme" interchangeably.

After the syntactic derivation is complete, the derivation is sent to Phonological Form and Logical Form. Logical Form operates according to standard formal semantic assumptions (compositionally, with operations like quantifier raising etc.). The Encyclopedia is another one of the DM lists that houses information that used to be in the lexicon—in the case of the Encyclopedia, it is the semantic information. As Harley (2014) phrases it, the Encyclopedia provides "instructions for interpreting

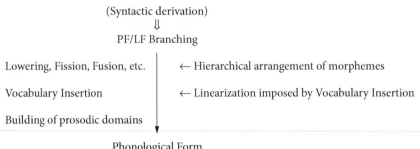

(Syntactic derivation)
⇓
PF/LF Branching

Lowering, Fission, Fusion, etc.   ← Hierarchical arrangement of morphemes

Vocabulary Insertion   ← Linearization imposed by Vocabulary Insertion

Building of prosodic domains

Phonological Form

FIGURE 1.2 The architecture of PF (inspired by Embick and Noyer 2001: fig. 1)

terminal nodes in context" (p. 228). For example, the Encyclopedia contains the instructions to interpret the root √CAT in a nominal context as a "feline mammal, four legs, meows, subject of many internet memes, etc."

Turning now to the PF branch, "Morphology" is the subcomponent of the grammar where morphological operations occur. One of these operations is Vocabulary Insertion, whereby syntactic feature bundles are given morphophonological content, i.e. they are exponed by the insertion of Vocabulary Items (this idea is referred to as Late Insertion; cf. the Separation Hypothesis of Beard 1995a).

There are several stages of PF, as shown in Figure 1.2. Directly after the PF/LF Branching, hierarchical structure is still present and certain morphological operations that manipulate feature bundles can occur. Such operations include Lowering, which lowers one feature bundle to adjoin to another (Embick and Noyer 2001), Fission, which splits off a feature from a feature bundle and grants it its own node (Noyer 1997 among many others), and Fusion, which combines two feature bundles into one node (Halle 1997 among many others).

Next, the Vocabulary Items are inserted (the terminal nodes are provided with phonological content), and the structure is linearized. Various post-linearization operations (e.g. Local Dislocation, a switch in linear order between two nodes; Embick and Noyer 2001, Embick 2003) also take place, and these operations are conditioned by precedence relations. Finally, prosodic domains are built, and the PF derivation finishes with a complete phonological and linear representation (although see Pak 2008 on how the prosodic part of the model may present difficulties).

Vocabulary Insertion is the process whereby it is decided which Vocabulary Item should be inserted at a particular feature bundle. It will play a large role in the book, so it is worthwhile to spend some further time on it. Vocabulary Insertion is a very local process: it applies to one feature bundle at a time, and only one Vocabulary Item can be inserted for any given feature bundle. A Vocabulary Item is a relation between a phonological string and information about where the string can be inserted. The information about where the string is inserted is made up both of features and contextual restrictions. Some Vocabulary Items for the past tense in English are shown in (4).

(4) a. T, [PAST]   ↔ -t / { √LEAVE, √BEND,...}
     b. T, [PAST]   ↔ -ed   (Embick and Marantz 2008)

The Vocabulary Items in (4) are in competition to realize the feature bundle T, [PAST]. Two main principles determine which Vocabulary Item wins a given competition: the Pāṇinian Principle (also known as the Elsewhere Condition) and the Subset Principle (Halle 1997). The Pāṇinian Principle states that a more specific rule is applied before a less specific rule, and it suffices to determine the winner in (4). If the context is met to insert Vocabulary Item (4)a (i.e. the root is √LEAVE or √BEND), then it must be inserted, since it is more specific than Vocabulary Item (4)b (because it has a contextual restriction). The Subset Principle determines the winner in other cases.

(5) **Subset Principle**

   (i) The phonological exponent of a Vocabulary Item is inserted into a position
        if the item matches all or a subset of the features specified in that position.
   (ii) Insertion does not take place if the Vocabulary Item contains features not
        present in the morpheme.
   (iii) Where several Vocabulary Items meet the condition for insertion, the item
        matching the greatest number of features specified in the terminal mor-
        pheme must be chosen.   (Halle 1997: 428)

The Subset Principle ensures that a Vocabulary Item cannot be inserted that contains features not present in the morpheme. However, the Vocabulary Item might contain fewer features than are present in the morpheme, in which case the Vocabulary Item is referred to as "underspecified." The Subset Principle also states outright that Vocabulary Items that match the most features with the given morpheme win.

   Many of the concepts just introduced will be discussed in more detail at various points throughout the book. However, this sketch of the core ideas suffices before they are presented in context.

1.2.3 *Lexical decomposition*

The assumptions in Section 1.2.2 form the core of DM, but much DM research has also pursued the idea that lexical categories are composed of a category-neutral root and a category-determining head, an idea also known as lexical decomposition (see e.g. Marantz 1997, 2001, Arad 2003, 2005, Embick and Noyer 2007, Embick and

Marantz 2008, Harley 2014).[2] For example, a verb like *hammer* consists of a root
√HAMMER, and a functional head *v* that "verbalizes" it.

(6)   vP   **Category Neutrality: Verbal**

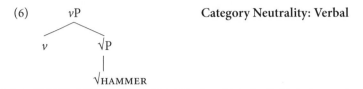

This also goes for nouns, which consist of a root and the nominalizing functional
head *n*.

(7)   nP   **Category Neutrality: Nominal**

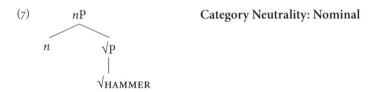

(7) results in the nominal *hammer* 'a tool for pounding nails' whereas (6) results in
the verb *hammer* 'to pound (something)'.

The empirical motivation for lexical decomposition is provided by the well-known
differences between lexical and syntactic word formation. Word formation in the
lexicon is more prone to phonological and semantic irregularities (e.g. special
phonological processes, idiomatic meanings), whereas syntactic word formation is
morphophonologically regular and has semantically predictable meaning. However,
in DM, there is no lexicon or lexical processes, so the contrast must be captured in a
different way. Marantz (2001, 2007) and Arad (2003, 2005) specifically propose that
"lexical" word formation corresponds to word formation from roots—the combination of a category-defining head (*n*, *v*) with a root. "Syntactic" word formation
corresponds to word formation from words—the combination of some head with a
categorized word (i.e. *n*P, *v*P). In subsequent research, the predictions and consequences of this proposal have been explored (see e.g. Embick 2010 on contextual
allomorphy). Even though some of the original claims have been disputed (see e.g.
Harley 2014 on the domain of semantic interpretation), lexical decomposition has
become a major approach to syntactic categories in modern morphosyntax. The aim
of this book is to explore the role of the categorizing head *n* in expressing gender
features in nominals.

Throughout the book, the roots in syntactic trees are labeled by a word in the
language in question after a square-root sign, as in (6) and (7). In early DM, however,

---

[2] It must be noted that this idea was not entirely new (see e.g. van Riemsdijk 1990 on *n*), nor do only
Distributed Morphologists subscribe to it (see e.g. Lowenstamm 2008). See also Borer (2005) for a similar
approach, although she argues (pp. 20–21) against the specific DM analysis adopted here.

roots were indicated only by a square-root sign in the syntax, and were assumed to be undifferentiated. Marantz (1995) argued that roots do not compete for Vocabulary Insertion, i.e. that any root could be inserted at a root node (as long as its licensing conditions were met). In other words, to the grammar, it does not matter whether 'hammer' or 'wrench' is inserted at a root node, just as long as both of them are licensed under a *n*.

This approach to roots, however, makes the prediction that there will be no root suppletion. If roots do not compete for insertion, then different forms of a root will not compete with each other for insertion at a particular context (e.g. the Vocabulary Item *person* will not be able to compete with *people* in a plural context). Although the idea that roots never undergo suppletion has been defended (see e.g. Marantz 1997), I agree with those who have argued that root suppletion is attested (see especially Harley 2014), and therefore I do not subscribe to the idea that roots do not compete.

Nevertheless, the representations in (6) and (7) suggest that the phonological content of a root is present from the beginning of the derivation. If this is true, then there is again a problem with root suppletion (if the phonological content of a root is present from the beginning of a derivation, how could roots ever be suppletive?—see Harley 2014). A solution is at hand, though: I assume that roots are identified by non-phonological indices/labels in the syntax, following much recent research (Pfau 2000, 2009, Embick 2000, Embick and Noyer 2007, Acquaviva 2009, Harley 2014). The index for a root is exponed at PF via Vocabulary Insertion (where different root allomorphs can compete for insertion) and interpreted at the Encyclopedia in a given context. I will represent indices numerically. (8) shows the syntactic representation, Vocabulary Item, and one possible interpretation of the root identified as √HAMMER in (6) and (7).

(8) a. √169   **syntactic representation**
     b. √169 ↔ hammer   **Vocabulary Item**
     c. [$_{nP}$ *n* [√169]] is interpreted as a type of tool with a   **Semantic interpretation**
        long narrow handle and a hard, specially shaped head,
        often used for pounding nails, etc . . .

I will continue to represent roots in individual trees and in the prose with the words of the language in question, but this is only for expository/clarificational purposes.

1.2.4 Summary

Overall, I assume the syntax operates as per Minimalist assumptions, and I take a Distributed Morphology approach to the grammar. This includes distributing listed information across the grammar, and having syntactic feature bundles be exponed post-syntactically via Vocabulary Insertion. I also assume lexical decomposition: lexical categories are decomposed into category-neutral roots and category-defining heads.

1.3 Limitations

This book aims to develop a broadly applicable analysis of gender, but there are certain necessary limitations on its scope. For example, the book does not engage directly with most of the puzzles related to gender agreement (see e.g. Wechsler and Zlatić 2003, Carstens 2011, Matushansky 2013). From one perspective, gender agreement is a separate phenomenon from gender assignment. The mechanisms that enforce gender agreement have been the focus of much morphosyntactic research on their own, i.e. research that is not concerned with gender assignment. However, from another perspective gender agreement is closely related to gender assignment. Most nominals do not have overt gender markers, so the only evidence that a noun has a particular gender is the gender agreement with that noun on other categories. The discussion of gender agreement in this book will therefore be limited to puzzles that relate to gender assignment.

Overall, the book will not advocate a particular theory of gender agreement. There will be little discussion of the mechanics of agreement (whether it requires a syntactic Agree relation or is entirely post-syntactic, whether the mechanisms for verbal agreement and DP-internal agreement are different, etc.). I also largely set aside puzzles relating to hybrid nouns (Corbett 1991: ch. 8, Matushansky 2013) and to gender resolution (Corbett 1991: ch. 9), i.e. how conjoined noun phrases agree when each noun phrase has a different gender. The most sustained discussion of gender agreement is in Chapter 10, where it is argued that agreement is with the highest gender feature in the nominal phrase.

The book also does not engage with gender-related puzzles of nominal ellipsis (see e.g. Bobaljik and Zocca 2011, Merchant 2014). The general approach to gender in Bobaljik and Zocca (2010) is very compatible with the analysis of gender developed in the book, and at the end of Chapter 8, I briefly discuss how some results from nominal ellipsis support the idea that gender is not on Num. However, fleshing out the details requires more focus on ellipsis than there is space for here, and I leave this topic for future research.

The book also is limited in empirical scope for practical reasons. I assume that gender is a unitary phenomenon across languages, and that its properties can be investigated in various languages with broadly generalizable conclusions. However, to be clear, this is an assumption. It is a separate and interesting research question whether some phenomenon that ostensibly fits the definition of gender may be in fact a different phenomenon (see e.g. Wiltschko 2012 on reanalyzing Ojibwe gender as nominal aspect).

Another restriction in empirical scope is that the book focuses on languages with two or three genders. This was a conscious choice so that more space could be devoted to topics like the interaction of gender and number, and the role of gender in nominalizations. However, the choice is not as limiting as it may initially seem. Two- and three-gender languages provide more than enough richness and complexity to get the analysis off the ground, push it forward, and ultimately test its predictions. Additionally, two- and three-gender languages are the most common types of gender systems. Corbett (2011a) surveys 112 languages with gender systems, and of these, 75 have two or three genders (67%). Nichols (1992) surveys 45 languages with gender systems, of which 26 have two or three genders (57%). Since it can be reasonably concluded that two- and three-gender languages are the majority of languages with gender systems, the analysis automatically covers most languages with gender systems even when it is restricted to only these languages. However, I do not intend to downplay the potential contribution of languages with more than three genders, and I hope that the proposals here can be extended in future research to these languages (see Chapter 11 for more specific thoughts on how this could be accomplished).

Finally, this research is focused squarely within the theoretical linguistic tradition and will not engage directly with sociolinguistic or psycholinguistic approaches to gender. However, in Chapter 11, I offer some final thoughts on how the results of the book might be affected by social factors. Also, in the conclusion of Chapter 8, I lay out a promising connection between the results of this book and the conclusions of some psycholinguistic work on gender.

1.4 The lay of the land: chapter previews

The book can be viewed as falling into three parts. The first part consists of two chapters on the gender system of the Ethiosemitic language Amharic; these chapters serve to lay out the primary analysis of the book in detail. The Amharic gender system is mostly based on natural gender, but there are also a small number of nouns with arbitrary gender. Amharic's gender system is hence different from most previously analyzed gender systems, and it raises important questions about whether natural gender features should be in the morphosyntax and if so, how they relate to arbitrary gender features. In Chapter 2, I describe its gender system and argue that previous morphosyntactic approaches face serious difficulties in trying to account for it.

In Chapter 3, I introduce the n analysis in detail, as well as my assumption that natural gender features are interpretable and arbitrary gender features are uninterpretable. I walk through the mechanics of it for Amharic, showing how it captures all the generalizations identified in Chapter 2. I also present direct evidence from Amharic that gender features are on n, looking at the interaction of gender and number, the interaction of gender and nominal vocalic pattern, and the role of gender in nominalizations. The second half of Chapter 3 fleshes out the analysis, exploring the nature of licensing conditions and setting in context my assumptions about the interpretability of gender features.

The second part (Chapters 4–7) widens the empirical domain, showing how all the two- and three-gender systems predicted by the analysis that I developed for Amharic are attested. Chapter 4 refines the definition of gender introduced in Section 1.1 as a precursor for discussing gender in a cross-linguistic context. Chapter 5 focuses on two-gender languages with the simplest possible inventory of gendered *n*s given my assumptions. I provide two case studies of languages that have this inventory: Dieri (Pama-Nyungan; Australia), which has a masculine default gender, and Zayse and Zargulla (Omotic; Ethiopia) which have a feminine default. I also identify a type of gender system based on biological sex that is predicted never to occur, and I show how one language that at first appears to have this gender system (Lealao Chinantec (Otomanguean; Mexico)) is instead based on animacy.

In Chapter 6, I focus on two-gender languages that contain at least one *n* with an uninterpretable (arbitrary) gender feature. I present three examples: Spanish (Indo-European (Romance); Spain, Central and South America), Maa (Nilo-Saharan (Nilotic); Kenya), and the Algonquian language family (Canada, United States). I argue that Spanish has a *n* with an uninterpretable feminine feature (like Amharic, which I compare it to), that Maa has a *n* with an uninterpretable masculine feature, and that Algonquian languages have a *n* with an uninterpretable animacy feature.

In Chapter 7, I turn to three-gender languages. I first examine Mangarayi (non-Pama-Nyungan; Australia), which has the simplest inventory of gendered *n*s. I chart the differences and similarities between Mangarayi and the languages of Chapter 5 in that Mangarayi has three genders whereas Dieri, Zayse, and Zargulla have two genders. I then move on to Wari' (Chapacuran; Brazil), which is the three-gender counter part of Maa (Chapter 6) in that it has one uninterpretable masculine feature. Finally, I investigate Lavukaleve, a three-gender language that provides evidence for two *n*s with uninterpretable features. The chapter closes with an excursus on the complexities of default gender in three-gender languages.

The third part turns the focus to gender being on *n*, exploring the interaction of gender and number (Chapter 8), the place of gender in nominalizations (Chapters 9 and 10), and the relationship between gender and declension class (Chapter 10).

Chapter 8 centers on the fact that some nouns in certain languages change gender in the plural, i.e. a noun has Gender X in the singular and Gender Y in the plural. I argue that even though gender seems to be dependent on number in these cases, gender is not on the Num(ber) head in the syntactic derivation. I demonstrate how a gender-on-*n* proposal accounts for the fact that number seems to be conditioning gender via in-depth case studies of two languages: Somali (Afroasiatic (Cushitic); Somalia) and Romanian (Indo-European (Romance); Romania). For Somali, I argue that all plurals are formed via *n*, and this explains why switching numbers can (but need not) involve switching genders. For Romanian, I argue in favor of the standard analysis of the gender-switching nouns as unspecified for gender; I show how this plays out in a *n* approach to gender, and how it results in the gender of such nouns being dependent on number.

In Chapter 9, I demonstrate how gender on *n* predicts that nominalizations will at least be capable of being gendered. I provide data from a range of languages, both ones previously encountered in the book and ones not mentioned before, that demonstrates that this prediction is borne out. I further identify three correct predictions of this approach, including that nominalizations that lack *n* should receive the default gender. I then address two potential problems for the analysis, including the fact that gender features seem to be exponed separately from a nominalizer in some languages, and I propose some solutions.

Chapter 10 has two goals, both related to further exploring the implications of having gender features located specifically on *n*. First, I investigate nominals that contain multiple, stacked *n*s, i.e. multiple gender features. I show how the highest *n* determines the gender of the nominal, and develop an explanation of this fact based on independently motivated assumptions about morphosyntactic cyclicity. I also briefly consider diminutive morphology and show how it supports the idea that the highest *n* determines the gender. The second goal of the chapter is to briefly consider declension class, which is often inserted post-syntactically at/near *n* in the Distributed Morphology literature. I demonstrate that declension class/pattern is not isomorphic with gender, but that gender can affect the choice of declension class—as predicted if it is adjoined to *n* and gender is on *n*.

Chapter 11 concludes, returning to the questions about gender posed in Section 1.1 and reviewing how the book has answered them. It also identifies key areas of future research—open questions that will hopefully lead to further advances in our understanding of the complex morphosyntax of gender.

2

The Amharic gender system and previous approaches to gender

2.1 Introduction

In order to introduce and justify a gender feature on n, I investigate over the next two chapters the gender system of the language Amharic (Afroasiatic (Semitic); Ethiopia). In this chapter, I show how Amharic relies on both natural and arbitrary gender in its gender system (Section 2.2), in ways that are difficult for previous gender approaches to explain (Section 2.3). In Chapter 3, I present evidence from Amharic that n is the appropriate locus for gender, using data from the interactions of gender and number, gender and nominalization, and gender and declension class.

2.2 Gender in Amharic

I start with some basic background on Amharic as a language, since it is the focus of the next two chapters and Amharic data recur throughout the book. Genetically, Amharic is an Ethiosemitic language and a member of the Afroasiatic language family. It is the national language of Ethiopia, taught in schools and used in national newspapers and government publications.[3] Lewis et al. (2013) report that there were approximately 21 million speakers of Amharic in Ethiopia according to the 2007 census, with approximately 15 million monolingual. There are also significant Amharic-speaking diaspora populations in Europe, Israel, Canada, and the United States. All unattributed data are from my own fieldwork in the South San Francisco

---

[3] There are approximately 80 languages spoken within Ethiopia, including 13 other Semitic languages (see above), many Cushitic languages (including Oromo, Sidamo and Afar), many Omotic languages, and several languages from the Nilo-Saharan family. In recognition of these many languages, Ethiopia has no official language, but Amharic, with its "national" status, is by far the most prominent politically and is used as a lingua franca. For a wide-ranging discussion of language in Ethiopia, see Bender et al. (1976).

The Morphosyntax of Gender. First Edition. Ruth Kramer.

Bay region and the Washington, DC area, and the majority of the remaining data are from Leslau (1995), the foremost reference grammar of the language.[4]

Amharic has maintained a relatively low profile in theoretical generative linguistics, from the early studies of Bach (1970), Hetzron (1970), Fulass (1966, 1972), and Manahlot (1977) to a cluster of work in the late 1980s and early 1990s (see e.g. Mullen 1986, Yimam 1988, 1996 et seq., Tremblay and Kabbaj 1990, Halefom 1994, Amberber 1996). In the past ten years, a formal semantic interest in Amharic has flowered due to work on indexical shifting (Schlenker 1999, 2003a, 2003b, Anand 2006), and a corresponding focus on Amharic syntax has taken shape (see e.g. Demeke 2001, 2003, Ouhalla 2000, 2004, Henderson 2003, den Dikken 2007, Beermann and Ephrem 2007, Yabe 2007, Eilam 2009, Kramer 2009, 2010, 2012, 2014a, 2014b, Kramer and Eilam 2012, Baker 2012). None of these sources (with the exception of Kramer 2009, 2014b) provides an analysis of the gender system, though, and I turn next to the facts of gender assignment.

2.2.1 The facts

Amharic distinguishes two genders, conventionally labelled "masculine" and "feminine" (Leslau 1995: 161). This is typical for a Semitic language (Rubin 2010: 34) and for many, if not all, Afroasiatic languages as well (see e.g. Zaborski 1992, Hayward 2000). There is no consistent morphophonological correlate of gender (Leslau 1995: 161, Cohen 1970: 74), with one exception discussed below. Therefore, gender is indicated by agreement on e.g. definite markers, demonstratives, and verbs. Masculine and feminine definite markers are shown in (1).[5]

(1)   **Amharic definite marker**
       a. *-u*   the.MS
       b. *-wa*   the.FS

When the gender of an Amharic noun needs to be indicated in this book, it will appear with the appropriate definite marker.

The Amharic system for assigning gender is heavily reliant on natural gender. Specifically, the gender of an animate noun is assigned exclusively according to its natural gender (Leslau 1995: 161ff., Hartmann 1980: 278ff., Appleyard 1995: 33). Some male/female pairs have different roots; mostly these are kinship terms (father/ mother) and domesticated animals (bull calf/heifer).

---

[4] A handful of examples are from the Amharic internet (with the link an accompanying footnote), and from the Walta Information Center Tagged Amharic News Corpus (cited as from Walta; see Demeke and Getachew 2006 for more details on the corpus).

[5] The definite markers could each be decomposed into a D morpheme /u/ and a gender marker. The masculine definite marker would thus consist of /u+∅/ and the feminine definite marker consists of /u+a/ which surfaces as [wa]. In the analysis, I do not represent the definite marker as decomposed, in order to keep the representations simple and in order to be in accordance with the previous Amharic literature.

(2) **Different-root nominals**[6]

a.	abbat	'father'	h.	innat	'mother'
b.	bal	'husband'	i.	mist	'wife'
c.	wändɨmm	'brother'	j.	ɨhɨt	'sister'
d.	aggot	'uncle'	k.	akɨst	'aunt'
e.	wäyfän	'bull calf'	l.	gidär	'heifer'
f.	bäre	'ox'	m.	lam	'cow'
g.	dɨngulla	'stallion'	n.	bazra	'mare'

I am assuming that these pairs have different morphological roots, but similar pairs of items in other languages have sometimes been treated as suppletive (see e.g. Osthoff 1899, Markey 1985, Mel'čuk 1976). However, there is evidence that these pairs are not suppletive from the relevant non-gendered term, e.g. 'parent,' 'calf,' etc. The non-gendered term in almost every case above is (i) either a phonologically distinct form (e.g. *tʼɨdʒdʒa* 'calf', *wäladʒ* 'parent') or (ii) unattested (e.g. there is no equivalent of the English word *sibling*). Either scenario is suspicious from the perspective of a suppletive analysis; the purported root shared by the pair would either leave no morphophonological trace across three slots of the paradigm or it would never surface with a non-gendered meaning. I conclude that the pairs in (2) are not morphologically related via suppletion, and continue to refer to them as different-root nominals.

Different-root nominals are only a small subset of the animate nominals in Amharic.[7] The vast majority have the same root for both males and females, whether for humans (e.g. *tämari* 'student') or animals (e.g. *wɨʃʃa* 'dog'). The female version is feminine and the male version is masculine.

(3) **Same-root nominals**

    a. tämari-w[8]   tämari-wa

        student-DEF.M   student-DEF.F

        'the (male) student' 'the (female) student'

---

[6] I do not classify *säw* 'man' and *set* 'woman' as different-root nominals. They are derived etymologically from the same Ge'ez root /sbʔ/ (unlike most of the different-root nominals, e.g. *wändɨmm* and *ɨhɨt* come from different roots; see Leslau 1969). They also behave differently from other different-root nominals in that the male form (*säw*) can be used for the superordinate term, i.e. with the meaning 'person' (it is common cross-linguistically for 'man' also to be used as a superordinate for 'person'; I assume that the choice of the male form as the default is due to social factors: see Ch. 11). Neither the male form nor the female form can be used as the superordinate for the other different-root nominals, even when there is not a lexicalized form of a gender-neutral term (e.g. when there is no word for 'sibling').

[7] There are also a few nominals that behave like different-root nominals but are not paired, i.e. they are limited to one gender. For example, *mäsfɨn* 'duke' is only used for males and there is no counterpart 'duchess.'

[8] The masculine definite marker *-u* is realized as *-w* after a vowel.

b. muʃɪrra-w   muʃɪrra-wa
   wedding.participant-DEF.M   wedding.participant-DEF.F
   'the groom'   'the bride'

c. hakim-u   hakim-wa
   doctor-DEF.M   doctor-DEF.F
   'the (male) doctor' 'the (female) doctor'

d. halafi-w   halafi-wa
   person.in.charge-DEF.M   person.in.charge-DEF.F
   'the (male) person in charge' 'the (female) person in charge'
   Walta hed12a2   Walta hed01a2[9]

e. wɪʃʃa-w   wɪʃʃa-wa
   dog-DEF.M   dog-DEF.F
   'the (male) dog' 'the (female) dog'

f. awraris-u   awraris-wa
   rhinoceros-DEF.M   rhinoceros-DEF.F
   'the (male) rhinoceros' 'the (female) rhinoceros'

Several kinship terms are also same-root nominals including *ayat* 'grandparent,' *amat* 'parent-in-law,' *warsa* 'sibling-in-law,' and *zämäd* 'relative.'

The default gender is masculine. For example, if the natural gender of the referent is unknown, then the nominal is masculine. In (12), the speaker does not know the natural gender of the baby, but uses a masculine definite marker.

(4) his'an-u   wänd   näw   set?
     baby-DEF.M male   be.3MS.S female?
     'Is the baby a he or a she?'[10]   (Leslau 1995: 164)

Additional evidence for a masculine default is that the nominal 'nobody' takes masculine agreement (cf. Roca 1989).

(5) balläfäw sammɪnt betäkrɪstiyan   mannɪmm al-hed-ä-mm
     last   week   church   nobody   NEG-go-3MS.S-NEG
     'Last week, nobody went to church.'   (Leslau 1995: 122)

Exceptionally, certain animals are feminine if their gender is unknown/irrelevant (Leslau 1995: 166, Hartmann 1980: 281, Cohen 1970: 75).[11]

---

[9] These examples are from the Walta Information Center Tagged Amharic News Corpus (Demeke and Getachew 2006). See fn. 4.

[10] The noun *his'an* 'baby' is a same-root nominal, i.e. it can be either masculine or feminine depending on whether it refers to a male or female infant.

[11] Other such animals include *ɨbab* 'snake,' *asa* 'fish,' *nɨb* 'bee' (all from Leslau 1995) as well as *zɨnb* 'fly' and *t'ɨntʃäl* 'rabbit' (from my own fieldwork).

(6) **Feminine-default nouns**
     a. bäk'lo-wa   b. ayt'-wa   c. k'äbäro-wa   d. ʃärärit-wa
        mule-DEF.F   mouse-DEF.F   jackal-DEF.F   spider-DEF.F
        'the mule'   'the mouse'   'the jackal'   'the spider'

If the natural gender of the referent for one of these animal nouns is known, though, it overrides the feminine default.

(7) ayt'-u
     mouse-DEF.M
     'the male mouse'

This demonstrates that natural gender, if known, always determines the gender of an animate nominal.

As for inanimate nominals, almost all of them are masculine (Leslau 1995: 161, Cohen 1970: 74).

(8) **Masculine nouns (inanimate)**
     a. mot   'death'   f. wɨdɨddɨr   'competition'
     b. kɨbɨr   'honor'   g. bet   'house'
     c. wänbär   'chair'   h. dɨmmɨr   'total, sum'
     d. dɨngay   'stone'   i. wäräda   'district'
     e. kɨbäb   'circle'   j. gazet'a   'newspaper'

Only a handful of inanimate nouns are treated as feminine; some examples are given in (9).

(9) **Feminine nouns (inanimate)**
     a. mäkina   'car'   e. s'ähay   'sun'
     b. azurit   'whirlpool'   f. kätäma   'city'
     c. agär   'country'   g. betä krɨstiyan   'church'
     d. mɨdɨr   'earth'   h. tʃʼäräk'a   'moon'

It is difficult to calculate the exact number of feminine nouns, since nouns are not listed in Amharic dictionaries with their gender (which indicates how small a role arbitrary gender plays in Amharic). After surveying the gender sections of three grammars (Leslau 1995, Hartmann 1980, Cohen 1970), as well as performing some basic searches in the Walta Information Center Tagged Amharic News Corpus (Demeke and Getachew 2006), my best estimate is that there are about twenty to thirty feminine nouns.

As for gender morphology, masculine gender is never morphologically marked (unsurprisingly). Feminine gender is also not universally associated with a particular affix, unlike in some other Afroasiatic languages like Ancient Egyptian (where feminine gender is marked by a *-t* suffix; see e.g. Gardiner 1957). A feminine *-t* or *-at* suffix has been reconstructed in Proto-Afroasiatic and is one of the common features across Afroasiatic languages in general (see e.g. Zaborski 1992, Hayward 2000). A descendant of this suffix remains in Amharic: in some same-root animate nominals, the female form can take the suffix -*it* (Leslau 1995: 163–4, Hartmann 1980: 280).

(10)   **Same-root nominals with -*it***

a.	lidʒ	lidʒ-it	e.	mämhɨr	mämhɨr-t
	'boy, child'	'girl'		'teacher'	'female teacher'
b.	mänäkʷse	mänäkʷs-it[12]	f.	t'ot'a	t'ot'-it
	'monk'	'nun'		'ape'	'female ape'
c.	ʃimagille	ʃimagill-it	g.	igäle	igäl-it
	'old man'	'old woman'		'so-and-so'	'female so-and-so'
d.	muʃirra	muʃirr-it			
	'groom'	'bride'			

This is not a highly productive process, since it is not possible for all animate nouns, e.g. **tämar-it* 'female student' and **hakim-it* 'female doctor.' It is also not deterministic; a noun can be feminine without -*it* even if it could have the -*it* suffix: (3)b *muʃirra-wa* '(the) bride' is just as good as (10)d *muʃirrit*.

In general, the suffix -*it* is neither a necessary nor a sufficient condition for feminine gender in Amharic, regardless of animacy (Leslau 1995: 163–4, Cohen 1970: 74). Nouns can be feminine without ending in -*it*, and nouns can be masculine and end in -*it*.

(11)   **Feminine, no -*it***   **Masculine, end in -*it***

s'ähay	'sun'		kulalit	'kidney'
agär	'country'		särawit	'army'
tämari-wa	'the (female) student'		mogzit-u	'the (male) tutor' (Cohen 1970: 74)

Finally, the suffix -*it* does not convert inanimate nominals to feminine arbitrary gender. In Hebrew, adding a feminine suffix (-*et*, -*it*) to an inanimate masculine noun derives a semantically related feminine noun (Ritter 1993).

(12)

a.	magav	magev-et	**Hebrew**
	'wiper'	'towel'	
b.	maxsan	maxsan-it	
	'warehouse'	'magazine'	(Ritter 1993: 796, (2))

---

[12] The final vowels in these nouns are deleted when the -*it* suffix is added in order to avoid hiatus. This is similar to other kinds of nominal suffixes, which also trigger deletion of the final vowel on the stem which they attach to (Leslau 1995: 36).

For example, *magav* without any suffixes has the meaning 'wiper,' but *magev* with a feminine suffix *-et* means 'towel.' In Amharic, however, adding *-it* to an inanimate masculine noun results in a diminutive interpretation of the nominal[13] (i.e. adding an interpretation that the nominal is small and/or cute, among other readings; see Leslau 1995: 167–8), not a new, semantically related nominal.

Moreover, if the "feminine suffix" is removed from nominals that end in *-it* like *färärit* 'spider' or *azurit* 'whirlpool,' the result is not a related masculine noun. There is in fact no such word as *färär* in Amharic, and *azur* is a verbal form (the masculine imperative of the verb *zorä* 'to turn,' which is morphologically related to *azurit*). In sum, then, the suffix *-it* has a rather limited role: it is a non-productive means of indicating only female natural gender only on certain same root nominals.

A last piece of gender-related morphology is the set of gender "specifiers" that indicate natural gender (Leslau 1995: 164–6, Cohen 1970: 76, Hartmann 1980: 279). For human nouns, the specifiers are *wand* for males and *set* for females.

(13) a. wänd ayat   male grandparent   'grandfather'
      b. set ayat   female grandparent   'grandmother'

There are a few additional specifiers only for animal nouns which denote either male or female gender, but the lexical items are different from those used for human nouns. There seem to be two options for analyzing the gender specifiers. First, they could be adjectives, like 'male' and 'female,' but more differentiated than in, say, English. Second, they could be nominal classifiers, similar to those found in Mayan languages, Bantu languages and many other language families (see Chapter 4).

There is some indication that the adjective analysis is correct. The specifiers exhibit the same morphosyntactic behavior as adjectives (e.g. the definite marker attaches to them; Leslau 1995: 165) and they can be predicates of a copular clause (see (4)). Also, most classifier systems operate over several more criteria than gender (animacy, shape, size, etc.) and do not usually coexist with a masculine/feminine two-gender system. I thus assume the gender specifiers are adjectives, and do not treat them further.

2.2.2 *Summary, typology, diachrony*

Looking at the facts as a whole, Amharic assigns gender mostly based on natural gender, i.e. biological sex (or the lack thereof). Arbitrary gender is only relevant in Amharic for the small number of feminine inanimate nouns, and the even smaller number of feminine-default animals. Otherwise, the natural gender (or lack thereof)

---

[13] This is true under the assumption that, in a nominal like *bet-it-u* 'the small house', *-it* is the feminine/ diminutive suffix and not part of the definite article. In Leslau (1995), it is claimed that the feminine definite marker may surface as *-itu* (also *-itwa*), but it is unclear whether these forms are truly feminine definite markers or combinations of *-it* and a definite article.

determines the gender of a nominal in Amharic according to the descriptive rules set
out in (14):

(14)   **Gender assignment rules in Amharic**
   a. If a nominal refers to a male referent, the nominal is masculine.
   b. If a nominal refers to a female referent, the nominal is feminine.
   c. If a nominal refers to a referent whose natural gender is unknown, or which
      does not have natural gender, the nominal is masculine by default.

It is useful to consider briefly how Amharic fits into Corbett's (1991) classification of
the systems of gender assignment in the world's languages. Corbett draws a fundamental distinction between semantic systems of assignment, where most nouns are
assigned gender according to semantic principles, and formal systems of assignment,
where most nouns are assigned gender according to morphological or phonological
principles. Both kinds of systems are found in a variety of languages and language
families, and semantic and formal criteria can overlap in a particular language (see
Chapter 11 for further discussion).

Amharic is best described as either a "strict semantic" or a "predominantly
semantic" system (Corbett 1991: 13), where the gender of most nouns is assigned
via semantic principles but there are certain sets of exceptions.[14] It is certainly not the
case that phonology or morphology determine the gender of a noun in Amharic—
there are no phonological regularities about which nouns are assigned which gender
and the only morphological indication of gender (the *-it* suffix) is neither necessary
nor sufficient to deduce gender.

The semantic principles are clear, though, as stated in (14). (14)ab in particular
seem to be virtually exceptionless.[15] There are, of course, a small number of exceptions to (14)c—there is a "residue" of inanimate nouns that are assigned feminine
gender. Similarly, there are a small number of animal nouns for whom feminine is
used when the gender is unknown and which (again) must be memorized.

The small residue of inanimate feminine nouns suggests that Amharic may have
had a gender system based on arbitrary gender in the past, and changed to one more
based on natural gender over time. In this respect, it is illustrative to look at the
history of gender in English. In the past millennium, English changed from a
language that relied on arbitrary gender and natural gender to a language that relies
almost exclusively on natural gender (i.e. in Modern English, inanimate nominals are
not sorted into two or more arbitrary genders, and pronouns and nominals referring

---

[14] It is unclear whether the number of exceptional nouns in Amharic is enough to render it "predominantly semantic."

[15] The major exception is the use of diminutive forms (which are all feminine) to refer to male animates
(with some kind of emotional impact: affection, mockery, etc.). See Chs 3, 9, and 10 for more information
on diminutives.

to animate nominals have the natural gender of their referents; for recent perspectives on the shift, see Curzan 2003 and Platzer 2005). It is commonly believed that the loss of gender morphology on both nouns and modifiers caused or at least greatly abetted the loss of arbitrary gender. Without morphological cues about nominal gender, it is difficult for a learner to determine (i.e. acquire) the gender of a nominal.

The ancient Ethiosemitic language Ge'ez (spoken during the Axumite empire, first written down around the 4th century BCE, now the liturgical language of the Ethiopian Christian church) is not a direct ancestor of Amharic; it belongs to the North branch of Ethiosemitic with Tigre and Tigrinya, whereas Amharic is part of the South branch with Harari and the Gurage languages. However, it offers some tantalizing clues about what an earlier stage of Amharic might have been like, and suggests that changes occurred which facilitated the loss of arbitrary gender in Amharic.[16]

Ge'ez had both masculine and feminine gender, but it is difficult to ascertain whether there were more feminine inanimate nouns than there are in Amharic.[17] It is clear though, that Ge'ez had pervasive gender agreement. Adjectives generally agreed in gender (Lambdin 1978: 68), many (if not all) of the verbs show distinct feminine and masculine forms in the singular and in the plural (see e.g. the perfect verbal paradigm in Lambdin 1978: 50, and the imperfect verbal paradigm in Lambdin 1978: 144), and cardinal numbers showed gender agreement. Amharic, in contrast, does not have consistent gender agreement for adjectives, and has lost gender agreement entirely on plural verbs and cardinal numbers. There is still some gender agreement in Amharic (on definite markers, demonstratives, and singular verbs), but the loss of some gender agreement might have facilitated or triggered a shift away from arbitrary gender, similar to the loss of agreement in the history of English.

Moreover, there is some evidence for this scenario in that the shift to natural gender is nearly complete for younger speakers (less than 25 years old). They tend to treat any feminine inanimate noun as a diminutive (see Chapter 3), and they treat feminine-default animal nominals like same-root nominals (i.e. with a masculine default). This means some younger speakers have not acquired arbitrary gender; they

---

[16] There are written records of earlier forms of Amharic, some dating as far back as the 1300s. However, Demeke (2013) does not note any differences between the gender system of Old Amharic (pre-18th c.) and Modern Amharic. Therefore, it is necessary to look further back in time to speculate about the origin of the Amharic gender system.

[17] Lambdin (1978: 26-7) and Tropper (2002: 69-70) observe that the gender of certain inanimate nouns seems to vary in Ge'ez; but this statement should be taken with a grain of salt. Gender usage varies across texts (meaning that gender may be consistent for a particular author) and some feminine nominals appear to be expressive in use (i.e. diminutives). Both these factors could seriously inflate the number of words whose gender seems to vary. Tropper also observes that one gender tends to be dominant for any given word, increasing the chance that variation may be due to expressiveness or individual author idiosyncrasies.

treat any non-female-denoting noun as masculine by default, and thus the Amharic gender system for them is entirely semantic.

In sum, the Amharic gender system heavily relies on natural gender (or the lack thereof) to assign genders, and possibly evolved from a system with more arbitrary gender in Ge'ez via the loss of gender agreement. In the next section, I start to tackle how to morphosyntactically analyze gender in Amharic—reviewing several previous analyses to show how they struggle with the Amharic facts.

2.3 The morphosyntax of gender: previous approaches

In mainstream syntactic theory, agreement is treated as a relation which is established during the syntactic portion of the derivation. Thus, in order for gender agreement to occur, gender features must be present during the narrow syntax (see also Pfau 2009 for empirical evidence from speech errors that gender features are in the syntax). If gender features must be present in the syntax, though, a gender feature must be one of the features on/of some terminal node in the syntactic derivation. The question is: which one? This is one of the driving questions of the book: what is the locus of gender features in the syntax?[18]

Intuitively, gender seems to be an inherent property of nouns. The gender of a noun is generally consistent no matter how it is inflected: for case, number, definiteness, etc.[19] This intuition has led to many proposals that the gender feature is in the lexical entry for any given noun, i.e. on the nominal head N in the syntax, as shown schematically in (15) for a feminine noun.

(15)

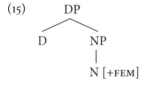

However, it has occasionally been claimed that the gender feature can or must originate elsewhere than on the noun, and I discuss these proposals first in Section 2.3.1. I then return to the idea that gender is on N, first from a lexicalist viewpoint (Section 2.3.2) and then from a Distributed Morphology perspective (Section 2.3.3).

---

[18] Under a post-syntactic approach to agreement (e.g. Bobaljik 2008), gender features could be inserted in the morphology before the agreement relation as dissociated features. The question would remain, though: where in the hierarchical structure would they be inserted?

[19] Although there are cases where plural number seems to cause a switch in the gender of a noun. See Ch. 8.

2.3.1 *GenP and NumP*

In Picallo (1991), it is argued that gender heads its own projection, i.e. Gen(der)P. In Ritter (1993), it is proposed that a gender feature can be a part of the Num head within NumP, which typically houses number inflection. In this section, I first discuss how a GenP analysis is not supported empirically and is conceptually problematic. I then show how a NumP analysis is not appropriate for Amharic gender features.

On the basis of data from Catalan, Picallo (1991) proposes that GenP immediately dominates NP and that the Gen head is the source of gender inflection for all nominals. Picallo argues for an articulated DP structure where NumP, which contains number inflection, dominates GenP.

(16)

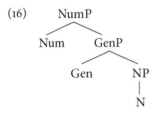

If N raises through Gen to Num, Gen is successfully predicted to be closer to the stem than Num (Stem-Gen-Num). However, this is not an argument for a gender projection per se. Gender morphology will also be closer to the stem than number morphology if gender is simply a feature on N, and N subsequently moves to Num.

Picallo also observes that when a noun has multiple arguments, the noun precedes all the arguments, e.g. *novelles* 'novels' in (17).

(17)   les novelles d'en Pere de Nabokov
        'the novels of Pere of Nabokov'
        (Picallo 1991: 283, (7a); *Pere* is a male name)

She assumes that *en Pere* 'Pere' is base-generated in the specifier of GenP and *Nabokov* is base-generated in the specifier of NP. She then argues that the noun raises past these arguments through Gen to Num, and this results in the N-initial order. However, the starting assumptions about argument position here are unmotivated. It seems equally likely that *Nabokov* would be the complement of the noun *novelles* and that *Pere* would be in Spec,NP—in which case, the noun would travel past them both by moving to Num, without a need for GenP.

(18)   [$_{NumP}$ Num [$_{NP}$ Pere [$_{N'}$ novelles [$_{DP}$ Nabokov]]]]

Even if two specifier positions turned out to be required for data like (17), there is no necessary link between the existence of an extra functional projection to house the specifier and that functional projection being the source of gender morphology.

Overall, the same predictions could be achieved concerning the Catalan data without GenP being present.

Moreover, GenP would be a projection that has no consistent semantics. Arbitrary gender on inanimates is uninterpretable, and Chomsky (1995: 349–55) argues against including projections in the syntax that only contain uninterpretable features (e.g. Agr nodes). In more recent work, Picallo (2006, 2007, 2008) has developed a different analysis of gender that addresses this issue, and I discuss it briefly in Chapter 3.

Ritter (1993) argues explicitly against GenP,[20] proposing that gender can be fully accounted for as a feature either on N or on Num depending on the language (N for Hebrew, Num for the Romance languages). The linchpin of her argument against GenP for Hebrew is that a structure like (16) indicates that gender is an inflectional affix on the noun, just like number. In Hebrew, though, gender suffixes are clearly derivational, e.g. a new, related nominal can be formed by adding a feminine suffix to a masculine inanimate noun (see Section 2.2; Ritter assumes that derivational morphology is attached in the lexicon).

However, for Romance languages, Ritter claims that changing the gender of an inanimate noun does not systematically result in a new related noun. She thus concludes that gender is inflectional in Romance, but argues that it is housed in NumP and not GenP for two reasons: (i) plural nouns in Romanian switch genders, i.e. Num must have gender and number specifications anyway, and (ii) in Walloon, gender and number are spelled out together as the realization of a Num head, separately from a nominal head that is not inflected for either.

I will not take issue here with the claim that gender is in NumP for Romance for now, although see Chapter 8 on Romanian. However, the empirical observations that Ritter uses as the basis of her arguments do not hold in Amharic. First, there is no gender switching in plural nouns like in Romanian. Adjectival agreement with a plural nominal does not often encode gender distinctions in Amharic, but when it does, it encodes the same gender the nominal has when it is singular.

(19) a. afrikawi-yan wändɨmm-otʃtʃ-atʃtʃin-imm   b. afrikawi-yat ɨhit-otʃtʃ-atʃtʃin
      African-M.PL brother-PL-our-TOP   African-F.PL sister-PL-our
      'our African brothers'[21]   'our African sisters'[22]

wändɨmm 'brother' is a masculine noun, and when it is pluralized and modified by an adjective that ends in the suffix -*awi*, there is plural masculine agreement on the

---

[20] See also di Domenico (1997: 136, as cited in Picallo 2007: 9) and Alexiadou (2004) for further argumentation against GenP.

[21] From http://ectvamharic.blogspot.com, accessed 1 Oct. 2008.

[22] From http://etiopiainitalia.blogspot.com, accessed 1 Oct. 2008.

adjective. In the same way, when an adjective that ends in *-awi* modifies the plural feminine noun *ɨhɨt* 'sister,' it takes plural feminine agreement.[23]

As for the data that Ritter uses from Walloon, a little more detail is needed to show how it is not relevant for Amharic. Ritter follows Bernstein (1991) in assuming that, because nouns are not inflected for number in Walloon, they do not move to Num. She also assumes (again following Bernstein) that the feminine plural marker *ès* on adjectives is the realization of a Num head with inherent gender features.

(20)   les belès feyes
        the pretty girls
        (Ritter 1993: 801, (13a))

Thus, number and gender features can be realized as one morpheme when the noun is not inflected for number (the *-es* on *fey* 'girl' is purely orthographic), and this is a prediction of Ritter's theory that gender is a feature of Num. However, nouns in Amharic are inflected for number, so the argument from Walloon cannot even get started in Amharic. Moreover, Num is associated only with regular plural morphology, and regular plural morphology never varies according to the gender of the nominal (as it might be expected to if Num also housed gender features; see also discussion in Chapter 3 on gendered plurals). Overall, then, there is no evidence indicating that gender features are located on Num in Amharic.

2.3.2 Gender on the noun: lexicalism

In this section, I return to the intuition that gender features are part of the nominal head N. The simplest theory of gender is perhaps that gender is a feature that is idiosyncratically listed in the lexicon on each noun. I will call this the "fully listed" analysis, since gender is listed for each (non-derived) noun in the language. The syntactic representation of gender would be as in (21), taking the Amharic noun *ɨhɨt* 'sister' as an example.

---

[23] Plural definite markers and demonstratives do not encode gender, which may misleadingly appear to indicate that the gender of the plural nominal is masculine or not present (the definite marker is always "masculine," the demonstratives have special plural forms that do not vary for gender). The evidence from (22), though, shows that the gender of the nominal is retained, and simply not reflected in the plural forms of these elements.

(21) NP
 |
 N [+FEM]

ihɨt = 'sister (fem.)'

The fully listed analysis is appealing its simplicity, but is not empirically tenable. For Amharic, it would not capture the nearly exceptionless generalization that male entities have masculine gender and female entities have feminine gender. In other words, there would be no formal connection between male natural gender and masculine agreement, and female natural gender and feminine agreement. Even beyond Amharic, one of the main insights of typological research on gender is that all gender systems have a "semantic core"—a set of nouns by which gender is assigned due to the semantics of the noun (e.g. its natural gender; see Chapter 4). A fully listed analysis of gender could not capture any connection between semantics and (grammatical) gender, and it would falsely predict that there are languages where gender is assigned idiosyncratically to each noun, completely disconnected from the semantics.[24]

Additionally, many languages, including Amharic, contain nouns that can have either masculine or feminine gender, depending on the natural gender of the referent (Corbett 1991: 181–2, Wechsler and Zlatić 2003, Alexiadou 2004). They are sometimes referred to as "common-gender" nominals, and I referred to them as "same-root" nominals above (see the list of nouns in (3)). It clearly would be undesirable to have two homophonous, synonymous nouns in the lexicon for each of these cases, one with masculine gender and one with feminine gender.

Finally, as observed in Kayne (2005), gender as a feature listed on individual nouns would go against the Chomsky–Borer hypothesis about linguistic variation, since there would be cross-linguistic variation in the features on a *lexical*, not functional, head (e.g. as noted in Chapter 1, the word 'morning' is masculine in French, feminine in Hausa, and neuter in Russian). For all of these reasons, a simple analysis of gender where it varies idiosyncratically for each noun is untenable.

Nevertheless, some previous work does adopt a lexical approach to gender, in all cases with modifications or additions to the fully listed analysis in order to address some of these objections. In this strand of work, gender is either listed on or assigned to a noun in the lexicon, with the choice of listing or assigning varying by noun.

---

[24] Occasionally, natural gender is set aside entirely from a morphosyntactic investigation of gender, i.e. it is assumed that biological sex is related to but different from the gender we see in language (see e.g. Bernstein 1993a: 117, Picallo 2008: 50). This does not seem like the right approach if the theory of gender is meant to encompass languages like Amharic, which have almost nothing but natural gender, and it cannot capture the robust cross-linguistic generalization that gender is always rooted in nominal semantics.

Relevant analyses in this vein include Roca 1989 (Spanish), Harris 1991 (Spanish), Ralli 2002 (Greek), Riente 2003 (Italian), Alexiadou 2004 (Spanish, Italian, Hebrew, Greek), and Carstens 2010, 2011 (Romance and Bantu). Although these analyses avoid the flaws of a fully listed approach, I argue that they still have some serious conceptual problems as well as difficulty accounting for the facts of Amharic gender assignment.

Abstracting away from the details, these analyses are almost all structured similarly. They make a distinction between natural gender (male/female, only for animates) and "grammatical gender" (masculine/feminine, for all nouns, the "true" gender feature that shows up in the syntax and the morphology). Nouns are listed in the lexicon with either specified or unspecified grammatical gender. A noun with unspecified grammatical gender is assigned grammatical gender via a lexical rule that refers either to some semantic property of the noun (e.g. its natural gender) or to the natural gender of its discourse referent (with different analyses making different choices here). Some sample nouns in the Spanish lexicon under this type of analysis are shown in (22).

(22)   **Nouns in the Spanish lexicon (Roca 1989, Harris 1991, Alexiadou 2004)**
       Nouns with specified grammatical gender
       a. Inanimates (*domicilio* 'house.M' vs. *residencia* 'residence.F')
       b. Animate nominals that have a fixed gender (*persona* 'person.F')

       Nouns with unspecified grammatical gender
       a. Different-root nominals (*mujer* 'woman,' *hombre* 'man')
       b. Common gender nouns (*estudiante* 'student,' *patriota* 'patriot,' *testigo* 'witness')

Inanimate nouns have their grammatical gender fully specified (= listed) in the lexicon since their gender is not assigned on the basis of any semantic property.[25] So do animate nominals whose gender does not depend on the natural gender of the referent (e.g. *rana* 'frog' is always feminine in Spanish, regardless of the natural gender of the frog in question).

Different-root nominals have specified natural gender (e.g. *mujer* 'woman' has the feature [FEMALE] in the lexicon), but their grammatical gender is unspecified and must be assigned via a lexical rule that connects natural and grammatical gender. To take an example, one such rule is called "Human Gender" in Harris (1991) (see also Roca 1989: 28, (46), Ralli 2002: 538, (31b), Riente 2003: 7, (9), Carstens 2010: 37 (9b)). This rule converts a female natural gender feature to a feminine grammatical feature for human nouns (Spanish does not sex-differentiate most animals).

---

[25] However, Carstens (2010, 2011) proposes that certain inanimates whose gender correlates with certain semantic properties are assigned gender via a lexical rule (e.g. mass nouns are feminine in Italian).

(23)   **Human gender rule: Spanish**

   [FEMALE] → f / __ [HUMAN]   (Harris 1991: 51, 32a)

As for males, Harris (1991) and most other approaches treat all masculine morphology as the result of a lack of a gender feature, so male different-root nominals
simply are never assigned grammatical gender.

   Common gender nouns are the most complicated in these analyses. In most cases,
they have both unspecified natural gender and unspecified grammatical gender in the
lexicon. For Harris (1991) and Carstens (2010), there is a "Human Cloning" rule that
generates male and female versions of each such noun in the lexicon.[26]

(24)   **Human cloning rule: Spanish**

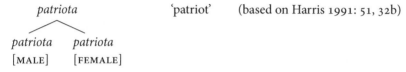

   patriota   'patriot'   (based on Harris 1991: 51, 32b)

   patriota   *patriota*
   [MALE]   [FEMALE]

This rule essentially makes common-gender nouns into different-root nominals; (23)
subsequently assigns feminine grammatical gender to the female version, and the
male version receives no grammatical gender feature.

   Recall that a fully listed lexical analysis misses the generalization that female-
denoting nouns are feminine whereas male-denoting nouns are masculine. These,
more sophisticated lexical analyses do capture this generalization by "converting"
natural gender (male/female) to the gender feature used in the syntax via rules like
(23). Thus, the analyses establish a connection between the semantics of a noun and
its gender in the syntax.

   From the perspective of minimizing the number of operations the grammar has to
go through, though, the extra step "converting" natural gender to a syntactic feature
seems unwarranted. If natural gender is the gender relevant to agreement, why not
have it be present in the syntax so it can trigger agreement directly? Moreover, in
Amharic and many other languages with natural gender-based gender systems, this
'conversion' would happen *for every animate noun*. This seems overly complicated
and unnecessary if there is a way to have the "female" feature itself trigger feminine
gender, which I develop below. In essence, these analyses "decouple" natural gender
and grammatical gender, which seems unintuitive for languages like Amharic and is
also unnecessary formally. Amharic is hardly the only language that relies heavily on
natural gender; nearly half of the languages surveyed by Corbett (2011c) have

---

[26] Roca (1989) and Ralli (2002) assume that there are two underlying representations/stem allomorphs
associated with common gender nouns, i.e. they do not connect the female and male versions via rule. This
seems to unnecessarily complicate the lexicon, which would have two semantically identical and phonologically near-identical entries/stems which differ only in natural gender.

"semantic" gender assignment systems where gender assignment is based primarily or predominantly on biological sex (and/or other interpretable semantic properties).

Another downside of these analyses is that the gender of common gender nouns ((22)d) is sometimes assigned based on the sex of the discourse referent via a lexical (presyntactic) rule. In Riente (2003), a redundancy rule assigns feminine gender if the referent is female. In Alexiadou (2004), a noun with unspecified gender enters into an agreement/concord relationship with its referent (the mechanics of the relationship are unclear). However, it seems implausible for the discourse referents of a given derivation to be accessible to operations in the lexicon, at least in a standard minimalist syntax. To put it another way, information does not usually flow from the syntax/semantics derivation to the lexicon.

Besides these conceptual problems, the analyses also struggle with the "feminine-default" animals of Amharic. Recall that some animal nouns have an unusual default feminine gender that is "overridden" by natural gender.

(25)   **Feminine-default animal noun: Amharic**

    a. ayt'-wa   b. ayt'-u

       mouse-DEF.F   mouse-DEF.M

       'the mouse, the female mouse'   'the male mouse'

The gender of feminine-default animals thus seems to be simultaneously specified (feminine, like (22)b) and unspecified (corresponds to the natural gender of the referent, like (22)d). These lexical systems are not structured to account for nouns where natural gender 'overrides' an idiosyncratically assigned gender.

I will use Harris (1991) to illustrate the point, but it also holds for Ralli (2002) and Riente (2003).[27] In Harris (1991), the only way to generate a distribution where the same noun (= root) bears different genders corresponding to different natural genders is by applying the Human Cloning rule ((24)). Presumably, when such a noun is used for an entity whose gender is unknown/irrelevant (the default case), the noun has not undergone Human Cloning. The noun will thus receive no value for grammatical gender in Harris's (1991) system; it will not trigger the Human Gender rule ((23)) and the lack of value for grammatical gender will trigger masculine morphology. Thus, the analysis predicts that the default for any same-root nominal (any word that participates in Human Cloning) will be masculine, and that nouns like the feminine-default animals in Amharic should not exist.

Even if we added a special rule just for feminine-default animals like *ayt'* and *k'äbaro* 'jackal,' the wrong prediction is still made.

---

[27] Alexiadou (2004) does not discuss defaults in detail. Roca (1989) analyzes female superordinates in Spanish (see Ch. 6) as deriving from two separate lexical entries, which is undesirable for Amharic words like *ayt'* 'mouse.'

(26) **Feminine default rule**
   [ ] → f / *ayt', k'äbäro*, etc.

This rule would assign feminine grammatical gender to specific words when their grammatical gender was otherwise unspecified. However, in Harris's analysis, male entities also do not have grammatical gender features. Thus, Harris (1991) predicts that a male form for *ayt'* would also surface as feminine, contrary to fact (see (25)b).

Carstens (2010, 2011) adopts an analysis similar to Harris (1991), in which lexical rules relate semantic features to grammatical genders. In the presyntactic lexicon, a rule gives any noun with a female feature feminine gender, and any noun with a male feature masculine gender. Nouns have inherently specified natural gender features, or receive a natural gender feature via the 'Human Cloning' lexical rule used in Harris (1991). Carstens does not discuss default gender, but it is straightforward to posit some additional default rules in her system as in (27).

(27) **Default rules inspired by Carstens (2010, 2011)**
   a. [α natural gender] → masculine
   b. [α natural gender] → feminine / *ayt', k'äbäro*, etc.

These rules would apply after Human Cloning, and would assign to most nouns masculine grammatical gender when natural gender is unspecified; however, a handful of nouns (the feminine-default animals) would be assigned feminine gender when their natural gender is otherwise unspecified (and I assume the Pāṇinian Principle: the more specific rule applies when its context is met).

However, this approach significantly complicates the analysis of default gender in general. If there is a separate default rule for natural gender, it is entirely coincidental that the default rule for all other categories in Amharic also assigns masculine gender (see e.g. discussion in Harris 1991: 43). Moreover, this analysis still suffers from the conceptual problems identified above: the decoupling of natural and arbitrary gender, and the gender of discourse referents being available in the presyntactic lexicon. Finally, since Carstens does not discuss defaults, this analysis is also speculative. The rules in (27) are not found in Carstens (2010, 2011), and this is understandable since these papers focus on gender agreement, not gender assignment. Carstens's proposals are thus an excellent starting point for developing a lexicalist approach to gender, but, in their current form, they do not constitute an analysis of gender that is fully fleshed out enough to cover Amharic.

All of the analyses discussed in this section are lexical in that they assume that most nouns are listed with a gender feature and that other nouns receive gender via lexical rules. In the next section, I explore a novel, non-lexical approach to the morphosyntax of gender that accounts for Amharic and avoids the difficulties faced by earlier analyses.

2.3.3 *Gender on the noun: Distributed Morphology*

In Distributed Morphology, the adoption of category-neutral roots has led to a more detailed structure for lexical heads like N. The increase in complexity ultimately allows for a more nuanced analysis of gender in Amharic that makes explicit the relationship between natural gender and arbitrary gender.

In the Distributed Morphology literature and elsewhere (see e.g. Marantz 1997, 2001, Arad 2003, 2005, Embick and Noyer 2007, Embick and Marantz 2008), the idea has been pursued that all lexical categories are made up of a category-neutral root and a category-determining head. To recap from Chapter 1, a verb like *hammer* consists of a root √HAMMER that could theoretically be either a noun or a verb, and a functional head *v* that "verbalizes" it.

(28)

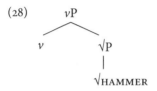

This also goes for nouns, which consist of a root and the nominalizing functional head *n*.

(29)

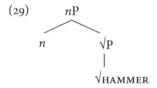

(28) results in the nominal *hammer* 'a tool for pounding nails' whereas (29) results in the verb *hammer* 'to pound (something)'. The upshot of this approach is that there now seem to be two possible heads on which the gender feature could be: the root or *n*. I argue in the remainder of this chapter that gender features should not be located on the root, and then make an extended case for gender being on *n* in Chapter 3.

2.3.3.1 *Gender is not on the root*   Recall that some animate nouns (the same-root nominals) do not change in form depending on gender.

(30) a. hakim-u   doctor-DEF.M   'the male doctor'
      b. hakim-wa   doctor-DEF.F   'the female doctor'

If gender were encoded on the root, there would have to be two roots for all the same-root nominals, one [−FEM] and the other [+FEM].

(31)   √HAKIM [−FEM]

      √HAKIM [+FEM]

This might be acceptable if only a small number of nominals were ambiguous, but ambiguity is in fact quite common. As noted above, different-root nominals tend to be limited to either kinship terms or select domestic animals, whereas the ambiguous, same-root nominals can refer to almost every other kind of animate human and animal (e.g. *profesor* 'professor,' *täkässaf* 'defendant,' *dɨmmät* 'cat').

An even more troubling consequence of having two separate roots for ambiguous nominals would be that the two roots would not be morphologically related. There would be a large number of roots in Amharic that would be coincidentally identical in terms of morphophonology and meaning, except for their gender. This kind of massive repetition of information is clearly undesirable.[28]

Also, recall the problematic feminine-default animals where feminine arbitrary gender is "overridden" by masculine natural gender; this overriding is difficult to treat in a root-based approach to gender. Even if each of these animals were associated with two roots, one masculine and the other feminine (as discussed with reference to (31)), there is no clear way to associate the *feminine* root with *lack* of natural gender (especially since lack of natural gender results in masculine arbitrary gender elsewhere in the language). Essentially, a root approach cannot capture the interplay between natural and arbitrary gender that the facts demonstrate, and I conclude that a root-based approach to gender is not viable.

2.3.3.2 Gender is on n   It is more plausible that gender is a feature on the nominalizing head *n*. This would mean that assigning gender to a root plays an essential part in turning that root into a nominal, which seems intuitively correct. In order to match up the right root with the right type of *n* (= the right gender), there must be some type of licensing condition, such that a root is licit in the context of a masculine or feminine *n* (see e.g. Acquaviva 2009).[29] This immediately allows for a simple treatment of same-root nominals (*tämari* 'student'); they have no licensing conditions.

Additionally, the relationship between gender and the root has several of the characteristics of the relationship between a categorizing head and the root (Marantz 2001). For example, gender is root-specific (different roots take different

---

[28] A seemingly viable solution would be for same-root nominals to have an unvalued gender feature that can be valued as either [+] or [−]. Presumably, agreement with some natural gender feature would value the feature on the root, similar to the lexicalist accounts above. Armoskaite (2011) develops this kind of analysis for Lithuanian, proposing that same-root nominals have an unvalued gender feature on their roots which is valued "by the discourse context" (p. 169). However, this approach runs into the same problem as the lexicalist accounts: the feminine-default animals would have to have an unvalued gender feature and a valued gender feature (for the default case) at the same time.

[29] The specific form of these licensing conditions is explored in Ch. 3.

genders, i.e. different types of *n*s). Moreover, there are paradigmatic gaps in root and *n* combinations (not all roots are possible with all genders, i.e. all types of *n*s). This lends credence to the idea that gender is a feature on a categorizing head like *n*.

Crucially, gender on *n* is different from having gender on the Gender head of a GenderP, even though both proposals involve gender features housed on a syntactic projection. The purpose of *n* is to nominalize roots and phrases—it has a broader reason to be in the derivation than just being a locus for gender features. I also assume that the category feature of the *n* is interpretable (it carries instructions for the semantic computational system; see Chapter 3), and thus *n* is never a head with only uninterpretable features like Gen.

Several previous works on gender have explored the idea that gender is a feature on *n*, including Lecarme (2002) (for Somali), Ferrari (2005) and Kihm (2005) (for Bantu and Romance), Lowenstamm (2008) (for French and Yiddish), and Acquaviva (2009) (for Italian).[30] Lowenstamm (2008) assumes that *n* has gender features, with there being as many versions of *n* in a particular language as the language has genders. Kihm (2005) proposes that *n* is where Class is located, Class being a kind of super-category that includes gender, noun class as found in Niger-Congo languages, and numeral classifiers like those found in Chinese (see also Ferrari 2005 for an approach very similar to Kihm's). Acquaviva (2009) argues against diacritic features on roots in general, and lays out explicitly how there must be licensing conditions connecting roots and types of *n*s.

Although I build on this body of work (e.g. in the use of licensing conditions), almost all of these analyses fail to discuss how the gender features on *n* relate to natural and arbitrary gender.[31] In practical terms, this means that the *n* analyses on the market have difficulty accounting for Amharic. Most pressingly, the feminine-default animals remain problematic. If the feminine-default animals are treated like

---

[30] There are three additional non-lexical approaches to gender that deserve mention: Percus (2011), Josefsson (2006), and Armoskaite and Wiltschko (2012). Percus assumes that gender is a feature merged during the derivation, and develops roughly the same approach to the interpretability of gender features as developed here (although he ultimately rejects it: see Ch. 3). In her account of Swedish gender, Josefsson also assumes that gender features are merged during the derivation of a nominal phrase. However, neither Percus (2011) and Josefsson (2006) focuses on the exact syntactic location of the gender features (Percus suggests that they are somewhere in the *n*P but not necessarily *n*s, Josefsson does not take a stand). Armoskaite and Wiltschko (2012) propose that gender is equivalent to aspect in the nominal domain, and develop a proposal that specifically accounts for "flexible" gender, i.e. when a noun has more than one gender. However, flexible gender can be captured in a *n* approach as well; see the proposals in Ch. 3 for Amharic same-root nominals and in Ch. 9 for nominalizations.

[31] In Kihm (2005), technically, *n* houses inflection class features in Spanish that are (partially) determined by natural gender features available pre-syntactically. Thus, the analysis is quite similar in structure to the lexicalist analyses from Sect. 2.3.2 that treat both arbitrary and natural gender (and it suffers from the conceptual problems outlined there). However, it is difficult to judge whether it can extend to Amharic because it is not obvious how it accounts for default gender or fixed gender nouns (e.g. different-root nominals, epicenes in Spanish). Ferrari (2005: 65, 114) briefly mentions rules connecting grammatical and natural gender, but does not provide any details.

same-root nominals (no licensing conditions), then it is unclear how they receive feminine gender as a default. If they are treated as licensed only in the context of *n* [+FEM], then it is unclear how they could ever have masculine gender (i.e. when they refer to a male referent). The *n* analyses are thus one-dimensional in their approach to gender, many of them assuming that nouns always receive gender arbitrarily. So, although the *n* analyses are on the right track, some kind of modification or addition is needed to account for both natural and arbitrary gender in this approach.

A separate but related set of analyses proposes that gender features are located on both the root and *n* (Kramer 2009, Steriopolo and Wiltschko 2010, Atkinson 2012, Duek 2014). These analyses avoid the empirical problems described in Section 2.3.3.1 that follow from having gender *only* on the root. However, there are several reasons to think that gender is *never* a feature on category-neutral roots.[32]

First, within the lexical decomposition literature, features on roots are either generally disallowed (Borer 2005, Acquaviva 2009) or limited to features that are inactive syntactically and semantically (Embick and Noyer 2007)—unlike gender, which participates in agreement relations. Moreover, gender as a phenomenon is specific to a particular lexical category (nouns), and putting category-specific information on roots severely undermines the idea that roots are category-neutral (cf. Acquaviva 2009). Gender would also be the only such feature on roots—other potentially root-specific features like declension class have been analyzed as being inserted at a category-defining head, often post-syntactically (see e.g. Oltra-Massuet 1999, Embick and Halle 2005); the insertion of a declension class feature can be conditioned by root identity, but the feature need not be on the root itself. Finally, putting gender on roots would make root features an area of cross-linguistic variation, which contradicts the Chomsky–Borer hypothesis that variation is limited to features on functional heads. (See Section 2.3.2.)

Moreover, there is no empirical phenomenon that requires gender to be on a root. I show in Chapter 3 that the Amharic facts which were the topic of Kramer (2009) can be reanalyzed as purely involving *n*. I argue in Chapter 6 that a Romance-type system can be captured using only *n* (as in Atkinson 2012 and Duek 2014), and in Chapter 7 that a Russian-type gender system can be captured using only *n* (as in

---

[32] Recent work by Lowenstamm (2014) reanalyzes derivational affixes as roots themselves. Faust (2013) takes up a version of this idea for gender, proposing that feminine affixes in Hebrew are roots that are adjoined to roots. However, Faust (p. 429) acknowledges that putting a gender feature on any root is conceptually problematic, since it seems to nominalize the root. In a related vein, Lowenstamm (2012) and Fathi and Lowenstamm (2014) argue for a bipartite approach to gender in French: a high gender projection which determines agreement (ClassP or GenP, above *n*P), and a low gender "profile" which affects morphological form (a root, adjoined to a root). However, in French, Fathi and Lowenstamm convincingly show that the low gender is not always identical to high agreement gender. Thus, I tentatively suggest that Lowenstamm's high gender is actually gender on *n*P, whereas low gender is declension class; the low "gender" profile is thus related to gender and expected to influence morphological form (see Ch. 10), but is not isomorphic to gender.

Steriopolo and Wiltschko 2010). Overall, then, it is unlikely that gender is ever on roots, and there remains to be seen an argument showing why gender *must* be on the root, not just why it *may* be there. In Chapter 3 I develop a *n* analysis for Amharic that avoids the root-gender problems and accounts for natural and arbitrary gender.

3

A *n* analysis of gender

3.1 Introduction

In Chapter 2, I described the Amharic gender system and surveyed previous approaches to gender, concluding that Amharic is difficult to account for under most previous analyses. In this chapter, I develop an analysis of the Amharic gender system where gender features are located on *n* which successfully generates the data and addresses both natural and arbitrary gender (Section 3.2). The analysis makes certain empirical predictions about the interaction between gender and other types of *n* in Amharic—these are identified, tested, and shown to be borne out in Section 3.3. In Section 3.4, I develop further two key components of the analysis: licensing conditions and the interpretability of gender features. Section 3.5 concludes with some big-picture discussion and provides a transition to the second part of the book, where data from other types of gender systems will test the mettle of a *n*-based analysis.

3.2 The morphosyntax of gender: a new approach

In this section, I develop an analysis of the Amharic gender system from a Distributed Morphology perspective. I propose that the gender feature is located on *n*, but crucially comes in two different types: interpretable for natural gender and uninterpretable for arbitrary gender (cf. Kramer 2009, Percus 2011, Matushansky 2013). This allows the analysis to capture the full range of Amharic gender while keeping gender features within the nominal and taking into account both types of gender (natural and arbitrary).

Three ingredients are necessary to analyze the Amharic gender system. The first ingredient is that natural gender is an interpretable gender feature housed on some types of *n*. These types are shown in (1).

(1) **Types of *n* (incomplete list)**
  a. *n* *i* [+FEM] Female natural gender
  b. *n* *i* [−FEM] Male natural gender
  c. *n*   No natural gender (or natural gender irrelevant/ unknown) = "plain" *n*

The Morphosyntax of Gender. First Edition. Ruth Kramer.
© Ruth Kramer 2015. Published 2015 by Oxford University Press.

A *n* with an interpretable [+FEM] feature is interpreted as female natural gender, a *n* with an interpretable [−FEM] feature is interpreted as male natural gender, and a *n* with no gender feature is interpreted as having no natural gender (or the speaker is choosing not to convey the natural gender of the referent). I will refer to this last type as "plain" *n*.

The second ingredient is the licensing conditions mentioned in Chapter 2: licensing conditions determine which roots combine with which flavor of *n* (Acquaviva 2009; see Section 3.4.1). For example, an Amharic different root nominal (e.g. *mist* 'wife' and *bal* 'husband') is licensed under one of either *n*[+FEM] or *n*[−FEM].

(2)

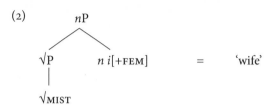

= 'wife'

(3)

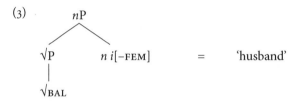

= 'husband'

Same-root nominals (e.g. *tämari* 'student') are licensed under any *n* in (1). When they combine with (1)a, they make a female student, with (1)b, a male student, and (1)c a student whose gender is unknown.

(4)

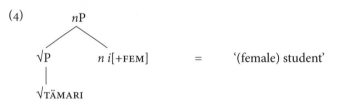

= '(female) student'

(5)

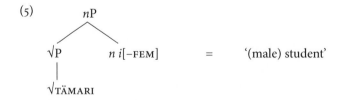

= '(male) student'

(6)

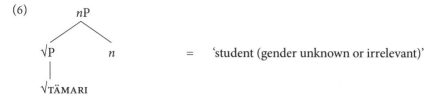

=   'student (gender unknown or irrelevant)'

The nominal in (6) will be realized with masculine agreement since masculine is the default, and it is worth saying a bit more about how this is accomplished.

As laid out in Chapter 1, I assume morphophonological exponents are inserted after syntax. These exponents (henceforth "Vocabulary Items") are pairings of a piece of morphophonology with a set of features. A one-to-one match between the feature bundle in the syntax and the features of the Vocabulary Item is not required in order for insertion to take place; in other words, Vocabulary Items are often underspecified with respect to the feature bundles that they realize. Vocabulary Items compete for insertion at a particular feature bundle according to the Subset Principle (Halle 1997): insert the Vocabulary Item that matches the most features on a feature bundle, without containing any features not present in the bundle (see Chapter 1 for a full statement of the Subset Principle). The Vocabulary Items for the definite marker, which realizes gender agreement, are in (7).

(7)   **Vocabulary Items for the definite marker**[33]
   a. D, [DEF], [+FEM] ↔ -*wa*
   b. D, [DEF] ↔ -*u*

I assume that definite D agrees in gender with *n* by whatever mechanism is responsible for concord (see e.g. Norris 2014). A definite D with a [+FEM] feature will be realized as (7)a -*wa*. A D with a [−FEM] feature will be realized as (7)b -*u*, since (7)b -*wa* has a non-matching feature. A D with no gender feature will also be realized as (7)b -*u*, since (7)a -*wa* has a feature ([+FEM]) not present on the feature bundle. Overall, any non-feminine D will be realized with the "masculine" exponent as the elsewhere case. In general, then, the analysis predicts correctly that if a nominal is interpreted as having a female referent, it will trigger feminine gender agreement, and if it is interpreted as having anything else (male, unknown natural gender), it will trigger masculine gender agreement.

This raises a question for the syntactic relation Agree, though: what does a probe with an unvalued gender feature do when it encounters a goal that lacks a gender

---

[33] If the definite marker is decomposed into a separate exponent for definiteness and a separate exponent for gender (see Ch. 2), the Vocabulary Items will look slightly different. I assume that gender agreement between the D and the noun results in an Agr node being adjoined to the D (see e.g. Embick and Noyer 2007, Halle and Matushansky 2006). The feminine exponent will expone [Agr,+FEM] in the context of [D, [DEF]] and have the morphophonology -*a*. The other exponent will expone only the category Agr in the context of [D,[DEF]] and will have null morphophonology.

feature? I assume that Preminger's (2009, 2011, 2014) failed agreement obtains: the agreement operation is obligatory, but in contexts like this the probe's feature fails to receive a value because the potential goal lacks the relevant features. The probe must then be exponed via (7)b, since (7)a has a valued gender feature and will not match the probe with (still) unvalued gender agreement.

Returning to the main thread of the analysis, recall that certain female animate nominals take the suffix -*it*.

(8) a. lidʒ   lidʒ-it   b. t'ot'a   t'ot'-it
        'boy, child'   'girl'   'ape'   'female ape'

I assume that -*it* is a possible exponent for an animate n[+FEM] in the context of certain roots, as shown by the Vocabulary Item in (9).

(9)   **Vocabulary Item for the feminine suffix**
      n, [ANIMATE], [+FEM] ↔ -*it* / {√LɨDʒ, √T'OT'A . . . }

The suffix -*it* will play a crucial role below in the discussion of nominalizations and gender.[34]

So far we have seen how the analysis handles most of the animate nominals, but there remain the inanimates and the feminine default animal nouns. Starting with the inanimates, the masculine inanimates (e.g. *bet* 'house') in fact come for free. They are licensed under 'plain' n since they do not have natural gender.

(10)

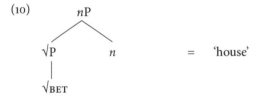

This will result in masculine gender as a default, exactly like when the natural gender is unknown/irrelevant for an animate nominal ((6)). All that is left is the third and final ingredient of the analysis for the feminine default animals and the feminine inanimates.

I propose that the feminine arbitrary gender on inanimates and feminine default animals is the result of an uninterpretable [+FEM] feature on n, (11)d.

---

[34] It may seem as if the VI for -*it* will block insertion of any other VI at a female n for these roots. This prediction would be false—it is possible to have *lidʒ* mean 'girl' without -*it* being present, i.e. with a null VI inserted at the n[+FEM]. However, see Embick and Marantz (2008: 13) for an approach to blocking that provides a solution for this problem.

(11)   **Types of *n* (complete)**
    a. *n*   *i* [+FEM]   Female natural gender
    b. *n*   *i* [−FEM]   Male natural gender
    c. *n*   No natural gender (or natural gender irrelevant/unknown)
    d. *n*   *u* [+FEM]   Feminine arbitrary gender

There are often uninterpretable and interpretable versions of the same feature (e.g. number on nominals and on T), even on the same head (e.g. Pesetsky and Torrego 2007: Q feature on C), so it is not unexpected to posit that gender also has uninterpretable and interpretable versions. Feminine inanimate nominals (e.g. *s'ähay* 'sun') are licensed only under this *n u*[+FEM].

(12)

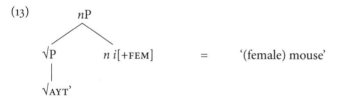

They surface with the same kind of agreement as a female nominal because they have a [+FEM] feature (albeit an uninterpretable one).

Turning finally to the feminine default animals, they are licensed under the interpretable *n*s ((1)ab) when their natural gender is known, similar to a same root nominal.

(13)

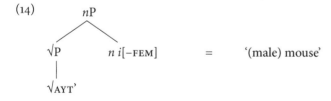

(14)

nP
√P   *n i*[−FEM]   =   '(male) mouse'
|
√AYT'

However, when their natural gender is not known/relevant, they are licensed under the uninterpretable *n*[+FEM] (and not a "plain" *n*).

(15)

nP
√P   *n u*[+FEM]   =   'mouse'
|
√AYT'

Thus, when the natural gender of a feminine default animal is known, the nominal will have the natural gender of the referent. When the natural gender is unknown, it will have feminine gender.

Overall, this is a gender assignment system which is almost entirely based on natural gender as an interpretable feature on *n*, and "masculine" forms as a default for anything that does not have a [+FEM] on *n*. The system accounts for the residue of feminine arbitrary gender in the language using an uninterpretable version of the same feature on the same head: *n u*[+FEM].[35] It is more successful than previous analyses in that all the Amharic facts are accounted for while keeping gender features associated with the nominal projection. Additionally, the current analysis is explicit about the (un)interpretability of gender features, allowing the gender feature of some nouns to be interpretable and of other nouns to be uninterpretable. Overall, the analysis provides a way to integrate gender into the currently dominant syntactic theory in a way that makes sense both for gender as a phenomenon and within the theory.

In the next sections, I support the analysis with additional analysis and delve more deeply into some of its key components. I present additional evidence from Amharic that gender is on *n* in particular (and not any other syntactic head), and discuss in depth licensing conditions and the (un)interpretability of gender.

3.3 Further evidence for *n* as the locus of gender

The analysis makes certain predictions about the interaction between gender features and various types of *n* in Amharic. In this section, I test and verify these predictions, adding further empirical support to the idea that *n* is the syntactic locus of gender. Amharic is a particularly appropriate language to test the predictions of a *n* analysis of gender, since it partially relies on *n* to generate plural nouns. The analysis thus predicts that plurals formed via *n* should be capable of formally varying with gender, since *n* will have both a gender and a plural feature in such cases. The analysis also predicts that the gender marker -*it* will be in complementary distribution with the irregular plural *n*. Another predictions is that nominalizing morphology should be capable in principle of having gender features. Finally, insofar as nominal pattern (as in root-and-pattern morphology) is a feature inserted at *n*, Amharic nominals are predicted to have their patterns vary depending on gender. I will show how all of these predictions are borne out.

First, though, some background on the plural system of Amharic is necessary. Amharic has both a regular plural suffix -*otʃtʃ* and a set of irregular pluralization

---

[35] Why are there no human nominals licensed under uninterpretable *n*[+FEM]? Perhaps this is because natural gender is more relevant and more detectable for humans than animals. Cf. Spanish, where most animals have fixed gender, but only 4 human nominals do (Harris 1991).

strategies (different suffix, partial reduplication, phonotactic changes, some combination of these strategies, etc.). A regular plural is in (16)a and an irregular plural that takes a different suffix is in (16)b.

(16) a. bet-otʃtʃ   b. näfs-at
         house-PL   soul-PL
         'houses' = Regular plural   'souls' = Irregular plural

In my previous work (Kramer 2009, 2012, to appear), I have presented evidence that irregular plural morphology does not compete with the regular plural suffix for morphophonological insertion at the same node. For example, there are double plurals (e.g. *näfs-at-otʃtʃ* 'souls'), and every nominal with an irregular plural can be alternatively regularly pluralized (e.g. *näfs-otʃtʃ* 'souls'). Irregular plurals also show characteristics of the local relationship between a categorizing head and its root (Marantz 2001; see Chapter 2), whereas regular plurals do not.

In Kramer (2009, 2012, to appear) I proposed that plurality is "split" across two syntactic loci in Amharic: irregular plural morphology is a realization of *n* (cf. Lecarme 2002, Acquaviva 2008), whereas regular plural morphology is the realization of Num. The derivation of a double plural under this approach is in (17).

(17)

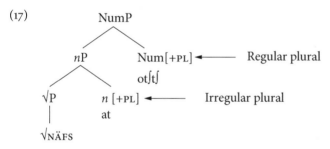

The irregular plural suffix is a realization of a plural *n*, whereas the regular plural suffix is a realization of Num.

If *n* has a plural feature as well as a gender feature, it is predicted that (*ceteris paribus*) (i) irregular plurals in Amharic will be capable of varying with gender, and (ii) regular plurals will not be (since they do not have gender). Both predictions are borne out. As shown in (18), certain irregular plurals are gendered: they take separate masculine (*-an*) and feminine (*-at*) suffixes.

(18) **Gendered irregular plural**
         a. kʼiddus 'saint'
         b. kʼiddus-an 'saints' (masc. pl. or mixed group)
         c. kʼiddus-at 'saints' (fem. pl.)

However, no regular plurals vary with respect to gender; both masculine and feminine nominals take *-otʃtʃ*.

(19) **Masculine**   **Feminine**
  a. bet-otʃtʃ   'houses'   e. mäkina-wotʃtʃ 'cars'
  b. nägär-otʃtʃ   'things'   f. agär-otʃtʃ   'countries'
  c. abbat-otʃtʃ   'fathers'   g. innat-otʃtʃ   'mothers'
  d. tämari-wotʃtʃ '(male) students'   h. tämari-wotʃtʃ '(female) students'

The restriction of gendered plurals to irregular plurals is puzzling unless gender is a feature on *n*, thus creating a feature bundle that has both gender and number features.[36]

Gender and number also interact tellingly with respect to the female suffix *-it*. Nominals ending in *-it* are freely regularly pluralized (recall that every nominal has a regular plural).

(20) a. mänäk^{w}s-it-otʃtʃ   b. arog-it-otʃtʃ
         monk-FEM-PL   old.person-FEM-PL
         'nuns'   'old women'

      c. muʃirr-it-otʃtʃ   d. t'ot'-it-otʃtʃ
         wedding.participant-FEM-PL   ape-FEM-PL
         brides   female apes

However, nominals ending in *-it* cannot be irregularly pluralized.

(21) Singular   Irregular plural   *Feminine irregular plural
      a. mänäk^{w}se(-it) mänäkos-at   *mänäkos-it-at, *mänäkos-at-it
         monk(-FEM)   monk-PL
      b. mämhɨr(-t)   mämhɨr-an   *mämhɨr-t-an, *mämhɨr-an-t
         teacher(-FEM)   teacher-PL

In (21)a, the root √MÄNÄK^{w}SE 'monk' can be nominalized and feminized with the addition of *-it* to mean 'nun.' The root can be irregularly pluralized with the *-at* suffix, but the plural *-at* suffix and the feminine *-it* suffix cannot co-occur. A similar case involves the root √MÄMHɨR 'teacher' in (21)b: it can be feminized via a suffix, but that suffix cannot co-occur with its irregular plural suffix. Crucially, the irregular plurals

---

[36] Although I have not pursued this option for ease of exposition, it is possible to decompose the gendered plural suffixes *-at* and *-an*: *-a* would be the plural exponent, *-t* feminine, and *-n* masculine. It is unclear whether this kind of decomposition is broadly desirable since it is only possible for the *-at* and *-an* that nominalize adjectives (*k'ɨddus* is the adjective for 'holy'). The *-at* and *-an* suffixes that nominalize roots are each compatible with either gender. In any event, under this analysis, a form like *k'ɨddus-a-t* 'female saints/holy ones' would have two stacked *n*s—the bottom one a *n*[+PL] realized as *-a*, and on top of that a *n* [+FEM] realized as *-t*. This analysis is compatible with a *n*-approach to gender, although the argument is slightly different than the main text. Under standard assumptions about DP structure, *n*s can be stacked freely, i.e. a *n*[+PL] will be able to be below a gendered *n*. However, a NumP cannot ever be below a *n*. Thus, it is predicted that a gender exponent (*-n/-t*) can be farther from the root than the irregular plural exponent (as in *k'ɨddus-a-t* 'female saints'), but it can never be farther from the root than a regular plural exponent.

here are not gendered: *mänäkosat* can refer to monks or nuns, and *mämhïran* can be used to refer to male or female teachers. Thus, it is not the case that *-it* is competing with, say, the *-t* in *-at*.

This asymmetry is predicted if gender features are on *n*. The feminine suffix and the regular plural suffix are independent heads in the syntax (*n* and Num, respectively) and do not compete for morphophonological insertion at the same slot. However, the feminine suffix and any irregular plural affixes compete for insertion at the *n* node. Only one Vocabulary Item (either the feminine suffix or an irregular plural marker) may be inserted.[37] Overall, the otherwise mysterious contrast between (20) and (21) falls out if gender is on *n*.

However, it is worth mentioning an alternative explanation for this contrast that still relies on gender being on *n*. Under a non-split analysis of plurality, the irregular and regular plurals would both be realizations of Num. The irregular plurals would be root-conditioned allomorphs of Num, where the regular plural would be the default/elsewhere allomorph. If it is assumed that Num must be adjacent to the root in order to have its allomorphy conditioned by the root (as in e.g. Embick 2010), then an overt gender exponent (e.g. *-it*) between the root and Num will force the insertion of the non-root-conditioned allomorph (*-ot/t/*). I leave the evaluation of this alternative explanation to future work on the locality conditions on allomorphy. However, both the split and non-split analyses of these facts rely on gender features being on *n*, so regardless of their ultimate explanation, these facts support a *n* approach to gender.

Another piece of evidence that gender is on *n* comes from nominalizations. In general, *n* is used not just to nominalize roots, but also to nominalize other syntactic categories (Marantz 2001, Arad 2003, 2005).[38] For example, a *n* can combine syntactically with a *v*P to create a deverbal noun, with a *a*P to form a deadjectival noun, and even with another *n*P to form a denominal noun.

If *n* has a gender feature when it combines with roots, it is possible that it carries a gender feature when it combines with phrases (see e.g. Kihm 2005, Ferrari 2005, Ferrari-Bridgers 2008, Markova 2010, Markovskaya 2012, Soare 2014). This prediction is borne out, for both interpretable and uninterpretable gender features. For example, an adjective derived from the name of a country (e.g. *Ethiopian*) can be nominalized

---

[37] It is natural to ask why the irregular plural "wins" the competition, i.e. why the plural suffix is inserted and not the feminine suffix when *n* is plural. One solution is to appeal to a feature hierarchy (see e.g. Noyer 1997: lxxv). In cases where there is a "tie" in which Vocabulary Item to insert at a morpheme, the individual features of the Vocabulary Items are inspected with reference to an independently-motivated feature hierarchy, and the Vocabulary Item that uniquely has the feature highest on the hierarchy (or which has the fewest nodes in the hierarchy) "wins" and is inserted. In all the feature hierarchy approaches, plural features are ranked above gender features, and thus the irregular plural would be inserted rather than the feminine suffix.

[38] Sometimes it is ambiguous whether *n* is attaching to an already formed *x*P or to a root. I will assume *n* is attaching to an already formed *x*P in all the examples below for concreteness.

by the animate, interpretable *n* suffix *-it* to make a noun that refers to a person of a particular gender from that country.

(22) a. ityop'p'iy-awi   b. ityop'p'iy-aw-it[39]
          Ethiopia-ADJ   ethiopia-ADJ-FEM
          'Ethiopian (adj.)'   'Ethiopian woman'

The derivation of (22)b is given in (23).[40]

(23)

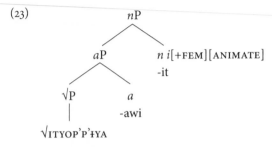

I return to the interaction of nominalizations and gender in much more detail in Chapters 9 and 10.

To take another Amharic example, Amharic has a highly productive diminutive formation for both inanimate and animate nominals (Leslau 1995: 167–9). There is no consistent phonological correlate of diminutivization, but all diminutivized nominals trigger feminine agreement. The nominal *bet* 'house' is masculine, as shown in (24)a, but can be diminutivized to trigger feminine agreement on the definite marker and on the verb ((24)b).

(24) a. bet-u   **Non-diminutive**
          house-DEF.M
          'the house'

      b. bet-wa   t-amir-all-ätʃtʃ   **Diminutive**
          house-DEF.F   3FS.S-be.cute-AUX-3FS.S
          'The (adorable little) house is cute'

Diminutivization is a kind of denominal noun formation, and diminutive morphemes have been independently argued to be realizations of *n* (Wiltschko 2006, Wiltschko and Steriopolo 2007, Steriopolo 2008). Diminutive nominals trigger feminine agreement in Amharic without any interpretation of female natural gender, and

---

[39] The final vowel in the stem is deleted when the *-it* suffix is added in order to avoid hiatus. This is similar to other nominal suffixes that are vowel-initial, which also trigger deletion of a stem-final vowel (Leslau 1995: 36).

[40] I assume that the adjective *ityop'p'iy-awi* 'Ethiopian' is deradical, but it could also be denominal (i.e. derived from the *n*P *ityop'p'iya* 'Ethiopia'). It does not matter to the argument here which option is correct.

thus can be analyzed as nominalization via an uninterpretable [+FEM] feature on the diminutivizing *n*.

(25)

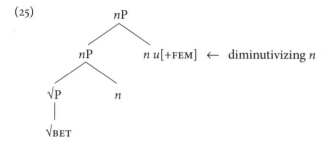

n u[+FEM] ← diminutivizing n

Therefore, both kinds of gendered *n* (interpretable and uninterpretable) can be used to nominalize *x*Ps in Amharic, lending support to the idea that gender is generally on *n*.[41]

Finally, I turn to a less conventional instantiation of *n*: nominal pattern. As a root-and-pattern language, Amharic is conventionally analyzed as forming nouns from a consonantal root plus one of a large number of nominal patterns (see e.g. the descriptions in Hartmann 1980 and Leslau 1995). For example, there is a consonantal root /l b s/ which means 'to wear' when combined with a verbal pattern. This same root can be combined with one or more nominal patterns to form semantically related nouns, e.g. 'clothing' and 'cover (of a book).'

(26)   Root: / l b s/

   Verb: läbbäsä   'to wear (a garment)'

   Noun 1 : libs   'clothing'

   Noun 2 : libas   'covering, cover of a book'

   Noun 3 : libbis   'worn clothing, second-hand clothing'   (Kane 1990: 78ff.)

The Noun1 pattern is thus $C_1iC_2C_3$, the Noun2 pattern is $C_1iC_2aC_3$ and the Noun 3 is $C_1iC_2C_2iC_3$.

Across many (if not all) Semitic languages, noun formation via root and pattern morphology is far less systematic than verb formation. For example, Arad (2005) observes that in Hebrew there are approximately seven verbal patterns, but over fifty nominal patterns (including patterns that have suffixes and prefixes). Arad also notes that several hundred nouns fall outside of those fifty nominal patterns and are not built from a consonantal root for a variety of reasons (mostly because they are loanwords). Moreover, unlike their verbal counterparts, most nominal patterns do

---

[41] This analysis of diminutive gender raises the interesting question of what happens when a given nominal has more than one gender feature, e.g. if a different-root nominal like *bäre* 'ox,' which is licensed under a *n*[−FEM], is diminutivized. Cohen (1970: 77) reports that the resulting gender is feminine (*yɨtʃtʃ bäre* 'this.F (cute) ox'). It is common (although not universal) that the gender feature on a diminutive morpheme determines the gender of the nominal, and see Ch. 10 for a detailed discussion of gender and diminutives, including which gender "wins" when multiple gender features are in the *n*P.

not convey anything about the semantics of the noun, which leads Arad (2005: ch. 2) to propose that the patterns only exist to turn consonantal roots into pronounceable strings and are inserted at PF.

In Amharic, nominal patterns are similarly difficult to pin down. There are a few productive deverbal noun formations that are associated with particular patterns, e.g. the infinitive, the instrumental, etc. (see Fulass 1966, Leslau 1995: 217). However, the rest of the nominals seem to divide into two classes like Hebrew. There is a large set of nominal patterns (including prefixes and suffixes) used to derive most of the nouns, and then a smaller set of non-derived nouns (see Leslau 1995: 216ff., Hartmann 1980: 223–38 for descriptions along these lines). The nominal patterns do not have systematic semantic interpretations.

It thus seems appropriate to analyze Amharic root and pattern morphology in the way that Arad analyzes Hebrew root and pattern morphology: the nominal patterns are inserted at PF in order to turn consonantal roots into licit phonological representations. Arad proposes that verbal patterns are inserted at the verbalizing head v, so nominal patterns by analogy will be inserted at n. This approach then predicts that the choice of a nominal pattern in root-and-pattern morphology could be conditioned by gender.

This prediction is borne out: there are a few nominals in Amharic that vary in pattern depending on gender.[42]

(27) | **Root** | **Male: CiCuC** | | **Female: CiCiCt** | |
|---|---|---|---|---|
| a. √NGS | nɨgus | 'king' | nɨgɨst | 'queen' |
| b. √LʔL | lɨʔul | 'prince' | lɨʔɨlt | 'princess' |
| c. √KʼDS | kʼɨddus[43] | 'saint (m.)' | kʼɨddɨst | 'saint (f.)' |

Each pair of nouns shares the same root, but has different patterns for natural gender. The male pattern has [u] as the second vowel, whereas the female pattern has [ɨ] as the second vowel and a -*t* suffix.

How this works analytically is that each of the consonantal roots in (27) is licensed under both of the interpretable n's: n[+FEM] and n[−FEM]. At PF, the pattern is inserted as a realization of one of the ns, with the particular pattern varying depending on the gender feature in n. The morphosyntactic representation of *nɨgus* 'king' and the Vocabulary Items that compete for insertion at the n node are given in (28) and (29).

---

[42] These nouns are inherited or borrowed from Ge'ez, which uses a feminine -*t* suffix generally (Leslau 1995: 162).

[43] The gemination in the second consonant here is because /k d s/ is a Type B root. I do not include it in the template for simplicity of exposition. See Leslau (1995: 224, 280). See also the root √KBR, which has male/female adjective versions: *kɨbur* 'honored (for a male referent)', *kɨbɨrt* 'honored (for a female referent)'.

(28)   *n*P

$\sqrt{}$NGS   *n* [–FEM]   ← Insert nominal pattern here

(29) a. *n* [–FEM] ↔ CiC(C)uC / __ {$\sqrt{}$NGS, $\sqrt{}$LʔL, $\sqrt{}$KʼDS ... }
      b. *n* [+FEM] ↔ CiC(C)iCt / __ {$\sqrt{}$NGS, $\sqrt{}$LʔL, $\sqrt{}$KʼDS ... }

Since the nominal pattern is inserted at *n* and is capable of being conditioned by gender, we have additional evidence that gender features are on *n*. I assume that all of the nouns which have identifiable patterns in Amharic are derived via root-and-pattern morphology, but (as noted in Chapter 1) I will generally use full words in the trees for clarity.[44]

To sum up, there is significant evidence for gender being on *n* in Amharic. Only irregular plurals vary formally for gender because they are the only plurals formed via *n*. The feminine suffix *-it* is in complementary distribution with the irregular plural suffixes, since they both compete for insertion at the same node (*n*). Finally, nominalizations can carry gender features in Amharic and gender can vary based on nominal patterns, further confirming *n* as the locale for gender in the syntax. For now, though, some conceptual issues need to be discussed further concerning the *n* analysis.

3.4 Licensing conditions and interpretability: refining the analysis

The analysis in Section 3.2 relies on licensing conditions to match up roots and *n*s, and assumes that gender is sometimes interpretable and sometimes uninterpretable as a feature. In this section, I explore first where these licensing conditions are located in the grammar (Section 3.4.1). I then present a basic definition of interpretability and compare my approach to previous approaches to the (un)interpretability of gender (Section 3.4.2).

---

[44] This assumption affects some of the previous data—specifically the data on other Vocabulary Items that can be inserted at *n*. If *n* is realized by a vocalic pattern, how is *n* realized at the same time by the feminine suffix *-it* for a noun like *mänäkos-it* 'nun' or a plural suffix *-at* for a noun like *mänakosat* 'monks, nuns'? There are at least three possible solutions: (a) the vocalic pattern is inserted as a dissociated morpheme which is triggered by *n* but does not expone *n*, (b) *n* undergoes the Fission operation (Noyer 1997) whereby a subset of its features are realized as a separate Vocabulary Item, (c) there are two *n*s: a bottom *n* near the root that is realized as the vocalic pattern, and an upper *n* that is realized as the feminine suffix or the plural suffix. It seems most plausible that Option (a) is correct, on analogy with Distributed Morphology approaches to declension class (see e.g. Embick and Halle 2005, Embick and Noyer 2007); in these approaches, a declension class node is inserted post-syntactically at/near a categorizing head. See Ch. 10 for further discussion of a *n* approach to gender and declension class.

3.4.1 Licensing conditions

Recall that there are four different "flavors" of *n* that are relevant for gender assignment in Amharic.

(30)   **Types of *n***
    a. *n   i* [+FEM]   Female natural gender
    b. *n   i* [−FEM]   Male natural gender
    c. *n*   No natural gender (or natural gender irrelevant/unknown)
    d. *n   u* [+FEM]   Feminine arbitrary gender

(30)ab result in female and male natural gender when they combine with a root, whereas (30)d results in feminine arbitrary gender. (30)c (the 'plain' *n*) has no gender features, and results in masculine gender by morphological default.

Different types of roots were paired with different *n*s in the analysis. Table 3.1 crosses roots with *n*-type to show which roots are licensed under which *n*'s. Different-root nominals like *innat* 'mother' and *abbat* 'father' are licensed only under the interpretable *n*s—each root choosing either feminine or masculine. Same-root nominals like *hakim* 'doctor' can be interpretably feminine or masculine, or take a plain *n* when gender is unknown. Feminine default animals are very similar to same-root nominals since they are licensed under both of the interpretable *n*s, but they are licensed under the uninterpretable *n*[+FEM] when gender is unknown. Finally,

TABLE 3.1. **How roots are licensed in Amharic**

	n i [+FEM]	*n i* [−FEM]	*n*	*n u* [+FEM]
Different root: feminine *innat* 'mother'	✓	✗	✗	✗
Different root: masculine *abbat* 'father'	✗	✓	✗	✗
Same root *hakim* 'doctor'	✓	✓	✓	✗
Feminine default *ayt'* 'mouse'	✓	✓	✗	✓
Inanimate: feminine *s'ähay* 'sun'	✗	✗	✗	✓
Inanimate: masculine *wänbär* 'chair'	✗	✗	✓	✗

inanimates are never licensed under one of the interpretable *ns*—just plain *n* (masculine default) or the uninterpretable feminine *n* arbitrarily.

The analysis encodes many generalizations about gender assignment in Amharic. It captures the fact that all female-referring nominals are feminine because interpretable femaleness is exponed as feminine morphological gender. It captures the fact that all male-referring nominals are masculine, and that nominals that do not have natural gender (plain *n*) are almost all masculine, since "masculine" morphology must be used to expone any morpheme that does not have a [+FEM] feature. Finally, the analysis stipulates that some roots have feminine gender either by default when natural gender is unknown, or arbitrarily (as for the inanimates).

However, it remains to be seen what specific grammatical mechanism pairs up the roots with particular *ns*. In Distributed Morphology, mechanisms that match roots and category-defining heads are usually referred to as licensing conditions (see e.g. Harley and Noyer 1998, 1999, 2000, Siddiqi 2009, Acquaviva 2009). Thus, in Section 3.2, I proposed that different *ns* are matched up with particular roots via licensing conditions, as first proposed in the context of gender by Acquaviva (2009). However, the licensing conditions were left somewhat vague. In this section, I briefly explore the nature of licensing conditions, focusing on how they are encoded in the grammar.

I propose that the licensing conditions be split into two sets: (i) licensing conditions that are related to semantics and (ii) licensing conditions that are arbitrary (unrelated to any property of the root, *n* or resulting *n*P). I discuss the semantic licensing conditions in Section 4.1.1, and the arbitrary licensing conditions in Section 4.1.2.

3.4.1.1 Semantic licensing conditions   Recall that each different-root nominal is licensed under one of the interpretable *ns*. These licensing conditions are semantic in that the *n* that a root combines with has an impact on semantic interpretation (i.e. causes the *n*P to be interpreted as male or female; see Section 4.2). Because these licensing conditions affect interpretation, I propose that they are encoded in the Encyclopedia as conditions on the semantic interpretation of a root in a context. For example, √ɨNNAT ('mother') is only interpretable at the Encyclopedia under a *n*[+FEM].

(31)   **Semantic licensing condition: 'mother'**
       [*n*[+FEM] [√ɨNNAT]] = 'female parent'

If the Encyclopedia receives any other *n* combined with √ɨNNAT, it will be unable to interpret the structure and the derivation will crash.[45]

---

[45] Another option would be to assume that it is infelicitous for √ɨNNAT to compose with any *n* but *n i* [+FEM], similar to the infelicity triggered by *colorless green ideas sleep furiously*. However, this approach would struggle to explain why √ɨNNAT could not compose with plain *n*, which is compatible with humans and might yield a felicitous reading of 'ungendered parent' if it combined with a root like √ɨNNAT, contrary to fact.

It could be argued that a generalization is missed here. It seems that roots that have a "female" component as part of their meaning (like √ɪNNAT 'mother') are always licensed under n[+FEM], whereas roots with a "male" component (like √ABBAT 'father') are always licensed under n[−FEM]. One possible solution would be to link up a "female" or "male" meaning component in the Encyclopedia entry for the root directly to the n choice, such that any "female root" is only interpretable under n[+FEM] and any "male root" under n[−FEM].[46] However, I believe such an approach would be misguided.

In the analysis outlined here, there is no need to separate out a gendered piece of meaning for the root. Licensing a root in a particular nominal context is what makes it be interpreted as male or female; there is no inherent male-ness or female-ness to the roots themselves (this approach has the added benefit of keeping the roots free from features that are associated with particular categories, like gender). It is true that natural gender (femaleness/maleness) correlates with being licensed under an interpretable n[+FEM] or n[−FEM], but that is because these features themselves are what trigger female/male interpretation, presumably at LF before the Encyclopedia is accessed (see Section 4.2). Morphologically, these features then trigger feminine exponents (for n[+FEM]) or masculine/default exponents (for n[−FEM]).[47]

Turning now to the same-root nominals and feminine-default animals, they can combine with both interpretable ns. Thus, there is no need to specify **any** semantic licensing conditions for these nominals. The Encyclopedia entry for a root like √HAKIM would be:

(32)   [√HAKIM] = 'doctor'

The last category of nominals remaining are the inanimate nominals. Their gender features are generally considered to be irrelevant for semantic interpretation (see Section 4.2 for some dissenting views). In the analysis in Section 3.2, this fact is captured because "masculine" inanimates lack gender features altogether, and feminine inanimates have a semantically uninterpretable gender feature.

---

[46] This would result in an analysis fairly similar to the lexicalist approaches discussed in Ch. 2 that have lexical rules like "[female] → [feminine]."

[47] Interpreted strictly, the analysis predicts that if a root like √ɪNNAT 'mother' is used in a non-nominal context, it will not trigger a female interpretation. However, I could not locate any non-nominal instances of such roots. Within Amharic, *ɪnnat* and *abbat* can be adjectivalized to *ɪnnat-awi* 'motherly' and *abbat-awi* 'fatherly.' However, *-awi* is only used to adjectivalize nouns (Leslau 1995: 240), and thus the structure would be [$_{aP}$ -awi [$_{nP}$ n[+FEM] [√ɪNNAT]]]. Also, according to a consultant and several Amharic dictionaries, there are no verbs 'to mother' or 'to father' in Amharic (and no verbs corresponding to other different-root nominals, e.g. 'to brother' or 'to sister'); this is not surprising if the only way to make such a verb would be to build it from a noun, since there are limited morphological resources in Amharic for converting nPs to verbs.

It may be that certain roots in general have very limited interpretations such that they can only be interpreted under a particular categorizing head (although they can be categorized again after that to form, e.g. a denominal adjective or denominal verb). The number of roots like this is probably small for any given language—the list of different root nominals in Ch. 2 is nearly complete for Amharic (there are perhaps 5 additional examples).

However, licensing conditions must not only correctly match up a root and *n*—they also must make sure that other *n*s cannot combine with the root. In the case of inanimates, it must be ensured somehow that roots that denote inanimates when nominalized do not combine with any of the *n*s that carry interpretable gender features. There are at least two viable options for accomplishing this goal.

The first option is a feature co-occurrence restriction on the feature bundles in the pre-syntactic lexicon (this option is adopted in Kramer 2009: 133–4; see Gazdar et al. 1985 on feature co-occurrence restrictions). Interpretable gender features are restricted such that they only co-occur with the feature [ANIMATE].

(33)   **Feature co-occurrence restriction: interpretable gender only for animates**
      a. n *i* [+FEM] → [ANIMATE]
      b. n *i* [−FEM] → [ANIMATE]

(33) keeps inanimate nominals from being associated with natural gender features, since it forces any interpretable *n* to also contain an animate feature. However, the restriction does not state anything about the distribution of the animate feature. I assume that there are two presyntactic feature bundles that contain plain *n*: one with an animate feature (used for animate nominals whose natural gender is unknown or unimportant to the speaker) and one with an inanimate feature (or perhaps just lacking an animate feature; used for masculine inanimates). (33) captures the fact that inanimate nominals are never compatible with natural gender, while still allowing masculine inanimate nominals and animate nominals whose natural gender is unknown to trigger the same type of agreement.

The second option for keeping natural gender from the inanimates is a semantic licensing condition, ensuring that the root for 'table,' 'bed,' 'idea,' etc. is only capable of being interpreted in the context of a *n* that lacks interpretable gender features (cf. Harley and Noyer 1998, 1999, 2000). This is shown for the Amharic root √BET 'house' in (34).

(34)   **Semantic licensing condition: 'house'**
      [*n* [√BET]] = 'house'

I assume that this licensing condition is the same for all inanimate-denoting roots, even if they are licensed under *n u* [+FEM], because the semantics ignores uninterpretable features (see Section 4.2). Essentially, this licensing condition conveys the idea that a house is not the type of entity in the real world that can ever have natural gender.

I will not decide between these two options here for a couple of reasons. First, I suspect that the empirical evidence necessary to allow this decision falls outside of the purview of this book, perhaps involving the "playful" or emotive use of natural gender for inanimate entities (see e.g. Corbett 1991: 12–13 on the use of animate pronouns for inanimate objects in English). Second, evaluating these two options will be easiest once our understanding of the nature of the Encyclopedia has progressed.

I therefore leave both options open for now, with the understanding that one of them suffices to keep inanimates from being licensed with the interpretable *n*s.

Overall, then, different root nominals have very strict semantic licensing conditions ((31)), same root nominals and feminine default nominals do not have any semantic licensing conditions (that are related to gender; (32))), and inanimate nominals are prevented from being interpreted as male/female through either a feature co-occurrence restriction ((33)) or a semantic licensing condition ((34)).

3.4.1.2 Arbitrary licensing conditions   Like semantic licensing conditions, arbitrary licensing conditions are root-specific; they match a particular root with a particular *n*. However, unlike semantic licensing conditions, they are idiosyncratic—essentially a chance association between a root and a *n*. They represent the most "listed" or "lexical" aspect of gender as a phenomenon.

Almost all of the previous work on licensing conditions has assumed that they are conditions on the Vocabulary Insertion of roots, i.e. on root exponence (see e.g. Harley and Noyer 1998, 1999, 2000, Siddiqi 2009, *pace* Acquaviva 2009). From this perspective, arbitrary gender is encoded as a fact about the exponence of a particular root. For example, in Amharic, *bet* 'house' is only capable of being exponed in the context of "plain" *n*, whereas *s'ähay* 'sun' is only capable of being exponed in the context of *n* [+FEM].

(35)   **Vocabulary Insertion at a root = arbitrary licensing condition (inanimates)**
    a. √BET ↔ [bet] / *n*
    b. √s'ÄHAY ↔ [s'ähay] / *n* [+FEM]

This is a suitably arbitrary analysis; it is merely listed whether a certain *n* is included in the context for exponence of a root.[48] I assume that a Vocabulary Item cannot be inserted if its context is not met, so if, for example, √BET is combined with *n* [+FEM] syntactically, then it will be impossible for it to be exponed since its context is not met. This assumption is quite similar to the Subset Principle—specifically, to how a Vocabulary Item cannot be inserted if it contains features that are not present in the terminal node from the syntax.[49]

Different-root nominals do not have any arbitrary licensing conditions.[50]

(36)   √ɨNNAT ↔ [innat]

---

[48] (35) cannot replace the semantic licensing conditions on inanimates because I assume PF does not care about whether features are interpretable. If this assumption is correct, (35)b would allow for 'sun' to combine with *n i* [+FEM].

[49] I also must assume that if no suitable Vocabulary Item can be inserted at a root, the derivation crashes at PF.

[50] It is worth asking whether an inanimate nominal could lack arbitrary licensing conditions. I argue in Ch. 6 that this phenomenon is attested in Spanish: certain inanimate nominals are compatible with either gender (often with a slight shift in meaning). I also speculate there on why this phenomenon is absent from Amharic (essentially, the distribution of *n* [+FEM] is too limited in Amharic).

A root like *ɨnnat* 'mother' is licensed under only one *n* at the Encyclopedia. So, PF need not care which *n*s it combines with since only one will ever be licit for the Encyclopedia.

Same-root nominals and feminine-default nominals have no semantic licensing conditions, but there is one licensing condition that seems arbitrary for these nominals: the *n* that is licensed when gender is unknown/irrelevant. For same-root nominals, this is *n*, whereas for feminine-default nominals, it is *n u*[+FEM]. This information could be listed in the context for the exponence of the associated roots, as shown in (37) for *hakim* 'doctor' (same-root nominal) and *ayt'* 'mouse' (feminine-default nominal).

(37)   **Same-root and feminine-default arbitrary licensing conditions (to be rejected)**
　　　a. √HAKIM ↔ [hakim] / {*n*, *n i* [+FEM], *n i* [−FEM]}
　　　b. √AYT' ↔ [ayt'] / {*n u*[+FEM], *n i* [+FEM], *n i* [−FEM]}

However, such an approach misses a key generalization: when gender is unknown/irrelevant, plain *n* is used to license almost every root.[51] In other words, it is left unexplained why only a few roots have restrictions like (37)b, and Amharic is not alone in this restriction. Other languages with occasional feminine defaults only have a handful of nominals that behave that way (see e.g. Spanish (Chapter 6), Maa (Chapter 6), and Romanian (Chapter 8)).

Instead, I propose that, like different-root nominals, same-root nominals in fact have no arbitrary licensing conditions.

(38)   **Same-root nominals: no arbitrary licensing conditions**
　　　√HAKIM ↔ [hakim]

This makes the difference between same-root and different-root nominals boil down to semantic licensing, which seems intuitively correct. 'Mother' must be feminine because of its meaning, whereas 'doctor' has no such association with biological gender. This predicts that similar lexical items will be different-root and same-root across languages, and the later chapters in this book will show that this is loosely borne out: basic kinship terms tend to be different-root, whereas professions tend to be same-root.

The same-root nominals are very much a default case: they have neither semantic nor arbitrary licensing conditions. Feminine-default nominals similarly have no semantic licensing conditions, but I propose that they do have arbitrary licensing conditions that keep them from combining with plain *n*, as shown in (39).

(39)   **Feminine-default nominal: arbitrary licensing condition**
　　　√AYT' ↔ [ayt'] / {*n* [+FEM], *n* [−FEM]}

---

[51] This approach also requires PF to see the difference between interpretable and uninterpretable features (see fn. 48).

Only one piece remains: keeping a *n* that is *u*[+FEM] from combining with a same-root nominal. There are multiple ways to encode this, and like the discussion of inanimates above, I put off choosing between them until we know more about this part of the grammar. One option would be to have the animate *n u*[+FEM] syntactically select only for a handful of roots (e.g. √AYT'). Another option would be for the Vocabulary Item that realizes animate *n u*[+FEM] to be insertable only in the context of a very small list of roots.[52] Either way, animate *n u*[+FEM] is prevented from combining with all but a small number of roots.

This approach to arbitrary licensing conditions raises a number of interesting questions which I can touch on only briefly. First, it raises the question of learnability. Certainly the most complex licensing conditions belong to the feminine-default nominals; learners not only have to learn an arbitrary licensing condition, but also must learn that the distribution of animate *n u* [+FEM] is highly limited. It is perhaps unsurprising that only a handful of roots are capable of being learned in this way across languages.

Second, this approach raises the question of root allomorphy conditioned by gender. Since the exponence of a root is conditioned by the gender identity of the *n* that categorizes it, the exponence of a root may accordingly vary by gender. I argue in Chapter 6 that this is attested in Spanish, e.g. *padre* 'father' and *madre* 'mother.'[53]

Finally, this approach allows for root allomorphy conditioned by categorizing head. If *n* conditions root allomorphy, then we might predict that roots would have different allomorphs when in the context of a different categorizing head. This is borne out in English verbal/nominal pairs like *destroy* ~ *destruct-ion*, as discussed in e.g. Harley and Noyer (1999).

I conclude that the root exponence approach to arbitrary conditions is on the right track, in that it captures the Amharic gender system and leads us to interesting questions and promising predictions about the nature of root allomorphy.

3.4.1.3 Summary   I have shown that licensing conditions are generally encoded via conditions on interpretation at the Encyclopedia, or conditions on realization at PF. It is expected to find licensing conditions in multiple locations in the grammar, so to speak. In a Distributed Morphology framework, listedness and root-specific statements are distributed throughout the grammar, whereas in lexicalist approaches they are concentrated in the pre-syntactic lexicon (and I showed in Chapter 2 that this is inadequate to account for Amharic). DM provides the flexibility to capture the nuanced interplay of default and listedness that gender licensing requires in Amharic.

---

[52] This requires there to be a way to distinguish this *n* [+FEM] from the interpretable *n* [+FEM] at PF.

[53] For the sake of completeness, it is worth noting that I have not come across any cases of root allomorphy for gender with an inanimate nominal. I leave this as an open question.

TABLE 3.2. **Amharic licensing conditions**

	Licensing Condition(s)
Different root *innat* 'mother' *abbat* 'father'	Semantic: root can only be interpreted under either n[+FEM] or *n* [–FEM]; see (31)
Same root *hakim* 'doctor'	• No semantic restrictions (related to gender); see (32) • No arbitrary restrictions; see (38) • Prevented from combining with *n u*[+FEM] via syntactic selection or conditions on exponence (see Section 3.4.1.2)
Feminine default *ayt'* 'mouse'	• No semantic restrictions (related to gender); see (32) • Arbitrary restriction: root licensed only under *n* [+FEM] and *n* [–FEM] (see (39))
Inanimate *s'ähay* 'sun' *bet* 'house'	• Either feature co-occurrence or semantic restrictions (see (33) and (34)) • Arbitrary restriction: root licensed under either *n* [+FEM] or *n* (see (35))

Acquaviva (2009) proposes a basic licensing conditions approach to gender where certain *n*s can only be exponed in the context of certain roots. He has the following reservations about a licensing conditions approach to gender:

(40)   . . . expressing the gender of a noun as a statement of co-occurrence between a root and a certain content for *n* is not particularly enlightening or predictive. (Acquaviva 2009: 17)[54]

In separating out semantic and arbitrary licensing conditions, this analysis renders licensing conditions (I believe) more enlightening and more capable of making predictions.

I close this section with Table 3.2, showing the licensing conditions required for each root.

3.4.2 *The interpretability of gender features*

In the analysis in Section 3. 2, I proposed that a gender feature can be either interpretable or uninterpretable. In this section, I expand a little on my assumptions about interpretability, and then evaluate previous approaches to gender and semantic interpretability.

---

[54] Acquaviva (2009: 17) also comments that the approach "does not provide a formal expression of the stable association of most roots with gender, class, or other diacritics. This seems to be a weakness, in so far as a noun's idiosyncratic marking should have a formal grammatical encoding, as distinct from a mere statement." However, it is unclear to me what the difference is; a statement is a type of formal grammatical encoding.

As per Chomsky (2000, 2001), I assume that a feature is interpretable when it is legible at the syntax–semantics interface, i.e. LF (I also assume that LF is separate from the Encyclopedia; see Chapter 1, and Harley and Noyer 1999). More specifically, I assume that interpretable features trigger some kind of effect at LF (e.g. insertion of a denotation) such that their presence/absence (or change in +/– value) changes the interpretation of a linguistic structure. A brief definition of "interpretability" in this approach is set out in (41) (cf. Zamparelli 2008: 170).

(41)   **Definition of interpretability**
        A feature is interpretable iff its presence/absence changes the interpretation of
        a linguistic structure, i.e. if it is legible at LF.

According to this rough diagnostic, natural gender is an interpretable feature. Depending on its value (and its presence/absence) it changes the interpretation of a nominal to be male or female, i.e. it is legible and causes a denotation to be inserted (see Percus 2011: 169–70 for a version of this argument using Italian data). For example, the feature i [+FEM] is interpretable because it causes a denotation to be inserted at PF that has the effect of interpreting a nominal as female.[55] Combining the root √HAKIM with a n i[+FEM] results in the interpretation 'female doctor,' whereas combining the same root with a n i[–FEM] results in the interpretation 'male doctor.'

In contrast, arbitrary gender is uninterpretable. The feature u[+FEM] is illegible at LF, i.e. no denotation is inserted for it and thus it does not affect interpretation. Combining the root √s'ÄHAY with a u[+FEM] results in the non-gendered meaning 'sun,' and combining it with a plain n would still result in the non-gendered meaning 'sun' (see Section 3.4.1 for how PF determines which n combines with the root in this case).

In some versions of Minimalism, uninterpretable features that are unchecked (not agreed with) cause the derivation to crash (Chomsky 2000, 2001). Under the present analysis, arbitrary gender is uninterpretable and unchecked—it does not enter into an Agree relation with an interpretable gender feature. However, the assumption that uninterpretable features must be checked/deleted/eliminated before the syntax–semantics interface has been questioned (Legate 2002, Pesetsky and Torrego 2007: fn. 15, Epstein et al. 2010, and esp. Carstens 2010, 2011 for gender). In many of these approaches, it is *unvalued* features that cause a crash, and uninterpretable features are simply ignored by the semantics. I will hereby adopt this slight modification: all unvalued features cause the derivation to crash (most likely at the PF interface,

---

[55] I do not advance a particular analysis of the LF denotation of interpretable gender features here, since that would take the discussion too far afield. See Kramer (2009), Percus (2011), Matushansky (2013), Merchant (2014) for some previous approaches. See also Heim and Kratzer (1998), Sauerland (2004, 2008), and Yanovich (2012) on the semantics of phi features, especially on pronouns.

regardless of interpretability) and valued uninterpretable features are ignored at LF. Since arbitrary gender is valued and uninterpretable, it will not cause a crash, and I assume that the interpretational algorithm at LF simply passes over material it cannot assign a denotation to.[56]

The analysis argued for here is somewhat unusual in its treatment of gender and interpretability. Setting aside Kramer (2009, 2014), there are only two previous proposals (to the best of my knowledge) suggesting that natural gender is interpretable and arbitrary gender is uninterpretable, namely, Percus (2011) and Matushansky (2013). I first discuss these two approaches, and then turn to proposals that treat gender as either always interpretable or always uninterpretable.[57]

Percus (2011) is a careful, thorough case study of the semantic interpretation of gender features in Italian. In broad strokes, much of the discussion is very congruent with the approach here. For example, he treats gender features as generally interpretable, but capable of being not interpreted under specific conditions (e.g. in the context of particular nouns). In fact, Percus (pp. 183–4) considers an analysis similar to the approach developed here. However, he decides against pursuing it, since it predicts that some nouns could have a feminine default, incorrectly for Italian. In Amharic, feminine-default nouns are of course attested, and in Section 3.4.1 I showed how licensing conditions ensure that masculine is the default for most nouns, and feminine for a few (Italian can also be accounted for in the present analysis if it simply lacks any nouns with the licensing conditions in (39)).[58]

Matushansky (2013) develops a theory of agreement that generates and explains mixed agreement, e.g. when the masculine noun *vrač* 'doctor' in Russian can (but need not) trigger feminine agreement on some or all agreement targets when it refers to a female doctor. As part of the assumptions of the analysis, Matushansky treats

---

[56] Alternatively, it could be that the failure to enact an obligatory operation causes a crash; see Preminger (2014).

[57] A wholly alternative approach would be to dispense with the feature diacritics "interpretable" and "uninterpretable." There would be four ns, two of which have a denotation which references natural gender (n_1 [+FEM], n_2 [–FEM]) and two of which still have a denotation but one which does not reference natural gender (n_3 "plain" n, n_4 [+FEM] another feminine n). However, there would have to be some way for LF to determine which denotation to insert at n [+FEM], unless it is sensitive to the subscript-numeral diacritics used for expository purposes. Nevertheless, it would be preferable for the analysis to be free of the "uninterpretable" and "interpretable" diacritics, and I hope the simple semantic proposals here that keep the diacritics around lead to more serious efforts.

[58] Percus ultimately adopts a relatively complex analysis that can be extended to languages with feminine default nouns, but which I do not pursue here for a few reasons. First, it relies on the grammar being able to access a female or male component of the meaning of roots, whereas I assume the Encyclopedia entries of roots are inaccessible. Moreover, it requires two very powerful constraints: (i) the Tidiness Condition: "Don't leave a gender feature uninterpreted when a minimally different noun with the same root and a different gender feature exists and has the resulting denotation" (p. 178), and (ii) No Needless Feature Deletion: "Don't leave a feature uninterpreted when you could arrive at the same result by using an interpreted feature" (p. 185). Both of these seem to be transderivational (depending on the nature of the lexicon), and No Needless Feature Deletion seems to require look-ahead.

"semantic" phi features like natural gender as interpretable, whereas "grammatical phi features" like arbitrary gender do not contribute to the semantic interpretation. Matushansky (2013: 284–5) also assumes that same-root nouns lack gender features, as argued for above. However, the analysis has similar drawbacks to Carstens (2010, 2011) (see Chapter 2): natural gender is "converted" into arbitrary gender, and there is no discussion of defaults.

Most of the previous research that takes a stand on the interpretation of gender has argued that gender is either (i) always interpretable or (ii) always uninterpretable. I review each type of approach in turn.

I first review approaches that argue that gender is always interpretable, starting with an overview and then focusing on proposals in Picallo (2006, 2007, 2008). A handful of analyses explicitly claim all gender features are interpretable, including Dowty and Jacobson (1980) and Pesetsky and Torrego (2007: fn. 29; cf. Bouchard 1984: 14–17).[59] These approaches claim that the sheer fact of categorizing a noun in a particular way is interpretable, even though the categorization does not change the meaning of the noun with respect to the "real world." In other words, the fact that the word for 'sun' in Amharic is feminine is an interpretable "fact" about the mental object sun. It is a fact about the mental object that represents the celestial body around which the earth orbits that the word for that mental object is feminine in Amharic.

As Legate (2002) observes, though, these approaches somewhat avoid the main issue in that they do not treat the gender feature itself as interpretable; it is the higher-order property of having a valued gender feature that is "interpretable." Moreover, recall that interpretability is defined as a feature being interpretable at LF ((41)). However, the way in which arbitrary gender is interpretable in these approaches involves a different level of the grammar—sometimes referred to as Domain D (Chomsky 1981)—which connects denotations and variables in LF with mental representations. Under these approaches, the gist is that as a mental object in Domain D, 'sun' has as a property that it is feminine in Amharic. This type of "interpretability," though, is substantially different from a feature that triggers the insertion of a denotation at LF. I conclude that arbitrary gender is not interpretable, at least not in the same way that other syntactic features are interpretable.[60]

Perhaps tellingly, the idea that gender must be interpretable has been put forth only because it necessarily follows from other, more central assumptions that the

---

[59] See also Carstens (2000) and Sessarego and Gutiérrez-Rexach (2011), who assume without comment that all gender features are interpretable on nouns.

[60] There is one empirical phenomenon that seems to indicate that arbitrary gender is interpretable: pronoun reference. It is well known that pronouns must agree in arbitrary gender with their referents, just as they agree in natural gender with their referents (see e.g. Picallo 2008). Nevertheless, I consider pronoun "agreement" to be substantially different from other types of agreement, and set it aside generally for this book (see Ch. 4).

authors want to maintain. That all gender is interpretable has never been argued for as a data-driven necessity.[61] However, recent work by Picallo (2006, 2007, 2008) takes up the idea that there is something interpretable about the sheer fact of categorization, and it is worth reviewing this approach briefly. Picallo (2007, 2008) proposes a unified analysis of sex-based gender systems (e.g. Romance languages), noun class systems (e.g. Bantu languages), and noun classifier systems (e.g. Jacaltec (Mayan)). Each of these systems has a functional category c which contains an interpretable feature [CLASS] (cf. Kihm 2005, Ferrari 2005). In sex-based gender systems, the class category c takes an NP complement whose head N has an uninterpretable gender feature.

(42)

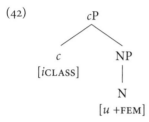

Framed in terms of present assumptions, cP will be below nP and NP is equivalent to the root. The class category c enters into an Agree relationship with N/the root and checks/values its uninterpretable gender feature. The relationship between c and N is similar to the relationship between T and V in English in certain frameworks (e.g. Pesetsky and Torrego 2007): T is inserted with interpretable tense features, and V is inserted with uninterpretable tense features that are checked/valued by T and ultimately spelled out on V. Put another way, [+/–FEM] on N is the formal exponent of the interpretable class feature. In noun class systems and noun classifier systems, the noun class affix and the classifiers are realizations of the c head.

Picallo's innovative approach pursues a middle road between lexicalist approaches to gender (gender on N) and the semantic approaches that focus on the interpretability of categorization. However, it suffers from the same drawback of interpretable approaches: it is unclear how exactly the categorization feature interpreted, especially at LF.[62] The analysis also does not take into account natural gender (which Picallo 2008: 50 deliberately sets aside), i.e. there is no relationship between the interpretability of categorization and the interpretability of natural gender features.

Finally, this approach to gender has some (at least initially) troubling empirical predictions. The Class head and the gender feature on the noun are never

---

[61] Dowty and Jacobson (1988) want to defend the idea that all agreement (including gender agreement) is semantic, and Pesetsky and Torrego (2007) want to defend the idea that all syntactic features are interpretable in at least one location per derivation.

[62] Picallo (2008: 50) suggests that c "translates to the grammatical system non-linguistic processes of entity categorization," but does not discuss further how the categorization feature is interpreted.

morphophonologically realized at the same time, unlike most Agree relationships. Also, the analysis provides no way of accounting for a major empirical difference between noun classifiers on the one hand and noun class systems and sex-based systems on the other. Noun classifiers do not trigger agreement, whereas noun classes and sex-based genders do (see Chapter 4), but there is no formal distinction between them in this approach.

Overall, the analyses that treat all gender as interpretable are unsuccessful, mostly because it is not convincing that gender features are interpreted (at least like other syntactic features). It is somewhat less common to claim that all gender features are uninterpretable; I start with the suggestions in Asudeh and Potts (2004), and proceed to the proposals in Carstens (2010, 2011).

Asudeh and Potts (2004) is the clearest defense of a position that has had some support over the years in gender research (cf. Bernstein 1993a: 117, Picallo 2008: 50), namely, that there are too many exceptions to the generalizations that connect natural gender and grammatical gender for grammatical gender to have anything to do with semantics at all. Put in more specific terms, generalizations like "male-referring nominals are masculine" and "female-referring nominals are feminine" have too many exceptions to serve as a basis for an analysis.

(43) a. mädchen   'girl.N'   **German**
      b. persona   'person.F'   **Spanish**

For example, in (43)ab 'girl' is neuter in German, and 'person' is feminine in Spanish regardless of the referent. While it is difficult to make precise exactly how many exceptions are "too many," it cannot be denied that exceptions do exist. However, I believe treating these exceptions as lethal to a semantic approach to gender throws the baby out with the bathwater for the following reasons.

First, even in languages with exceptions (e.g. Spanish), the vast majority of nominals follow the generalizations. For example, there are very few human nouns in Spanish that are not masculine when male and feminine when female (Harris 1991: 40, Roca 1989: 18[63]). More tellingly, there are many languages whose gender systems have vanishingly few or no exceptions to the semantic generalizations. Notably, this set of languages includes Amharic (see Chapter 2), but Amharic is far from being the only member. Nearly half of the languages with gender surveyed in Corbett (2011c) have "semantic" gender assignment systems where the assignment of gender to nominals is based primarily or predominantly on biological sex and/or other inter-pretable semantic properties. In fact, one of the most robust generalizations about gender cross-linguistically is that every gender system assigns gender at least partially on a semantic basis (Corbett 1991), as will be explored more fully in Chapter 4. There

---

[63] In contrast, most animals in Spanish have a fixed gender regardless of sex, but this is because Spanish does not generally represent non-human natural gender in the grammar; see Ch. 6.

is no such thing as a gender system that is not based on a semantic feature. Given these facts, I conclude that it is invalid to treat exceptions as evidence that gender is always uninterpretable. The generalizations that relate gender features and semantic properties are cross-linguistically and intra-linguistically very robust.

However, there is a way to capture the semantics–gender connection even in an analysis where gender features are uninterpretable: lexicalism. In a lexicalist approach which assigns gender in the lexicon pre-syntactically, it is possible to have rules that connect a female feature to feminine gender, and a male feature to masculine gender. Then, in the syntax, the feminine and masculine features them-selves are uninterpretable. This is the approach developed in Carstens (2010, 2011), and the assumption that the feminine/masculine features are uninterpretable could easily be added to pre-minimalist lexicalist analyses like Harris (1991). However, as I argued in Chapter 2, the best worked-out version of this analysis in Harris (1991) struggles to account for Amharic, and Carstens (2010, 2011) is not developed in enough detail to determine if it will be successful. I conclude that an all-uninterpret-able approach to gender features is not a fruitful direction to pursue.[64]

In this subsection, I have looked at alternative approaches to the (un)interpret-ability of gender features. The analysis developed in this book is essentially a compromise: certain gender features are interpretable, and certain gender features are not. However, in most previous analyses that are explicit about gender and interpretability, gender features are treated as entirely interpretable or entirely uninterpretable. The "entirely interpretable" analyses are unconvincing in that arbi-trary gender cannot be interpretable at LF. The most straightforward "entirely uninterpretable" analysis ignores valid generalizations relating gender to semantic features across languages, and the lexicalist approaches that captures these general-izations cannot cover Amharic, as argued in Chapter 2.

3.5 Conclusion

This chapter has served as the focal point for the *n* analysis of gender for Amharic. Section 3.2 developed the analysis and showed how it applies to various types of nominals. The analysis received additional empirical support in Section 3.3 from a variety of Amharic phenomena. The discussion of licensing conditions in Section 3.4.1 provided a formalization of these crucial components of the analysis.

---

[64] A different type of objection is raised by Zamparelli (2008). He considers Italian nouns like *bambino* 'male child' and *bambina* 'female child' to have different roots, and the roots contribute the natural gender meaning. The gender features relevant for agreement are uninterpretable. However, see Percus (2011) for arguments against this stance from words like *musicista* 'musician' in Italian, which are compatible with either gender but clearly only have one root.

Section 3.4.2 laid out my assumptions about interpretability and compared them to previous research.

Now that the *n* analysis has been developed to some degree of empirical and theoretical detail, it is time to test it with a broader range of data. First, I will survey gender systems cross-linguistically (Chapter 4) and then proceed to present how the analysis works for other types of gender systems (Chapters 5, 6, and 7).

4

Defining gender

4.1 What gender is, and what gender isn't

The purpose of this brief chapter is to clarify a typological definition of gender as a prelude to the cross-linguistic case studies in subsequent chapters. In Chapter 1, I defined gender in the following way:

(1) **Definition of gender (preliminary version)**
Gender is the sorting of nouns into two or more classes, as reflected in agreement morphology on determiners, adjectives, verbs, and other syntactic categories.

This definition is the "industry standard" in gender research, at least since Corbett (1991) (Corbett credits Hockett 1958: 231 for the definition; see also Greenberg 1978: 49, Nichols 1992, Comrie 1999: 457, Matasović 2004: 19–20, Velupillai 2012: 165). Under this approach, gender is a way of describing the sub-categorial behavior of nouns. In this chapter, I scrutinize the typological definition of gender, first discussing its component parts, then clarifying what phenomena it designates as "gender" and what phenomena it excludes (I do not discuss how to define "gender" in terms of the analysis in Chapter 3; see Chapter 11 for some thoughts on that). I close this chapter with a friendly amendment to (1) that recognizes the important role that natural gender plays across languages.

The definition in (1) has three main parts: there must be at least two genders; gender is restricted to nouns; and the genders (nominal sub-categories) are differentiated from one another via agreement patterns. The minimum of two genders is simple to justify: if all nouns agree in the same way, then there is no need to describe the nouns as anything other than a single category defined by sheer nounhood, not as sub-classes. As for the restriction to nouns, it is possible to identify sub-classes of verbs and adjectives (and other syntactic categories) based on varying linguistic behavior in certain contexts (e.g. a sub-class of verbs takes a certain set of inflections, predicative adjectives behave differently than non-predicative adjectives in copular clauses). However, their differences do not manifest in different agreement patterns on other elements because nouns are (usually) the only category in a language that controls agreement (Corbett 2006a: 35). Therefore, sub-categorial differences among verbs and adjectives are not considered to be genders.

The Morphosyntax of Gender. First Edition. Ruth Kramer.
© Ruth Kramer 2015. Published 2015 by Oxford University Press.

Under (1), it is truly the agreement patterns that are crucial in identifying a gender system and differentiating the genders. Notably, it is not sufficient or necessary to morphologically mark a noun for its gender; this is because in many languages there is no consistent morphological correlate of particular genders (see Velupillai 2012: 165 for a clear statement of this).

Consider a schematic example: take two nouns in Language A—let's say Noun 1 and Noun 2. Noun 1 and Noun 2 trigger different agreement patterns: Pattern 1 and Pattern 2. From these facts alone, we can say that Language A has a gender system, and that Noun 1 and Noun 2 have different genders: Noun 1 is in Gender X and Noun 2 is in Gender Y ((2)).

(2) a. Noun 1   Agreeing category pattern 1   = Noun 1 is Gender X
     b. Noun 2   Agreeing category pattern 2   = Noun 2 is Gender Y

A natural language example from French is in (3).

(3) a. la   petite   vache   **French**
        the.F   small.F   cow

     b. le   petit   taureau
        the.M   small.M   bull

In (3)a, the determiner is *la* and the adjective has a final *-e*, whereas in (3)b the determiner is *le* and the adjective lacks a final *-e*. In other words, the nouns 'cow' and 'bull' trigger different agreement patterns on the definite determiner and the adjective within a nominal phrase. This allows us to say that French "has" a gender system, and that 'cow' and 'bull' belong to different genders (conventionally, feminine and masculine).[65]

Contrast the French data in (3) with the Hungarian data in (4).

(4) a. a   kicsi   tehén   **Hungarian**
        the   small   cow

     b. a   kicsi   bika
        the   small   bull

The definite article *a* and adjective *kicsi* are identical for (4)a and (4)b, i.e. there is no differing agreement behavior across the two nouns. In fact, it is the case for any pair of nouns in Hungarian that they do not differ in the forms of agreeing elements (if they have the same number and person; more on this below). Therefore, Hungarian as a language "lacks" a gender system, and it is in fact conventionally described this way (see e.g. Dryer and the WALS author team 2011, Rounds 2001). Note that the

---

[65] Nothing in the definition of gender restricts the elements that show gender agreement: adjectives, determiners, verbs, etc.—all are fair game and none are privileged. See Nichols (1992: 137) for some typological data on the frequency of agreement with different types of targets across languages.

words for 'cow' and 'bull' are distinct in Hungarian and each carry a component meaning of biological sex—cows are female bovines, bulls are male bovines. However, since this does not affect agreement patterns, the language is not considered to "have" gender in that it does not have a gender system (see further discussion on this point in Chapter 11).

In general, the presence or absence of agreement not only allows us to identify languages with gender systems, but also allows us to determine whether a particular noun sub-classification phenomenon falls under the rubric of gender. I briefly review several noun sub-classification phenomena that are *not* genders under (1) (classifiers, declension classes), as well as several phenomena that *are* gender under (1) (pronominal-gender-only systems, "noun class" systems).

4.1.1 Classifiers and declension class are not genders

There are two phenomena which clearly involve noun classification but do not involve agreement, and thus they do not qualify as "genders." The first phenomenon is noun classifiers; morphosyntactically independent from the noun and often invariant, classifiers are elements that serve to put nouns into semantically based categories often depending on animacy, shape, or any number of semantic distinctions. For example, in Minangkabau (Austronesian (Malayic); Indonesia), there are separate classifiers for trees and for fruits, which can be applied to the same word.

(5)   a. batang   limau   b. buah   limau
         tree.CL   lemon   fruit.CL   lemon
         'lemon tree'   'lemon fruit'   (Velupillai 2012: 172)

Classifiers do not change the agreement behavior of the noun (i.e. a noun with classifier X does not agree differently from a noun with classifier Y, *ceteris paribus*), so they are a separate phenomenon from gender as per (1). However, many if not most languages with classifier systems lack a gender system,[66] leading some to think that (at least numeral) classifiers are a precursor to developing a gender system (see e.g. Greenberg 1978; see also Aikhenvald 2000 and Gil 2011 on classifiers in general).

Another phenomenon which involves noun classification but not agreement is declension class, also known as inflection class. Declension class is a way of sorting nominals depending on how they inflect for number and case, found in many Slavic languages (Russian: Corbett 1991; Serbian-Croatian: Wechsler and Zlatić 2003), Greek (Alexiadou 2004), Latin (Comrie 1999), Spanish (Harris 1991), and others.

---

[66] Upon crossing the "numeral classifier" feature (Gil 2011) and "number of genders" feature (Corbett 2011a) in WALS , there are 133 languages classified by both features. Of these 133, 30 have obligatory or optional numeral classifiers. Of those 30, 27 have 0 genders (i.e. they do not have a gender system), 1 has 2 genders, and 2 have 3 genders. Thus, at least initially, it seems that classifier languages usually do not have gender systems.

Nouns in different declension classes do not necessarily trigger different agreement patterns. For example, Latin *anima* 'soul' is Declension Class 1 whereas *lēx* 'law' is Declension Class 3, but both nouns trigger the same agreement patterns (feminine; see Maidhoff 2009: 17ff.). Therefore, declension class does not meet the definition of gender established in (1).

The relationship between gender and declension class can be complex, though. In contrast to the classifier languages, the canonical languages with nominal declension class (including those listed above) all have gender systems, and the gender system interacts with declension class in intricate ways. I return to this issue in Chapter 10, once the analysis of gender proposed in the book has been fully articulated.

The definition in (1) is clear about agreement: gender must involve agreement, and this excludes classifiers and declension class from being considered genders. However, there is nothing in the definition that identifies the features in which the nouns agree. This allows certain less canonical phenomena to be considered gender, and I discuss them in the next section.

4.1.2 *Noun class and pronominal gender are gender*

The French data in (3) correspond to what many people think when they think of gender: two genders (maybe a third: neuter), related to biological sex somehow. But nothing in (1) is that limiting. Gender need not involve biological sex according to (1) (the word 'gender' derives from the Latin word *genus* which means only 'kind' or 'sort' and not 'biological sex'; Greenberg 1978, Corbett 1991: 1), and there is only a set minimum of genders (two), with no maximum. In fact, looking beyond biological sex allows for a language to have more than two to three genders, and this book will consider any noun classification system to be gender as long as it is reflected in agreement patterns, regardless of the number of genders or whether they are based on biological sex.

This is hardly a novel move: languages that fit this profile are almost always included in typological gender studies (e.g. Corbett 1991). But it is worth stating this explicitly because such languages are often described within their own literatures as having "noun class"—not gender. For example, Caucasian languages often have two to eight genders traditionally referred to as "noun classes" (Corbett 1991: 25). These genders affect agreement, and they are differentiated via a mixture of animacy and biological sex (and possibly other factors). For example, Lak (Nakh-Daghestanian) has four genders: one for male humans, one for female humans, one for other animates and a few inanimates, and a final gender for all other nouns (Corbett 1991, Velupillai 2012).

A last important example is Algonquian languages. Unlike Caucasian languages, Algonquian languages are often described as having gender, perhaps because most if not all Algonquian languages only have two genders. However, gender in Algonquian languages is different from gender in e.g. French in that it is entirely based on animacy, regardless of biological sex (see Chapter 6; Goddard 2002). The two genders are thus "animate" and "inanimate." I still count these languages as having gender as per (1) since animacy distinctions affect agreement patterns (see e.g. Corbett 1991: 20 on Ojibwe), and I discuss how their gender systems fit into the picture here in Chapter 6.

A less clear-cut case is languages where gender is only reflected in formal distinctions among the pronouns, also known as pronominal-gender languages. One such language is English, which distinguishes biological sex and animacy in the 3rd person singular pronouns: *he, she, it.* The question is: does English "have" a gender system? The answer to that question depends on how "agreement" in (1) is defined. If agreement is interpreted loosely, referring to any phenomenon where there is covariation in features between two elements, then yes, pronouns "agree" with their antecedents and English has gender. This is the traditional line taken in the typological literature; such languages are included in gender surveys like Corbett (1991).

However, if "agreement" is interpreted strictly as referring to the Agree relation (Chomsky 2000, 2001) or another formal approach to agreement, then it is fairly clear that pronouns do not enter into an Agree relation with their antecedents. Most notably, the relationship between the pronoun and its antecedent does not meet the locality restrictions on Agree (e.g. the target must c-command the controller). There are also some signs that pronominal gender is empirically different from gender agreement with other types of targets. For example, it is much more likely to agree with the natural gender of the referent, even if the nominal that refers to that referent has arbitrary gender grammatically (Corbett 1991: 226). I thus set aside pronominal gender systems for the majority of the book (see Audring 2009 and references therein for a recent perspective on pronominal gender).

4.1.3 *Gender is not like other phi-features*

So far, (1) has served well: it allows us to determine whether a language has a gender system. However, strictly speaking, (1) does not differentiate gender from other features involved in agreement, most often number and person (cf. Greenberg 1978: 50). For example, two nouns with different numbers will also trigger different agreement patterns on adjectives, verbs, etc., but those two nouns do not necessarily have different genders. Consider some French data again in (6).

(6) a. la   vache   **French**
         the.F   cow

     b. les   soeur-s
         the.PL   sister-PL

     c. les   frère-s
         the.PL   brother-PL

The definite determiner is *la* in (6)a whereas it is *les* in (6)bc. In the absence of any other information, we could conclude that *vache* is a different gender than *soeur* and *frère*, and *soeur* and *frère* have the same gender. However, this is false; it is clear from agreement patterns in the singular that *vache* and *soeur* are both feminine, whereas *frère* is masculine. It is number that differentiates the agreement patterns across the nominals in (6).

In order to distinguish gender from other agreement features like number, Corbett (1991: 148) suggests that the nouns to be compared must have their morphosyntactic form held constant, i.e. plural nouns must be compared with plural nouns, singulars with singulars, etc. However, another way of distinguishing gender is through semantics; I believe incorporating the semantics of gender into the definition renders the definition more contentful and emphasizes the central role that natural gender plays in gender systems cross-linguistically.

At first glance, it may seem specious to connect gender to semantic properties at all. Examples are readily accessible where the gender of a nominal seems to have nothing to do with its biological sex or animacy. For example, in Spanish, the noun *domicilio* 'house' is masculine despite not having biological sex, and the noun *persona* 'person' is always feminine regardless of the biological sex of the referent.

However, one of the most robust discoveries from typological research is that gender systems are always rooted in nominal semantics. All gender systems have what I will call a "semantic core," a robust generalization or generalizations that connect semantic properties to genders (see e.g. Aksenov 1984, Corbett 1991: 63, Nichols 1992: 129, Dahl 2000, Corbett 2006b: 751–2, Matasović 2004: 22). Dahl (2000) further observed that the semantic core of a gender system always references at least some of the animate nominals. Languages vary in whether the relevant semantic property is biological sex (like Amharic), animacy (like Algonquian languages; see Chapter 6), human-ness (like Bantu languages; see Chapter 11), or possibly others. There may be some exceptions to the semantic core (e.g. *persona* in Spanish), but no language assigns genders to nouns completely randomly or completely formally; there is always a core set of nouns for which semantics determines how they receive gender (e.g. Spanish *madre* 'mother', *hija* 'daughter,' *mujer* 'woman,' *nuera* 'daughter-in-law,' *abuela* 'grandmother').

In comparison, the semantics of number (very roughly) involves the cardinality of units denoted by the noun, and the semantics of person involves discourse participation—identifying the speaker, the addressee, and any non-participants in the conversation. I therefore propose the following revision to the definition in (1):

(7) **Definition of gender (final version)**
     Gender is:
     (i)   the sorting of nouns into two or more classes;
     (ii) assigned depending on biological sex, animacy, and/or human-ness, for at least some animate nouns;
     (iii) reflected by agreement patterns on other elements (e.g. adjectives, determiners, verbs, auxiliaries).

It is possible that (7)ii may prove to be too strict. For example, it rules out a language whose semantic core is "all animal nouns receive Gender X" whereas all other nouns receive Gender Y. It is doubtful that such a language exists, but if one were to be located, it may be that (7)ii would be better phased as "gender assigned depending on any animate feature that is part of the animacy hierarchy" (see e.g. Lockwood and Macaulay 2012 on hierarchies).

In sum, we have seen that the definition in (7) allows us to identify a language as having a gender system and to identify how many genders a language has. It includes many languages traditionally described as having noun classes, but excludes classifiers and declension class. The final revision makes gender necessarily involve a semantic property, reflecting the key typological finding that all languages with gender systems have a semantic core.[67]

4.2 Conclusion

Now that there is a definition of gender, the scene has been sufficiently set for the case studies that test the predictions of the analysis in the next few chapters. Chapters 5 and 6 both concern languages with two genders. In Chapter 5, I focus on two-gender languages that lack uninterpretable gender features, unlike Amharic. In - Chapter 6, I cover languages that have one uninterpretable gender feature, looking at Spanish, Maa, and Algonquian languages. In Chapter 7 I turn to three-gender languages, showing how they can have zero, one, or two uninterpretable gender features.

---

[67] Note that this definition excludes the complex "noun classes" in Kiowa (Harbour 2007, 2011). The agreement classes of Kiowa nouns are capable of being analyzed just in terms of number features (some of which are on Num, and some of which are on *n*), with no need to depend on biological sex or animacy. They are also characterizable in terms of non-number-related semantic features (Harbour 2011: 578), but none of those features involve animacy or biological sex.

5

Case study 1: Two genders, three *n*s

5.1 Introduction

In the analysis of Amharic in Chapter 3, I identified four different "flavors" of *n* which are relevant for gender. They are repeated in (1).

(1) **Types of *n***
    a. *n* *i* [+FEM]   Female natural gender
    b. *n* *i* [−FEM]   Male natural gender
    c. *n*   No natural gender (or natural gender irrelevant/unknown)
    d. *n* *u* [+FEM]   Feminine arbitrary gender

Since category-neutral roots are interpreted as gendered in the context of a gendered *n*, a language that interprets any nominalized root as female/male/unsexed must minimally contain (1)abc.[68] In this chapter, I identify the types of gender systems predicted by (1) for languages that distinguish two genders, and show how the predictions that the analysis makes are borne out.[69]

If a language contains only (1)abc and makes distinctions only between two genders morphologically, there are two main possible gender systems, shown in Table 5.1.

TABLE 5.1. **Two genders, three *n*s**

Gender 1	Gender 2	Description	Example language
a. *n*[+FEM]	*n*[−FEM] *n*	Females vs. all other	Dieri
b. *n*[−FEM]	*n* [+FEM] *n*	Males vs. all other	Zayse and Zargulla

---

[68] See Ch. 11 for some discussion of what this means for languages that lack gender systems.
[69] I focus on *n*s that select for roots, setting aside until Ch. 9 *n*s that select for other categories (*n*s that nominalize verbs, adjectives, nominals, etc.).

The Morphosyntax of Gender. First Edition. Ruth Kramer.
© Ruth Kramer 2015. Published 2015 by Oxford University Press.

If a language has one form for agreement for female nouns and another type of agreement for all other nouns, then it is Type (a) in Table 5.1. If it has one form for agreement for male nouns, and another type of agreement for all other nouns, then it is Type (b). There are attested languages with each type of gender system sketched in Table 5.1, and I present case studies of each type of system in Section 5.2. Type (a) is instantiated by the Australian language Dieri (Section 5.2.1) and Type (b) by the Omotic languages Zayse and Zargulla (Section 5.2.2).

Missing from Table 5.1 is a language that contrasts plain *n* with female and male *n*s—such a language could be described as having an animacy contrast (inanimate plain *n* vs. animate, sex-differentiable female and male *n*s). However, given the three-way contrast in biological gender features assumed here, I explain in Section 5.3 how it is impossible to configure the Vocabulary Items such that the same exponent realizes both male and female *n*s. I thus argue that languages with an animacy-based gender system are better accounted for with animacy features (not biological sex features), and show how this makes correct empirical predictions for the Otomanguean language Lealao Chinantec.

Crucially, this chapter and subsequent chapters are not an exhaustive study of all the possible gender systems among the world's languages. I focus on testing the predictions of the analysis, both positive (if a predicted type of gender system is attested) and negative (if a type of gender system which is predicted **not** to exist is attested). This approach leaves a major set of questions open, namely, whether the gender systems of the world can or cannot generally be predicted by the analysis (and/or how the analysis would have to be modified to generate them). Investigating that set of questions rigorously would have to involve a broad and detailed typological survey of gender systems—which would be beyond the purview of this book. Hopefully, this type of large-scale testing of the analysis from a typological perspective will be pursued in the future. However, this chapter and subsequent chapters are intended to show the promise of the analysis in explaining the variation in gender systems across languages, and the general validity of the analysis in that the positive and negative predictions it makes are borne out.

5.2 Masculine default or feminine default

In Chapters 2 and 3, I argued that Amharic contains a *n* with an uninterpretable gender feature. However, as discussed in Section 5.1, this type of *n* is not required in order for a language to have a gender system as defined in Chapter 4. Without an uninterpretable gender *n*, a language is still capable of interpreting entities as female/male/unsexed, and still can condition Vocabulary Insertion due to biological sex features (i.e. still can have gender agreement).

Removing the uninterpretable *n* results in gender systems that are often described as "semantically based" where gender assignment to animates is done purely by biological sex. Males are masculine, and females are feminine. The question then is: what gender is assigned to the non-sexed nouns (inanimates and any animates that lack biological sex)? The two possibilities were shown in Table 5.1: in languages of Type (a), it is masculine, leading to a masculine default; in languages of Type (b), it is feminine, leading to a feminine default.

In this section, I present detailed case studies of Dieri (Type (a)) and Zayse and Zargulla (Type (b))—describing their gender systems and then presenting a basic *n* analysis. These languages show that the predictions of *n* analysis are borne out: that there are languages that lack an uninterpretable gender *n*, and either masculine or feminine can be the default gender.

5.2.1 Masculine default: Dieri

5.2.1.1 Description of the Dieri gender system
Dieri (Pama-Nyungan (Karnic[70])) is spoken in the northeast of the state of South Australia, near Lake Eyre.[71] As of 2011, the few remaining fluent speakers were all above the age of 50, but a language revitalization effort is ongoing in the community, led by the Dieri Aboriginal Corporation (see http://dieriyawarra.wordpress.com/). Although there has been little theoretical linguistic analysis of Dieri morphosyntax (exceptions include Austin 1981b, Goddard 1982), there is a clear and thorough grammar (Austin 1981a, 2011) which serves as the main source for the data in this section.[72]

Dieri has two genders, referred to as feminine and non-feminine (Austin 2011: 64). Nouns referring to female animates—both human ('woman,' 'girl,' etc.) and animal ('female dog,' 'female kangaroo,' etc.)—trigger feminine forms. Non-feminine forms are used when referring to all other entities (male animates like 'boy' and 'male dog,' inanimates like 'nest' and 'string'). Definite determiners and certain case markers show gender distinctions, and I will focus on definite determiners in the following discussion.[73]

The case and gender paradigm for definite determiners is set out in Table 5.2; there is no syncretism, although it is possible that certain forms are derived from others. As the title of the table indicates, these forms are also used as 3rd person singular

---

[70] See Bowern (2001) and references therein on the classification of Karnic within Pama-Nyungan and the internal organization of the Karnic subgroup.

[71] Dieri is the name that the community prefers (Austin 2011: 7), but the language is also referred to as Diyari or Diari.

[72] See also the sketches of (portions of) the Dieri gender system in Alpher (1987), Corbett (1991), Sands (1995), Dahl (2000), Dixon (2002), and Audring (2009). All of these are based on Austin (1981a).

[73] The case markers are much more limited in empirical scope than the determiners: all determiners agree in gender, but it is only case markers on proper nouns and certain kinship terms that show gender distinctions (Austin 2011: 52–4, 56–7, Dixon 2002: 464).

TABLE 5.2. **Definite determiners/3rd person singular pronouns in Dieri (Austin 2011: 65)**

	Ergative	Nominative	Accusative	Dative	Locative allative	Ablative
Feminine	nhandru	nhani	nhanha	nhangkarni	nhangkangu	nhangkangundru
Non-feminine	nhulu	nhawu	nhinha	nhungkarni	nhungkangu	nhungkangundru

pronouns (which thus also show gender/case distinctions).[74] Only singular determiners are shown, since there are no gender distinctions in the plural.

Female humans like *wilha* 'woman' in (2) and *mankarra* 'girl' in (3) always trigger feminine agreement on definite determiners (accusative *nhanha* and nominative *nhani* respectively).[75]

(2) ngathu **nhanha wilha** karlka-yi
1S.ERG 3FS.ACC woman.ACC wait.for-PRES
'I wait for the woman.'   (Austin 2011: 157, (350))

(3) **nhani-ya** **mankarra** ngumu marla
3FS.NOM-near girl.NOM good very
'This girl is very good.'   (Austin 2011: 112, (157))

Nouns that refer to female animals also trigger feminine agreement, as in (4) for the noun *nhanthi ngandri* 'mare.'

(4) **nhani** **nhantu ngandri**
3FS.NOM horse mother
'the mare'   (Austin 2011: 98)

In contrast, male humans and male animals trigger non-feminine agreement. The noun *kanku* 'boy' has a non-feminine determiner *nhawu* in (5) (contrast the nominative feminine determiner *nhani* for 'mare' in (4)).

(5) **nhawu** **kanku** wirari-yi mankarra-wurla-ngu
3NFS.NOM boy.NOM go.about-PRES girl-DUAL-LOC
'The boy is going about with two girls.'   (Austin 2011: 132, (243))

---

[74] It is relatively common cross-linguistically, and particularly common in Australian languages, for definite determiners and 3rd person pronouns to be (at least partially) homophonous. See e.g. many Romance languages where the definite determiners partially or fully overlap with 3rd person object clitics. See Blake (2001) on determiners and pronouns in Australian languages in particular.

[75] The determiner *nhani* has a deictic suffix *ya* which denotes proximity to the speaker; see Austin (1982) on deixis in Dieri in general.

According to Austin (2011), male animals also trigger non-feminine agreement, although I was unable to locate an unambiguous example of a male animal in Austin (2011) and other works on Dieri (e.g. Murray and Austin 1981, Austin 1981b, Austin 1982).

Inanimates lack biological sex, and they are all treated as non-feminine.[76]

(6) **nhawu**   **thurru**   karta-nga-yi
     3NFS.NOM   fire.NOM   crack-PROD-PRES
     'The fire is crackling.'   (Austin 2011: 170, (392))

(7) **nganhi** **nhinha-ya**   **yawarra**   yatha-yi
     1S.NOM   3NFS.ACC-near   language.ACC   speak-PRES
     'I speak this language.'   (Austin 2011: 119–20, (184))

In (6), the inanimate nominal *thurru* 'fire' has a non-feminine nominative determiner. In (7), the inanimate and abstract nominal *yawarra* 'language' has a non-feminine accusative determiner (with a deictic suffix).

What happens where an animate has unknown gender? Or its gender is irrelevant? In at least some cases, the nominal has non-feminine gender. Consider (8).

(8) nhawu-rda   kupa   muntya
     3NFS.NOM-VICIN   child.NOM   sick
     'This (male) child (here) is sick.'   (Austin 1982: 275, (3))[77]

The noun *kupa* 'child' has a non-feminine definite determiner *nhawu* (with a deictic suffix). However, the sentence is ambiguous: it can mean 'this male child is sick' or 'this child is sick.' The latter is an interpretation where the referent 'child' is not specified for gender. Thus, gender unknown/irrelevant readings are possible with non-feminine gender agreement.

Overall, then, Dieri has a gender system according to the definition in Chapter 4: gender sorts nouns into two classes (see Austin 2011: 40, who explicitly states that nouns are sub-categorized for gender), depending on biological sex (female vs. male/none), as reflected in agreement patterns on the definite determiner (and on case markers).

5.2.1.2 Analysis of the Dieri gender system   To place the analysis of Dieri in context, it is useful to compare Dieri to the gender system that has so far been the main focus of inquiry in the book: Amharic. Amharic and Dieri have fundamentally similar gender systems: they have the same number of genders (two), the main semantic feature relevant to gender assignment is the same (biological sex), they have the same semantic core (male entities are masculine, female entities are feminine), and they brook no exceptions to the core.

---

[76] Plants are also treated as non-feminine (e.g. *pathara* 'box tree,' Austin 2011: 194, (489)).
[77] Glossing slightly changed to be consistent with data from Austin (2011).

The two languages diverge, though, in arbitrary gender assignment. Dieri uses the same Vocabulary Item that appears in agreement with male-referring nouns for agreement with entities that lack biological sex. Amharic can almost be described in the same way: the vast majority of entities that lack biological sex have the same Vocabulary Item appearing in agreement contexts as male-referring nouns. However, there is a small but persistent minority of nouns that have a different Vocabulary Item (feminine gender) despite lacking biological sex, i.e. the feminine inanimates and the feminine default animals.

This difference between the two languages is predicted if Dieri lacks (1)d: the *n* with uninterpretable feminine features. In Dieri, then, a nominal will never be capable of triggering feminine agreement without being interpreted as biologically female, and this is empirically correct. The list of *n*s for Dieri is thus as in (9).

(9) **Dieri *n*s**
   a. *n* [+FEM]   female biological sex
   b. *n* [–FEM]   male biological sex
   c. *n*   no biological sex

For each type of *n*, there are certain roots that are only licensed under that *n*. For example, a root like √THURRU 'fire' is licensed only under the "plain" *n*. A root like √MANKARRA 'girl' is licensed only under *n*[+FEM] and thus is only interpreted as female (see also *ngandri* 'mother,' *kaku* 'elder sister'), whereas a root like √KANKU 'boy' is licensed only under *n*[–FEM] and obligatorily male (see also *kaka* 'mother's brother,' *mathari* 'initiated man'). 'Girl' and 'boy' are different-root nominal pairs like those seen in Amharic from Chapter 2, i.e. roots with similar meanings that are morphophonologically unrelated and different in gender. Like the different-roots in Amharic, each member of the pair is licensed under only one interpretable *n*.

Recall that Amharic also contains same-root nominals, where the same root is used for both genders (e.g. *tämari* 'student'); those roots are licensed under all three *n*s in (9): female *n*, male *n*, and plain *n* (when the natural gender is unknown). There is some evidence that Dieri has same-root nominals, too. (8) shows that the root √KUPA can be licensed under *n*[–FEM] (interpreted as 'male child') and under *n* (interpreted as 'child'). P. Austin (p.c.) confirms that *kupa* can also be used to refer to a female child as well, and thus triggers feminine agreement (although speakers prefer to use *kanku* 'boy' and *mankarra* 'girl' if the sex of the child is known/ relevant). The same is true for the root √PULUKA: licensed under *n*, it means 'cattle,' under *n*[–FEM] it means 'bull,' and under *n*[+FEM] it means 'cow' (P. Austin, p.c.).

Since Dieri lacks uninterpretable gender, the basic licensing conditions between *n*s and roots are simple to encode. They are all semantic, i.e. conditions on the interpretation of a root at the Encyclopedia (assuming that inanimates have semantic licensing conditions; see Chapter 3). Some sample, extremely simplified Encyclopedia entries are

in (10). For example, (10)a conveys that √MANKARRA is only capable of being interpreted as 'female young person' at the Encyclopedia if it is in a *n*[+FEM] context.

(10)   **Dieri Encyclopedia entries for 'girl,' 'boy,' and 'fire'**
    a. [*n* [+FEM] [√MANKARRA]] = 'female young person'
    b. [*n* [−FEM] [√KANKU]] = 'male young person'
    c. [*n* [√THURRU]] = 'fire'

For Amharic, I argued that conditions on Vocabulary Insertion determined whether
a root was licensed under plain *n* or uninterpretable *n*[+FEM]. That is because this
decision is arbitrary—unconnected to the interpretation of the root in question.
However, in Dieri, all inanimates combine with the same *n* and they are prohibited
from combining with female *n* and male *n* for semantic reasons (i.e. in the Encyclopedia they are specified as combining only with *n* as in (10)c). There is simply no
need for the grammar to specify which unsexed *n* the inanimates combine with, since
there is only one unsexed *n*, with the result that all licensing conditions are semantic.

Turning now to gender agreement in Dieri, the three semantic options for gender
(+, −, and lacking a feature altogether) end up as two morphophonological genders
via underspecification of Vocabulary Items. Dieri is very similar to Amharic in this
respect: for every target of gender agreement, there is one potential exponent
(Vocabulary Item) marked [+FEM] and one potential exponent (Vocabulary Item)
with no gender features. For example, I assume that the following Vocabulary Items
compete for insertion at a nominative definite determiner (syntactic feature bundle:
[D], [DEF], [NOM]).[78]

(11)   a. [D], [DEF], [NOM], [+FEM] ↔ nhani
     b. [D], [DEF], [NOM] ↔ nhawu

If the nominative definite determiner has agreed with a noun that has *n*[+FEM]
(however this agreement is accomplished), then it will have a [+FEM] feature and (11)
a will be inserted. If it has agreed with a noun that has *n*[−FEM], then it will have a
[−FEM] feature and (11)b will be inserted (because Vocabulary Item (11)a does not
match the features on the syntactic feature bundle). Finally, if it has agreed with a
noun that has plain *n*, then (11)b will also be inserted since (11)a would have one more
feature ([+FEM]) than the syntactic feature bundle.

In sum, Dieri's gender system is (a) capable of being accounted for by a *n* approach
to gender and (b) in fact predicted to occur. Moreover, Dieri is not the only system of
its kind. There are several other languages whose gender systems operate along the
same principles, including the fellow Karnic language Pitta-Pitta (Pama-Nyungan
(Karnic); Australia; Blake 1979: 193–4), the language Awtuw (Sepik-Ramu; Papua

---

[78] It is possible that the determiners could be further morphologically decomposed such that *nha-*
corresponds to [D], [DEF] and the suffixes *-nhi* and *-wu* express gender and case distinctions.

New Guinea; Feldman 1986) and the Omotic languages Dizi and Wolaytta (Afro-asiatic (Omotic); Ethiopia; Allan 1976 and Beachy 2005 on Dizi, Wakasa 2008 on Wolaytta).[79] I now move forward to two languages that are the mirror image of Dieri in terms of gender, with feminine gender as the default.

5.2.2 Feminine default: Zayse and Zargulla

5.2.2.1 Description of the Zayse and Zargulla gender systems   Zayse and Zargulla (Afroasiatic (Omotic)) are two closely related languages spoken in southwest Ethiopia. It is sometimes claimed that they are dialects of the same language (Lewis et al. 2013: lemma *Zaysete*), but Amha (2007, 2009, 2012) distinguishes them, and observes that there are morphological and lexical differences between them. The 2007 Ethiopia census lists 18,000 speakers of Zayse and no separate entry for Zargulla; the 1994 census reported 7,800 speakers of Zargulla (Amha 2007).[80]

The main source for Zayse is Hayward's (1990) 140-page grammar sketch. There is no grammar of Zargulla, but there are a fair number of papers on the language (see e.g. Yimam 1994, Amha 2007, 2008, 2009, 2010). I also draw on the handful of papers on gender in Omotic languages, many of which involve Zayse and/or Zargulla (Hayward 1989, Amha 2010, 2012).

Like many (if not all) Afroasiatic languages, Zayse and Zargulla have two genders: masculine and feminine (Zayse: Hayward 1990: 248; Zargulla: Amha 2010: 61). Verbs and definite determiners show gender agreement in both Zayse and Zargulla (Hayward 1990: 248, Amha 2012: 447), and some case markers and demonstratives do as well in Zargulla (Amha 2010, 2012: 445).[81] In the following examples, verbal agreement and definite determiner agreement are used to indicate gender distinctions.

---

[79] Pitta-Pitta and Awtuw have been claimed to be pronominal gender languages, but in both languages the pronouns may be used as determiners, quite similarly to Dieri (see Blake 1979: 214, (101) for an example; Blake 2001: 415–16 for analysis of Pitta-Pitta; see Feldman 1986: 121–3 for Awtuw). See Audring 2009 on why (predominantly) pronominal agreement systems might be particularly prone to gender systems based only on interpretable gender features for animates.

[80] The ethnolinguistic and political situation of these languages is rather complicated. Zargulla speakers refer to themselves as Gamo and their language as Gamotso; I continue to use the name Zargulla (which is their name for the region) following Amha (2007, 2009, 2010, 2012). Confusingly, there is another ethnic group that also calls itself Gamo and their language Gamotso nearby, but the two Gamotso languages are not mutually intelligible and in fact are in different branches of the Omotic sub-group Ometo. The second Gamotso language is known as Gamo in the linguistics literature. To make matters worse, the Ethiopian government treats all people who call themselves Gamo as one administrative unit, with the result that Zargulla speakers are taught Gamo in school and Zargulla has become threatened (Amha 2010; as evidenced by its disappearance between the 1994 and the 2007 censuses). Zayse was placed in a different administrative unit with several Cushitic languages. See Freeman (2006) and Amha (2010) for further details.

[81] See Amha (2010) on how the verbal/copular markers *-tte* and *-tta* are in the process of changing from gender markers to markers of assertion.

Many Omotic languages have gender systems similar to Amharic, where gender is assigned almost entirely based on biological sex and masculine gender is assigned by default to (almost) all inanimates (Hayward 1989, Amha 2012: 443). Zayse and Zargulla at first seem similar in that gender is assigned based on biological sex: male entities are masculine, and female entities are feminine. In (12), 'a man' triggers one form for agreement on the verb, whereas in (13) 'a woman' triggers a different form of agreement.

(12) Ɂats-í   gel-á-tte-s-inne   **Zargulla**
      man-NOM   enter-INT-FOC-**3MS**-PAST
      'A man entered.' (Amha 2012: 446, (18a))

(13) biššo-y   gel-á-tte-š-inne   **Zargulla**
      woman-NOM   enter-INT-FOC-**3FS**-PAST
      'A woman entered.' (Amha 2012: 446, (18b))

The same goes for animals: in (14)a, the noun 'lion' means 'male lion' when it takes a masculine determiner, whereas in (14)b with a feminine determiner it means 'lioness.'

(14) a. Ɂe-gármá-y   b. Ɂi-gármá-y   **Zayse**
         DEF.M-lion-NOM   DEF.F-lion-NOM
         'the male lion.NOM'   'the lioness.NOM'
         (Hayward 1990: 276)   (Hayward 1990: 276)[82]

However, Zayse and Zargulla differ from other Omotic languages in how they assign gender to inanimate nouns. The vast majority of inanimates in other Omotic languages are masculine, but **all** such nouns in Zayse and Zargulla are feminine (Hayward 1990: 248, Amha 2012: 446). For example, the noun 'garment' triggers feminine verbal agreement; compare (15) to (13).

(15) nas'ála-y   bóot-ó-tte-š-inne   **Zargulla**
      garment-NOM be.white-INT-FOC-**3FS**-PAST
      'The garment became white/clean.' (Amha 2012: 446, (18c))

In (16), the nouns 'house' and 'water' also trigger feminine agreement on the determiner.

(16) a. Ɂi-waatsé-y   b. Ɂi-keets-í   **Zayse**
         DEF.F-water-NOM   DEF.F-house-NOM
         'the water.NOM' (Hayward 1990: 248)   'the house.NOM' (Hayward 1990: 248)[83]

---

[82] The nominative suffix has been changed from *[j]* to *-y* to be consistent with data from Amha (2012). Note also that I have slightly clarified Hayward's translation. H translates (14)a as 'the lion,' but this can refer to either a male or a female lion in English. Hayward notes earlier (1990: 248) that masculine is only used for male animates in Zayse, so the masculine-triggering lion in (14)a must be interpreted as male and I have accordingly adjusted the translation.
[83] Transcription standardized to be consistent with Amha (2012).

The fact that all inanimate nouns are feminine suggests that feminine is the default gender in Zayse and Zargulla.

Several additional pieces of evidence support this analysis. For example, weather *it* in Zayse (Hayward 1990: 249) and Zargulla (Amha 2012: 447) triggers feminine agreement, as in (17).

(17) móož-á-tte-š-inne   **Zayse**
      be.cold-INT-FOC-3FS-PAST
      'It got cold (the weather).' (Hayward 1990: 249)[84]

Moreover, Hayward (1990: 276) observes that animals whose biological sex is irrelevant/unknown are treated as feminine in Zayse, and A. Amha (p.c.) confirms that this is also true for Zargulla. This is analogous to masculine being used as the default for (most) non sex-differentiated animals in Amharic (see Chapter 2).

Finally, tentative evidence suggests that humans which are not sex-differentiated are also treated as feminine. Consider (18).

(18) ʔíso-í   túlle   ʔatsí-tta   **Zargulla**
      3FS-NOM   deaf   person-COP.3FS
      'She is a deaf woman/person.' (A. Amha, p.c.)

Amha (p.c.) reports that consultants translate (18) as either 'she is a deaf woman' or 'she is a deaf person,' which accords with the theory that 'person' in its sex-neutral interpretation is feminine.

I conclude that feminine is the default gender in Zayse and Zargulla, in accordance with the conclusions of Hayward (1989, 1990) and Amha (2010, 2012). Zayse and Zargulla thus are the mirror image of Dieri: instead of reusing masculine for non-sexed entities (inanimates and non-sexed animates), they reuse feminine gender.

5.2.2.2 Analysis of the Zayse and Zargulla gender systems   A feminine default gender system, like the one in Zayse and Zargulla, is predicted to occur under a *n* approach to gender. Zayse will have the same set of *n*s as Dieri, but the Vocabulary Items which realize gender agreement will be differently configured. The relevant set of *n*s is repeated in (19).

(19) **Zayse and Zargulla *n*s**
      a. *n* [+FEM]   female biological sex
      b. *n* [−FEM]   male biological sex
      c. *n*   no biological sex

For each type of *n*, there are certain roots that are only licensed under that *n*. For example, in Zargulla, a root like √NÁSʼALA 'garment' is licensed only under the

---

[84] Transcription and glossing adjusted to be consistent with Amha (2012).

"plain" *n*. In Zayse, a root like √ ʔíNDO 'mother' is licensed only under *n*[+FEM] and thus is only interpreted as female, whereas a root like √ʔADDÁ 'father' is licensed only under *n*[−FEM] and obligatorily male. 'Mother' and 'father' are different-root nominal pairs like those seen in Amharic and Dieri above. Also, just as in Dieri, the basic licensing conditions between *n*s and roots are all semantic, i.e. conditions on the interpretation of a root at the Encyclopedia (see Chapter 3 and Section 5.2.1).

As for gender agreement, male/female/unsexed is realized as two genders via underspecification of Vocabulary Items, very similar in overall structure to Dieri. However, the specific features on the relevant Vocabulary Items are different from Dieri. For example, I assume that the following Vocabulary Items compete for insertion at a definite determiner in Zayse (syntactic feature bundle: [D], [DEF]).[85]

(20) **Zayse definite determiner**
      a. [D], [DEF], [−FEM] ↔ ʔe
      b. [D], [DEF] ↔ ʔi

Vocabulary Item (20)a includes [−FEM], whereas (20)b does not have a gender feature. This will result in (20)a being inserted for every male-agreeing determiner, whereas (20)b is inserted at all other determiners (female-agreeing, inanimate, unsexed animate). Thus, the agreement form used for females will be used in all non-sexed contexts, and this is what we find in Zayse (and Zargulla).

This type of system is predicted to occur in that there are no known restrictions on how a language can "package" gender features with Vocabulary Items. If some language can contrast a [+FEM] VI with a VI that lacks gender features (as in Dieri), then it should be possible for some language to contrast a [−FEM] VI with a VI that lacks gender features.

Zayse's and Zargulla's gender systems are easy to address under a *n* approach, and confirm the predictions of a *n* approach: they have masculine for male-referring nouns, and use feminine gender for all others by morphological default. This type of gender system may seem striking, but feminine-default languages similar to Zayse and Zargulla are not unusual cross-linguistically; many Pama-Nyungan languages have feminine defaults (e.g. Kala Lagaw Ya; Bani 1987; see Alpher 1987 for an overview), as do a large subset of Dravidian languages (e.g. Ollari; Bhattacharya 1957).

5.3 Animacy-based gender systems and a negative prediction

5.3.1 Introduction

Section 5.2 presented gender systems where the masculine gender associated with the male *n* is default (Dieri) and gender systems where the feminine gender associated

---

[85] It is possible that the determiners could be further morphologically decomposed such that ʔ- corresponds to [D], [DEF] and the suffixes *-e* and *-i* express masculine and feminine respectively.

with the female n is default (Zayse, Zargulla). However, there have been no examples presented of gender systems where the plain n triggers one exponent for gender agreement, and the male and female ns together trigger a different exponent.

In fact, given certain fundamental assumptions about Vocabulary Insertion, and the fact that gender features make a three-way distinction, this type of gender system is predicted to be impossible. To see why, consider the hypothetical language L. L has gender agreement on definite determiners that uses Exponent X for plain n nominals and Exponent Y with male and female nominals. L would thus have the following Vocabulary Items for realizing definite determiners.

(21)   **Hypothetical language L : Vocabulary Items for definite determiner**
    a. [D], [DEF] ↔ X
    b. [D], [DEF], [+FEM], [−FEM] ↔ Y

Recall from Chapter 1 that the matching between a morpheme and a Vocabulary Item is restricted by the Subset Principle, repeated in (22).

(22)   **Subset Principle**
    (i) The phonological exponent of a Vocabulary Item is inserted into a position if the item matches all or a subset of the features specified in that position.
    (ii) Insertion does not take place if the Vocabulary Item contains features not present in the morpheme.
    (iii) Where several Vocabulary Items meet the condition for insertion, the item matching the greatest number of features specified in the terminal morpheme must be chosen. (Halle 1997: 428)

The crucial clause is (22)ii, which ensures that Vocabulary Items have the same or a subset of the features of the syntactic feature bundle. A definite determiner that agrees with a female nP will have a [+FEM] feature, but the VI (21)b would not be able to be inserted at such a feature bundle, since (21)b contains a [−FEM] feature as well (a feature not present in the feature bundle). The same goes for a definite determiner that agrees with a male nP, since (21)b also has a [+FEM] feature. Thus, languages that contrast plain n with male and female ns are predicted to be unattested.[86]

---

[86] Such a system could potentially arise if a language (call it L') had three Vocabulary Items for D (one plain, one with [+FEM], and one with [−FEM]) and the VIs for [+FEM] and [FEM] were accidentally homophonous.

(i)   **Hypothetical Language L': Vocabulary Items for definite determiner**
    a. [D], [DEF] ↔ X
    b. [D], [DEF], [+FEM] ↔ Y
    c. [D], [DEF], [−FEM] ↔ Y

I have yet to confirm that there is a natural language like L'. Perhaps it would be difficult to acquire such a system unless the [+FEM] and [−FEM] features were each associated with their own distinct exponent on some other agreement target (cf. Müller 2004's Syncretism Principle).

However, *contra* this prediction, there do exist gender systems that treat both male and female entities as having the same gender and unsexed entities having a different gender. Such systems can be broadly described as animacy-based: male and female entities are both treated as having one gender (animate), and inanimate entities have a different gender (inanimate). In this section, I first lay out a typical example of this type of system: Lealao Chinantec (Section 5.3.2). I then return to the question of how to analyze this type of gender system (5.3.3), contrasting an approach based on animacy features with the one above based on biological sex features. I demonstrate how an animacy approach and a biological sex approach make subtly different predictions, and then show that the animacy based approach's predictions are borne out in Lealao Chinantec. I conclude that, at least at a first pass, the Subset Principle combined with the *n* analysis of gender is correct in ruling out gender systems configured as in (21).

5.3.2 *The gender system of Lealao Chinantec: description*

Lealao Chinantec (henceforth LC; Otomanguean (Western); Mexico) is a Chinantecan language spoken in northeastern Oaxaca, especially in the town of San Juan Lealao. Rupp (2009) reports that that there are about 2,000 speakers. There is a grammar of LC (Rupp 1989), as well as a smattering of theoretical linguistic papers (see e.g. Rupp 1990 on phonology, Roberts 2011 on word order). There has been almost no research on the gender system, with the notable exception of Rupp (2009), which describes animacy agreement in Lealao and Ozumacín Chinantec. Rupp (1989, 2009) are the main sources for this section.

LC distinguishes two genders, traditionally called "animate" and "inanimate." It has robust gender agreement: verbs as well as many NP-internal elements (adjectives, quantifiers, deictics, etc.) agree in gender with the noun. Animate agreement is often realized by adding an *-i* or *-y* suffix, whereas inanimate agreement is often phonologically null (the choice of *-i* or *-y* is arbitrary (J. Rupp, p.c.); I preserved whichever suffix was on the reported data). In the examples below, agreement on verbs, adjectives, numerals, and quantifiers shows the relevant gender distinctions.

Humans and nouns denoting "all known animal life" (Rupp 1989: 20) trigger animate gender agreement. An example with a female human is in (23), where the verb has a suffix *-i* showing the subject is animate. Note that tone is notated by

The best potential candidates for L' that I have located are Danish, Swedish, Norwegian, and Dutch. In these languages, sex-differentiable nouns receive one gender ("common" gender), but masculine and feminine forms are distinguished in the pronoun system. However, there are various complicating factors (e.g. in Danish, plants are also "common" gender, the full pronoun paradigm has a four-gender distinction: masculine, feminine, common and neuter, etc.), and these complications require a more elaborated analysis than there is space for here.

superscript numerals (1 = highest) following Rupp (2009), but the transcription is otherwise mostly faithful to Rupp (1989).[87]

(23) na³-kiʔ⁴²-i   mí⁄³
      STA-fall-**AN**   woman
      'The woman is fallen (by someone).'   (Rupp 1989: 27, (126))

In (24), the same agreement suffix -*i* is used when the subject is a male human. (Note that the language has optional classifiers which do not affect agreement and are thus not genders as per Chapter 4.)

(24) ma³-hú̠³-i   hmii³   mi¹-liuʔ²
      PAST-die-**AN**   father   CL1-little
      'The child's father died.'   (Rupp 1989: 87, (405))

All animals are also treated as animate. In (25), the noun 'dog' triggers an animate agreement suffix on a modifying adjective.

(25) dsɨɨ³   dxú⁴-y
      dog   good-**AN**
      'good dog'   (Rupp 2009: 10)

All nouns besides humans and animals are inanimate. For example, (26) forms a minimal pair with (23). When the subject is inanimate as in (26), the verb lacks the animate agreement suffix -*i*.

(26) na³-kiʔ¹   ñú²
      STA-fall   house
      'The house is fallen (by someone).'   (Rupp 1989: 27, (125))

(27) in turn forms a minimal pair with (25). When the head noun is inanimate, the adjective lacks the -*y* suffix.

(27) mih³   dxú⁴
      clothing   good
      'good clothing'   (Rupp 2009: 10)

Exceptionally, there are five inanimate nouns which are treated as animate: 'sun,' 'moon,' 'rainbow,' 'star,' and 'cross' (Rupp 2009: 5). However, that is because these entities (at least the meteorological phenomena) are treated as animate according to Chinantec oral traditions. LC is thus different from Algonquian languages, which are often mentioned as a paradigmatic example of an animacy-based gender system. Many

---

[87] Exceptions: nasalized vowels are underlined, the high central vowel is consistently represented as a barred i, vowel length is represented by orthographic gemination, and the palatal nasal is represented as an [n] with a tilde.

(if not all) Algonquian languages treat a rather large number of semantically inanimate nouns as if they have arbitrary animate gender; Goddard (2002: 195–6) includes a list approximately 55 such nouns in Ojibwe and (quoting a grammar) notes that there are a "vast number of others" (see Chapter 6 for further discussion). This is quite a different scenario from the handful of "exceptions" in Lealao Chinantec, which are probably not truly exceptional since they are considered to be animate by speakers.

Overall, then, Lealao Chinantec can be classified as having a gender system according to the definition in Chapter 4: gender sorts nouns into two classes, depending on animacy, as reflected in agreement patterns on verbs and adjectives (among many other categories). More details about how gender is assigned in Lealao Chinantec, including default gender, will emerge in the following section.[88]

5.3.3 *The gender system of Lealao Chinantec: analysis*

Given the fairly straightforward animacy-based gender system of Lealao Chinantec, there are two possible analyses of the facts. Under an "animacy analysis," there are two Vocabulary Items for any given gender target: one with an animate feature, and one with an inanimate feature. This is shown for a hypothesized adjectival agreement Vocabulary Item in (28) (*a* = adjective head).[89]

(28)   **Adjectival agreement Vocabulary Items: animacy analysis**
    a. *a*, [+ANIMATE] ↔ -y/-i
    b. *a*, [−ANIMATE] ↔ Ø

Alternatively, under the "biological sex" analysis, one Vocabulary Item has biological sex features whereas the other does not.

(29)   **Adjectival agreement Vocabulary Items: biological sex analysis**
    a. *a*, [+FEM] [−FEM] ↔ -y/-i
    b. *a* ↔ Ø

The biological sex analysis is predicted not to be able to occur, since it would be impossible to insert the correct Vocabulary Items according to the Subset Principle. Fortunately, the biological sex analysis and the animacy analysis make two different empirical predictions, and we will see that the predictions of the animacy analysis, but not the biological sex analysis, are borne out in Lealao Chinantec.

The first area of different predictions is about entities that are animate but not sex-differentiable. Corbett (2011b) observes that, in terms of biology, "sex distinctions

---

[88] Note that, as far as I could determine, there are no agreement targets that distinguish biological sex in Lealao Chinantec.

[89] See Ch. 6 for discussion of whether the animacy feature should be privative or binary; it does not matter for this analysis.

TABLE 5.3. **Predicted genders**

	Animacy analysis	Biological sex analysis
Insects	Possibly animate	Inanimate
Plants	Possibly animate	Inanimate
Unsexed animates	Animate	Inanimate

extend to insects and plants, but no language has been reported as including reference to their biological sex within a grammatical system." Under a biological sex analysis, then, insects and plants are predicted to have inanimate gender. That is, they will lack [+FEM] and [−FEM] features and thus will trigger the null exponent of agreement. Under an animacy analysis, though, it is at least possible for insects and plants to be treated as animates, depending on where the language draws the line on what counts as animate.

A second empirical phenomenon that differentiates the two theories is the case of humans and animals with unknown gender. A biological sex analysis predicts that, since the *n* in these cases lacks a gender feature, the resulting nouns will have the same gender as non-sexed entities, i.e. inanimates. This pattern is familiar from Amharic, Dieri, Zayse, and Zargulla. However, an animacy analysis predicts that since such *n*'s have an animacy feature, the resulting nouns will be animate. These predictions are summed up in Table 5.3. In LC, there is clear evidence that the predictions of the animacy analysis are borne out, and those of the biological sex analysis are incorrect.

To start, LC treats plants as inanimate (Rupp 2009: 4), which does not differentiate the analyses. However, crucially, LC treats insects as animate. In (30), the object 'grasshoppers' triggers an animate agreement suffix -*y* on the verb (transitive verbs agree with their objects in gender: Rupp 1989: 21).

(30) Ḷih³   ba²   ga³-cuh³-y
      grasshopper   AFFIRM   HAB-eat.3-AN
      'He eats grasshoppers.'   (Rupp 2009: 6)

Thus, the predictions of the animacy approach are borne out, and the predictions of the biological sex approach are not.[90]

Moreover, there are numerous examples in Lealao Chinantec of human-denoting nouns with indeterminate gender which are treated as animate. In (31), the non-sexed noun 'child' triggers the animacy suffix -*y* on the numeral 'four.'

---

[90] Another potential example is shrimp, which are most likely not differentiated by biological sex in any language. However, they are treated as animate in Lealao Chinantec (J. Rupp, p.c.).

(31)   chiú³-y   mi¹-liuh²
        four-AN   CL1-little
        'four children'   (Rupp 2009: 4)

In (32), the non-sexed noun 'person' triggers the animacy suffix *-y* on the quantifier 'all.'

(32)   liáh⁴ji³-y   dsa³
        all-AN   person
        'all the people'   (Rupp 2009: 9)

I conclude that an animacy approach is superior, since its predictions are borne out in Lealao Chinantec. Therefore, the predictions of the *n* analysis are upheld: there is no language like L where male/female contrasts with plain *n*.[91,92]

5.4 Conclusion

All the predictions that the *n* analysis makes for two-gender languages with no uninterpretable gender features are upheld. Such languages can draw a contrast in gender assignment between female-referring nouns and all others (Dieri), or male-referring nouns or all others (Zayse and Zargulla), but they never draw a contrast between female/male referring nouns and inanimate nouns. I showed that Lealao Chinantec, a language whose gender systems superficially resembles this last type of contrast, in fact is best analyzed as based on animacy features and not biological sex features at all.

In all of the languages that I have presented thus far, there are no uninterpretable gender features. In Dieri and Zayse/Zargulla, where gender is based on biological sex, *n* is either male, female, or lacks a gender feature altogether (with the unsexed cases triggering the default gender). In LC, *n* has either an interpretable animate feature or an interpretable inanimate feature. However, some languages do have uninterpretable gender features, as we saw with Amharic in Chapters 2 and 3. I proceed in Chapter 6 to explore the predictions of a *n* analysis for two-gender languages with uninterpretable gender.

---

[91] Crucially, it is not the case that animacy systems like LC lack biological sex features entirely. Indeed, in order to interpret any nominal as sexed (as LC does, since it has words for 'father,' 'mother,' etc.), biological sex features on *n* must be present (see Ch. 3). The difference may be that the biological sex features are not relevant for gender-related exponence at PF in LC. See Ch. 11 for discussion of this issue with respect to languages that lack gender entirely.

[92] The same argument applies to languages where gender is assigned based on human-ness, i.e. there is one gender for humans and one gender for non-humans. Languages with this type of system include the Caucasian language Tabarasan (Corbett 1991: 24) and the Austronesian language Palauan (Nuger 2010). The key test case for these languages is how unsexed humans (humans that lack gender features) are treated. If they have the "human" gender, then the language will not be Language C. If they have the "non-human" gender, then the language is Type C. For Palauan, at least, it is clear that it is not Type C. Unsexed animates like the word 'person' still trigger e.g. human demonstratives (Nuger 2010: 100).

6

Case study 2: Adding an uninterpretable gender feature

6.1 Introduction

Chapter 5 focused on two-gender systems based on biological sex. Such systems require three *n*s at a minimum to explain the possible semantic interpretations of a root with respect to biological sex: a female *n*, a male *n*, and a non-sexed *n* to generate female nouns, male nouns and nouns that lack biological sex respectively. However, what if a language has more than the minimum *n*s needed semantically for biological sex? That is, what if a language has a *n* with an uninterpretable feature? Gender systems that contain such a *n* are the focus of this chapter.

Recall that the feature which encodes biological sex is [+/−FEM]. This means that there are two possible uninterpretable gender features: *u* [+FEM] and *u* [−FEM]. Considering only cases where a language has one uninterpretable gender feature (see Section 6.5 and Chapter 7 for discussion of multiple uninterpretable gender features), there are two possible sets of *n*s that can comprise the pre-syntactic lexical items—one with an uninterpretable feminine feature, and one with an uninterpretable masculine feature. The two sets are laid out in Table 6.1.

Adding an uninterpretable feature has one main effect: unsexed entities no longer all have the same, default gender. We saw in Chapter 5 that all inanimates are masculine in Dieri, and all inanimates are feminine in Zayse and Zargulla. In a language with an uninterpretable gender feature, it is possible for inanimates to be

TABLE 6.1. Two genders, four *n*s

Set 1: Uninterpretable feminine	Set 2: Uninterpretable masculine
n i [+FEM]	*n i* [+FEM]
n i [−FEM]	*n i* [−FEM]
n	*n*
n u [+FEM]	*n u* [−FEM]

The Morphosyntax of Gender. First Edition. Ruth Kramer.
© Ruth Kramer 2015. Published 2015 by Oxford University Press.

licensed under the non-default gender and still be interpreted as unsexed. This also holds for any unsexed animates; nominals like 'person', as well as animate entities whose biological sex is irrelevant/unknown, become capable of having non-default gender.

In Chapters 2 and 3, we saw an example of a language with Set 1: Amharic. Amharic has a masculine default, but also contains some feminine inanimate nominals (e.g. *s'ähay* 'sun') and a few animals which have a feminine default when their natural gender is unknown (e.g. *ayt'* 'mouse'). In this chapter, I first take an in-depth look at a language where *u*[+FEM] is licensed more liberally across the inventory of roots: Spanish (Section 6.2). I briefly consider the question of variation in the extent to which *u*[+FEM] is licensed in Section 6.2.3. In Section 6.3, I present a language that has Set 2: Maa (Nilo-Saharan (Nilotic); Kenya). In Section 6.4 I return to animacy systems, and argue that (i) animacy is a privative feature and (ii) the gender system of Algonquian languages includes a *n* with an uninterpretable animate feature.

6.2 Uninterpretable feminine gender: Spanish

6.2.1 *The gender system of Spanish: description*

Spanish (Indo-European (Romance)) is spoken in Spain as well as throughout large portions of Central America, South America, and the United States. There are perhaps 400 million speakers globally (Lewis et al. 2013). I focus here on the dialect of Spanish spoken in Europe. Spanish differs from many of the other languages considered so far in that it has an extremely rich descriptive tradition and has been the focus of generative linguistic research for decades. Of necessity, the discussion here does not aim towards comprehensiveness—just a serviceable survey. Although there are many papers on Spanish gender, the main sources that discuss gender assignment from a generative, theoretical perspective are Klein (1989), Roca (1989, 2000, 2005), Harris (1991), Aronoff (1994), Lloret and Viaplana (1997), Alexiadou (2004), and Picallo (2008) (see Chapter 2, which discusses the analyses developed in many of these papers). These sources were supplemented by the reference grammar by Butt and Benjamin (2011) and the intuitions of native speaker consultants.

Spanish has two genders, referred to as masculine and feminine. Gender distinctions are morphologically evident in determiners and adjectives, among other categories. I will use determiners to indicate gender below: *el* is masculine and *la* feminine.

As the names of the genders suggest, nouns referring to male entities are masculine, and nouns referring to female entities are feminine. Spanish resembles Amharic in that it has pairs of nominals where different roots have different biological sexes, as in (1), as well as roots that are compatible with either biological sex (same-root nominals) as in (2).

(1) **Spanish different-root nominals**
   a. el hombre 'the man'   la mujer 'the woman'[93]
   b. el yerno   'the son-in-law' la nuera 'the daughter-in-law'
   c. el caballo 'the stallion'   la yegua 'the mare'

                                    (Butt and Benjamin 2011: 1–2)

   d. el caballero 'the gentleman' la dama 'the lady'   (H. Campos, p.c.)

(2) **Spanish same-root nominals: invariant**
   a. el/la soldado   'the soldier'
   b. el/la artista   'the artist'
   c. el/la adolescente   'the adolescent'
   d. el/la estudiante   'the student'
   e. el/la rehén   'the hostage'   (Butt and Benjamin 2011: 2–3)

There are also certain entities for which the same root is used across genders, but where the final vowel of the noun differs: -*o* in the masculine and -*a* in the feminine.

(3) **Spanish same-root nominals: vowel change**
   a. el abuelo   'the grandfather'   la abuela   'the grandmother'
   b. el amigo   'the male friend'   la amiga   'the female friend'
   c. el candidato 'the male candidate'   la candidata 'the female candidate'
   d. el perro   'the male dog'   la perra   'the female dog'
   e. el oso   'the male bear'   la osa   'the female bear'

                                    (Butt and Benjamin 2011: 2)

However, following previous research, I assume that -*o* and -*a* are not morphological expressions of gender; they are theme vowels (also known as declension class markers) whose realization is partially conditioned by gender. There is a substantial literature on the complex relationship between gender and declension class in Spanish (see e.g. Klein 1989, Harris 1991, Aronoff 1994, Lloret and Viaplana 1997, Alexiadou 2004, Picallo 2008), and I sketch an analysis of Spanish declension class in Chapter 10. For now, the most important observations it that these are same root nominals where the root is e.g. √ABUEL, √AMIG, etc.

There are also many male/female paired nouns in Spanish that are morphologic-ally related in a different way, e.g. *duque/duquesa* 'duke/duchess,' *bailarín/bailarina* 'dancer,' *actor/actriz* 'actor/actress,' and *monje/monja* 'monk/nun.' These nouns are most likely same-root pairs as well, although I will not catalogue/analyze them in detail here and I leave open the possibility that some of the pairs are not morpho-logically related (see discussion in e.g. Lang 1990: 188–9).

---

[93] *Mujer* also is attested in the different root pair *marido* 'husband' ~ *mujer* 'wife.' See fn. 98.

As the examples so far have shown, the vast majority of entities treated as sexed in Spanish are human, as well as a handful of animals. If animals are distinguished for biological sex, they are most likely to exhibit the *-o/-a* alternation (there are about ten to fifteen such animals, mostly domesticated), and least likely to use the same root for both genders like the nouns in (2) (although *tigre* 'tiger/tigress' is attested; *gorila* 'gorilla' and *jirafa* 'giraffe' are also used colloquially as same-roots; Butt and Benjamin 2011: 4, 7). As we will see below, all other animals are treated as unsexed; but first I turn to the inanimate nominals.

Unlike in Dieri and Zayse/Zargulla, nouns referring to inanimate entities are either masculine or feminine in Spanish.[94] Masculine or feminine gender is assigned arbitrarily to inanimates; there are no correlations between meaning and gender, or between the phonological shape of the noun and gender (setting aside generalizations based on the theme vowels).[95] Examples of masculine and feminine inanimates are given in (4).

(4)   **Spanish inanimates**

a.	el libro	'the book'	f.	la pluma	'the pen'
b.	el tiro	'the shot'	g.	la mano	'the hand'
c.	el amor	'the love'	h.	la flor	'the flower'
d.	el dogma	'the dogma'	i.	la verdad	'the truth'
e.	el plátano	'the banana'	j.	la manzana	'the apple'

(Butt and Benjamin 2011)

Spanish also has same-root inanimates. Instead of the change in gender corresponding to a change in natural gender, though, it signals a change in the interpretation of the root. Sometimes the two meanings are semantically related ((5)ab),[96] and sometimes not ((5)cd).

(5)   **Spanish same-root inanimates**

a.	el cerezo	'the cherry tree'	la cereza	'the cherry'
b.	el editorial	'the editorial'	la editorial	'the publishing house'

---

[94] There are also a few nouns which are compatible with either gender with no change in meaning, e.g. *mar* 'sea.' The main point is that Spanish has two genders available for inanimates, unlike Dieri and Zayse/Zargulla.

[95] There are pockets of semantic and morphophonological regularity, detailed in Butt and Benjamin (2011) and catalogued in much of the second-language-learning literature on Spanish. However, almost all of the semantic regularities are instances of metonymy where the gender of a noun is the gender of some elided/assumed noun (e.g. the names of companies are feminine because the noun *compañia* 'company' is feminine; see Butt and Benjamin 2011: 7–8, 10). Also, almost all of the morphophonological regularity boils down to either (a) generalizations about word class markers or (b) generalizations about the gender of particular derivational suffixes (on this last point, see esp. Morin 2010 and discussion of nominalizations in Chs 9 and 10).

[96] Some semantic relations are more common, e.g. there are many pairs of masculine tree and feminine fruit like (5)a. However, there are also many tree/fruit pairs that do not fit this pattern, e.g. *higuera* 'fig tree' (f.) and *higo* 'fig' (m.) (Harris 1991: 36). See Harris (1991) for further examples.

c. el paso	'the step'	la pasa	'the raisin'
d. el coma	'the coma'	la coma	'the comma'

(Butt and Benjamin 2011: 8, 15, Alexiadou 2004)

Plants are treated as unsexed, i.e. arbitrarily masculine (*el tulipán* 'the tulip') or feminine (*la rosa* 'the rose').

The majority of animals (e.g. 'kangaroo,' 'swan,' 'frog') and a handful of human nouns ('person,' 'victim,' 'angel') are treated as unsexed, like plants and inanimates. They are unsexed in that each of these nouns has an arbitrary gender that remains the same regardless of the natural gender of the referent.

(6) **Spanish fixed-gender animals**

a. el canguro	'the kangaroo'	d. la araña	'the spider'
b. el castor	'the beaver'	e. la ballena	'the whale'
c. el sapo	'the toad'	f. la rana	'the frog'

(Butt and Benjamin 2011: 6)

(7) **Spanish fixed-gender humans**

a. el ángel	'the angel'	c. la persona	'the person'
b. el genio	'the genius'	d. la víctima	'the victim'

(Butt and Benjamin 2011: 6)

For example, *persona* 'person' triggers feminine agreement forms even when it refers to a male entity. I will refer to these as fixed-gender nouns.

Finally, the default gender in Spanish is masculine (Prado 1982, Roca 1989). Recall that there were two arguments for a masculine default in Amharic: (i) the nominal 'nobody' triggered masculine agreement, and (ii) a same-root noun takes masculine agreement when the natural gender of its referent is unknown. The same type of evidence indicates that Spanish has a masculine default. In (8), 'nobody' is the subject and the agreement on the predicate adjective *malo* 'evil' is masculine (technically, the *-o* is a declension class marker, but it indicates masculine agreement).

(8) Para   él,   nadie   es   mal-o
     for   him,   nobody   is   evil-M
     'For him, nobody is evil.'   (Roca 1989: 14)

In (9), *hijo* 'child' is unsexed, since the gender of the referent can later be specified as either female or male. Nevertheless, *hijo* triggers masculine agreement on the indefinite determiner (and has a masculine-associated theme vowel; cf. *hija* 'daughter').

(9) sólo   tuvo   un   hijo,   y   le   salió   {niña/niño}
     only   she.had   one.M   child,   and   it   turned.out girl/boy
     'She only had one child, and it was a girl/boy.'   (Roca 1989: 17)

Additional evidence for a masculine default comes from a third 'gender' in Spanish traditionally called the neuter. Neuter forms include the determiner *lo*, the pronouns *ello* and *lo*, and the demonstrative pronouns *esto*, *eso*, and *aquello*. The determiner does not take nominal complements, e.g. *lo bueno* 'the good (thing).' Moreover, the pronouns are never used with overt nominal antecedents (Picallo 2008: 50), and they refer to non-nominal entities as in (10).

(10)   No,   no   lo   sabíamos
        no   NEG   it.N   we.know
        'No, we didn't know (that).'   (Butt and Benjamin 2011: 90)

Since most of the neuter forms are pronouns, they fall outside of the purview of this book (see Section 6.2.2 for the neuter determiner). However, it is worth asking what gender the neuter pronouns themselves trigger on e.g. predicate adjectives, which do not have neuter forms. In such cases, the agreement is always masculine, e.g. on *estupendo* in (11).

(11)   Esto   es   estupend-o
        this.N   is   stupendous-M
        'This is stupendous.'   (Roca 1989: 14, (23b))

Thus, masculine is used to "fill in the paradigm" for gender agreement when a neuter pronoun is agreed with. I conclude, along with all other gender researchers on Spanish, that masculine is the default gender.

However, there are at least two same-root nouns for which the default seems to be feminine. As in Amharic, they are animal nouns.

(12)   **Spanish feminine-default animals**
        a. el gallo   'rooster'   la gallina   'hen, chicken'
        b. el macho/cabrón   'billy-goat'   la cabra   'she-goat, goat'
                    (Butt and Benjamin 2011: 1–2, as well as elicitation with consultants)

The feminine forms in (12) can be used to refer to either an ungendered instance of the animal in question or a mixed group (see Roca 1989 on the latter), as well as a female instance of the animal. If the animal in question is male, though, the masculine form is used.

Before concluding, it is worth returning briefly to different-root nominals in Spanish. Recall that, in Chapter 2, I argued that the Amharic different-root nominals are **not** related morphologically via root suppletion—as their name suggests, they are derived from different roots. The main evidence for this analysis was that neither of the paired roots can be used as a superordinate term that denotes the meaning which the roots share. For example, neither *abbat* 'father' nor *innat* 'mother' can be used for 'parent' (a separate root is used: *wälädʒ*). Rather than have a three-way suppletive paradigm, it seems that *abbat* 'father' and *innat* 'mother' (albeit related in meaning) are morphosyntactically derived from different roots.

However, a close investigation of Spanish different root nominals reveals that they can be sorted into three groups depending on the presence and the gender of a(ny) superordinate term.[97]

(13)   **Masculine superordinate**
    a. padre   'father'   madre 'mother' padre   'parent'
    b. hombre 'man'   mujer 'woman' hombre 'person/mankind'
    c. caballo 'stallion' yegua 'mare'   caballo 'horse'

(14)   **Feminine superordinate**
    a. carnero 'ram'   oveja 'ewe'   oveja 'sheep'
    b. toro   'bull'   vaca   'cow'   vaca   'bovine (of either gender)'

(15)   **Different-root or no superordinate**
    a. marido 'husband'   mujer 'wife'   esposo/a 'spouse'
    b. yerno   'son-in-law' nuera 'daughter-in-law' (No superordinate term)

Given this evidence, I tentatively suggest that the nouns in (13) and (14) are derivationally related via suppletion—and thus are same-root nominals. The majority have a masculine default, but some have a feminine default. The only true different-root nominals in Spanish are then *yerno/nuera* 'son/daughter-in-law,' *marido* 'husband,' and possibly *mujer* 'wife.'[98] I speculate that this is because Spanish is unusually rich in morphological means for deriving differently sexed-nominals from the same root: such nominals can be zero-derived ((2)), derived via *-o/-a* alternation ((3)), derived via a different derivational alternation, and derived via suppletion ((13) and (14)).

Overall, then, Spanish has masculine and feminine genders. Male entities are masculine, and female entities are feminine. Inanimates are arbitrarily either masculine or feminine. Most human entities are sexed and accordingly masculine or feminine according to natural gender, but most animals are unsexed and have a fixed arbitrary gender. Masculine is the default, although there are a handful of feminine default animals. There are few confirmed cases of different-root nominals.

6.2.2 The gender system of Spanish: analysis

Given the data in Section 6.2.1, I analyze Spanish as having four *n*s—Set 1 from Table 5.1.

---

[97] The formation of such a list requires one to separate out nominals which are plausibly derivationally related (which I would classify as same-root) from those which are not (e.g. *hombre/mujer*). Some cases are not clear-cut, though, and I leave for more fine-grained research on Spanish derivational morphology to determine whether pairs like *principe/princesa* 'prince/princess' share a root or not.

[98] *Mujer* 'wife' is a different-root nominal if the root for 'wife' and the root for 'person' happen to be exponed with the same Vocabulary Item when licensed under *n i*[+FEM]. Alternatively, the root for 'person' could be interpreted as either 'woman' or 'wife' when it appears with a *n i*[+FEM].

(16)   **Spanish *ns***

    a. *n i*[+FEM]

    b. *n i*[−FEM]

    c. *n*

    d. *n u*[+FEM]

Since the gender system of Spanish is based on biological sex, it has the three *ns* needed to create the semantic contrast for such a system: female, male and plain ((16) abc). However, there is also evidence that it has a *n* with an uninterpretable feminine feature. The default gender is masculine, yet some inanimates (e.g. *la pluma* 'the pen') and some unsexed animates (e.g. *la persona* 'the person') have feminine gender. These inanimates and animates are not interpreted as female, so they must combine with a *n* that does not have an uninterpretable gender feature, yet triggers the insertion of feminine agreeing forms—that *n* is (16)d.

The Vocabulary Items for the Spanish definite determiners are quite similar to Amharic definite determiners.[99]

(17)   **Spanish definite determiner VIs**

    a. [D],[DEF],[+FEM] ↔ *la*

    b. [D],[DEF] ↔ *el*

One VI has a [+FEM] feature so it is inserted in the context of females and inanimates/unsexed animates that have *u*[+FEM], and the other VI has no gender features so it is inserted in all other contexts: males, all other inanimates and unsexed entities. This results in a "masculine" (more precisely, non-feminine) default.[100]

This configuration of *ns* in the syntax and Vocabulary Items generates much of the data seen above. To start with roots licensed under interpretable *ns*, each same-root nominal with a masculine default (e.g. *estudiante* 'student') is licensed under (16)a, (16)b, and (16)c. Each same-root nominal with a feminine default (e.g. *gallina*

---

[99] I set aside feminine nouns that start with a stressed [a] and appear with *el*, e.g. *el agua* 'the water.' I assume the choice of masculine article is phonologically-conditioned. See Wolf (2008) for analysis and references, and see Embick (2010) for approaches to phonologically conditioned allomorphy in DM.

[100] One might wonder how the neuter determiner *lo* (as in *lo bueno* 'the good (thing)') fits into (17). I follow Picallo (2008) in assuming that neuter forms in Spanish are not just genderless but numberless as well. In contrast, *el* and *la* have number: they are singular, i.e. not used for plural nouns. So, one way of adding *lo* to (17) would be:

(i)   Spanish definite determiner VIs

    a. [D],[DEF],[+FEM][−PL] ↔*la*

    b. [D],[DEF][−PL] ↔*el*

    c. [D],[DEF] ↔ *lo*

The neuter determiner *lo* is inserted when the determiner lacks both gender features and number features. In such a context, *la* and *el* cannot be inserted since they each include a number feature. This leaves many questions open (especially about the nature of agreement on determiners), but hopefully it has shown that adding *lo* is not an insurmountable task for the analysis.

'chicken') is licensed under (16)a, (16)b, and (16)d. The different-root nominal *yerno* 'son-in-law' is licensed under (16)b, the 'male' n whereas *nuera* 'daughter-in-law' is licensed under (16)c, the 'female' n.

Inanimates are licensed under either the plain n and are masculine or under n u[+FEM] and are feminine (but in neither case are they interpreted as having biological gender). Note that same-root inanimates are predicted under a n analysis, since the combination of n with a root necessarily results in idiosyncratic meaning (Harley 2014)—the root cannot be interpreted without being categorized. Thus, it is not unusual that different ns should trigger different interpretations of the root. I leave it open whether the cases where the semantic relation is more opaque between the two genders should be analyzed as same-root or as two roots which are coincidentally exponed via homophonous Vocabulary Items.

As for the fixed-gender nouns, they are licensed like the inanimates: under plain n (masculine, e.g. *el ángel* 'the angel') or n u[+FEM] (feminine, e.g. *la persona* 'the person'). Although these nouns are animate, they do not convey any information about natural gender, i.e. they are not biologically sexed, exactly like inanimates.[101] The licensing conditions needed for Spanish are summed up in Table 6.2.

TABLE 6.2. **Licensing conditions for Spanish**

	n i [+FEM]	n i [−FEM]	n	n u [+FEM]
Different root: masculine *yerno* 'son-in-law'	✗	✓	✗	✗
Different root: feminine *nuera* 'daughter-in-law'	✓	✗	✗	✗
Same root: masculine default *estudiante, hijo, hombre*	✓	✓	✓	✗
Same root: feminine default *gallina, oveja*	✓	✓	✗	✓
Fixed gender: feminine *pluma, persona*	✗	✗	✗	✓
Fxed gender: masculine *libro, ángel*	✗	✗	✓	✗

---

[101] If the natural gender for a fixed-gender animate (or for certain plants) needs to be expressed, adjectives meaning 'male' or 'female' are added and the gender remains the same (e.g. *la rana macho* 'the male frog,' *la víctima masculina* 'the male victim'). It may be that these adjectives lack the proper features to qualify as gender agreement controllers.

The gender system of Spanish is thus capable of being analyzed in a *n* approach, and provides further support for the 'Set 1' type of language which was already instantiated by Amharic. However, there are many differences between the Amharic and Spanish systems, and I discuss why and how these differences may have arisen in Section 6.2.3.

6.2.3 Comparing Spanish and Amharic

Spanish and Amharic have largely similar gender systems. Both are based on biological sex where males are masculine and females are feminine. Both have large numbers of same-root nominals, some of which have masculine defaults and a handful of which have feminine defaults. Both have masculine and feminine inanimates. Due to these similarities, it is straightforward to use the ingredients of the analysis developed so far to analyze the Spanish gender system.

However, there are two significant differences between the Spanish and Amharic gender systems. The first difference is twofold: Amharic has many fewer feminine inanimates than Spanish, and Amharic lacks nouns where gender changes the meaning of the root idiosyncratically (referred to as "same-root inanimates" above). In terms of the analysis developed here, this can be captured by saying that the proportion of roots that are licensed only under *n u*[+FEM] is much larger in Spanish. I speculate that this is because Amharic is 'losing' the syntactic feature bundle *n u*[+FEM]: over time fewer and fewer roots are being learned as licensed under *n u*[+FEM]. This explains why there are fewer feminine inanimates, and the lower proportion of feminine inanimates may be why there are not "same-root inanimates" (perhaps there are simply not enough masculine/ feminine contrasts for this phenomenon to appear). Moreover, younger speakers of Amharic (under 25 years old) tend to treat any feminine inanimate noun as a diminutive, and to treat feminine default animals like same-root nominals. Overall, Amharic is transitioning into a gender system where natural gender is the only determining factor in gender assignment, exactly like Dieri: all female entities have feminine gender, and all other nominals have masculine gender by default.

The second main difference between Amharic and Spanish is that Amharic lacks fixed-gender nouns—i.e. it has no animate nominals that are always treated as unsexed. In contrast, Spanish does contain fixed-gender nouns, e.g. *persona* 'person,' which are always feminine. In general, as described and analyzed in Chapters 2 and 3, natural gender is a more direct factor in Amharic gender assignment than in Spanish gender assignment. In Amharic, animates always have their own natural gender when known/relevant (this is also true for Dieri and Zayse/Zargulla), whereas in Spanish, animates need not have their own natural gender. From the perspective of this analysis, this restriction seems to be most easily stated over semantic licensing conditions.

(18)   **All animates are sexed in Amharic**
    In Amharic, if a root is licensed under a *n* that contains an animate feature,
    then it must be capable of being licensed under at least one *n* that contains
    either [+FEM] or [−FEM].

This ensures that all animate nominals are capable of being interpreted as at least
male or female, even if in a particular context they may not be (e.g. if natural gender
is irrelevant/unknown). It also allows for a root to be licensed under both of these
features (albeit with different *n*s). In order to account for the cross-linguistic variation, it must be that (18) simply does not hold as a restriction within the Spanish
Encyclopedia. Refining and formalizing this restriction on the interpretation of roots
(especially from a cross-linguistic perspective) requires a better understanding of the
structure of the Encyclopedia and the nature of licensing conditions (see Chapter 3).
I thus leave it for future work to focus more narrowly on these tasks.[102]

6.3 Uninterpretable masculine gender: Maa

so far, two languages have been presented that instantiate Set 1: Amharic (Chapters 2
and 3) and Spanish (Sections 6.2.1 and 6.2.2). Both have a *n* with an uninterpretable
feminine feature. However, there remains another set of possible *n*s—Set 2—which is
identical to Set 1 except that the uninterpretable feature is masculine, i.e. [−FEM] (see
Table 6.1).

    In this section, I argue that the language Maa (Nilo-Saharan (Nilotic); Kenya/
Tanzania) has Set 2, further confirming the predictions of a *n* analysis.

    First, though, it is helpful to think through what the gender system resulting from
Set 2 would look like. Recall that the uninterpretable feminine *n* in Set 1 results in
feminine inanimates as well as a handful of feminine default same-root nouns in
Spanish and Amharic. Nevertheless, the masculine forms are the default for both
languages (encoded by the Vocabulary Items for gender agreement targets having
either a [+FEM] feature or no feature at all). Overall, then, the uninterpretable
feminine *n* allows for the formation of nouns that are unsexed but nevertheless do
not have the default gender.

    In a Set 2 language, the uninterpretable masculine *n* will allow for the formation of
nouns that are unsexed and masculine. If a language has a masculine default and no
other uninterpretable features, this has no effect, since all nouns that are unsexed are

---

[102] Another difference is that Spanish seems to use suppletion to derive sex-related pairs, whereas
Amharic does not (instead, such pairs are derived via separate roots). This difference is not as deep, insofar
as there are not considered to be systematicities in which morphological devices are recruited for certain
phenomena across languages (e.g. some languages use prefixing to express certain categories, others use
suffixing, others use ablaut).

predicted to be masculine anyway. Such a language would be indistinguishable from Dieri (see Chapter 5), where all inanimates and unsexed animates are masculine.

However, in a language with a feminine default, the effects of an uninterpretable masculine *n* would be observable. There would be, in such a language, good reason to think that feminine is the default gender, but there would also be masculine inanimates and masculine unsexed animates.

I submit that Maa is such a language. Multiple sources agree that feminine is the default/unmarked gender in Maa (Tucker and Mpaayei 1955, Payne 1998, Koopman 2003, Newell 2005). In Chapter 5, I presented data on the feminine-default languages Zayse and Zargulla, where all inanimates and unsexed animates are feminine. Unlike Zayse and Zargulla, Maa contains some masculine inanimate nouns and some masculine defaults for same root nouns. Maa is thus the Set 2 counterpart of Amharic/Spanish, with a clear default but some unsexed entities receiving the non-default gender. In Section 6.3.1, I present the Maa gender system, and outline its analysis in a *n* approach in Section 6.3.2.

6.3.1 *The gender system of Maa: description*

Maa is a Nilotic language spoken in Kenya and Tanzania by around a million speakers (Lewis et al. 2013). It is sometimes referred to as "Maasai," but strictly speaking "Maasai" refers to a particular ethnic group (who speak Maa), and Maa as a language is spoken by other ethnicities as well (Sommer and Vossen 1993). There is a small cluster of theoretical linguistic research on Maa, and for this section I draw on the description in Hollis (1905) and Tucker and Mpaayei (1955), as well as the gender-focused discussions in Payne (1998), Newell (2005), and Shirtz and Payne (2012, 2013). The transcription of tone follows Tucker and Mpaayei (1955) and Payne (1998).

The main gender distinction in Maa is between feminine and masculine gender (Tucker and Mpaayei 1955: 3; there is also a very small third gender that contains two place-related nouns—see below). Gender distinctions are morphologically marked on demonstratives as well as other categories, and each noun also has a "gender clitic" that indicates its gender. I remain agnostic about the proper analysis of the gender clitic, but I use it as an indicator of gender in the examples below, glossed as GC. The masculine gender clitic is typically *ɔl-* and the feminine gender clitic is typically *ɛn-* (see Tucker and Mpaayei 1955: 3–4 for a list of the phonologically conditioned alternations of the clitics).

The semantic core of Maa is similar to all of the previous languages examined in that nouns interpreted as male humans and male animals are masculine, and nouns interpreted as female humans and female animals are feminine (setting aside augmentatives and diminutives; on which, see below). Maa has both different-root nouns ((19)) and same-root nouns ((20)) expressing these distinctions.

(19) a. ɔl-ayíónì   GC.M-boy   'boy'   **Different root**
      en-títo   GC.F-girl   'girl'
      (Tucker and Mpaayei 1955: 3, 285, 293)

   b. ɔl-búŋàì   GC.M-bull.calf 'bull calf'
      ɛn-táwúó   GC.F-heifer   'heifer'
      (Tucker and Mpaayei 1955: 286, 294)

(20) a. ɔl-apʊtánì   GC.M-wife's.parent 'wife's father'   **Same root**
      ɛnk-apʊtánì   GC.F-wife's.parent 'wife's mother'
      (Payne 1998: 173)

   b. ol-derónì   GC.M-rat   'male rat'
      en-derónì   GC.F-rat   'female rat'
      (Tucker and Mpaayei 1955: 3)

There are very few animates with a fixed gender regardless of their natural gender
(one crucial exception is (27)b), so I tentatively assume that Maa is largely like
Amharic in that natural gender (when known/relevant) determines the gender of
the human or animal.

Inanimates in Maa are either masculine ((21)) or feminine ((22)).

(21) **Masculine inanimates**
   a. ol-óríkà   'small three-legged stool'   (Hollis 1905: 9[103])
   b. o-rinká   'club'
   c. o-sóít   'stone'
   d. ol-kítíkótó   'path'
   e. ol-dóínyó   'mountain'   (Tucker and Mpaayei 1955: 3, 5)

(22) **Feminine inanimates**
   a. e-remét   'spear'
   b. ɛn-kímá   'fire'
   c. e-rórêt   'lawn'
   d. enk-óítóí   'road'
   e. en-dóínyó   'hill'   (Tucker and Mpaayei 1955: 3, 5)

To the best of my knowledge, there is no correlation between morphophonological
form and gender in inanimates (besides the gender clitic), but most sources mention
that masculine is associated with large size and/or strength whereas feminine is
associated with small size and/or weakness (see e.g. Tucker and Mpaayei 1955: 3,
Payne 1998). To take one example, 'mountain' in (21)e is masculine but the same form
with feminine gender in (22)e is 'hill' (= small mountain).

---

[103] Transcription follows Tucker and Mpaayei (1955: 308).

However, the correlation is not categorical. There are inanimate entities that are masculine and small (e.g. (21)a) as well as entities that are feminine and large (compare (22)d 'road' to (21)d 'path'). Moreover, the correlation also appears with animate nouns, i.e. even female-referring/male-referring nouns can have the opposite gender from their natural gender and receive the corresponding evaluative interpretation. For example, *ɔl-aláshè* is 'brother,' and it can take the feminine gender clitic *ɛnk-aláshè* and be interpreted as 'weak brother' (Payne 1998: 172).

I therefore suggest that Maa has a masculine augmentative and a feminine diminutive that are quite similar to the Amharic feminine diminutive (Chapter 3): the head which has the evaluative interpretation has its own gender feature, and the evaluative gender is taken as the gender of the DP as a whole; in other words, it "overrides" the gender associated with the root-selecting *n*, most likely because only the highest gender feature is agreed with. I focus only on root-selecting *n*s until Chapters 9 and 10, so I put aside these facts for now.

Thus far, Maa looks rather similar to Amharic and Spanish; but unlike these languages, feminine gender is the default (Tucker and Mpaayei 1955, Payne 1998, Koopman 2003, Newell 2005). First of all, when the gender of an animate entity is unknown, feminine gender is used in many cases. (19) contains the words for 'boy' and 'girl,' which are a different-root pair. However, *ɛn-kɛrái* 'child' (a young human of indeterminate gender) is feminine (Tucker and Mpaayei 1955). This is particularly striking compared to the word for 'child' in Dieri (Chapter 5), Amharic (Chapter 2) and Spanish (see (9)), which is masculine in each language.

Moreover, in Maa, many animals have a feminine default, including 'rhinoceros,' 'rat,' and 'goat.'

(23) a. ɛ-mônỹ   GC.F-rhinoceros 'rhinoceros'
      b. en-derónì GC.F-rat   'rat'
      c. en-kíné   GC.F-goat   'goat' (Tucker and Mpaayei 1955: 303, 304, 293)

Again, the feminine animals are not fixed-gender: they are feminine when gender is irrelevant/unknown, but masculine when a male rhinoceros, rat, or goat is referred to (Tucker and Mpaayei 1955: 3, Payne 1998: 160).

Additionally, gender of an unknown entity is feminine, as shown in the form of demonstratives (see also Payne 1998: 172–3, fn.14).

(24) áínyɔɔ   ɛndá?
      what   that.F
      'What is that?'   (Tucker and Mpaayei 1955: 17)

In (24), the speaker does not know the gender of the object referred to since the speaker does not know the identity of the object, and yet there is feminine agreement on the demonstrative. In Amharic, the same sentence has a masculine demonstrative and masculine agreement on the copular verb, as shown in (25).

(25) ya   mɪndɪn   näw?
      that.M   what   be.3MS.S
      'What is that?

Payne (1998, p.c.) also observes that many borrowings into Maa (at least of inanimates) are assigned feminine gender, and that the vast majority of (non-agentive) nominalizations are feminine. Although there is not space to treat borrowing or nominalizations here, these facts suggest that unsexed entities (whether sex is unknown, as yet unencoded in the language, or irrelevant) are feminine in Maa, i.e. feminine is the default gender.

Further evidence that feminine is the default gender comes from the "third" gender in Maa, sometimes referred to as the 'place' gender (Tucker and Mpaayei 1955: 15). This gender is only triggered by two nominals: 'place' and 'where.' Descriptively, these two nominals have a different set of agreeing forms for certain targets than masculine and feminine nouns. In (26), the demonstrative for 'place' is different in form than the demonstrative for 'boy' (masculine) and 'knife' (feminine).

(26) a. ɛlê ayíónì   'this boy'
      b. ɛnâ álɛ́m   'this knife'
      c. enê wúéjì   'this place'   (Tucker and Mpaayei 1955: 17)

I assume that there is a feature which encodes place agreement and which is unrelated to biological sex (perhaps, [LOCATIVE]). However, not all agreement targets have Vocabulary Items for the full set of three morphosyntactic distinctions (masculine, feminine, locative). For example, the possessive agreement forms make only two morphophonological distinctions, and the agreement on the possessor with 'place' is *feminine* (Tucker and Mpaayei 1955: 20). This is further indication that feminine is the default in Maa—it "fills in" the paradigm for the sub-gender. Compare the Spanish neuter forms discussed in Section 6.2.1, which trigger masculine agreement on e.g. predicate adjectives: since masculine is the default in Spanish, masculine is used to 'fill in' the paradigm for neuters.

Despite this wealth of evidence that feminine is the default gender in Maa, there are a few cases of unsexed entities with masculine gender. Some animals have masculine defaults (as mentioned above), and 'person' is masculine (the same root is used for 'man').

(27) a. ɔl-kɔrɔí   GC.M-colobus.monkey 'colobus monkey'
                                       (Tucker and Mpaayei 1955: 287)
      b. ol-tuŋánì GC.M-person   'person'   (Tucker and Mpaayei 1955: 301)

Moreover, Payne (1998: 170–71) observes that a few nominalizations are masculine, and most importantly, there are masculine inanimates (see (21)). This is unlike the previous feminine default languages that I introduced—Zayse and Zargulla—where all inanimates are feminine.

Overall, then, Maa has two genders that correspond to biological sex in humans and animals (plus a very small third gender for locatives). It has a feminine default for unsexed entities, including animates of unknown/irrelevant gender and inanimates, but also uses masculine for some unsexed entities, too.[104]

6.3.2 *The gender system of Maa: analysis*

The facts just summarized are all predicted if a language has Set 2 of the possible *n*s: female *n*, male *n*, plain *n*, a *n* u[−FEM], and a feminine default. I assume that the feminine default is encoded just as in Zayse and Zargulla. Sample Vocabulary Items for the gender clitic are in (28), using [GC] to stand in for whatever morphosyntactic feature bundle the gender clitics expone.

(28)   **Vocabulary Items: Maa gender clitic**
        [GC], [−FEM] ↔ *ɔl-*
        [GC] ↔ *ɛn-*

The Vocabulary Items in (28) ensure that the VI used for female animates (*ɛn-*) is the default, used in any non-male situation.

As for licensing, female animates result from licensing a root under the female *n*, and male animates result from licensing a root under the male *n*. Inanimates are combinable with either plain *n* (surfacing as feminine) or *n* u[−FEM] (surfacing as masculine). An unsexed animate has the same licensing conditions: it combines with plain *n* (feminine, e.g. 'child') or *n* u[−FEM] (masculine, e.g. 'person').

The set of licensing conditions for Maa are in Table 6.3. I tentatively assume that the two different root nominals are truly not morphologically related (like Amharic, not like Spanish), since the superordinate terms I was able to locate all involve a third root (*ɛn-kɛ́ráí* 'child' and *ɔl-áshê* 'calf'; Tucker and Mpaayei 1955: 286). Table 6.3 summarizes the licensing conditions between *n* and the root for Maa.

Overall, then, Maa is the feminine default "mirror image" of Amharic/Spanish, similarly to how Zayse and Zargulla were the mirror image of Dieri. This type of language is predicted by the analysis, and the fact that it exists is further evidence that the *n* approach is on the right track.

---

[104] It is worth noting that plural gentilics (e.g. *Europeans, (the) Maasai*) are masculine when denoting a mixed-gender group or used generically (D. Payne, p.c.). I suspect that this is because the word *ol-órèrè* 'people' is masculine (even when referring to a group of women (D. Payne, p.c.)), but I leave the encoding of the connection between this noun and the gentilics to future research that is more grounded in Maa morphosyntax.

TABLE 6.3. Licensing conditions for Maa

	n i [+FEM]	*n i* [−FEM]	*n*	*n u* [−FEM]
Different root: masculine ɔl-ayíónì 'boy'	✗	✓	✗	✗
Different root: feminine en-títo 'girl'	✓	✗	✗	✗
Same root: feminine default ɛn-kɛráí 'child'	✓	✓	✓	✗
Same root: masculine default ol-toŋánì 'person'	✓	✓	✗	✓
Inanimate: feminine e-remét 'spear'	✗	✗	✓	✗
Inanimate: masculine o-sóít 'stone'	✗	✗	✗	✓

6.4 Uninterpretable animacy: Algonquian

So far in this chapter, the focus has been on gender systems based on biological sex. However, if gender systems based on biological sex can contain uninterpretable features, it is predicted that (*ceteris paribus*) gender systems based on animacy can also contain uninterpretable features. I submit that this situation is in fact attested in the gender system common to many (if not all) Algonquian languages. In Section 6.4.1 I lay out the facts, and in Section 6.4.2 I develop an analysis of the typical Algonquian gender system that crucially relies on an uninterpretable animacy feature.

6.4.1 *The gender system of Algonquian: description*

Algonquian languages are spoken across the United States and Canada, from California to the East Coast and upwards into Canada from Labrador to Alberta. The Algonquian family is usually divided into four parts: Eastern Algonquian (a genetic sub-group including Micmac, Passamaquoddy, and Massachusett), Central Algonquian (an areal sub-group, with shared innovations due only to contact, including Fox, Ojibwe, Cree, and Menomini), Plains Algonquian (an areal sub-group; Cheyenne, Arapaho, Blackfoot), and the two Algonquian languages spoken in California (possibly an areal sub-group: Wiyot, Yurok). For the discussion in this section, I focus mostly on the Eastern and Central Algonquian languages, especially Fox.

There is a relatively rich literature on Algonquian languages, and Algonquian gender in particular has been the focus of much previous work. I rely on Dahlstrom

(1995) and Goddard (2002) for the initial facts, supplemented by Kilarski (2007), Quinn (2004), and Mithun (1999).

All Algonquian languages have two genders, conventionally called animate and inanimate. Gender distinctions are encoded on several different categories. In Fox, for example, DP-attached number markers agree in gender.

(29)   **Number markers show gender distinctions in Fox**

	Singular	Plural	
Animate	-a	-aki	
Inanimate	-i	-ani	(based on Dahlstrom 1995: 55)

At least some if not all Algonquian languages also mark gender on demonstratives. Verbs additionally agree in gender, although the nature of the agreement marker is contentious; it is unclear whether it is truly agreement or some other type of verbal morphology (see e.g. Quinn 2006 on Penobscot; Johansson 2008 and Ritter and Rosen 2010 on Blackfoot).

The animate gender includes living entities (e.g. people, animals, insects) whereas the inanimate gender includes non-living entities (e.g. objects). Some examples of animate nouns are given in (30), and inanimate nouns in (31), both from Fox (following Algonquian transcription conventions, a raised dot indicates vowel length). The animate nouns all have a final -*a*, whereas the inanimate nouns all have a final -*i*, following (29).

(30)   **Animate nouns in Fox**
   a. neniwa   'man'
   b. ihkwe·wa   'woman'
   c. anemo·ha   'dog'
   d. mahkwa   'bear'
   e. a·mo·wa   'bee'   (Dahlstrom 1995: 56)

(31)   **Inanimate nouns in Fox**
   a. ahkani   'bone'
   b. mahkwayi   'bear skin'
   c. ta·htapakwi 'leaf'
   d. aseni   'stone'
   e. ana·kani   'bowl'   (Dahlstrom 1995: 59–60)

Most trees and plants in Fox are inanimate ((32)), but some are animate ((33)).

(32)   **Inanimate trees and plants in Fox**
   a. ahte·himini   'strawberry'
   b. ani·pi   'elm'
   c. mano·mini   'rice'
   d. wa·pikoni   'squash, pumpkin'
   e. pe·škone·wi·hi   'flower'   (Dahlstrom 1995: 60)

(33)   **Animate trees and plants in Fox**
    a. wi·tawi·ha   'raspberry'
    b. mi·twi·wa   'cottonwood'   (Dahlstrom 1995: 60)

The default gender in Algonquian is inanimate (Corbett 1991: 206, Dahlstrom 1995, Quinn 2004, Goddard 2002; see also Dawe-Sheppard and Hewson 1990). For example, for Menomini, Bloomfield (1962: 26–7) observes that "reference to indifferent objects, gestures, events, circumstances and the like is made in inanimate gender," i.e. linguistic objects that do not have gender features are treated as inanimate. Consider the example in (34), where a clause has been nominalized.

(34)   **Default gender is inanimate (Menomini)**
Eneh	sa	se·hkas-e-yan
that.INAN.S	PARTICLE	hate-1.O-1/2S

'the fact that you hate me'
                         (data from Bloomfield 1962: 27, glossing from Corbett 1991: 206)

Clauses lack gender, yet the demonstrative associated with the nominalized clause (*eneh*) is inanimate.[105]

The facts presented so far are uncontroversial in the Algonquian gender literature. However, there is one last part of the gender system to be described, and it has inspired a heated debate. Many if not all Algonquian languages contain a set of nouns which trigger animate agreement, but are interpreted as inanimate objects (see Goddard 2002: 224–5 for evidence in favor of inanimate interpretation). A partial list from Fox is in (35); note the final *as*.

(35)   **Semantically inanimate but animate-agreeing nouns in Fox**
    a. ni·ča·pa   'doll'
    b. wi·tawi·ha   'raspberry'
    c. mi·kona   'feather'
    d. ato·wa   'blood clot'
    e. owi·wi·na   'horn; braid'
    f. oto·neno·ha   'kidney'
    g. amehkwaya   'beaver skin'
    h. ahpenya   'potato'

---

[105] A more direct diagnostic for default gender would be a sentence like 'What is that?' in reference to an entity whose animacy is unclear, in an Algonquian language that has animacy distinctions for demonstrative pronouns (e.g. Nishnaabemwin, a dialect of Ojibwe (Valentine 2001: 923)) . However, I was unable to locate any examples of this type in the literature, perhaps because the context is somewhat unnatural. While it is straightforward to imagine scenarios where biological sex is unclear (e.g. a person is far away in the distance, a student did not write their name on a paper), it is harder to imagine scenarios where animacy is unclear. If such a sentence were to be elicited, the analysis predicts that the inanimate demonstrative pronoun would be used. I leave this as a prediction to be tested.

i.	mesa·hkwa	'ear of corn'	
j.	ako·na	'snow'	
k.	ana·kwa	'star'	
l.	mehte·ha	'bow'	
m.	mi·seče·ha	'peach'	(Dahlstrom 1995)

If Fox is similar to Ojibwe, there may in fact be a "vast number" of this type of noun (Goddard 2002: 196; see also Darnell and Vanek 1976 for a list of such nouns in Cree, Straus and Brightman 1982 for Cheyenne, Bloomfield 1962: 29–36 for Menomini, and Armoskaite 2011 for some examples from Blackfoot). Crucially, there are no nouns in Algonquian that display the opposite behavior, i.e. interpreted as animate but triggering inanimate agreement.[106]

To the best of my knowledge, there is no phonological generalization that would unite the nouns in (35) and provide a basis for treating them as animate (setting aside, of course, the animate gender marker itself). However, it has been very controversial whether there is some semantic property in common between the nouns in (35) and the rest of the animate-agreeing nouns.

In relating the history of the controversy, Kilarski (2007) divides the debate into two camps. The first camp (see e.g. Bloomfield 1933: 271–2, Greenberg 1954: 15–16, Armoskaite 2011, Mathieu 2012) treats the nouns in (35) like feminine inanimates in languages like Amharic and Spanish—having a gender that is purely arbitrary and unrelated to semantics. The second camp has argued that there is indeed some semantic feature F which is common to all nouns that trigger "animate" agreement, where F is most commonly referred to as "power" (Hallowell 1960, Darnell and Vanek 1976, Black-Rogers 1982, Straus and Brightman 1982).[107]

I will adopt the approach of the first camp for two reasons. First, the studies which have attempted to clarify the mapping between entities with "power" and those with animate gender have been unable to exhaustively characterize the set of nouns with animate gender (this point has been observed in Black-Rogers 1982, Dahlstrom 1995, Kilarski 2007, and Armoskaite 2011; see Darnell and Vanek 1976, Straus and Brightman 1982, Black-Rogers 1982 for specific examples of this type of study).

---

[106] There are two kinds of exceptions to this claim, neither of which pose a serious challenge. The first kind of exception is a noun which is expected to be animate (e.g. 'grandfather') triggering inanimate gender when it refers to an inanimate object in a narrative (see e.g. Goddard 2002). It is common for nouns to shift gender within a narrative depending on the animacy of the referent, and I suggest in Ch. 9 that such cases are a root being licensed under different *n*s. The second kind of exception is two nouns interpreted as animate ('game' in the sense of game animals and 'kin') that are grammatically inanimate in Fox (Dahlstrom 1995: fn. 2); however, both of these are collectives and collectives are generally inanimate in Algonquian (Goddard 2002, Mathieu 2012).

[107] Another important approach to Algonquian gender is to reanalyze it as nominal aspect, as argued in Wiltschko (2012) and Ritter (2013) for Blackfoot. However, there may be a split among Algonquian languages in this respect. Mathieu (2012) argues that animacy in Ojibwe is gender, not nominal aspect, and Ritter (2013) argues the same for Plains Cree. I do not include data from Blackfoot in this discussion.

In each study, there are many ad hoc associations between "power" and certain nouns with animate gender, most likely because a full list of entities with "power" is impossible to obtain (Black-Rogers 1982, Kilarski 2007). Black-Rogers (1982) further observes that some "power"/animacy associations may be diachronically motivated, and that this results in the gender assignment being as arbitrary as Bloomfield, Greenberg, and others originally proposed. If it is impossible to fully characterize the set of animate-agreeing nouns as having "power," then the fundamental problem that the animate-agreeing nouns do not have a consistent semantics remains unsolved.

The second argument against the gender-as-power position is from Goddard (2002). Goddard observes that many nouns interpreted as inanimate vary in whether they agree as animate across Algonquian languages, despite the fact that the entity denoted has the same cultural status across the communities (see also Valentine 2001: 116 for gender variation even within a language community). Consider (36).

(36) 'tobacco'

    a. Animate: Fox *ase·ma·wa*, Cree *ciste·ma·wa*, Menomini *neʔnema·w*, Ojibwe *asemaa*

    b. Inanimate: Munsee *kwašáhte·w*, Unami *kwšá·tay*, Eastern Abenaki *wətamáweyi*

                                           (Goddard 2002: 200–201)

The word for 'tobacco' is animate in Central Algonquian languages, but inanimate in other Algonquian languages. Yet, Goddard writes, "the cultural role and status of tobacco differed little among the Algonquian peoples" (p. 201). He includes nine such examples of nouns with stable cultural status and differing gender across Algonquian languages, and notes that the list could be "greatly extended" (p. 201). This seems like a strong indication that cultural status/attitude does not determine gender, and shifts the burden of proof onto showing how (for example) tobacco is treated/regarded differently in the (36)a languages vis-à-vis the (36)b languages.[108]

I will move forward under the following assumptions, following the first camp above: the nouns in (35) are interpreted as inanimate but they trigger animate gender agreement. There is no single cultural feature in common to all such nouns in a particular language, i.e. they receive animate gender arbitrarily.[109]

---

[108] However, Goddard (2002) concludes by positing more or less the same type of gender system as a "power" approach: one gender is "high" and the other is "low," and certain communities assign "high" to some inanimates due to a "cultural component" (p. 224). Without further specifying this cultural component, it is difficult to see how this is different from the "second camp" of analyses.

[109] There is one caveat here: careful investigation by Dahlstrom (1995) and Quinn (2004) has revealed complex semantic relations among all the animate nouns. For example, Dahlstrom develops a Lakoff-inspired approach where the central members of the animate gender are animate, and most other members are related radially to the central members through some shared semantic property. However, there is no one feature that can be pointed to as characterizing the set of animate nouns. Following a suggestion by Quinn (p.c.), I will assume that these small semantic relations that connect the animate nouns are not part

Overall, then, Algonquian languages have two genders—animate and inanimate—where all semantically animate nouns have animate gender and most semantically inanimate nouns have inanimate gender. A subset of the semantically inanimate nouns trigger animate agreement, and for the reasons identified above, I adopt the position that such nouns are interpreted as inanimate and trigger animate gender agreement.

6.4.2 *The gender system of Algonquian: analysis*

I now turn to the analysis of the Algonquian gender system. I start by comparing Algonquian to the other animacy-based gender system previously encountered—the gender system of Lealao Chinantec. I show that the semantically-inanimate-but-animate-agreeing nouns indicate that Algonquian requires a different kind of analysis, and consider several alternatives before arguing for an approach where animacy features are privative and the [ANIMATE] feature can be uninterpretable.

In Chapter 5, I sketched an analysis of the gender system of Lealao Chinantec, which is animacy-based like Algonquian. In Lealao Chinantec, humans and animals are animate, and all other nouns are inanimate.[110] Semantic animacy thus maps directly onto agreement-relevant animacy, which supports Lealao Chinantec having the *n*s below.

(37)   **Lealao Chinantec *n*s**
      a. *n ↔ i* [+ANIMATE]
      b. *n ↔ i* [−ANIMATE]

Roots found in the words 'woman' and 'dog' are licensed under (37)a and are interpreted as animate, whereas roots found in the words 'house' and 'clothing' are licensed under (37)b and interpreted as inanimate. There are two Vocabulary Items for any category that participates in gender agreement: one with an animate feature and one with an inanimate feature. The animate Vocabulary Item is inserted upon agreement with (37)a and the inanimate Vocabulary Item is inserted upon agreement with (37)b.

At first, a similar approach seems viable for Algonquian. For Fox, roots found in the words 'woman' and 'dog' (see (30)) would be licensed under a *n* like (37)a, whereas roots found in the words 'bone' and 'bowl' (see (31)) would be licensed under a *n* like (37)b. There would be two Vocabulary Items for e.g. singular Num (see (29)), one with [+ANIMATE] and one with [−ANIMATE].

However, this approach runs into a problem in Algonquian with the semantically inanimate but animate-agreeing nouns like 'raspberry,' 'feather,' and 'star' in Fox (see (35)). These nouns are interpreted as inanimate, which indicates they are licensed

---

of the generative grammar per se, at most serving as non-categorical preferences in the pairing of a root with a *n* that has an uninterpretable animacy feature.

[110] There are only 5 exceptions—5 "inanimate" nouns that trigger animate gender. However, there is evidence that these nouns are interpreted as animate for speakers. See Ch. 5.

under (37)b. However, they trigger the same agreement as animate nouns, which means they must contain an animate feature.

In Chapters 3 and 5, I analyzed similar nouns in Amharic, Spanish, and Maa. Amharic and Spanish each contain nouns that are interpreted as unsexed (licensed under plain *n*) but trigger feminine agreeing forms (contain [+FEM]). Maa has similar nouns that are interpreted as unsexed but trigger masculine agreeing forms (contain [−FEM]), despite the feminine default. The solution adopted for these languages was that these nouns have *uninterpretable* gender features that do not affect interpretation but do trigger agreement.

On a par with Amharic and Maa, it seems as if the 'raspberry'-type nouns in Algonquian could have an uninterpretable animacy feature that would trigger animate agreement. However, if so, the 'raspberry' nouns would contain a *n* with two gender features that have opposite values ((38)).

(38)   ***n* for semantically inanimate, agreeing animate noun (non-final)**
       n
       i   [−ANIMATE]
       u   [+ANIMATE]

The *n* has an uninterpretable animate feature for agreement purposes, but an interpretable inanimate feature for semantic interpretation.

The question is how to determine which feature is the controller of agreement.[111] Setting aside sheer stipulation, one answer to this question could rely on a prominence hierarchy ((39)) where animacy is ranked higher than inanimacy.

(39)   **Animacy hierarchy**
       Animate > Inanimate

The higher-ranked feature would then be required to be the controller of agreement.

It is uncontroversial for animacy to be more prominent than inanimacy on prominence hierarchies (see e.g. Dawe-Sheppard and Hewson 1990, Valentine 2001: 267 on Algonquian, and Lockwood and Macaualay 2012 for an overview of prominence hierarchy research). However, from a Minimalist/Principles and Parameters perspective, prominence hierarchies have been argued to be epiphenomenal (see e.g. Wiltschko 2008a, Richards 2008). There is no evident way to incorporate a hierarchy into these frameworks, especially into Minimalism, where Universal Grammar is assumed to be as restricted as possible. Accordingly, there have been many successful reanalyses of hierarchy effects in terms of independently motivated principles and

---

[111] In his detailed analysis of Kiowa noun class, Harbour (2007) proposes that certain syntactic heads can contain two instantiations of the same feature with opposite values. However, this only arises in his approach when a target of agreement receives two different values from two different controllers. It is never the case for an agreement controller like a *n*P.

operations (see the references above as well as Halle and Marantz 1993, Bruening 2001, Brown et al. 2004, Béjar and Rezac 2009, and many others). I therefore do not pursue a hierarchy solution to the 'raspberry'-type nouns here—instead, I propose an alternative approach to animacy as a feature.

Specifically, I propose that animacy is a privative feature—either present as [ANIMATE] or absent altogether (see Ritter 2013 for a similar proposal for Plains Cree; see Harley and Ritter 2002, Toebosch 2003, 2011 for evidence that animacy is privative from other languages). The relevant *n*s under this proposal are shown in (40).[112]

(40)   **Animacy *n*s in Algonquian on a privative approach to animacy features (incomplete list)**
    a. *n   i* [ANIMATE]
    b. *n*

I assume that (40)a triggers an animate interpretation when combined with a root, whereas (40)b entails a default interpretation (as per the theory of privative features where the absence of a feature entails the default; see e.g. Harley and Ritter 2002, Dresher 2003 for detailed discussion). The default gender is inanimate in Algonquian (see Section 6.4.1), so roots licensed under (40)b will be interpreted as inanimate.[113]

With these assumptions in place, it is easy to see how roots found in the words 'woman' and 'dog' would be licensed under (40)a and those in 'bone' and 'bowl' under (40)b. Thus far, a privative approach is as successful as a binary approach The privative approach pulls ahead with respect to nouns like 'raspberry'—inanimate-interpreted but animacy agreeing. Such nouns require there to be one more type of *n* – one with an *un*interpretable animacy feature.[114] This *n* is in (41)c.

---

[112] Several arguments have been advanced against privative features in Minimalism; see e.g. Adger (2010), Adger and Svenonius (2011), Harbour (2011). One of the most compelling arguments comes from Adger and Svenonius (2011). They observe that, in Minimalism, a probe must specify that it is looking for a certain type of feature; this is normally encoded as the probe having version of that feature which is unvalued. Thus, features on goals must be valued in order to value the probe, i.e. features on goals not be privative. Although it would be hard to restrict, one technical fix would be for animacy to have only a plus value on goals; this would render it valued but (I believe) would lead to the same conclusions as treating it as truly privative (i.e. value-less). Moreover, it is worth emphasizing that privativity is not just a quick fix for the analysis here: it is empirically supported because it predicts the lack of semantically animate nouns that have inanimate gender (see later on in this section and Ritter 2013).

[113] Cf. Quinn (2006: ch. 2) for a *v* approach to verbs in Algonquian languages that has many similarities to this analysis of the nominal system.

[114] Another option is that all the nouns like 'raspberry' are derived—specifically, that they are denominal nouns formed by adding a *n* with an uninterpretable animate feature to a plain *n*P ((i)):

    (i)   [*n u* ANIM [*n* [√]]]

(i) would be interpreted as inanimate, but would trigger animate agreement as per Chapter 10 on nominalizations.

Evidence in favor of this approach would be that, for every noun like 'raspberry,' there is an inanimate noun with the same root (i.e. with a related interpretation and morphophonological expression). In fact, some of the nouns like 'raspberry' do seem to share a root with an inanimate noun (see Goddard 2002: 214).

(41) **Animacy *n*s in Algonquian on a privative approach to animacy features (complete list)**

   a. *n* *i* [ANIMATE]
   b. *n*
   c. *n* *u* [ANIMATE]

The root associated with *wi·tawi·ha* 'raspberry,' then, is licensed under (41)c (the singular marker *-a* has been removed from the root).

(42)

```
        nP                    =     'raspberry' (Fox)
       ╱  ╲
      n      √P
   u [ANIM]   │
          √WI·TAWI·H
```

Since the *n*P has no interpretable animacy feature, it is interpreted as inanimate by default. However, it still contains an animacy feature, which causes animate agreeing forms to be inserted for, e.g. number markers. The relevant Vocabulary Items for Fox plural markers appear in (43).

(43) **Vocabulary Items for Fox plural markers**

   a. [Num], [+PL], [ANIM] → -aki
   b. [Num], [+PL] → -ani

Any agreement target with an animacy feature causes *-aki* to be inserted, whereas all others cause *-ani* to be inserted. This predicts that both nouns like 'woman' and nouns like 'raspberry' will trigger the insertion of "animate" exponents.

   As Ritter (2013) observes, another argument in favor of a privative approach is that it explains why nouns are never interpreted as animate but agree like inanimates (see Section 6.4.1). There is simply no inanimate feature that could be said to be uninterpretable for these hypothetical nouns. In order to be interpreted as animate, they would have to be formed via a *n* bearing an interpretable animate feature, which would lead to animate agreement (just like the noun 'woman').

However, some of the nouns like 'raspberry' seem to be only semantically related to an inanimate noun (often providing a special/specific instance of an inanimate noun), and are morphophonologically unrelated (Goddard 2002: 215–16). Moreover, some of the nouns like 'raspberry' seem to be unrelated to any inanimate noun at all; in Fox, body parts, crops, skins, and trees can be either animate and inanimate without one gender clearly being derived from another (Goddard 2002: 217–21). Given this array of facts, it seems that the evaluation of whether (i) is correct requires significant Algonquian expertise, and I necessarily set it aside. This approach is, however, less promising than the analysis pursued in the main text, since it offers no explanation for why only semantically inanimate nouns can agree as animate, but semantically animate nouns cannot agree as inanimate.

In sum, Algonquian provides an example of a language family that uses an uninterpretable animacy feature, and I have argued, following Ritter (2013), that animacy is a privative feature. It is clear, then, that uninterpretable features in a gender system extend to animacy features as well as biological sex features, as predicted (*ceteris paribus*) by the proposal on gender developed so far.[115]

I close with a housekeeping note and an interesting prediction. The housekeeping note is that it is perfectly plausible to analyze Lealao Chinantec in a privative approach to animacy features. It will have just the *n*s in (40), i.e. it will lack uninterpretable animacy features. This makes the relationship between Lealao Chinantec and Algonquian similar to the relationship between, say, Dieri and Amharic. Lealao Chinantec and Dieri have a subset of the *n*s of Algonquian and Amharic, respectively, and the extra *n*s in Algonquian and Amharic have uninterpretable gender.

The interesting prediction of a privative approach to animacy is the following. If the animacy feature were binary, then it is predicted that at least some language would have an animate as the default gender, similar to how the binary approach to biological sex predicts some language has feminine as the default gender (a prediction which is borne out in languages like Zayse, Zargulla, and Maa; see Chapter 5 and Section 6.3). In an animate default language under a binary approach to animacy, one of the two Vocabulary Items for any given target would have a [−ANIM] feature and the other would not. However, under a privative approach, the only possible default is the inanimate gender because there is no [−ANIM] feature in the syntax to expone. Although this prediction will have to wait to be confirmed, some preliminary support comes from Harley and Ritter (2002); they treat inanimate as the default in a feature hierarchy based on a broad cross-linguistic survey of pronouns.

6.5 Conclusion

In this chapter, I examined *n* systems that include one uninterpretable feature, and showed how the two types of languages that the analysis predicts are attested. Amharic and Spanish are examples of languages which have not just female, male, and unsexed *n* but also a *n* with an uninterpretable feminine feature. I sketched the gender system of Spanish, and discussed how most of the differences between Amharic and Spanish boil down to Amharic being in the process of "losing" that

---

[115] Animacy as a feature has played a large role in the description and analysis of many grammatical phenomena besides gender—most prominently case assignment, cliticization, and verbal agreement (see e.g. Malchukov 2008 on case marking, Anagnostopoulou 2003 on cliticization, Sedighi 2005 on verbal agreement, Bentley 1999 and Comrie 1981: ch. 9 on a combination of these phenomena). There is not space to explore the consequences of a privative approach to animacy from all of these perspectives, especially because it is unclear whether the feature involved is truly animacy in all cases (see e.g. Adger and Harbour 2007, Ritter and Rosen 2010).

particular *n* (i.e. it is used to license very few roots). I presented Maa as an example of a language with female, male, and unsexed *n* as well as an uninterpretable masculine feature. Finally, I returned to animacy systems, touched on briefly in the previous chapter, and showed how Algonquian languages are a case of a gender system that uses an uninterpretable animacy feature. So far, the gender systems predicted by a *n*-based approach have all been attested.

Throughout the chapter, the discussion has been limited to two-gender systems that contain only one *n* with an uninterpretable feature. What if a two-gender system contained more than one such *n*, as in (44)?

(44)   a.   *n   i* [−FEM]
       b.   *n   i* [+FEM]
       c.   *n*
       d.   *n   u* [+FEM]
       e.   *n   u* [−FEM]

In a language that has this set of *n*s, there are three options for licensing inanimates and unsexed animates: under plain *n* (resulting in whatever the default gender is), under feminine uninterpretable *n* (feminine gender), and under masculine uninterpretable *n* (masculine gender). This language would be indistinguishable empirically from Amharic/Spanish or Maa, depending on the default. However, it is more complicated than any of these languages in that it has an additional type of *n*, and it is unclear why a learner would deduce the more complex inventory of *n*s in (44) when presented with data compatible with the less complex system for Spanish/Amharic and Maa.

One imaginable scenario in which a learner might in fact deduce (44) from a two-gender system is if the default gender was not the same in all contexts; perhaps it would be masculine in Context C, and feminine in Context D. Then all the roots licensed under *n* would have masculine gender in Context C and feminine gender in Context D, and they would be empirically distinguishable to the learner. Interestingly, I argue that this situation holds in Romanian (Chapter 8), but it is easier to explain once we have seen how languages with three genders work. Three-gender languages are accordingly the focus of the next chapter.

7

Case study 3: Three-gender languages

7.1 Introduction

In Chapters 5 and 6, I explored the predictions of a *n* approach to gender for two-gender systems. In this chapter, I widen the empirical focus to include languages that use three genders, and show how the analysis predicts that neuter is the default gender in such languages. In Section 7.2, I discuss Mangarayi, an Australian language that has only interpretable gender features on *n*—essentially the three-gender counterpart of Dieri, Zayse, and Zargulla (Chapter 5). In Section 7.3, I show how the analysis predicts the existence of a language where only one of the non-default genders (e.g. masculine or feminine) can be used for inanimates, the three-gender counterpart of Amharic and Maa (Chapter 6). This prediction is confirmed via the language Wari' (Chapacuran). I analyze in Section 7.4 the gender system of Lavukaleve (Papuan), whose gender system resembles the three-gender system commonly found in Indo-European languages (inanimates found in both masculine and feminine genders). Section 7.5 concludes, and Section 7.6 is an excursus on the nature of default gender in three-gender languages. Overall, I conclude that the three-gender systems predicted by a *n* approach are all attested, and that, despite some counterexamples, there is evidence that neuter is the default in these three-gender languages.

7.2 Three genders, three *n*s: Mangarayi

A gender system based on biological sex minimally requires three *n*s: a female *n* ((1)a), a male *n* ((1)b), and a *n* to form unsexed entities ((1)c).

(1) a. *n i* [+FEM]
     b. *n i* [−FEM]
     c. *n*

The most basic kind of such a gender system would have a different Vocabulary Item for each different *n* (at all gender agreement targets). This type of gender system is attested (and relatively common) among the world's languages, and I spend the remainder of this section describing and analyzing one language with this system: Mangarayi.

7.2.1 *The gender system of Mangarayi: description*

Mangarayi is a non-Pama-Nyungan Australian language spoken in northern Australia. Its classification/genetic affiliation among the non-Pama-Nyungan languages is complex (see Heath 1990, Merlan 2003, and Sharpe 2008 for some perspectives). The language is moribund; Merlan (1982) reports around twenty-two remaining speakers, about ten of whom were elderly at the time of writing (Lewis et al. 2013 report that there are now twelve speakers). The main source used here is the comprehensive grammar Merlan (1982), supplemented by Merlan (1981). There is a small amount of typological research that uses Mangarayi data (see e.g. Nichols 1992, Lehmann 2002), but there is very little theoretical linguistic research on the language, except for phonological investigations of its reduplication patterns. All previous research relies on data from Merlan (1982).

Mangarayi has three genders: masculine, feminine, and neuter (Merlan 1982: 56–8). The main agreement target for gender is case markers; adjectives also agree in gender since they agree in case with their associated nouns. Demonstratives agree in gender, although the formal difference between masculine and neuter has collapsed in most of the demonstrative paradigms (Merlan 1982: 110–11). Mangarayi has an ergative split based on gender: masculine and feminine have nominative-accusative case markers, whereas neuter has ergative-absolutive case markers (Merlan 1982: 56ff.). This is reflected in the glossing, e.g. masculine/feminine transitive and intransitive subjects are glossed as nominative, whereas neuter transitive subjects are glossed as ergative and intransitive subjects as absolutive.

The masculine gender includes male humans and higher animals, and the feminine gender includes female humans and higher animals. Mangarayi contains both different-root and same-root pairs of masculine and feminine nouns. (2) shows a different-root pair: masculine *biwa* 'boy' and feminine *muṛu* 'girl.'

(2) **ṇa-biwa**   ŋanju-gu,   **ŋaḻa-muṛu**   ŋaya-naŋgu
    M.NOM-boy   1S-GEN,   **F.NOM-girl**   3FS-GEN
    'The boy is mine, the girl is hers.'   (Merlan 1982: 63)

(3) contains a same-root nominal *bugbug* 'old person.' Note that the final [g] in the masculine form has nasalized—stop nasalization is a "pervasive" phonological process in Mangarayi (Merlan 1982: 205).

(3) nara-bayi   **ṇa-bugbuŋ-gu**   /   **ŋaya-bugbug**
    that-FOC   **M.GEN-old.person-GEN**   /   **F.GEN-old.person**
    'That is the old man's/old woman's.'   (Merlan 1982: 66)

Higher animals are either masculine or feminine depending on biological sex, e.g. a dog can be masculine as in (4), or feminine as in (5) (where the name referring to the dog has feminine case markers).

(4) **ṇa-muyg**   baŋga   ŋan-wa-b
    M.NOM-dog   close   3s/1s-go.to.see-PP
    'The dog came close to me.'   (Merlan 1982: 81)

(5) guṛʔ   Ø-ma-ṛi   **muyg-bayi**   ŋan-ŋalima
    sool   3s/3s-AUX-PC   **dog-FOC**   F.ACC-**Name**
    'He sooled the dog Nalima.'   (Merlan 1982: 49)[116]

The neuter gender includes all other entities: lower animals (e.g. 'snake' in (6)), insects, plants (e.g. 'tree' in (7)), and inanimate nouns (e.g. 'billabong' in (7) and 'language' in (8)).

(6) **Ø-bandi**   ŋa-ḍaṛaiwu-b   baŋgal-yi
    N.ABS-snake   1s/3s-find-PP   egg-PROP
    'I found a snake with eggs.'   (Merlan 1982: 72)

(7) **Ø-wumbawa Ø-ḷandi**   jir   Ø-jaygi-ni wuburgba   **ṇa-bundal-an**
    N.ABS-one   N.ABS-tree stand   3s-AUX-PC halfway   **N.LOC-billabong-LOC**
    'One tree was standing in the middle of the billabong.'   (Merlan 1982: 59)

(8) ŋan-guḍugu   buyʔ   wuḷa-wu-na   Ø-ŋani
    F.ACC-woman   show   3PL/3s-AUX-PP   **N.ABS-language**
    'They taught the woman language.'   (Merlan 1982: 64)

In sum, Mangarayi has a gender system according to the definition in Chapter 4: gender sorts nouns into three classes, depending on biological sex (female vs. male vs. none), as reflected in agreement patterns on case markers.

7.2.2 *The gender system of Mangarayi: analysis*

In this section, I show first how Mangarayi is analyzed under the approach to gender advanced thus far, and then how the analysis makes two correct predictions about Mangarayi's gender system. The n inventory for Mangarayi is given in (9). It is the same inventory needed for Dieri, Zayse, and Zargulla (Chapter 5).

(9) **Types of n (Mangarayi)**
    a. n i [+FEM]
    b. n i [−FEM]
    c. n

---

[116] 'Sool' is a transitive verb 'to cause to attack,' used for dogs in Australia and New Zealand (Oxford English Dictionary 2014).

Each type of *n* licenses roots in Mangarayi. For example, √MUṚU 'girl' is licensed only under (9)a and thus is necessarily interpreted as female, whereas √BIWA 'boy' is licensed only under (9)b and is necessarily interpreted as male. Other roots are licensed only under (9)c and are thus interpreted as unsexed, e.g. √BANDI 'snake' and √ḶANDI 'tree.'

As for gender agreement, each gender agreement target has three potential Vocabulary Items competing for insertion, where the gender features on the Vocabulary Items straightforwardly mirror the gender features on the *n* agreement controllers. I will use demonstratives as an example, since the case marker paradigms are quite morphologically complex—they involve prefixation and suffixation, as well as intricate syncretism patterns, and a better understanding of Mangarayi case assignment is necessary before the Vocabulary Items can be deduced. The distant demonstrative takes three forms in the nominative.

(10)   **Nominative distant demonstrative paradigm: Mangarayi**
   a. ṇina   Masculine
   b. ṇaḷina   Feminine
   c. nara   Neuter   (Merlan 1982: 110)

The Vocabulary Items for these are given in (11).

(11)   **Mangarayi nominative distant demonstrative**
   a. [DEM], [NOM], [DIST], [−FEM] ↔ ṇina
   b. [DEM], [NOM], [DIST], [+FEM] ↔ ṇaḷina
   c. [DEM], [NOM], [DIST] ↔ nara

Vocabulary Item (11)a includes [−FEM], which will result in (11)a being inserted for every demonstrative that agrees with a male-denoting nominal. Similarly (11)b includes [+FEM] which will result in (11)b being inserted for every female-nominal-agreeing demonstrative. Finally, (11)c is used for all other demonstratives, e.g. demonstratives associated with plants, inanimates, etc. This is where Mangarayi differs from Dieri, Zayse, and Zargulla: Mangarayi has separate Vocabulary Items for the agreement targets corresponding to each *n*, whereas Dieri, Zayse, and Zargulla have only two Vocabulary Items per agreement target to realize the three-way semantic distinction. (11)a corresponds to the masculine gender, (11)b to the feminine gender, and (11)c to the neuter gender.

This basic analysis makes two correct predictions about Mangarayi gender. First, if it is necessary to refer to a typically unsexed entity as sexed (e.g. mythologically, in a narrative, etc.), then the analysis requires that entity to trigger either masculine or feminine gender agreement, depending on the natural gender of the intended referent. It is not possible for a root licensed under plain *n* (which triggers neuter agreement) to convey any information about natural gender.

This prediction is borne out. Merlan (1982: 51) observes that "many mythological characters are designated by nouns which are ordinarily neuter, but in the mythic context are treated either masculine or feminine." For example, *gij* 'moon' is neuter when referring to the astronomical entity, but masculine as a mythic figure. Thus, the root √GIJ is interpreted as 'astronomical entity of the night sky' in the context of the plain *n* and 'male mythological figure' in the context of *n*[−FEM].

The second prediction concerns default gender agreement. Recall that plain *n* combines with a root to form unsexed animates (e.g. 'student') in Amharic, Dieri, Zayse, Zargulla, etc., with the result that these animates received the default gender (masculine for Amharic and Dieri, feminine for Zayse/Zargulla). If plain *n* licenses unsexed animates in Mangarayi as well, it is predicted that these nouns will trigger neuter gender agreement since the plain *n* has its own particular set of agreement targets (called neuter) in Mangarayi. The prediction is borne out, as seen in the noun *waŋgij* 'child.' This noun is translated as 'boy' when masculine ((12)) and 'girl' when feminine (F. Merlan, p.c.).

(12)   Ø-ḍaway   ṇa-waŋgij   Ø-ḍadima-ñ
        N.ABS-tail   **M.NOM-boy**   3S/3S-finish-PP
        'The boy finished the tail.'   (Merlan 1982: 26)

However, it can also be neuter, leading to the unsexed interpretation 'child.'

(13)   ... Ø-ma-ñ   gi-nara   Ø-waŋgij
        ... 3S-say-PP   ANA-DIS   **N.ABS-child**
        '... said the child.'   (Merlan 1982: 45)

The root √WAŊGIJ is thus licensed under *n*[−FEM] in (12) leading to male interpretation, under *n*[+FEM] in leading to a female interpretation, and under the plain *n* in (13) leading to an unsexed interpretation (and neuter gender).[117]

Overall, then, as expected, a gender system is attested which distinguishes three genders: masculine for male entities, feminine for female entities, and neuter for unsexed entities. Moreover, this kind of system is hardly rare among the languages of

---

[117] Unexpectedly, plurals that denote a mixed-gender group of humans trigger masculine agreement (see the paradigm in Merlan 1982: 89). However, most masculine and neuter forms are syncretic in the plural: plural-marked nouns take distinct case suffixes and are aligned in a nominative-accusative way, thus removing the contrast between masculine and neuter case-markers (Merlan 1982: 88–9).

There is one exception: Mangarayi has number-neutral nouns that are not plural-marked but can be interpreted as plural; the one example of a mixed-gender number-neutral noun that I was able to locate still displayed masculine gender. However, it involves the word 'man' being used with a plural interpretation to mean 'people,' and it is unclear whether the group of people denoted in this sentence were all male (see Merlan 1982: 96). Moreover it is unclear how the plural interpretation is retrieved from the number-neutral nouns in the first place (and thus what their internal structure is), so I set this data aside pending better understanding of the Mangarayi number system. See also the discussion of masculine defaults in three-gender languages in Section 6.

the world. A broad range of languages exhibit this type of gender system including Tamil (Dravidian; India and Sri Lanka; see e.g. Arden 1942), Abkhaz (North West Caucasian; Georgia; Hewitt 1979), Barasano (Tucanoan; Columbia, Jones and Jones 1991), and English (even though the gender system of English is only pronominal). Many of these languages (e.g. Tamil and Abkhaz) restrict masculine and feminine to human males and females (all animals are treated as neuter), although I will leave the explanation of this generalization for future research.[118] I proceed to consider a three-gender system that includes uninterpretable gender features.

7.3 Three genders, one uninterpretable feature: Wari'

In the previous chapters, I developed the idea that *n*'s can contain uninterpretable gender features. In particular, I presented evidence for two sets of *n*'s, where one of the *n*'s in each set contains an uninterpretable gender feature: Set 1 with an uninterpretable [+FEM] and Set 2 with an uninterpretable [−FEM]. These are reproduced in Table 7.1

TABLE 7.1. **Four *n*s: possible inventories**

Set 1: Uninterpretable feminine	Set 2: Uninterpretable masculine
n i [+FEM]	*n i* [+FEM]
n i [−FEM]	*n i* [−FEM]
n	*n*
n u [+FEM]	*n u* [−FEM]

---

[118] One facet of the gender system of Tamil deserves further comment. Tamil has three genders— masculine for males, feminine for females, and neuter for all other entities. All animal nouns are neuter, which means that they are all licensed under plain *n* in the present analysis. However, there are different roots for female and male instantiations of certain animals, e.g. *seeval* 'rooster' and *kooli* 'hen' (E. Surenthiraraj, p.c.; cf. Arden 1942). The analysis requires the *n*Ps for these animals to contain a *n*[−FEM] or *n*[+FEM] in order to be interpreted as male or female, but this should cause them to trigger masculine and feminine agreement respectively.

Since the animals are interpreted as male and female, so I will take it as a given that these animals are licensed under *n*[−FEM] or *n*[+FEM]. Something must go amiss, then, during the agreement process such that those features do not end up on the agreement target, and the default (neuter) forms are used. There are at least two ways in which this could be accomplished. First, the agreement mechanism could be sensitive only to elements that have [HUMAN] features, such that agreement would never successfully occur between a target and a *n*P that does not have a [HUMAN] feature. It is common for agreement to be restricted only to animates (see e.g. Comrie 1981: 184), so restricting it to humans seems plausible. The second way in which things could go amiss is that agreement could carry on as normal, but at PF the non-human agreement targets could be Impoverished for [+/−FEM] before Vocabulary Insertion, causing a "retreat to the default case" of neuter gender (see Halle 1997 on Impoverishment). Deciding between these depends on a detailed investigation of Tamil morphology, but suffice it to say, there are at least two likely explanations.

TABLE 7.2. **Four *n*s: possible inventories (with genders)**

Set 1: Uninterpretable feminine		Set 2: Uninterpretable masculine	
n i [+FEM]	feminine gender	*n i* [+FEM]	feminine gender
n i [−FEM]	masculine gender	*n i* [−FEM]	masculine gender
n	neuter gender	*n*	neuter gender
n u [+FEM]	feminine gender	*n u* [−FEM]	masculine gender

I argued in Chapters 3 and 6 that Amharic and Spanish have Set 1, and in Chapter 6 that Maa has Set 2. The main difference between languages with only interpretable gender features (Dieri, Zayse, Zargulla) and languages with interpretable and uninterpretable gender features (Amharic, Spanish, Maa) is that in the latter set, unsexed entities will be able to trigger non-default gender agreement. For example, all inanimates trigger masculine agreement (the default gender) in Dieri, whereas some inanimates trigger feminine in Amharic and Spanish despite the fact that masculine is the default gender in those languages.

For three-gender languages, a similar effect is predicted. A three-gender language with an uninterpretable gender feature will have some unsexed entities that do not trigger default gender agreement, i.e. that are not neuter. The sets of *n*s are repeated in Table 7.2 along with the gender that they are predicted to trigger for a three-gender language.

For both sets, female entities (licensed under female *n*) are feminine, male entities (licensed under male *n*) are masculine, and at least some unsexed entities are neuter (licensed under plain *n*). This is very much like Mangarayi, but the difference again is that *not all* unsexed entities will be neuter in these languages. In a three-gender language with Set 1, some unsexed entities will be feminine (licensed under *n u* [+FEM], trigger the insertion of agreement Vocabulary Items with [+FEM] features). In a three-gender language with Set 2, some unsexed entities will be masculine (licensed under *n u* [−FEM], and trigger the insertion of agreement Vocabulary Items with [−FEM] features).

This prediction is interesting, since languages with these types of gender system are not widely known. These languages would not have the familiar Indo-European three-gender system where unsexed entities are attested in both non-default genders (e.g. Russian, German). These languages would also be different from Mangarayi (and Tamil, Barasano, etc.), where all unsexed entities have the default gender. Instead, they strike an in-between position, allowing some unsexed entities to have one (and only one) of the non-default genders.

However, both these types of three-gender systems are attested, as the analysis predicts. For example, the Arakul' dialect of Lak (Caucasian; Russia) has three genders and Set 1 of *n*s (Khaidakov 1966, Friedman 1996). One gender contains females and a handful of unsexed entities (animals, inanimates = feminine gender in Set 1, Table 7.2), a second gender contains only males (masculine gender in Set 1, Table 7.2), and a third gender contains inanimates (including abstract nouns; neuter gender in Set 1, Table 7.2). Unfortunately, there is insufficient data available on this dialect in order to describe and analyze it in comparable detail to the other languages in this book. Therefore, it must suffice to record its existence, and leave its gender system (and the relationship between its gender system and the four-gender system of literary/standard Lak) for future research. However, there is much more data available for a language that has three genders and Set 2. The language is Wari' (Chapacuran; Brazil), and I describe and analyze its gender system in detail for the remainder of this section.

7.3.1 The gender system of Wari': description

Wari' is a Chapacuran language spoken in western Brazil in the state of Rondônia. The Chapacuran family includes a handful of other languages spoken in Brazil and Bolivia, and, despite a suggestion in Greenberg (1987), it is unrelated to the other Amazonian language families with gender (Arawan, Arawakan), or to any other language family (see Everett and Kern 1997: 3, Aikhenvald 2001: 223). The language has approximately 1,800 speakers (Everett and Kern 1997) and, as of 2006, it was being taught in schools and actively transmitted to later generations (Turner 2006).

There is one grammar (Everett and Kern 1997), and it is extremely comprehensive and serves as the main source for the data here. There is also a fair amount of linguistic research on Wari'. It has inspired some phonetic research, since it contains a very rare type of sound that (a voiceless apico-dental plosive followed by a voiceless bilabial trill; see Ladefoged and Everett 1996, MacEachern et al. 1997). There are also extended studies of Wari' intonation (Turner 2006) and Wari' discourse (Kern 1996). The syntactic and morphological research includes many papers by Everett (Everett 1998, 2005, 2009) and a handful by Birchall (2008, to appear). For the most part, though, the previous literature does not dwell on the gender system; exceptions include Aikhenvald (2001) and Birchall (2008), and are discussed further in Section 7.3.2.

Wari' has three genders, and Everett and Kern (1997) call them feminine, masculine, and neuter. Gender is never marked on the noun itself, but instead is indicated via verbal agreement (realized on a verbal inflectional clitic), possessor agreement (realized on a nominal clitic), complementizer agreement (Everett 1998: 693), preposition agreement, and demonstrative agreement (Everett and Kern 1997: 298, Birchall 2008).

The feminine gender includes only human females. For example, in (14), the noun *xi* 'mother' triggers feminine object agreement (bolded) on the post-verbal clitic.

(14)   xina-Ø   nana-**m**   xi-cacam
        lie.1S-VBLZ   3PL.RP/P-**3FS**   mother-3FPL[119]
        'They told their mother.'   (Everett and Kern 1997: 362, (689c))

The masculine gender includes all human males, about half of the animals and insects, some plants, and half of the inanimates. In (15), the human male *nem* 'my sister's husband' triggers masculine object agreement on the post-verbal clitic.

(15)   coromicat   'ina-**on**   nem   cara pane
        think   1S.RP/P-**3MS**   sister's.husband.1s   that.long.absent
        'I am remembering my long-absent brother-in-law.'
                                                     (Everett and Kern 1997: 154, (253c))

In (16), the monkey species *jowin* triggers masculine possessor agreement.

(16)   banana   **nucun**   jowin
        banana   3MS.POSS   jowin.monkey
        'the jowin monkey's banana'   (Everett and Kern 1997: 299, (562e))

From the description in Everett and Kern (1997), it seems that the gender of this species does not change depending on the gender of the referent, i.e. *jowin* is a masculine epicene. In (17), *wom* 'cotton' (here interpreted as a skirt) triggers masculine possessor agreement as well.

(17)   capija-**con**   wom
        mouth-**3MS**   cotton
        'the hem of the skirt'   (Everett and Kern 1997: 299, (562b))

Wari' contains both different-root and same-root nouns. Many kinship terms are different root, e.g. *'aji'* 'my elder brother' and *we* 'my elder sister' (Everett and Kern 1997: 436). The noun *xa'* 'younger sibling,' though, is same-root, triggering either masculine or feminine agreement depending on whether it refers to a younger brother or sister. In (18), *xa'* triggers masculine object agreement on the post-verbal clitic and is translated as 'brother.'

(18)   juc   wao   ra-**on**   co-xa'   ma
        push   swing   2S.RF-**3MS**   INFL-younger.sibling   2s
        'Swing your younger brother.'   (Everett and Kern 1997: 382, (733))

In (20), *xa'* triggers feminine object agreement on the clitic and is translated as 'sister' (note that *co* is an inflectional element added to certain non-1st-person-possessed kinship terms, and that *jajao* is a plural verb).

---

[119] Gloss clarified from Everett and Kern (1997) such that the null suffix is glossed as a verbalizer. Note that the 1st person singular form of the noun is nominalized (see Everett and Kern 1997: 359).

(19) jajao   'ina-**m**   xa'
     together.PL   1S.RP/P-**3FS**   younger.sibling.1s
     'I accompanied my younger sister.'   (Everett and Kern 1997: 231, (399a))

The neuter gender contains the remaining half of the animals and insects, most of the plants, and the remaining half of the inanimates. In (20), the animal *mijac* 'pig' triggers neuter object agreement on the post-verbal clitic.

(20) cao'   nana-**in**   mijac   'oro   wari'
     eat   3PL.RP/P-**3N**   pig   COLL   person
     'The people ate the pig.'   (Everett and Kern 1997: 326, (611))

In (21), the inanimate noun *wao'* 'small basket' triggers neuter possessor agreement (compare (17)).

(21) capija-in   wao'
     mouth-3N   small.basket
     'the rim of the small basket'   (Everett and Kern 1997: 299, (562a))

Everett and Kern (1997: 296) further observe that the neuter gender includes all nouns denoting objects "which were not familiar to the Wari' before their contact with civilization." I assume this is because all loanwords in Wari' are neuter (Everett and Kern 1997: 301, Birchall 2008).

Overall, then, Wari' has a gender system according to the definition in Chapter 4: gender sorts nouns into three classes, depending partially on biological sex (males are masculine, females are feminine), as reflected in agreement patterns on various elements.

7.3.2 *The gender system of Wari': analysis*

In this section, I first lay out the basic analysis of the Wari' gender system, along the lines of the analyses of previous gender systems, and then investigate default gender in Wari'. The *n* inventory for the Wari' gender system is in (22) (it is the same inventory as Maa in Chapter 6).

(22) **Types of *n* (Wari')**
     a. *n*   *i* [+FEM]
     b. *n*   *i* [−FEM]
     c. *n*
     d. *n*   *u* [−FEM]

Each type of *n* licenses roots. For example, √XI 'mother' is only interpreted as female and is thus only licensed under (22)a, whereas √NEM 'brother-in-law' is only interpreted as male and thus only licensed under (22)b. Wari' also has same-root roots like √XA' which can refer to either males or females; √XA' is accordingly licensed under

(22)a or (22)b. So far, Wari' seems very much like Mangarayi, but only human nouns have been considered. What about animals and inanimates?

Wari' treats all animals as unsexed entities, like inanimates—there is no evidence in Everett and Kern that shows animals receiving gender according to their biological sex. If animals are unsexed, then the question that closed the previous paragraph can be restated as: what about unsexed entities in Wari'? At this point, Wari' diverges from Mangarayi because there are two possible *n*s that unsexed entities can be licensed under: (22)c plain *n*, and (22)d with the uninterpretable masculine feature. This is unlike Mangarayi, which licensed all unsexed entities under the same, plain *n*. In Wari', then, there are both unsexed entities with neuter gender (licensed under plain *n* (22)c, e.g. √WAO 'small basket') and unsexed entities with masculine gender (licensed under (22)d, e.g. √WOM 'cotton'). Overall, then, Wari' instantiates a Set 2 language with three genders, which differs crucially from other three-gender languages because some unsexed entities do not have neuter gender.

As for gender agreement, there will be three Vocabulary Items for any given gender agreement target. One VI will realize targets that agree with a *n* [+FEM], one will realize targets that agree with a *n* [−FEM] (and include both male entities and unsexed entities), and one will realize targets that agree with plain *n*. I will use the verbal object marker as an example, assuming that object agreement is comprised of a bundle of *v* and phi features (see Chomsky 2001). The object marker has three forms in the 3rd person singular.

(23)   **3rd person singular object marker paradigm: Wari'**
    -on   MASCULINE
    -m   FEMININE
    -in   NEUTER   (Everett and Kern 1997: 334)

The Vocabulary Items for these are in (24).

(24)   **Vocabulary Items: 3rd person singular object marker: Wari'**
    a. v, [3], [−FEM] ↔ on
    b. v, [3], [+FEM] ↔ m
    c. v, [3] ↔ in

Vocabulary Item (24)a includes [−FEM], which will result in it being inserted for every object marker that agrees with a male-denoting nominal and every object marker that agrees with a nominal containing a root licensed under (22)d. VI (24)b includes [+FEM], which will result in it being inserted for every object marker that agrees with a female-denoting nominal. Finally, (24)c is used for the remaining unsexed entities, resulting in their bearing neuter gender. In fundamentals, Wari' differs from Dieri, Zayse, and Zargulla in the same way that Mangarayi does: it has three separate Vocabulary Items for the agreement targets *n*, whereas Dieri, Zayse, and Zargulla have only two Vocabulary Items per agreement target. However, Wari' differs from

Mangarayi in that it makes a four-way distinction among the *n*s, resulting in some roots which are licensed under different *n*s triggering the same type of agreement (masculine).

The analysis thus far makes an interesting prediction: that neuter will be the default gender of Wari'. Specifically, it predicts that any time an agreement target must be exponed that lacks a gender feature, a "neuter" Vocabulary Item will be inserted, since it lacks gender features (as in (24)c). There is some evidence that this is correct, and Birchall (2008) explicitly argues that neuter is the "functionally unmarked" gender in Wari'. I review the evidence below, then turn briefly to some surprising facts about defaults that will be discussed further in Section 7.6.

First of all, subordinate clauses in Wari' trigger neuter gender on agreement targets (Everett and Kern 1997: 296, Birchall 2008, Everett 2009: 383). In (25), the subordinate clause is the object of a preposition and the preposition has neuter agreement ('be happy' is expressed idiomatically as 'see my father').

(25) querec te   'ina-em   **pain**   ca   hwet   ma-pa' ca'
      see   father.1s 1S.RP/P-2S **PREP.3N**   INFL.N.RP/P   appear   2S-1S   this.N
      'I am happy that you came (lit. appeared) to me.'

                                                    (Everett and Kern 1997: 297, (557g))

Other agreement controllers that lack gender also trigger neuter agreement, including 'why,' 'not,' and non-referential words (Everett 2009: 385). Birchall (2008) further observes that wh-words trigger neuter gender when the gender of a questioned object is unclear.

(26) cain'   **ca**   tomi'   cama?
      what.N   INFL.N.RP/P   speak   3FS
      'What did she say?'   (Everett and Kern 1997: 51, (78b))

In (26), the complementizer/inflectional element *ca* is neuter in agreement with the wh-word.[120]

Another piece of evidence that neuter is the default comes from gender agreement with coordinated nominal phrases, also referred to as "resolution" (see e.g. Corbett 1991: ch. 9, Wechsler and Zlatić 2003, Hock 2009). I have set aside resolution data so far, since it seems to access the gender of discourse referents (often called "semantic agreement"), and their gender can be different from the gender features on *n*. For

---

[120] Birchall also argues that since all loanwords are neuter, neuter is the default gender. However, all the loanwords on which data are available are inanimate objects (Birchall 2008) and animals (J. Birchall, p.c.), and I suspect that any loanwords for humans would be masculine or feminine according to natural gender. Nevertheless, it is significant that the loanwords are all neuter and not masculine (despite some of the loans having masculine gender in Portuguese). It appears that non-native roots are only capable of being licensed under plain *n*, although I leave the formal encoding of this generalization to a study that focuses on loanword gender (see Corbett 1991 for some of the complexities therein).

Wari', I will continue to set aside data on resolution for human-referring subjects due to the influence of discourse referent biological sex. However, the discourse referent problem does not apply to non-human nominals in Wari', whose discourse referents do not have a biological sex that could conflict with the gender feature on *n*. Birchall (2008) observes that conjoined non-human masculine and neuter nouns trigger neuter agreement.

(27) 'om   ca   taraju xo'   camain' **cain**   'oro   me
      not:exist INFL.N.RP/P hear   correctly at:all   3SM-3N   COLL   bird.M
      'oro   jowin   cwa'   'oro   carawa   jimao.
      COLL   monkey.spec.M   this   COLL   animal.N   different
      'He doesn't hear correctly at all, the birds, the jowin monkeys, all different
      animals.'   (Everett and Kern 1997: 484, (92–4))

In (27), the object agreement on the bolded clitic is neuter, although it cross-references a conjoined DP that contains masculine and neuter nouns. So far, then, several converging pieces of evidence suggest that that neuter gender is used as the default, as predicted.[121]

The analysis also allows for a root to be licensed under the *n* with an uninterpretable [−FEM] feature and to denote a human entity (when nominalized). The resulting nominal would not convey any information about natural gender. This possibility is in fact attested in Wari': *wari'* 'person' triggers masculine agreeing-gender. For example, in (28), there is masculine subject agreement on the passive verbal clitic *tocwa*.[122]

(28) querec 'a   **tocwa**   wari'
      see   NEG.S   **PASS.3MS** person
      'The person was not seen.'   (Everett and Kern 1997: 40, (58a))

Along these same lines , the wh-word for humans, *ma'* 'who,' does not trigger neuter agreement (compare *cain'* 'what' in (26)). The complementizer/inflectional element that agrees with wh-words has only two forms: one for masculine/feminine and

---

[121] Everett (2005: 320–21) briefly proposes a morphological analysis of Wari' pronouns that bears on default gender. The pronouns in Wari' are periphrastic, consisting of a clitic plus a demonstrative. Everett (2005) puts forward realizational rules for the demonstrative portion—for example, for spatial distal demonstratives, the neuter form is *cain* and the elsewhere form is *cwain* (since *cwain* is used for both masculine and feminine). Insofar as this analysis is only about pronouns, it is less relevant to this book. However, the demonstratives that are part of the periphrastic pronouns are also generally used as demonstratives throughout the language. The analysis then can be interpreted as claiming that the default gender form for a spatial distal demonstrative is masculine/feminine *cwain*, since it is the elsewhere case. However, this seems to be incorrect—when demonstratives are used as wh-words, the neuter form *cain* can be used despite the fact that the gender of the referent is unknown (see (26)). See Sect. 4.3 for similar argumentation against an alternative analysis of Lavukaleve gender.

[122] The noun *wari'* 'person' has a different root than the noun for 'man' (*tarama'*) and the noun for 'woman' (*narima'*).

one for neuter. When it agrees with *ma'* 'who,' it takes the masculine/feminine form, as in (29).

(29) ma'   **co**   tomi'   na?
      who   **INFL.M/F.RP/P**   speak   3S.RP/P
      'Who is speaking?'   (Everett and Kern 1997: 45, (64a))

While it is impossible to determine whether *ma'* triggers masculine or feminine, the right facts can be generated if it contains an uninterpretable [−FEM] feature like 'person' as part of its feature bundle.

So far, the analysis makes correct predictions about default (and unspecified) gender, but the last component of Wari' defaults is more challenging. In Wari', mixed gender groups of males and females trigger feminine agreement. For example, when *wari'* 'person' is plural and refers to a group of men and women, it triggers feminine agreement, as shown on the object marker in (30).

(30) querec   'ina-**anam**   'oro   wari'
      see   1S.RP/P-**3FPL**   COLL   person
      'I saw the people (both men and women).' (Everett and Kern 1997: 295, (555c))

Crucially, the collective marker in (30) is not what causes the feminine agreement; nouns preceded by *'oro* trigger masculine agreement when referring only to males (see e.g. Everett and Kern 1997: 389, (745d)). The feminine gender of mixed groups is what causes Aikhenvald (2001) to refer to feminine as the "functionally unmarked" gender whereas neuter is the "default gender." Under the present analysis, it is not immediately clear how to ensure that a mixed gender group receives feminine gender, without (incorrectly) causing it to be interpreted as all-female.

Moreover, the analysis thus far seems to miss a generalization. Taking all the default facts together, Wari' uses neuter for non-human-denoting nominals that lack gender features (although data on animals is lacking), but uses masculine or feminine for human-denoting nominals that lack gender features. This is not predicted by the analysis as it stands, and I return to this generalization in Section 7.6. First, though, I present and analyze the gender system of a language with two uninterpretable gender features.

7.4 Three genders, two uninterpretable features: Lavukaleve

Wari' has one *n* with an uninterpretable masculine gender feature, and its counterpart, the Arakul' dialect of Lak (I assume) has one *n* with an uninterpretable feminine gender feature. However, in the Conclusion of Chapter 6 I sketched out a gender system that has two *n*s with uninterpretable gender features—one with [−FEM] and one with [+FEM]. The inventory is repeated in (31).

(31)   a. *n i* [−FEM]
       b. *n i* [+FEM]
       c. *n*
       d. *n u* [+FEM]
       e. *n u* [−FEM]

If a two-gender system has the inventory in (44), there will be three options for licensing inanimates and unsexed animates: under plain *n* (resulting in whatever the default gender is), under feminine uninterpretable *n* (feminine gender), and under masculine uninterpretable *n* (masculine gender). This language would be indistinguishable empirically from Amharic, Spanish, or Maa, depending on the default (masculine: Amharic and Spanish, Maa: feminine).

However, interestingly, the inventory in (44) is empirically distinguishable among the three-gender languages. The inanimates and unsexed animates in a three-gender language with (44) would have not just neuter gender (like Mangarayi) and not just neuter gender and masculine (like Wari'). The inanimates and unsexed animates would in fact be capable of being either neuter, masculine, or feminine, i.e. licensed under (44)c, d, or e.

This type of gender system is in fact rather familiar because (I submit) it is likely to be the gender system of German and Russian, among others. However, it is also found in less well-known languages; for this section, I present the gender system of Lavukaleve (Papuan; Solomon Islands) as the case study.

A reader might wonder why this section does not focus on German, Russian, or Greek—three languages whose gender systems are well studied and which (at least at first glance) have the same type of gender system as Lavukaleve. There are several reasons for this choice. On the practical level, there are complex interactions between declension class and gender in Russian and Greek (and possibly also German; see e.g. Alexiadou and Müller 2008). These complexities render the languages less than ideal candidates for a quick and clear case study.[123] Additionally, German, Russian, and Greek are all from the same language family and are relatively well-known; the soundness of the predictions of the *n* analysis is more striking if the same type of system also is attested in a completely different family and part of the world. Finally, it can only be beneficial to actively promote and publicize research on understudied and endangered languages. Of course, all languages are equal in the analyst's eye, but hopefully this small treatment of Lavukaleve will introduce readers to the excellent descriptive resources available on Lavukaleve and trigger further interest in Papuan languages (and I hope Sections 7.2 and 7.3 will do the same for Mangarayi and Wari').

---

[123] Moreover, most of the key sources on the gender systems of these languages are written in the languages themselves, and are thus less accessible to the non-specialist.

7.4.1 The gender system of Lavukaleve: description

Lavukaleve is an isolate spoken in the Russell Island subgroup of the Solomon Islands. It is a Papuan language, but Papuan is an areal group of languages, not a genetic family, and it remains unclear whether Lavukaleve is genetically related to any of the other Papuan languages (the best candidates are several other Solomon Island Papuan languages—Savosavo, Bilua, and Touo, Terrill 2003: 9; see also Terrill 2011 on language contact). Terrill (2003: 1) reports that 1,700 Lavukal people live in the Russell Islands, and that most of them speak Lavukaleve as their first language. However, the language faces serious encroachment from English and Solomon Island Pijin. Terrill (2003: 12) notes that many Lavukal families in the East Russells in particular do not speak Lavukaleve to their children.

Lavukaleve has a small but considerable descriptive literature, almost entirely due to the pioneering research of Angela Terrill. There is a substantial grammar (Terrill 2003) as well as many descriptive studies of specific topics (see e.g. Terrill 2004 on coordination, Meira and Terrill 2005 on contrastive demonstratives, Terrill 2006 on body parts, Terrill and Burenhult 2008 on spatial expressions). There is also some work on discourse-related issues (Terrill 2001: reference tracking, Terrill 2010: complex clause combinations) and on the preparation of published materials for a non-literate speaker community (Terrill 2002a). However, besides the grammar (Terrill 2003) and Terrill (2002b) (a survey of gender in the East Papuan languages in order to determine their inter-relationships), none of these works focus on gender. There is also very little theoretical linguistic research on Lavukaleve, with the exception of Hamann (2010), which is discussed in detail in Section 7.4.2.

Lavukaleve has three genders, named as masculine, feminine, and neuter in Terrill (2003). The language has rich gender agreement within the DP and in the verbal system. Adjectives, demonstratives, and definite articles all agree in gender with their head nouns (see Terrill 2003: 78, 172ff., and 91, respectively). Verbal object agreement is sensitive to gender (p. 243), although subject agreement is not (p. 141). A number of other heads also show agreement including focus markers (p. 271), postpositions (p. 150), and the "verbal agreement suffix" (which is used in various contexts; Terrill 2003: ch. 10). Note also that Lavukaleve has three numbers: singular, dual, and plural. Genders are distinguished in the dual (i.e. most targets have feminine dual, masculine dual, etc.) but not in the plural.

Humans, animals, plants, and all kinds of inanimates are found in each gender. The feminine gender includes female humans, certain animals, some plants/trees, and both concrete and abstract inanimates. In (32), the definite article and predicative adjective agree in feminine gender with *vovo* 'girl.'

(32) aka   vovo   **la**   **ho'bea**   ke
      then   girl   DEF.F   **good.FS**   EMPH
      'And the girl was beautiful.'   (Terrill 2003: 51, (21))

In (33), the object marker agrees with feminine *karokomua* 'gecko.'

(33) vela-nun   vela-nun   vela-nun   kini   karokomua   **o-o-le**
      go-DUR   go-DUR   go-DUR   ACT   gecko   **3FS.O-3S.S-see**
      'He went on and on and on, then he saw a gecko.'   (Terrill 2003: 76, (48))

As far as I can determine, all animals are treated as unsexed in Lavukaleve, i.e. (33) does
not denote a female gecko but instead all geckos are treated as feminine regardless of
biological sex. In other words, all animal nouns are fixed-gender (see above on Wari'
and also Chapter 6 on Spanish, where most animal nouns are fixed-gender).

Turning now to inanimates, in (34), *gu* 'wave' triggers feminine agreement on the
indefinite determiner and the main verb.

(34) ...hano   gu   **ro**   hale-re   **vo-a**
      ...then   wave   **one.FS** break-NONFIN   **come-FS**
      '...then a wave broke.'   (Terrill 2003: 80, (62))

The masculine gender contains male humans (as expected), but also contains
animals, plants/trees, and both concrete and abstract inanimates. In (35), *kalem*
'father' triggers masculine agreement on the following definite article.

(35) ...hano   lo-kalem   **na**   o-vo-e
      ...then   3DU.POSS-father **DEF.M**   3S.POSS-come-PSV
      '...then the father comes.'   (Terrill 2003: 70, (36))

Sokoroaem 'lizard' in (36) and *nganga* 'river' in (37) similarly trigger masculine
agreement on the definite article.

(36) sokoroaem   **na**
      lizard   **DEF.M**
      'the lizard'   (Terrill 2003: 167, (188))

(37) nganga   **na**
      river   **DEF.M**
      'the river'   (Terrill 2003: 152, (145))

Lavukaleve has both different-root and same-root nominals for human-denoting
nouns. For example, 'male giant' and 'female giant' are different-root—*bagatum*
(masculine) and *kom'ua* (feminine) (Terrill 2003: 135–6). Several kinship terms are
same-root: *man* is 'male-in-law' and *man-io* is 'female-in-law,' where *-io* is a suffix
associated with feminine gender generally (pp. 4 and 132).

Finally, the neuter gender contains plants/trees and both concrete and abstract
inanimates. Terrill (2003: 136) notes that it also contains one human noun *tu'tul*
'baby,' and a small number of animals (e.g. *lata* 'black-lipped clam'). An example of
the neuter noun *tu'tul* 'baby' triggering neuter object agreement is in (38).

(38) aira   lavea   la   aira   tu'tul   e-ma-a   la   o-ne
     woman   marriage   DEF.F   woman   baby   3SN.O-take-FS   DEF.F   3FS.O-with
     ngoa   lo-me
     stay   3S.S-HAB
     'A married woman stays with the woman who has delivered the baby.'
     (A. Terrill, p.c.)

In (39), the inanimate noun *lafi* 'water' triggers neuter agreement on the definite article.

(39) lafi   **ga**
     water   DEF.N
     'the water'   (Terrill 2003: 246, (376))

Compared to the languages previously described in this chapter, Lavukaleve is different from Mangarayi in that unsexed elements like 'wave' and 'river' can be feminine or masculine, and different from Wari' in that unsexed elements can be feminine.

With the exception of biological sex for humans, there are no categorical semantic generalizations about which nouns have which gender. Terrill (2003: 135–7) lists a number of correlations, but notes that they "are more in the nature of weak tendencies than predictive associations" (p. 137). There are many counterexamples to each correlation, and there are many semantic categories in which masculine, feminine. and neuter nouns are all attested (e.g. body parts; see Terrill 2006: tables 1, 2 and 3).

Terrill also records a number of morphophonological generalizations about gender assignment (Terrill 2003: 132–3). Some of these generalizations are clearly morphological (e.g. nouns ending in *-io* are feminine, where *-io* is used as a feminine nominalizer generally). However, others are less easy to explain (e.g. nouns ending in *-ae* are neuter). I return to phonological correlations with gender in Chapter 11, and move on to the basic analysis of Lavukaleve gender.

7.4.2 *The gender system of Lavukaleve: analysis*

I start this section by presenting the outlines of the analysis of Lavukaleve gender, proceed by showing how the predictions made about default gender are borne out, and conclude by evaluating the approach to Lavukaleve gender developed in Hamann (2010).

The *n* inventory for the gender system of Lavukaleve appears in (40).

(40) **Types of *n* (Lavukaleve)**
    a. *n*   *i*   [+FEM]
    b. *n*   *i*   [−FEM]
    c. *n*
    d. *n*   *u*   [−FEM]
    e. *n*   *u*   [+FEM]

All of these *n*s are necessary to license roots in Lavukaleve. For example, √KOM'UA 'female giant' is only interpreted as female and is thus only licensed under (33)a, whereas √BAGATUM 'male giant' is only interpreted as male and thus only licensed under (33)b. Roots that denote unsexed entities (including animals) when nominalized can be licensed under (40)c (neuter gender), (40)d (masculine gender), or (40)e (feminine gender). This allows for animals and inanimates to be found in each of these genders, as shown above. It also allows for the unsexed human-denoting root √TU'TUL to be licensed under (40)c and receive neuter gender. (I return later to humans whose natural gender is unknown and human-denoting nouns with uninterpretable masculine/feminine gender.) Overall, Lavukaleve instantiates the possible language laid out at the beginning of this section: it has three genders, and unsexed entities are found not only in one of the genders (like Mangarayi), and not only in two of the genders (like Wari'), but in fact in all three genders (feminine, masculine, and neuter).

As for gender agreement, just as in Wari' and Mangarayi, a typical target will have three Vocabulary Items: one VI for [+FEM], one for [−FEM], and one for plain *n* (I say "typical" here, since certain agreement targets display syncretism across genders, e.g. feminine and neuter agreement use the same form for agreement on *roi* 'which'; Terrill 2003: 458). As with Wari', I will use the verbal object marker as an example, and it has three forms in the third person singular, shown in (23).

(41)   **3rd person singular object marker paradigm: Lavukaleve**
    -a   MASCULINE
    -o   FEMININE
    -e   NEUTER   (Terrill 2003: 243)

The Vocabulary Items for these are given in (42).

(42)   **Vocabulary Items: 3rd person singular object marker: Lavukaleve**
    a. *v*, [3], [−FEM] ↔ a
    b. *v*, [3], [+FEM] ↔ o
    c. *v*, [3] ↔ e

Lavukaleve's five-way *n* inventory for the syntax reduces down to a three-way contrast morphologically, so large numbers of roots which are licensed under different *n*s in the syntax trigger the same gender agreement. For example, roots licensed under the "male" *n* ((40)b) and under the uninterpretable masculine *n* ((40)d) will trigger the insertion of the same gender exponent.

The analysis thus far makes a pair of interesting predictions regarding contexts that have triggered "default" gender in other languages. First, for any elements appearing in positions that trigger gender agreement but completely lack gender features (e.g. subordinate clauses), it is predicted that the gender agreement must be neuter. Such elements do not have [+FEM] or [−FEM] features, so no VI can be inserted that contains those features.

This prediction is borne out. As Terrill (2003: 144) observes, "in those cases in which gender agreement is controlled by an element which does not have gender, Lavukaleve obligatorily uses third person singular *neuter* agreement" (my emphasis). For example, the focus marker agrees with either the constituent it focuses (in the case of an argument) or some sub-part of that constituent (in the case of an entire clause) (Terrill 2003: 273). However, if the focus marker focuses an adjunct, a particle, a non-main verb, or the first part of a complex predicate, it always shows neuter agreement, regardless of the sub-parts of these constituents. In (43), the focus is on the PP adjunct *spepat vona* 'on spare parts.' The focus marker is 3rd person neuter singular, despite the fact that 'spare parts' is a plural noun (as shown in the plural object marker on the postposition *na* 'in').

(43) spepat   vo-na   **fi**   fo'foira   o-a-i
      spare.parts.PL 3PL.O-in   **3NS.FOC**   work   3FS.O-1S-do
      'I worked on spare parts.'
                                                          (Terrill 2003: 144, (126))

Therefore, neuter is the morphological gender triggered for elements that lack gender features, as predicted by the analysis.

The analysis also allows for the possibility of a *n*P or feature bundle denoting a human entity whose natural gender is not indicated to have neuter, masculine or feminine gender. Such a root would be licensed in the context of *n*, *n u*[−FEM] or *n u* [+FEM], and such a feature bundle would either have no gender features, *u*[−FEM] or *u*[+FEM]. This prediction is partially borne out, to the extent to which data is available.

First of all, it is clear that human-denoting nouns can be neuter and not convey anything about biological sex, e.g. *tu'tul* 'baby.' Terrill (2003: 144) specifically comments that when a particular baby is in question, which presumably leads to biological sex being known, then *vo'vou* 'boy' or *vovo* 'girl' is used instead. Moreover, the human-referring wh-word *ami* 'who' is masculine. For example, in (44), it triggers masculine agreement on the focus marker although the speaker (presumably) does not know the gender of the referent.

(44) ami   hin   lei-m   hin
      who   3MS.FOC   exist-MS   3MS.FOC
      'Who is it?'
                                                          (Terrill 2003: 456, (868))

This is further evidence for the existence of the feature *u*[−FEM] in the language, which is presumably part of the determiner feature bundle that is realized as *ami* 'who.'

I was unable to locate any human-denoting nouns or wh-words with unknown/ irrelevant gender triggering feminine agreement, but I suspect that this is due to the relatively small number of human-denoting nouns in the grammar (with the exception of kinship terms, which tend to indicate natural gender).[124] Alternatively, it may be that Lavukaleve has a similar constraint to Amharic (Chapter 6), where I proposed that if a root is licensed under a *n* that contains an animate feature, then it must be capable of being licensed under at least one *n* that contains either [+FEM] or [−FEM]. The neuter noun *tutul* 'baby' would be an exception to this constraint, but it may prove to be the only one. Overall, then, almost all of the predictions of the analysis with respect to default gender are confirmed, though it remains to be seen whether the language requires animate-denoting nouns to be sexed like Amharic does.[125]

An understanding of default gender is necessary in order to evaluate Hamann (2010)'s analysis of Lavukaleve gender. The broad goal of Hamann (2010) is to analyze the syncretisms within the Lavukaleve subject and object marker paradigms from a Minimalist/Distributed Morphology perspective. I focus here on the 3rd person object marker paradigm, since it shows gender distinctions (see Table 7.3).

TABLE 7.3. Lavukaleve object marker paradigm

	Singular	Dual	Plural
3 masculine	a-	la-	vo-
3 feminine	o-	lo-	vo-
3 neuter	e-	le-	vo

(Terrill 2003: 243)

---

[124] One red herring is *ruima* 'old man,' which is feminine (Terrill 2003: 142–4). Since *ruima* in fact conveys meaning about the biological gender of its referent (i.e. this is an old man, not an old woman), it does not have unknown/irrelevant gender, so it is not useful for the discussion above. In fact, a noun of this kind is predicted to be impossible—it should necessarily have masculine gender since it refers to a male human and is thus licensed under the interpretable *n* [−FEM].

However, I submit that the structure of *ruima* is complex. Given other facts of Lavukaleve, it is plausibly analyzed as containing the root √RUI, the male natural gender suffix *-m* (Terrill 2003: 125), and then a feminine triggering derivational suffix *-a* (Terrill 2003: 125)—where both suffixes are *ns*. The highest *n* would thus be feminine, and see Chapter 10 on how the highest gender-bearing *n* determines the agreeing gender for a nominal. Under this analysis, *ruia* 'old woman' would consist of the root √RUI, a female natural gender suffix *-a* (Terrill 2003: 125), and then the feminine derivational suffix. This would result in *rui-a-a*, but there is deletion to resolve hiatus at morpheme boundaries (Terrill 2003: 37), so *ruia* is in fact predicted. This analysis is tentative pending further understanding of Lavukaleve morphology, but it as at least reasonable that *ruima* is morphologically complex and thus not a counterexample. It seems to also be the case that *ruima* is in the process of becoming masculine; see Terrill (2003: ch. 6).

[125] Although plural agreement does not make gender distinctions, dual agreement does have separate masculine, feminine, and neuter forms (in most contexts). Another way to test for the default gender of Lavukaleve, then, would be to see what gender is triggered by a DP like 'the two people' where one person is a man and one is a woman. As far as I can determine, there are no such DPs in Terrill (2003). Terrill (2003: ch. 6) does briefly discuss gender resolution, where two conjoined DPs triggers dual agreement, but I set aside resolution for human nominals.

Hamann (2010) decomposes the 3rd person object markers. He proposes that *l-* is the exponent corresponding to dual whereas *v-* is the exponent corresponding to plural. This leaves *-a* and *-e* as the exponents corresponding to masculine and neuter gender respectively for both singular and dual, but what about *-o*? Since *-o* is used for all genders in the plural (and is used as the 3rd person subject marker regardless of gender), Hamann proposes that *-o* merely expones 3rd person. Thus, in his approach, this "feminine" form *-o* is the default (i.e. the least specified Vocabulary Item) for the 3rd person object markers.

This contradicts with the approach above. I assumed (as in Mangarayi and Wari') that neuter gender Vocabulary Items express no gender features, but this would predict that the neuter exponent *-e* would be the form with the widest distribution in the paradigm since it expones e.g. only 3rd person (see (42)c). In order to keep this from happening, Hamann has to assume different features for each gender than I have assumed throughout the book. Specifically, he assumes that the syntactic representation of each gender has a masculine and feminine feature, as shown in (45).

(45)   **Gender features (Hamann 2010: 211)**
    a. [+MASC], [–FEM] = masculine
    b. [–MASC], [+FEM] = feminine
    c. [+MASC], [+FEM] = neuter
    d. [–MASC], [–FEM] (excluded)

Taking this featural approach to gender, the resulting VIs for 3rd person singular object markers are shown in (46).

(46)   **VIs for 3rd person object marker: Lavukaleve (Hamann 2010)**
    a. [3][+MASC][+FEM] ↔ e
    b. [3][+MASC] ↔ a
    c. [3] ↔ o

Again, this is different than the VIs that I proposed for the Lavukaleve gender marker in (42) in that the exponent that expones the fewest features is the "feminine" exponent in (46)c, and the neuter (which expones the fewest in (42)c) actually expones the most features in (46)a.

The general approach to gender features in (45) does not address one of the key questions for this book—the interplay between arbitrary and natural gender. Setting this drawback aside, though, the Vocabulary Items in (46) and in (42) make different empirical predictions. The VIs in (46) predict that a controller which lacks gender features will trigger "feminine" gender *-o*, since the masculine and neuter exponents both require gender features in the morpheme from the syntax. However, the VIs in (42) predict that a controller which lacks gender features will trigger neuter gender. As Terrill (2003) observes, neuter is always the gender triggered by non-nominal controllers, supporting the analysis in this book and indicating that (46) is not on the right track.

Terrill (2003: 145) even presents a case where a non-nominal controller triggers neuter gender on the object marker in particular. In Lavukaleve discourse, when it is necessary to indicate that events carried on as they were for some time, the intransitive verb *me* 'continue' is used in a subordinate clause (along with the anterior suffix *-ge*). Intransitive verbs in a subordinate clause take object markers to indicate agreement with their subjects, and this kind of agreement is obligatory (Lavukaleve has a partially ergative agreement system in subordinate clauses; see Terrill 2003: 423ff.). Crucially, the agreement on *me* in this particular type of continuative subordinate clause is 3rd person singular *neuter*, even though there is no argument with which it agrees. For example, in (47), there is a neuter object marker on *me* 'continue.'

(47) aka   e-e-me-ge   a-o-ke   feu-ri
       then   3NS.O-SUBORD-continue-ANT   3MS.O-3S.S-push.off go.inland-CAUS
       'Then it went on (like that), then he pushed it [his canoe] up on shore.'

(Terrill 2003: 145, (129))

The neuter agreement demonstrates that the Vocabulary Items in (42) are correct.

Note also that the analysis developed here can still generate the object marker paradigm correctly, just with less syncretism than Hamann (2010). For example, in 3rd person object markers, the dual prefix can still be *l-*, but there must be a separate Vocabulary Item *vo-* that corresponds to plural object markers, i.e. *vo-* can no longer be decomposed into a plural marker and a 3rd person marker. Although it may be that this is a drawback of the present analysis, it is not clear what benefits accrue from forcing an analysis to have the maximum amount of syncretism possible—a system with maximal syncretism is perhaps easier to learn, but when it contradicts markedness patterns in the language (like default gender in Lavukaleve), it seems that an analysis that incorporates only some syncretism (but not every possible syncretism) is warranted.

7.4.3 Conclusion: Lavukaleve

In this section, we have seen a language that has three genders and two uninterpretable features—resulting in inanimate and unsexed entities being distributed throughout the genders. I showed how this type of language is straightforwardly accounted for in the gender analysis adopted thus far, and how it makes correct predictions about default gender.

Other examples of this type of gender system are readily available. For example, German also has three genders where inanimates and unsexed entities are distributed throughout the neuter, masculine, and feminine genders. Specifically, inanimates can be masculine (*der Tisch* 'the.M table'), feminine (*die Wand* 'the.F wall'), or neuter (*das Fenster* 'the.N window'; data from Durrell 2011: 1). Unsexed animates, even if they denote humans, can also be masculine (*der Mensch* 'the.м person') feminine (*die Geisel* 'the.ғ hostage'), or neuter (*das Kind* 'the.и child'; Durrell 2011: 2, 6–7). Russian and Greek also seem to be possible candidates for this type of gender system. Although it is unclear why this gender system seems common (there may be something particularly learnable about it, or it may be an accident of history), it suffices to say that again, the predictions of the analysis are borne out in that such a gender system is attested and is structured as expected.

7.5 Conclusion

In this chapter, I have shown that the *n* inventories that I proposed for two-gender, biological-sex-based gender systems in Chapters 3, 5, and 6 are also found in three-gender languages. The same inventory of three *n*s (male, female, plain) is found in Dieri, Zayse and Zargulla, and Mangarayi. The same inventory of four *n*s (male, female, plain, plus one *n* with an uninterpretable feature) is found in Amharic, Spanish, Maa, and Wari'. Finally, as discussed in section 7.4, a typical two-gender language cannot provide evidence for an inventory of five *n*s (male, female, plain, two *n*s with uninterpretable features), but a three-gender language easily can, and I argued that Lavukaleve in fact has this inventory. Thus, two- and three-gender languages provide evidence that all possible combinations of *n* inventories, given my assumptions about gender features, are attested.

The analysis also makes a strong prediction about three-gender languages: since neuter gender corresponds to the *n* without gender features, neuter will always be the default gender, i.e. the Vocabulary Item that lacks gender features will always be inserted when the feature bundle of the agreement target also lacks gender features. I presented evidence that bore this out for each language, although there were a few recalcitrant cases where it seemed that another gender was the default. I tackle these cases more fully in Section 7.6.

First, though, it is necessary to mention one topic I do not cover. In Chapters 5 and Chapter 6, I also addressed animacy-based gender systems—namely, Lealao Chinantec, and Algonquian languages. However, I do not address animacy-based gender systems in this chapter, primarily because there are not clear predictions about what such a system would be like. Biological gender makes a three-way distinction among the *n*s relevant for syntax/semantics (male, female, *n*), and languages vary in whether they have the Vocabulary Items available to maintain this distinction morphologically (three-gender language) or whether they collapse two of the distinctions (two-gender language). However, I treated animacy as only a two-way distinction (animate or inanimate), so it is unclear what a three-gender language system based strictly on animacy would look like, if it could exist at all.

One possibility is that the animacy feature would be "broken down" into more specific features like human, animal, and/or different kinds of inanimates. For example, there are attested three-gender systems that have one gender for humans, one for animals, and one for animates (e.g. Nzakara (Niger-Congo (Adamawa-Ubangi), Central African Republic); Tucker and Bryan 1966: 146–7). However, investigating this type of gender system requires a better understanding of the nature of animacy features than there is space to construct here (see also Chapter 11 on the nature of gender features). I leave this matter open for future research, with the hope that the proposals here will at least provide a starting point on which to base the investigation.

7.6 Excursus: default gender in three-gender languages

The analysis in the book so far has covered a lot of ground, but there is a loose end about default gender agreement that deserves to be tied off (if only approximately) before the close of this section. Many three-gender languages do not use the neuter gender as the default in certain cases; for example, Wari' uses feminine gender agreement for mixed-gender groups (see (30)). I propose that this is because there is resistance to sex-differentiable nouns having neuter gender. ("Sex-differentiable nouns" are the set of nouns in a language such that the language makes biological sex distinctions between at least some members of that set; e.g. human nouns and animal nouns are sex-differentiable in Amharic, human nouns and higher animals are sex-differentiable in Spanish, only human nouns are sex-differentiable in Wari'.) However, I show in this section that non-sex-differentiable nouns always trigger neuter agreement, exactly as the analysis predicts.

I review relevant data from the languages covered in this chapter in Section 7.6.1. In order to gain a fuller picture of defaults across three-gender languages, I add data from Russian, Icelandic, and Tamil to the mix in Section 7.6.2. In Section 7.6.3, I conclude that the generalization that neuter is not used for sex-differentiable nouns is a clear tendency, but not categorical, and I offer some suggestions on how to refine this generalization and to integrate it into the grammar in future research.

First, though, two clarifications are necessary. It is possible in principle for languages to license roots that denote sex-differentiable entities (when nominalized) under plain *n* or a *n* that lacks uninterpretable features. The resulting nominals express no information about natural gender even though they denote sex-differentiable entities. An example of this from Section 7.3 is the Wari' word *wari'* 'person,' which refers to humans (sex-differentiable in Wari'), and is masculine, but does not convey anything about the natural gender of the person referred to. The distribution of roots across *n*s is a highly complicated issue for any language, and it raises intra-language and inter-language questions about variation that I have purposely not pursued in great detail for any language other than Amharic (see Chapter 3; see also Chapter 6 comparing Amharic and Spanish). I do not further explore the licensing of this type of root in this section.

Instead, I use "default gender" for when an agreement controller has no gender features—because it is non-nominal (e.g. a clausal subject), because it is a same-root licensed with a plain *n*, or because it is interpreted as lacking natural gender and is not a root (e.g. wh-words, and pronouns like *nobody*; if it were a root, then the paragraph above applies). This encompasses both non-sex-differentiable and sex-differentiable controllers. I also include data from mixed-gender groups and resolution, where, strictly speaking, it is not obvious that these DPs lack gender features entirely. However, given the limited data available for many languages, I have cast the net a bit wider than is comfortable here, and I return to this issue in Section 7.6.3.

The second clarification is how this definition of default gender relates to the previous literature on default gender; see e.g. Corbett (1980, 1991, 2006a), Corbett and Fraser (2000a), Fraser and Corbett (1997), Evans et al. (2002), Sauerland (2008), Zamparelli (2008). Sauerland (2008) introduces a series of tests for the markedness of phi features that include many of the default diagnostics used here, including quantification over DPs whose referents have multiple natural genders and resolution. Sauerland tentatively concludes that neither masculine nor feminine are unmarked in German (i.e. they are marked, and neuter is unmarked), similar to the proposals here.

The remainder of the literature distinguishes: (i) normal case default and (ii) exceptional case default. In a lexicalist approach, the normal case default is the gender assigned to a noun whose lexical entry is underspecified for gender (see e.g. Fraser and Corbett's 1997 analysis of Arapesh). The normal case default is also thought to be the gender assigned to nouns with "reference problems" (Corbett and Fraser 2000a), like a same-root nominal whose referent has unknown/irrelevant gender. The exceptional case default is posited to be used for "evasive" forms (see 6.2 on Tamil) and for non-nominal controllers like clausal subjects.

From the perspective of the DM analysis developed here, the terms "normal case default" and "exceptional case default" do not map onto useful distinctions. Instead, I group together nouns that have reference problems with non-nominal controllers as both triggering default gender agreement, since they both lack gender features in the analysis. The equivalent of having a lexical entry be underspecified for gender in this approach is non-sex-differentiable roots that are licensed only under plain *n*. There is a sense in which they receive default agreement, since agreement targets with these nominals can only be exponed via the least specified Vocabulary Item. However, I have used these cases as a starting point for my analysis of a gender system, and then I test the prediction that the gender agreement that they trigger is used in all cases.

7.6.1 Default gender in Mangarayi, Wari', and Lavukaleve

In this section, I review the facts presented earlier concerning default gender in Mangarayi, Wari', and Lavukaleve. I start with Wari', for which the most information on gender defaults is available. Recall that Wari' uses neuter as the default gender for clausal subjects ((25)), non-human-referring wh-words ((26)), agreement with 'why,' 'not,' and non-referential words (Everett 2009: 385), and verbal agreement with a coordinated nominal phrase subject where one conjunct is masculine and the other neuter ((27)). This is as expected under the analysis.

However, Wari' has masculine human-referring wh-words ((29)) and feminine is the gender for mixed-natural-gender human groups ((30)). As already suggested, it is possible to explain (29) as the human-referring wh-word containing an uninterpretable masculine feature. However, also as noted above, this explanation misses the generalization that neuter is not used for default agreement only with the sex-differentiable nouns (i.e. humans).

There is some information on defaults in Lavukaleve and Mangarayi, but not an abundance. In Lavukaleve, the default gender is neuter for subordinate clause subjects ((43)), and for (potential) expletive subjects like ((47)). However, human-referring wh-words are masculine, as in Wari' ((44)). In Mangarayi, there is at least one case of an animate nominal receiving neuter gender when natural gender is unknown ((13)). However, even though the data is not clear, it appears that mixed-gender groups in Mangarayi are masculine (fn. 117).

Two broad generalizations emerge from the data thus far. They are set out in (48).

(48)   **Default gender generalizations**
   a. Default gender agreement is neuter for all non-sex-differentiable controllers.
   b. Default gender agreement is not neuter for all sex-differentiable controllers.

In Wari' and Lavukaleve, only humans are sex-differentiable; in Mangarayi, humans and animals are sex-differentiable (see e.g. (5)). (48)a captures the default gender agreement for e.g. subordinate-clause subjects in Wari' and Lavukaleve. (48)b covers the default gender agreement of e.g. mixed-gender groups in Wari' and Mangarayi. There is one major exception to (48)b. In Mangarayi, *waŋgij* 'child' is neuter when its gender is unknown in Mangarayi. I shall return to this exception, but first I broaden the data pool by considering defaults in a few additional three-gender languages.

7.6.2 *Default gender in Russian, Icelandic, and Tamil*

The data from Mangarayi, Wari', and Lavukaleve is valuable, but the variation it displays and the limited amount of information on e.g. Lavukaleve suggest that bringing in more data from other three-gender languages would be fruitful. I will focus on Russian, Icelandic, and Tamil because detailed data on defaults is available for each of these languages, and because these languages illustrate the range of ways that three-gender languages address default agreement. I will assume that Russian and Icelandic have gender systems that are basically structured like Lavukaleve (unsexed entities attested in all three genders), whereas Tamil is basically structured like Mangarayi (unsexed entities are only neuter).

At least at first glance, Russian is a clear case of a language that abides by (48) (sources consulted here include Corbett 1991, Fraser and Corbett 1995, Corbett and Fraser 2000a, Nikunlassi 2000, and Doleschal and Schmid 2001). Both humans and certain animals (domesticated ones, ones where sex differences are striking) are sex-differentiable (Corbett 1991: 34), but I will focus on gender default contrasts between human-referring and non-human-referring agreement controllers to keep the discussion manageable. Non-human-referring agreement controllers that lack gender features trigger neuter default gender. For example, weather predicates have neuter gender agreement, as in (49).

(49) byl-o   xolodn-**o**   **Russian**
      was-NS   cold-**NS**
      'It was cold.' (Corbett 1991: 204)

Moreover, infinitival subjects (Corbett 1991: 204) and non-human-referring wh-words also trigger neuter agreement. An example with a non-human-referring wh-word is in (50).

(50) čto   proizošl-**o**   **Russian**
      what   happen.PAST-**NS**
      'What happened?'

So, initial evidence suggests that (48)a holds for Russian: non-sex-differentiable agreement controllers trigger neuter agreement.

Initial evidence also suggests that (48)b holds for Russian. Sex-differentiable nouns do not trigger neuter gender agreement when natural gender is unknown or unclear; instead, they trigger masculine gender agreement. For example, the same-root nominal *sirota* 'orphan' triggers masculine agreement in a quantificational context (see also Doleschal and Schmid 2001: 264).

(51) **každyj** sirota   xočet   čtoby   u   nego bylo   bol'šaja sem'ja **Russian**
      every.M orphan wants   that   at   him   was   big   family
      'Every orphan wants to have a big family.'   (Nikunlassi 2000: 776)

The indefinite pronouns *kto-nibud'*, *kto-to*, *koe-kto*, *nekto* 'anybody, somebody' and *nikto* 'nobody, no one' also trigger masculine agreement (Doleschal and Schmid 2001: 264). Finally, the human-referring wh-word *kto* 'who' triggers masculine agreement; compare (52) to (50).

(52) kto   èto   **sdelal?**   **Russian**
      who   this   **did.M**
      'Who did this?'   (Corbett and Fraser 2000a: 83)

To be clear, I have not conducted an exhaustive search to confirm that Russian always uses masculine agreement for sex-differentiable controllers, and neuter agreement otherwise. However, the signs are promising that (48) holds for Russian.

As for Icelandic, at first it seems similar to Russian. For example, clausal subjects trigger neuter agreement ((53)), whereas sex-differentiable human-referring pronouns 'everybody' and 'nobody' trigger masculine agreement ((54)).

(53) að   María skuli   elska Jón   er ótrúleg-t   **Icelandic**
       that   Mary could.3s   love John   is unbelievable-NS.NOM
       'That Mary could love John is incredible.'   (Grönberg 2002: 170)

(54) Engin-n   má   yfirgefa hús-ið   **Icelandic**
       nobody-MS.NOM   may.3s   leave   house-DEF.NS.NOM
       'Nobody is allowed to leave the house.'   (Grönberg 2002: 170)[126]

However, contrary to (48)b, certain mixed-gender human-referring groups trigger neuter gender. For example, the pronoun to refer to such groups is neuter 'they' (Grönberg 2002: 170), and the expressions for 'mothers and sons' and 'fathers and daughters' are neuter (whereas 'fathers and sons' is masculine and 'mothers and daughters' is feminine; Grönberg 2002: 167). Moreover, the universal quantifier triggers neuter default gender for a human group.

(55) öll   velkomin   **Icelandic**
       all.NPL   welcome.NPL
       'All are welcome.'   (Grönberg 2002: 171)

(55) is taken from a church sign, and Grönberg notes that, interestingly, the masculine version (*allir velkomnir*) is more common in such contexts. Icelandic thus seems to abide by (48)a in that non-sex-differentiable controllers trigger neuter agreement, but it has exceptions to (48)b in that some sex-differentiable (i.e. human) controllers trigger neuter agreement, too—either in addition to, or instead of, masculine agreement.

I turn now to Tamil, in which only humans are sex-differentiable (see Asher 1982). All non-human agreement controllers (including animals) trigger neuter gender, as displayed in (56) for a weather predicate.

(56) DC-ile   sooda   irukki-di   **Tamil**
       DC-LOC   hot.INF   be-3NS
       'It is warm in DC.'

There is also at least one case where neuter is used for a human-referring controller. For Tamil, this is the wh-word 'who,' which triggers neuter agreement on the verb in (57).

(57) yaaru   athe   conn-adu   **Tamil**
       who   that   say-3NS
       'Who said that?'

---

[126] Glossing for these two examples is from M. Norris (p.c.).

Moreover, Tamil sometimes uses "evasive" forms when a gender default is necessary for a human-referring controller (the term "evasive" is due to Corbett 1991). "Evasive" forms occur when a language recruits forms from another paradigm to avoid having to choose a default gender. In Tamil, 'male student' is *manavan* and 'female student' is *manavi*. When a student of unclear gender is referred to, the honorific form *manavar* is used, even though no honorific interpretation is intended (cf. *they* in English being used to refer to a singular person of unclear gender).

(58) manavar   paricei-ye   paas   pandun-aange   **Tamil**
      student.HON   test-ACC   pass   do-3PL
      'The student (hon.) passed the test.'

Overall, then, Tamil conforms to (48)a in that non-human controllers trigger neuter, but flouts (48)b through human controllers triggering neuter agreement and the use of evasive forms.

7.6.3 *Suggestions for analysis and conclusion*

The generalizations identified in Section 7.6.1 are repeated in (59).

(59) **Default gender generalizations**
      a. Default gender agreement is neuter for all non-sex-differentiable controllers.
      b. Default gender agreement is not neuter for all sex-differentiable controllers.

It is clear from the data considered that (59)a is well-supported. Clausal subjects, non-human-referring wh-words, and other non-sex-differentiable controllers always have neuter gender in Mangarayi, Wari', Lavukaleve, Russian, Icelandic, and Tamil.[127] However, (59)b is not well-supported. Even though sex-differentiable controllers have non-neuter gender in certain contexts in most of these languages, some sex-differentiable controllers trigger neuter gender in certain contexts in Mangarayi, Icelandic, and Tamil. In other words, (59)a is nearly exceptionless, whereas (59)b has exceptions in Mangarayi, Icelandic and Tamil.

Nevertheless, (59)b clearly has some clout: it goes some way to describing defaults for sex-differentiable controllers in Mangarayi and Icelandic, and it is sufficient for Russian, Wari', and Lavukaleve. So it seem fair to say that across all these languages there is some kind of resistance to sex-differentiable nouns triggering neuter agreement, and the resistance seems to be closest to categorical in Russian, Wari', and Lavukaleve. The commonsense reasoning behind this is clear: insofar as neuter is a gender used only or primarily for non-sex-differentiable controllers (humans, in most of these languages), it has the whiff of an insult to cross-reference a sex-differentiable controller with a form that is used for non-humans.

---

[127] The only exception that I have found is the wh-word *man* 'what' in Lavukaleve, which triggers masculine agreement (Terrill 2003: 147).

However, encoding this preference in the grammar is a dicey business, and I must defer solving this problem to future research for a few reasons. First of all, this investigation is very pilot-like and most likely misses some key distinctions; it is mostly intended to show how complex the facts are about defaults in three-gender languages. In-depth study of a language is required in order to gain a full picture of the defaults it uses—grammars do not always suffice, and even those that include some default information rarely include every test. Moreover, languages differ in their default behavior in important ways, so careful investigation of many carefully chosen languages will be key. The conclusions may well turn out to be different once a broader range of languages are considered.

Moreover, I have used different tests across different languages according to the availability of the data, but different default diagnostics might have different explanations. Some tests focus on defaults with nominals, but others have wh-words and quantifiers as the agreement controllers. I also have used mixed-gender groups and resolution data, even though it does not necessarily follow that nominals in these contexts lack gender features.

Finally, determining the default in three-gender languages involves phenomena that are not easy for Minimalism/DM to treat or fall outside the scope of Minimalism/DM. I suspect that the kind of intralanguage variation that has been reported for Icelandic defaults may be common, and how it interacts with cases where the default is clear will be thorny to determine. Moreover, evasive defaults are used by many languages (Corbett 1991: 231ff.), and the insertion of a Vocabulary Item whose (seemingly) defining feature is not present in the syntactic feature bundle it expones (e.g. an honorific Vocabulary Item for Tamil) is not an easy morphosemantic nut to crack.[128] Finally, the explanation for why most of the non-neuter defaults are masculine is likely to involve extralinguistic social factors (see e.g. Hellinger and Bußmann 2001, and discussion in Chapter 11).

However, it is absolutely crucial to note that only (59)b has exceptions; (59)a holds absolutely, exactly as the analysis predicts. This makes it seem as though neuter truly is used for default agreement at some level, and in some cases that is disrupted (perhaps systematically, perhaps not) by the fundamental resistance to having sex-differentiable nouns trigger neuter agreement. Thus, with the caveat that non-neuter defaults for sex-differentiable nouns require an explanation beyond the reach of this book, considering a wider range of three-gender default data provides some support for the analysis above.

---

[128] One plausible approach to "evasive" defaults is to treat them as the realization of numberless (as well as genderless) feature bundles. See e.g. Picallo (2002, 2007) on the Spanish neuter, Giurgea (2014), and Ch. 8 on Romanian demonstratives. However, it is unclear how to map these approaches onto Tamil, where the putatively numberless honorific form triggers plural verbal agreement (at least without further investigation of number and markedness in Tamil).

8

Gender is not on Num

Evidence from Somali and Romanian

8.1 Introduction

In Chapters 4–7, I confirmed the predictions of a *n* approach to gender about possible (and impossible) gender systems for two- and three-gender languages. For this chapter and Chapters 9–10, I explore the predictions of a *n* approach to gender in terms of particular empirical phenomena related to gender: the interaction of gender and number in Chapter 8, the interaction of gender and nominalizations in Chapters 9 and 10, and the interaction of gender and declension class in Chapter 10. I originally looked at these phenomena for Amharic in Chapters 2 and 3, and in the following chapters I broaden the empirical base of by including other languages.

In this chapter, I focus on the fact that some nouns in certain languages change gender in the plural, i.e. a noun has Gender X in the singular and Gender Y in the plural. This is shown for Somali in (1) with switching between masculine and feminine gender.

(1)   **Somali**
      a. díbi   'bull (m.) '   b. dibí   'bulls (f.)'
      c. náag   'woman (f.)'   d. naag-ó   'women (m.)'   (Lecarme 2002)

In Chapter 2, I argued that gender is not on Num in Amharic. In this chapter, I argue that gender is not on Num in general, and I demonstrate how a *n* gender proposal accounts for the fact that number seems to be conditioning gender via in-depth case studies of two gender-switch languages: Somali (Section 8.2) and Romanian (Section 8.3). For Somali, I argue that all plurals are formed via *n*, and this explains why switching numbers can (but need not) involve switching genders. For Romanian, I argue in favor of the standard analysis of gender-switching nouns as unspecified for gender. I show how this plays out in a *n* approach to gender, and how it results in the gender of such nouns being dependent on number. Section 8.4 concludes.

Before diving in, though, there is one additional way in which gender and number interact that might initially seem to provide support for gender being on Num. Gender and number can be expressed simultaneously on the same exponent, i.e. as

The Morphosyntax of Gender. First Edition. Ruth Kramer.
© Ruth Kramer 2015. Published 2015 by Oxford University Press.

a portmanteau morpheme. For example, in Italian, the exponent -*i* expresses masculine plural and the exponent -*e* expresses feminine plural.

(2) a. ragazz-**i**   b. ragazz-**e**   **Italian**
        young.person-MPL   young.person-FPL
        'boys'   'girls'   (Alexiadou 2004: 34)

The fact that gender and number are realized by a single exponent could be seen as evidence that gender is a feature on the Num head.

However, it has been argued for many of these cases that the relevant marker should be decomposed, often into a plural exponent and a feminine exponent (see e.g. Lampitelli 2010 on Italian, Faust 2013 on Hebrew, Taraldsen 2010 on the Nguni sub-family of Bantu languages; but see Bernstein 1993a for anti-decomposition arguments for Walloon). Even if there is a clear-cut case of one single exponent for gender and number, though, it does not necessarily indicate that gender and number are on the same syntactic head. The Number head and the *n* head are adjacent, and thus will be local enough to affect each other's exponence. There are at least two ways in which they could relate that would result in a single exponent expressing both gender and number. First, they could undergo Fusion, which combines two terminal nodes into one terminal node before Vocabulary Insertion; this style of analysis has been proposed for Italian in Alexiadou (2004) and Acquaviva (2009). Num and *n* are also close enough to condition each other allomorphically, e.g. by Num being realized as a particular Vocabulary Item in the context of a particular *n*; this style of analysis has been proposed for Romance and Bantu in Bernstein (1993a) and Ferrari (2005) respectively. While it is not immediately obvious which of these will be successful for any given language, it is clear that a *n* approach to gender has multiple ways of accounting for languages where there seems to be one exponent for gender-number, many of which have already been argued for. Gender–number portmanteaux do not indicate that gender must be on Num.

8.2 Gender switch in Somali: all plurals are *n*

Recall from Chapter 3 that Amharic has "split" plurality: some plural exponents are inserted at Num, and some are inserted at *n*. Following Lecarme (2002), I argue in this section that Somali has plural exponents inserted only at *n*, and that this explains the strong connection between plurality and gender in the language. In Section 8.2.1, I lay out the gender system of Somali, which most closely resembles the gender system of Spanish of the languages discussed so far in the book (see Chapter 6). I then describe the complex Somali plural system in Section 8.2.2, including the interaction with gender. In Section 8.2.3 I present the arguments that all the plurals are formed via *n*, and I show in Section 8.2.4 how this analysis captures the relevant generalizations. Finally, I present two alternative analyses (a split approach to Somali plurality, and a Num-based analysis) and show their shortcomings. I close by discussing the cross-linguistic implications for number and gender marking.

8.2.1 *Gender in Somali: description and analysis*

Somali (Afroasiatic (East Cushitic)) is spoken by about 14 million people worldwide (Lewis et al. 2013). It is spoken in Somalia, Djibouti, Kenya, and Ethiopia, and there are significant expatriate populations of speakers in the United States, Canada and elsewhere. There is an ample descriptive tradition for Somali, and a fair amount of research has been done on the language from a theoretical linguistic perspective; see Green et al. (2014b) for an extensive bibliography of both descriptive and theoretical research The major grammars consulted for this case study were Saeed (1993, 1999), Orwin (1995), and Green et al. (2014a). Acute accent marks indicate high tone accent throughout.

Somali has two genders: masculine and feminine. Gender agreement is reflected on determiners, demonstratives, and verbs, among other categories (Saeed 1999: 55–6). Following the conventions of previous research, I will use determiners to indicate gender in the examples below. The feminine determiner is exponed as *-ta*, *-da*, *-dha*, or *-sha*, and the masculine determiner is exponed as *-ka*, *-ga*, *-a*, or *-ha* (phonological factors determine which allomorph is used).

Like other languages with biological-sex-based gender, nouns referring to male entities are masculine, and nouns referring to female entities are feminine (for human-referring, singular nouns). Somali has different roots for different biological sexes of the same type of animate, as in (3)ab, and it also has roots that are compatible with either biological sex (same-root nominals), as in (3)cd.

(3) Somali biological-sex-determined gender

Masculine			Feminine		
a.	nín-ka	'the man'	e.	náág-ta	'the woman'
b.	aabbá-ha	'the father'	f.	hooyá-da	'the mother'
c.	ínan-ka	'the boy'	g.	inán-ta	'the girl'
d.	damêer-ka	'the male donkey'	h.	daméér-ta	'the female donkey'

(acdegh from Green et al. 2014a, bf from Lecarme 2002)[129]

I assume the stress–tone differences between the male and female forms in (c) and (d) are because *n i*[+FEM] and *n i*[−FEM] are realized distinctly (see e.g. the description in Green et al. 2014a: 35).

---

[129] I follow the tone-marking conventions of whichever source the data is from. Most of the data is from Green et al. (2014a), which has the following conventions: "a short vowel linked to H tone is marked with an acute diacritic; a toneless vowel is not marked. A long vowel or diphthong linked to a H tone on the first of its two moras is marked by a circumflex diacritic... When a long vowel or diphthong has a H tone associated with the second of its two moras, speakers will pronounce the entire vowel H. Such vowels are marked v*ív*í (or sometimes vv*í*, depending on the particular example)" (p. 34).

Somali also has nouns referring to inanimate entities that arbitrarily have either masculine or feminine gender, and there seem to be a significant number of each gender. Examples of masculine and feminine inanimates are given in (4).

(4)   **Masculine inanimates**   **Feminine inanimates**
      a. baabûur-ka 'the truck'   d. mindí-da 'the knife'
      b. sánnad-ka 'the year'   e. galáb-ta 'the afternoon'
      c. ílig-ga   'the tooth'   f. káb-ta   'the shoe'   (Green et al. 2014a)

Many animals are treated as unsexed, like inanimates, in that they have the same gender regardless of the sex of the referent. Some examples are shown in (5).[130]

(5)   **Fixed-gender animals**
      a. túke   'crow (m.)'
      b. abéeso   'snake (f.)'   (Saeed 1999)[131]

Finally, the default gender in Somali is masculine. For example, the impersonal pronoun *la* 'one' triggers masculine agreement even when the speaker does not know the gender of the referent (Saeed 1999: 76).

The Somali gender system is similar to the Spanish gender system. The animate nominals can be different-root, or same-root, or have one fixed gender. The inanimate nominals are masculine or feminine arbitrarily, with more feminine nouns than are found in e.g. Amharic. The default gender is masculine. Because of these parallels, I will assume that the Somali gender system has roughly the same analysis as Spanish, i.e. the four-*n* inventory in (6).

(6)   **Somali *n*s**
      a. *n i*[+FEM]
      b. *n i*[−FEM]
      c. *n*
      d. *n u*[+FEM]

(6)ab are used for different-root and same-root nominals, e.g. √HOOYO 'mother' is licensed only under (6)a, whereas √INAN, the root for 'boy' and 'girl,' is licensed under both (6)a and (6)b. (6)c, the plain *n*, is used to form masculine inanimates and masculine fixed-gender animals, whereas (6)d, the uninterpretable [+FEM] *n*, is used to form feminine inanimates and feminine fixed-gender animals. I assume that gender agreement targets like the definite determiner have two Vocabulary Items, one with [+FEM] and the other with no gender features; this ensures that male nominals and nominals

---

[130] It is unclear whether there are any human nouns with fixed gender.
[131] Green et al. (2014a) consider the default tone of these nouns to be on the rightward syllable; the tone shifts leftward when there are no suffixes because of a preference for a word not to end in a high tone (pp. 37–8).

that lack gender features trigger the same, non-feminine (= masculine) gender agreement. Overall, the gender system of Somali is familiar and relatively straightforward, but as I will show in Section 8.2.2, the plural system is unusually elaborate.

8.2.2 *The plural system of Somali*

Descriptively, I will present the Somali system as containing eight different pluralization strategies. By "pluralization strategy," I mean an affix or non-concatenative change to a singular noun that triggers a plural interpretation. I present each of the strategies, and conclude with some key generalizations across them.[132]

The majority of nouns are pluralized via an -*o* suffix, but most previous research separates out two to three different classes of *o*-plurals. The first type of *o*-pluralization applies mostly to masculine nouns, and always changes them to feminine nouns. This plural suffix is -*o* after consonants, and -*yo* after vowels as well as after the segments [x], [c], [q] and often [s], [g], and [y]. The final consonant of the stem is often geminated. An example is in (7); note that final -*o* changes to -*a* when the definite marker is added, throughout the examples.[133]

(7) *o*-**plural: feminine**
   a. baabûur-ka   'the truck (m.)'
   b. baabuurr-ó   'trucks (f.)'
   c. baabuurr-á-da   'the trucks (f.)'   (Green et al. 2014a)

The second type of *o*-pluralization applies to masculine and feminine singular nouns, and always results in a masculine plural noun. There is no gemination and no epenthetic -*y* after certain consonants, but otherwise its exponence is identical to the first type of *o*-plural. An example of a feminine noun with this type of pluralization appears in (8), and a masculine noun in (9).[134]

(8) *o*-**plural: masculine, from feminine noun**
   a. náág-ta   'the woman (f.)'
   b. naag-ó   'women (m.)'
   c. naag-á-ha   'the women (m.)'   (Green et al. 2014a)

---

[132] Ever since Andrzejewski (1964), nouns in Somali have been described in terms of declensions or classes, although the number of classes and the criteria for membership have varied across researchers. One of the primary criteria that has been used for differentiating the classes is pluralization strategy, and in the footnotes I will correlate the pluralization strategies I present with class terminology from prior research.

[133] This type of *o*-pluralization is Class 2 for Orwin (1995), Saeed (1999), and Lampitelli (2013), and Class 1b for Green et al. (2014a).

[134] This type of *o*-pluralization is Classes 1 and 3 for Orwin (1995), Saeed (1999), and Lampitelli (2013), and Classes 1a and 1c for Green et al. (2014a). Previous research has separated this plural strategy into two strategies, primarily on the basis of its availability to both masculine and feminine nouns. I choose not to make this distinction, since the same exponents are used to express plurality for both the masculine and feminine nouns that it applies to.

(9)   *o*-plural: masculine, from masculine noun
    a. nâas-ka   'the breast (m.)'
    b. naas-ó   'breasts (m.)'
    c. naas-á-ha   'the breasts (m.)'   (Green et al. 2014a)

I will refer to the these pluralization strategies as the "*o*-plural:feminine" ((7)) and the "*o*-plural:masculine" ((8),(9)) henceforth.

Although the *o*-plurals are the most common pluralization strategies, there are six additional strategies and many of them are relatively frequent. For example, some nouns are pluralized via the addition of an -*a* suffix followed by a consonant which is reduplicated from the final consonant of the noun. These nouns are all masculine in the singular and their plurals are masculine as well.[135] I will refer to this strategy as the "reduplication-plural," and give an example in (10).[136]

(10)   **Reduplication-plural: masculine**
    a. tûug-ga   'the thief (m.)'[137]
    b. tuug-ág   'thieves (m.)'
    c. tuug-ág-ga   'the thieves(m.)'   (Green et al. 2014a)

Another type of plural is formed by moving the high tone accent of the singular to the final mora of the plural; this class is often referred to as prosodic plurals and I will accordingly call this strategy the "prosodic-plural." These nouns are always masculine singular and their plurals are always feminine. An example is given in (11).[138]

(11)   **Prosodic-plural: feminine**
    a. díbi-ga   'the bull (m.)'
    b. dibí   'bulls (f.)'
    c. dibí-da   'the bulls (f.)'   (Green et al. 2014a)

Yet another type of plural is formed by adding the suffix -*yaal*; this applies to nouns ending in -*e*, many (if not all) of which are derived (Saeed 1999: 62). All nouns that are pluralized in this way are masculine, and the resulting plurals are feminine. An example is in (12); the final *é* in the singular changes to *á* with the addition of suffixes.[139]

---

[135] Recent corpus work has uncovered a few cases where feminine singular nouns have reduplication-plurals (C. Green, p.c.); the resulting plural noun is still masculine. I set these cases aside until more is known about the extent to which feminine nouns are licit with the reduplication-plural, i.e. whether these are isolated instances or evidence for a pervasive change in progress.

[136] This is Class 4 for Orwin (1995), Saeed (1999), and Lampitelli (2013), Class 2 for Green et al. (2014a).

[137] It is not entirely clear whether 'the thief' with masculine gender must be a male thief. Christopher Green reports (p.c.) that 'the thief' with feminine gender is attested in Internet corpora.

[138] This is Class 5 for Orwin (1995), Saeed (1999), and Lampitelli (2013), Class 3 for Green et al. (2014a).

[139] This is Class 7 for Orwin (1995) and Saeed (1999), Class 4a for Green et al. (2014a), and not treated in Lampitelli (2013).

(12) *yaal*-plural: feminine

    a. aabaanduulá-ha   'the commander (m.)'
    b. aabaanduula-yáál   'commanders (f.)'
    c. aabaanduula-yáá-sha 'the commanders (f.)'   (Green et al. 2014a)

Some plurals are formed by adding the suffixes *-oyin* or *-yow* (it is unclear what determines the variation between the two suffixes). These plurals are added to nouns that are etymologically derived from a stem that includes a plural ending *-o*, e.g. *baakó* 'package.' All these nouns are feminine singular, and the resulting plurals are masculine.[140]

(13) *oyin/yow*-plural: masculine

    a. baaká-da   'the package (f.)'
    b. baakó-óyin   'packages (m.)'
    c. baakó-óyin-ka 'the packages (m.)'   (Green et al. 2014a)

Finally, there are two pluralization strategies that are less common, but still not infrequent. Some nouns are pluralized by the suffix *-aan*, perhaps a relic of an older Afroasiatic plural *-an* (Hasselbach 2007). These nouns are either masculine or feminine in the singular, and the resulting plurals are feminine.[141]

(14) *aan*-plural: feminine

    a. qálin-ka   'the pen (m.) '
    b. qalm-áán[142]   'pens (f.)'
    c. qalm-áán-ta 'the pens (f.) '   (Green et al. 2014a)

Some Arabic loan words retain their "broken" plurals—a form of pluralization specific to Semitic languages that involves changing the internal voweling and/or phonotactics (rather than suffixation). Interestingly, these nouns are treated homogenously in terms of their gender—they are all masculine in the singular, and feminine in the plural.[143]

(15) **Broken plural: feminine**

    a. búnduq-a   'the rifle (m.)'
    b. banaadííq   'rifles (f.')'
    c. banaadííq-da 'the rifles (f.)'   (Green et al. 2014a)

---

[140] This is Class 6 for Orwin (1995) and Saeed (1999), Class 4b for Green et al. (2014a), and not treated in Lampitelli (2013).

[141] No class in Orwin (1995), Saeed (1999), Class 5 for Green et al. (2014a), not treated in Lampitelli (2013).

[142] The other phonological effects here are general, and not specific to adding the plural *-aan* suffix. For example, the [i] is deleted due to syllable contraction (Saeed 1999: 26–7).

[143] No class in Orwin (1995), Saeed (1999), Class 5 for Green et al. (2014a), not treated in Lampitelli (2013).

TABLE 8.1. **Plural strategies in Somali**

Plural strategy	Gender of N In singular	Gender of N In plural
o-plural: feminine	Mostly M, a few F	F
o-plural: masculine	M, F	M
Reduplication-plural	M	M
Prosodic-plural	M	F
yaal-plural	M	F
oyin/yow-plural	F	M
aan-plural	M, F	F
Broken-plural	M	F

Table 8.1 summarizes all the plural strategies in Somali, including the gender of the nouns in the singular and plural.[144]

The first crucial generalization to draw from this table is that all possible relationships between a noun's gender in the singular and a noun's gender in the plural are attested. Some masculine nouns retain masculine gender (e.g. reduplication-plural), whereas others change to feminine (e.g. *o*-plural:feminine). Some feminine nouns retain feminine gender (e.g. *aan*-plural; see also fn. 144) whereas others change to masculine (e.g. *oyin/yow*-plural). There are differences in the frequency of each of these pairings (and an interesting question which I will not be able to pursue is *why* certain pairings are more common), but all the combinatorial options are at least possible. This point is particularly important because the Somali plural system is often held up as a paragon of polarity, i.e. as a system where nouns always switch genders in the plural. Although polaric plurals are common, the system includes many other gender/number pairings (see also discussion on this point in Lecarme 2002, Green et al. 2014a).

The second crucial generalization is that the data are not best described in terms of a noun retaining or switching genders in the plural, despite superficial appearances.

---

[144] I do not include the plurals of feminine Arabic borrowings (Green et al. 2014a: 86). An example is given in (i).

(i) a. saaxiib-*ád*-da   b. saaxxib-*áád*-da
        friend-FEM-DEF.F   friend-FPL-DEF.F

      'the female friend'   'the female friends'

The noun for 'friend' is borrowed from Arabic. Adding the suffix -*ád* ((i)a) renders it feminine and referring to a female friend. When the female form is pluralized, the noun is still feminine and the suffix -*áád* is used, as in (i)b. I set this data aside because the suffix -*áád* seems to be a portmanteau of gender and number, and it would take me too far afield to determine which analytical option of those sketched in Section 8.1 is correct in this case.

Instead, as originally observed by Lecarme (2002), the plural strategy imposes a gender on the noun, regardless of that noun's original gender. For example, the *o*-plural:masculine imposes masculine on masculine and feminine nouns, and the *aan*-plural imposes feminine gender on masculine and feminine nouns. Each of the plural strategies also consistently imposes one particular gender; that is, there is no variation in gender across nouns that are all pluralized via the same strategy.

Finally, the nouns retain their natural gender in the plural. In (8), the *o*-plural: masculine 'women' is interpreted as referring to female humans, despite triggering masculine agreement. In (11), the prosodic-plural 'bulls' is interpreted as referring to male bovines, despite triggering feminine agreement.

Taking these facts together, one plausible analysis of Somali would be that each plural strategy is a different Num, each Num carries a gender feature, and the Num gender feature overrides whatever gender is on *n*. This potential analysis is shown in (16) for *náag-o* 'women (m.).'

(16) **Gender-on-Num analysis of Somali (to be argued against)**

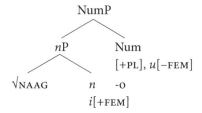

The "higher" gender would be the agreeing gender (as argued by Kramer 2009, de Belder 2011a, and Steriopolo and Wiltschko 2010; see also Chapter 10), but the lower gender would be interpretable and thus generate an interpretation of 'female human.'

Despite the initial plausibility of this analysis, there is evidence that number is on *n*, and not on Num in Somali. This provides support for the strongest version of the thesis of this book—that gender features are always on *n* (and never on Num). I present the evidence for a *n* analysis of Somali number in Section 8.2.3.

8.2.3 Plurality is on n in Somali: evidence

Four different pieces of evidence point towards number features being on *n* in Somali: root-specificity, selectional restrictions, non-determinism, and double plurals. I present each in turn. Lecarme (2002) was the first to argue for this position, and this discussion draws heavily from the evidence there.

First of all, almost all of the plural strategies are root-specific, i.e. it is arbitrarily stipulated which roots have which strategies (Lecarme 2002: 125). This kind of arbitrary relationship is characteristic of the relationship between a *n* and a root (see Arad 2003, 2005 on paradigmatic gaps), but it is more unusual for an inflectional head like Num. While it is true that a few plurals are root-specific in a Num-based system like English (e.g. *child ~ children*), root-specificity is much more pervasive in Somali. The clearly root-specific strategies include the *aan*-plural, the broken-plural, and the prosodic-plural; there are no generalizations about which roots undergo these plurals.[145] While the reduplication-plural is clearly limited to monosyllabic nouns (Saeed 1999, Lampitelli 2013), there are many monosyllabic nouns which do not undergo the reduplication-plural (see e.g. (8) and (9), compare with (10)). This makes it seem as if some morphophonological constraint ensures that only mono-syllabic nouns are licit in this strategy, but within that set it still must be stipulated by root which nouns actually undergo the reduplication-plural.

This leaves only the *yaal*-plural, the *oyin*-plural, and the *o*-plurals as the remaining strategies. As I will discuss next, the *yaal*-plural and the *oyin*-plural are *n*P-specific, so I set them aside for now. The *o*-plural:masculine is not root-specific for feminine nouns: it is the elsewhere pluralization strategy for any feminine nouns that are not pluralized with the *aan*-plural (in a way that I will make precise shortly). However, the *o*-plural:feminine and the *o*-plural:masculine for masculine nouns are root-specific. Of the masculine nouns not pluralized by the *aan*-plural, broken-plural, or prosodic-plural, some take the *o*-plural:feminine and some take the *o*-plural:masculine. Lampitelli (2013) claims that the masculine nouns that take the *o*-plural:masculine can be morphophonologically characterized as $[C(V)V_i\_CV_iC]$, but the two co-indexed vowels need not be identical and that the final C is not required (see (17)ac).

(17) a. béri-ga   'the day (m.)'
      b. bery-ó   'days (m.)'
      c. bery-á-ha   'the days (m.)'   (Green et al. 2014a)

Moreover, some roots that are disyllabic and fit Lampitelli's template take the *o*-plural:feminine, like *nácas* 'fool' in (18).

(18) a. nácas-ka   'the fool (m.)'
      b. nacas-yó   'fools (f.) '
      c. nacas-yá-da   'the fools (f.)'   (Green et al. 2014a)

I therefore conclude that it must be specified which masculine nouns undergo the *o*-plural:masculine and which roots undergo the *o*-plural:feminine. Overall, then, the *o*:plural:masculine for masculine nouns, the *o*-plural:feminine, the reduplication-plural,

---

[145] I set aside loanword status as a licit generalization about which roots have the broken-plural because not all Arabic loans undergo the broken-plural (Saeed 1999: 62) and not all broken-plurals are Arabic loans (Green et al. 2014a). Moreover, it cannot be assumed that all speakers are aware that the singular forms are loanwords from Arabic to begin with. I also set aside Lampitelli's (2013) characterization of prosodic-plurals as "not [CVC]" since this rules in many diverse syllable structures.

the prosodic-plural, the *aan*-plural and the broken-plural are root-specific in Somali, which is unexpected if these plurals are all derived via Num.

The second piece of evidence that Somali pluralization strategies are *n*s is that certain pluralization strategies are extremely choosy about which *n*Ps they combine with. For example, *yaal*-plurals only occur with stems that end in the derivational suffix *-e*, as in (19) (Saeed 1999, Lecarme 2002, Green et al. 2014a).

(19) a. bár   'teach (imperative)'
      b. bar-é   'teacher (m.)'
      c. bar-a-yáal   'teachers (f.)'   (Lecarme 2002)

Also, *oyin*-plurals occur only with nouns that end in a fossilized plural ending *-o* (see (13)), and I submit the fossilized plural ending *-o* is now treated as a non-plural *n* in the context of these roots. Thus, *oyin*-plurals occur only with *n*Ps that are headed by *-o*.[146]

These restrictions are highly reminiscent of (traditionally defined) derivational morphology, which also has strict selectional restrictions (see e.g. Fabb 1988 on English derivational morphology). Although the derivational/inflectional distinction has no theoretical status in Distributed Morphology, it often corresponds to the distinction between non-category-defining heads like Num (inflectional) and category-defining heads like *n* (derivational) (see e.g. Harley 2009). Thus, it seems likely that plurality in Somali is on *n*, since almost all the plurals that are not root-specific select for particular stems to combine with.

The third piece of evidence is that plural marking is non-deterministic for some roots in Somali, i.e. some roots have more than one plural strategy available to them (Lecarme 2002: 120). For example, the noun *túug* 'thief' can be pluralized with a prosodic-plural, a reduplication-plural or an *o*-plural:feminine.

(20) a. túug   'thief (m.)'   **Singular**
      b. tuúg-ta   'the thieves (f.)'   **Prosodic-plural**
      c. tuug-ág-ga 'the thieves (m.)'   **Reduplication-plural**
      d. tuug-á-da   'the thieves (f.)'   **o-plural:feminine**   (Lecarme 2002)

This is highly unusual, again, for an inflectional morpheme like Num. For example, in English, it is ungrammatical to pluralize *child* any other way than *children* (**childs*, **child*, **cheeld*, etc.). Nevertheless, it is not unusual for different derivational morphemes to combine with the same root or *x*P. For example, in English, the nouns *cover*, *coverage*, and *covering* (in the sense of *The covering flew off the wood pile*) are plausibly all derived from the same root √COVER combining with different *n*s.

---

[146] Lecarme (2002: 120) also includes an example of *-oyin* attaching to a derivational suffix that ends in *-o*. I leave for future work the questions of whether this derivational suffix is multi-morphemic and includes fossilized plural *-o*.

The final piece of evidence for Somali plural strategies being *n*s is that Somali has double plurals (Lecarme 2002: 121–2, Green et al. 2014a). Some examples are given in (21)–(23).

(21) a. nín   'man (m.)'   **Singular**
      b. nim-án   'men (m.)'   **Reduplication-plural**
      c. nim-an-yáal   'groups of men (f.)' **Double plural**   (Lecarme 2002)

(22) a. náag   'woman (f.)'   **Singular**
      b. naag-ó   'women (m.)'   **o-plural:masculine**
      c. naag-a-yáal   'groups of women (f.)'   **Double plural**   (Lecarme 2002)

(23) a. ílig   'tooth (m.)'   **Singular**
      b. ilk-ó   'teeth (f.)'   **o-plural:masculine**
      c. ilk-a-yáal   'sets of teeth (f.)'   **Double plural**   (Lecarme 2002)

The outermost plural in these examples is always a *yaal*-plural (Lecarme 2002 also includes some examples where the outermost plural is -*yow*). The inner plural is either a reduplicated-plural or an *o*-plural. The interpretation of the double plural is different than the singleton plural; it is the sum-plural of a group interpretation of the nominal (i.e. the plural of 'group of men').

In terms of whether plurals in Somali are on Num or *n*, it would be unusual for there to be multiple Num projections in the same DP, but it is quite common for there to be multiple *n*s (see e.g. nouns with evaluative morphology like diminutives (Chapter 10), English words like *revolu-tion-ary* where -*tion*, -*ary* can both be *n*s). The fact that multiple plural strategies can occur on the same noun is a strong indicator that at least some of the strategies are *n*s (see Section 8.2.5 for arguments against some plural strategies being Num's and some being *n*s).

Moreover, the group interpretation is expected if plurality is capable of being on *n*. Arabic has double plurals that also receive plural-of-group interpretations, and Zabbal (2002) proposes that the group meaning is contributed by a syntactic head that is situated close to the root, i.e. like *n*. If *n* is the cross-linguistic locus of group plurality, and multiple *n*s are allowed for a single root, then it is predicted that double plurals with group interpretations like those in (21)–(23) would occur in Somali. Naturally, this raises the question of why double plurals in Somali are (apparently) limited to group interpretations. I will offer somewhat of a mechanical solution below (-*yaal* subcategorizes for *n*[+GROUP]), but I tentatively suggest that double plurals are not semantically well-formed unless the bottom plural is interpreted as group (i.e. distinct from the sum-plural of -*yaal*). Thorough testing of this hypothesis will have to wait, though, for formal semantic fieldwork on Somali group nouns and plurals.[147]

---

[147] There is not much published data on group plurality in a non-double-plural context, but there is at least one indication that the analysis here is on the right track. The analysis predicts that at least some

Overall, in this section, I have presented four facts that make a Num-based analysis of Somali plurals unlikely. They are reiterated in (24).

(24) **Evidence for plurality on *n* in Somali**
   a. Almost all of the plural strategies are root-specific.
   b. Some plural strategies impose selectional restrictions.
   c. Some nouns have multiple plural strategies.
   d. There are double plurals, and they have plural-of-group interpretations.

I develop a *n*-based analysis of Somali plurals in Section 8.2.4, accounting for many of the effects seen above, and then briefly argue against some alternative analyses and close out the case study in Section 8.2.5.

8.2.4 *Somali plural system: analysis*

In Chapter 3 I argued that gender is on *n* in Amharic, since irregular plurals can express gender distinctions (and regular plurals do not). I developed an analysis where an irregular plural *n* in Amharic has both a plural feature and the gender feature required to license the root. For example, the *n* that combines with √K'ɪDDUS to form *k'iddus-at* 'female saints' has a plural and a feminine feature on it, as in (25).

(25)

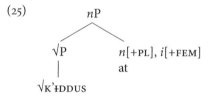

It is tempting to analyze Somali along the same lines as Amharic, with *n*[+PL] sister to a root and carrying gender features itself. This potential analysis is shown for *ínan* 'son, boy,' which takes an *o*-plural:feminine ((26)), in (27) (RED = reduplicant).

(26) a. ínan   'son, boy (m.)'
       b. inammó   'sons, boys (f.)'[148]

---

morphologically plural nouns would be able to be interpreted as groups (e.g. *naag-ó* could be interpreted as 'a group of women') and thus trigger singular agreement (compare Zabbal 2002 on broken plurals in Arabic, Kramer to appear on irregular plurals in Amharic). Prosodic-plurals do in fact sometimes trigger singular agreement on verbs, and it has been suggested that when they do so a "collective" interpretation is allowed (Saeed 1999: 61).

[148] As shown by the contrast above in (3)c, *n*[−FEM] is realized as a high tone on the penult in the non-derived word *ínan* 'boy,' but the plural form here has a high tone on the ultima (*inammó* 'sons'). I assume that the plural marker brings its own high tone on the ultimate syllable, and that there can only be one high tone per nominal (Saeed 1999: 41; see also Green and Morrison 2014). Affixes commonly "trump" the tone on the stem in Somali (Saeed 1999: 41), so it is expected that the plural marker high tone is retained and the high tone marking natural gender is eliminated.

(27)

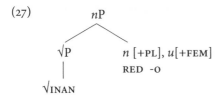

However, there are several reasons to doubt this starter analysis of the *n*-plurals of Somali.

First of all, the structure in (27) leaves no way for the plural noun to receive the male interpretation 'sons,' as opposed to a gender-neutral interpretation of 'children.' The male interpretation cannot be from the root, since the same root is used for 'girl, daughter' (see (3)c). There is simply no interpretable [–FEM] feature in (27) to trigger a male interpretation.

Additionally, there is a key empirical contrast between Amharic and Somali that is not captured if (27) is the structure for both. It is impossible for feminine suffixes to co-occur with irregular plurals in Amharic (see (28)), but feminine suffixes co-occur licitly with plural *n*s in Somali (see (29)).

(28) a. ityop'p'iy-awi-t   b. *ityop'p'iy-awi-t-at   **Amharic**
          Ethiopia-ADJ-FEM   Ethiopia-ADJ-FEM-PL
          'Ethiopian woman'   Intended: 'Ethiopian women'
          Feminine suffix   ***Feminine suffix + plural**

(29) a. abaabu-shó   b. abaabu-sho-óyin   **Somali**
          organize-NMLZ.F   organize-NMLZ.F-PL
          'female organizer (f.)'[149] 'female organizers (m.)'
          Feminine suffix   ✔ **Feminine suffix + plural**   (Lecarme 2002)

The Amharic data in (28) is easily explained if the feminine suffix and the plural suffix are competing for insertion at the same *n* slot: only one exponent can ultimately be inserted (the plural ultimately wins the competition here: *ityop'p'iy-awi-yat* Ethiopia-ADJ-PL 'female Ethiopians' is grammatical[150]). However, this leaves the Somali facts somewhat puzzling: barring a post-syntactic morphological operation that separates

---

[149] The morpheme decomposition here is a bit tricky. In the interests of full disclosure, the root is *abaabul* and the definite marker is *-to*, but due to assimilation with a stem-final *-l* the resulting consonant is *sh*.

[150] It is natural to ask why the irregular plural wins the competition, i.e. why the plural suffix is inserted and not the feminine suffix when *n* is plural. One solution is to appeal to a feature hierarchy (see e.g. Noyer 1997: lxxv). In cases where there is a "tie" in which Vocabulary Item to insert at a morpheme, the individual features of the Vocabulary Items are inspected with reference to an independently motivated feature hierarchy, and the VI that uniquely has the feature highest on the hierarchy (or which has the fewest nodes in the hierarchy) "wins" and is inserted. In all the feature hierarchy approaches, plural features are ranked above gender features, and thus the irregular plural would be inserted rather than the feminine suffix.

the feminine and plural features, they are not predicted to be capable of being realized by separate exponents.

The analysis in (30) solves both of these problems.[151] I propose that in Somali the n[+PL] is in fact one level higher in the hierarchical structure: it selects for a nP sister. The gender feature of the highest n is the gender of the nominal, as will be explored at length in Chapter 10. The structure of *inammó* 'sons' under this analysis is given in (30).

(30)

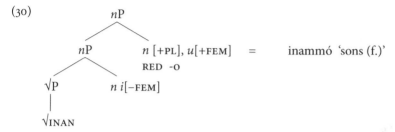

The bottom n has an interpretable [–FEM] feature, which causes the noun to be interpreted as referring to males. However, the upper, plural n has an uninterpretable feminine feature, causing the nominal to trigger feminine agreement.

(29) is now explained in that it is entirely possible for the two separate ns to be exponed separately. In (29), the lower n is realized as the feminine suffix *-sho* (closer to the root, as predicted by (30)), and the upper n as *-oyin* which determines the masculine gender of the entire noun (despite the overt feminine suffix).

The structure in (30) is in fact already predicted to occur given the analysis of gender and nominalization advanced here. We saw in Chapter 3 (and will return to in Chapter 9) that morphemes that nominalize xPs can carry their own gender features (e.g. diminutives are ns that nominalize nPs in Amharic, and they bring a feminine gender feature). So, if n[+PL] is attested in a language, it is capable (in principle) of having its "own" gender feature, stacking on top of the n required to license the root. This is exactly what we see in Somali: plural ns can carry their own gender, separate from a lower, root-nominalizing n.

Under this analysis, there is evidence for six different n[+PL]s in the syntax, that correspond to eight different Vocabulary Items (= plural strategies). This is shown in Table 8.2.

Viewed in this way, the complex plural system of Somali becomes neatly symmetric. There are two sub-classes of n: those that are feminine (top three rows of Table 8.2), and those that carry no gender features (and therefore trigger masculine agreement;

---

[151] I depart from Lecarme's analysis at this point. She proposes that the n[+PL] is inserted post-syntactically. However, it is unclear how other elements agree with the plural nominal if it does not have a gender feature in the syntax.

TABLE 8.2. **Analysis of the Somali plural**

Syntactic head	Selects for	Vocabulary Items/plural strategies
n_I [+PL], [+FEM]	M	• Broken-plural (root-specific) • Prosodic-plural (root-specific) • *o*-plural:feminine (root-specific)
n_{II} [+PL], [+FEM]	Ø	*aan*-plural (root-specific)
n_{III} [+PL], [+FEM]	*n* realized as *é*	*yaal*-plural
n_{IV} [+PL]	M	Reduplication-plural (root-specific)
n_V [+PL]	Ø	*o*-plural:masculine • Root-specific for masculine nouns • Remainder of feminine nouns not specified in *aan*-plural context
n_{VI} [+PL]	*n* realized as *ó*	*oyin*-plural

bottom three rows of Table 8.2). Each sub-class contains three flavors of *n*: one flavor selects for masculine nouns, one flavor has no selectional restrictions, and one flavor selects for particular *n*s (feminine: *yaal*-plural, masculine: *oyin*-plural).

The analysis also allows for straightforward explanations of selectional restrictions and the non-deterministic nature of the plural system. As for the selectional restrictions, all that needs to be said is that *-yaal* and *-oyin* select for particular *n*s, just like all the other plural strategies.[152] In fact, treating all the plurals as selecting for a *n*P allows for a unified analysis of *yaal/oyin*-plurals with the other types of pluralization.

As a first step in explaining non-determinism, I assume that root-specificity is encoded via contextual restrictions associated with Vocabulary Items. For example, the *aan*-plural is the VI in (31); it is restricted to appearing with the root √QALIN, etc.[153]

(31) n_{II}, [+pl], [+fem] ↔ -aan / {√QALIN, √SIYAASI, √MUSLIN . . .} (Green et al. 2014a)

---

[152] The analysis comes together most cleanly if all the *n*s realized as *-e* that *-yaal* selects for (and all the *n*s realized as *-o* that *-oyin* selects for) have one syntactic feature in common that *-yaal* can select for. I leave the investigation of this fact to a study devoted to Somali derivational morphology.

[153] It may seem that the root cannot condition plural *n* allomorphy since they are not adjacent (the *n* that carries the gender features to license the root intervenes). For example, in the theory of allomorphic locality in Embick (2010), the topmost *n* would be unable to have its allomorphy conditioned by the root (and vice versa). There are many possible solutions, though—if the plural *n* is non-cyclic (i.e. acts like Num, perhaps because the language lacks NumP altogether; see Sect. 2.5), then Embick (2010) predicts that it is able to be conditioned by the root (and vice versa). Another potential solution would be to appeal to spans, a set of contiguous syntactic heads in an extended projection (Svenonius 2012, Merchant to appear). Merchant (to appear) proposes that allomorphy can be conditioned by an adjacent span, i.e. that the root and the *n* immediately above the root together could condition the allomorphy of the plural morpheme.

To capture non-determinism, all that needs to be said is that some roots appear on multiple lists. For example, recall that √TUUG can be pluralized in several different ways.

(32)   a. túug   'thief (m.)'   **Singular**
       b. tuúg-ta   'the thieves (f.)'   **Prosodic-plural**
       c. tuug-á-da   'the thieves (f.)'   *o*-plural:feminine
       d. tuug-ág-ga   'the thieves (m.)'   **Reduplication-plural**

√TUUG is in the list of root-specific contextual restrictions for the prosodic-plural, the *o*-plural:feminine, and the reduplication-plural. The prosodic-plural and the *o*-plural:feminine are both inserted to realize the same syntactic head n_I [+PL], [+FEM]. Thus, I assume they have identical features as Vocabulary Items (same elements to the left of the double-headed arrow), and differ in their contextual restrictions and their phonological content (notated just as [tone] for the prosodic-plural), as in (33)ab.

(33)   a. n_I, [+PL][+FEM] $\leftrightarrow$ [tone] / {√TUUG, √DIBI...}   **Prosodic-plural**
       b. n_I, [+PL][+FEM] $\leftrightarrow$ -o / {√TUUG, √BAABUUR...}   *o*-plural:feminine
       c. n_{IV}, [+PL] $\leftrightarrow$ a[RED]/ {√TUUG, √AF[154]...}   **Reduplication-plural**

I assume that there is no ordering relation between (33)a and (33)b, since they are equivalently good matches to the syntactic feature bundle, and √TUUG is on both of their lists of contextual restrictions.[155] Thus, either can be inserted. The reduplication-plural is inserted to realize a different feature bundle: n_{IV}, [+PL]. Assuming that the syntax has sent this feature bundle to PF for realization,[156] (33)c will not compete with (33)ab since (33)ab contain a feature that the syntactic feature bundle lacks. Thus, the reduplication-plural will be inserted and overall, multiple pluralization strategies are available to one noun.

I close this section by returning to the three generalizations at the end of Section 8.2.2. The first generalization was that different plural strategies select for different genders. This comes for free in the present analysis: different plural *n*s can select for various types of *n*s depending on the gender feature on the *n* (although it remains unclear why only masculine nouns are actively selected for in terms of gender). The second generalization was that each pluralization strategy brings its own gender that "overwrites" the gender of the noun, and this is captured (i) because

---

[154] The root for 'language'; see Green et al. (2014a: 81).
[155] Note also that a feature hierarchy is irrelevant to determining the ordering relation; see fn. 150. I also assume that the grammar does not "count" how many roots are in a contextual restriction in order to determine whether one Vocabulary Item is more specific than another.
[156] I am assuming that the Roman numeral diacritics on *n*s are part of the identity of the *n*, and that a Vocabulary Item must match this diacritic. Therefore, if the syntax sends any other *n* (I, V, etc.), the VI in (33)c will still not be able to be inserted, since it will not match the diacritic.

plurals are *n*s which can host gender features generally and (ii) the highest *n* is the one whose features matter for agreement (see Chapter 10). The third generalization was that nouns retain natural gender in the plural, and this is captured because the lower *n* is still present in (30) to be interpreted.

Overall, then, analyzing the Somali plurals as formed via *n* explains many of their properties. It also allows for the discovery of significant symmetry in the nature of the plural *n*s in the syntax that then are realized via many different root-idiosyncratic pluralization strategies in the morphology.[157]

8.2.5 *Alternative analyses and conclusions*

In this section, I briefly consider two alternative analyses and then offer some concluding discussion. There are (at least) two alternative analyses of Somali plurality: a split-plurality analysis, and the Num-based analysis of Somali plurality in Lampitelli (2013). As discussed in Chapter 3, I have argued for a split analysis of plurality Amharic (Kramer 2009, 2012, to appear). By "split," I mean that there are two syntactic locations for plurality: the regular plural suffix in Amharic is a realization of Num, whereas the many possible irregular plural affixes/broken plurals are realizations of *n*. There are clear contrasts between regular plurals and irregular plurals in Amharic, including the fact that all nouns take a regular plural (as expected for productive, inflectional morphology like Num) and that irregular plurals are always closer to the root than the regular plural in a double plural (expected for *n* since it is sister to the root).

However, a split analysis of Somali is less successful, primarily because there is conflicting evidence about which plural strategy/strategies would correspond to Num. The strategies that are the most productive across nouns are the *o*-plurals, but there are (at least) two sub-types of *o*-plural and some of those are root-specific (unlike Num). The element farthest from the root in a double plural is *-yaal*, which makes it seem like Num, but recall that *-yaal* has strict selectional restrictions like a derivational morpheme. I conclude that there is no individual plural strategy which straightforwardly corresponds to Num in Somali, and that all plural strategies are realizations of *n*.

---

[157] One major issue remains, though. Recall that Somali has the same gender system as Spanish, where male-referring nouns are licensed under *n i* [–FEM] and masculine inanimate nouns are licensed under the plain *n*. This means that the two plural *n*s which select for "masculine" nouns actually each select both for *n* [–FEM] and *n*. It seems somewhat arbitrary that both of these plural *n*s would select only for those two gendered *n*s, and in general the approach to gender features that I have adopted struggles to express generalizations that hold across all masculine nouns. However, there have proven to be few such generalizations so far, there are only two *n*s in question in Somali (which is not a very great number of items to be arbitrary across), and the general distribution of selectional restrictions for plural *n*s in Somali is mysterious (why are feminine nouns never selected for?). I leave this issue open, then, with due acknowledgment of the potential issue this could raise for the analysis of gender features espoused here. See also Ch. 11.

Lampitelli (2013) claims that all plurals are formed via Num, and Num is always realized as *-o*. The *-o* exponent of Num then undergoes several different allomorphic rules to generate the different plural strategies. As shown in Section 8.2.3, a Num approach offers no explanation for the selectional restrictions of certain plural strategies, the non-determinism of plural strategies with respect to nouns, and the double plurals. Moreover, Lampitelli (2013) only covers certain plural strategies, namely, the *o*-plurals, the reduplication-plural, and the prosodic-plural; it is much more difficult to see how plurality is derived allomorphically from an *-o* exponent for the *yaal*-plural, the *oyin*-plural, the *aan*-plural, and the broken-plural.[158] Finally, Lampitelli (2013) accounts for the generalization that plural strategies impose their own genders by proposing an allomorphy rule that inserts feminine gender on all plurals (this rule is either blocked from applying, or the gender feature is deleted, in order to generate the plurals that impose masculine gender). However, an allomorphy rule that inserts gender is too late to affect agreement relations, which are established in the syntax. For all these reasons, I do not pursue a Num-based approach to Somali plurals as laid out in Lampitelli (2013).

In this section I have argued that all the plurals in Somali are derived via *ns*. This explains many of their properties, and immediately predicts that they will affect gender since *n* in general can carry gender features. There is no need to appeal to gender features on Num to account for the interaction of gender and number in Somali, and it is in fact less explanatory to do so. However, two open issues are worth remarking upon before moving on to the next case study.

First, it is worth asking whether Somali has a NumP at all. It is clear that NumP is not used for plurality in Somali, but NumP has been proposed to house cardinal numerals (Borer 2005) and quantifiers (Ritter 1991). Green et al. (2014a) argue that all cardinal numerals are nouns in Somali, so it may be (if quantifiers are not Num heads) that the language does indeed lack this projection (cf. Déprez 2005, Ghomeshi 2003 for other languages that may lack NumP).

Secondly, this approach leads to a typology of the morphosyntax of plurality. Languages can have wholly Num-based plurals (e.g. Spanish, where the-*s* plural occurs with all nouns, modulo some morphophonology), *n*-based plurals, or split plurality.

(34)   **Morphosyntactic typology of plurality**
   a. Num-based plurality (Spanish)
   b. *n*-based plurality (Somali)
   c. Split plurality (Amharic)

This typology, combined with gender being on *n*, has the welcome prediction that plurals will be able to affect gender in Somali, but not in Spanish. Identifying further

---

[158] Lampitelli (2014) proposes that the *yaal*-plural is a derivational morpheme, but it is unclear, then, why the other plurals are still treated as Nums.

predictions of this typology (and investigating whether they are correct) is a central goal for future research on cross-linguistic variation in plurality and gender, especially given the growing body of research on the idiosyncratic/"lexical"/non-inflectional properties of certain plurals cross-linguistically (see e.g. Lowenstamm 2008, Acquaviva 2008, Wiltschko 2008b, Harbour 2011, Ghaniabadi 2012, Butler 2012). Although it remains controversial which exact heads besides Num are capable of carrying plural features, many researchers have identified *n* as a source of alternative plurality, and hopefully its role in carrying gender features will assist in the exploration of this new empirical area.

8.3 Gender switch in Romanian: the neuter is real

In this section, I examine one of the best-known cases of gender switch in the plural: neuter nouns in Romanian. These nouns trigger masculine agreement in the singular, and feminine agreement in the plural. Because gender co-varies with number for these nouns, it is tempting (again) to locate the gender features on the Number head. In this section, however, I argue for the standard analysis of Romanian neuters, in which they are unspecified for gender. They thus receive default gender, and the singular default gender is masculine whereas the plural default gender is feminine. I demonstrate how this approach is compatible with gender features being on *n*, and how it is superior to an approach that puts gender features on Num. The analysis also harmonizes with the treatment of three-gender languages in Chapter 7, where neuter nouns in a variety of languages are analyzed as unspecified for gender. Overall, Romanian is treated as a three-gender language in terms of its inventory of *n*s, but a two-gender language in terms of its morphological resources for expressing agreement contrasts in gender.

   In Section 8.3.1, I lay out the basic facts about the Romanian gender system. I develop a Distributed Morphology analysis of Romanian in Section 8.3.2 that relies on gender being on *n*, building on the insights of the lexicalist analysis in Farkas (1990). In Section 8.3.3, I present arguments against some alternative analyses, including gender being on the Num head (Giurgea 2008, Croitor and Giurgea 2009 (in part)), Romanian having only masculine and feminine gender (Bateman and Polinsky 2010), and Romanian having number on *n* like Somali. I conclude in Section 8.3.4.

8.3.1 The Romanian gender system

Romanian (Indo-European (Eastern Romance)) is spoken by approximately 23 million people, primarily in Romania and Moldova (Lewis et al. 2013). It has a long and rich linguistic tradition, including much research by native speaker linguists. The gender system in particular has received much attention due to the unusual behavior of the neuter nouns. Citations to the theoretical literature appear at relevant points below, and I draw primarily from Maurice (2001) and Dobrovie-Sorin and Giurgea (2013; henceforth DSG) for the description of the gender system in this section.

Typically, I begin the description of a gender system with the number of genders it contains. However, neuter nouns make it more difficult to determine the number of genders in Romanian. Suffice it to say for now that there are either two or three genders, in a way to be made more precise shortly. Gender agreement is reasonably robust, occurring on indefinite determiners, demonstratives, adjectives, certain verbal forms, and other categories (see DSG 2013: 2, Maurice 2001: 231).

The gender system of Romanian at first glance seems very similar to Spanish (Chapter 6; see also Somali above); this is not surprising, since they are both Romance languages. Nouns referring to male entities are masculine and nouns referring to female entities are feminine (DSG 2013: 8; there are a few exceptions detailed below). Romanian has both different-root nouns ((35)) and same-root nouns ((36)) to express gender distinctions.

(35)   **Different-root nominals: Romanian**
    a. frate   'brother (m.)'   soră   'sister (f.)'   (DSG 2013: 7)
    b. taur   'bull (m.)'   vacă   'cow (f.)'   (Maurice 2001: 233)

(36)   **Same-root nominals: Romanian**
    a. complice   'accomplice (m. or f.)'   (Maurice 2001: 236)
    b. prieten(ă)   'friend (m., f. with *ă*)   (DSG 2013: 7)

In (35) and (36), the nouns which can have feminine gender have a final *-ă*. However, this morpheme is not, strictly speaking, a feminine gender marker. Following Chitoran (1996, 2002) and Iscrulescu (2003), I assume that all Romanian nouns have the structure in (37).

(37)   [[Root]-Vocalic.Morpheme]

Iscrulescu (2003) (and other sources cited therein) argue that the masculine nouns that seem consonant-final in fact have a final *-u*. The final *-ă* in the feminine nouns is a realization of the vocalic morpheme that is exclusively for feminine nouns, but feminine gender is not sufficient to condition the insertion of *ă*: the final *-e* vocalic morpheme is used for either gender as in (36)a. Further evidence that the vocalic morpheme, while sensitive to gender, is not a gender suffix itself is that it co-occurs with overt gender suffixes, like *-iț* in (38).

(38)   a. pictor   'painter (m.)'
    b. pictor-iț-ă   'painter (f.)'   (Maurice 2001: 234)

The vocalic morphemes are thus most likely declension class markers, similar to Spanish final *-o/-a* (see Chapter 10 for an analysis of Spanish declension class). It would take the discussion too far afield to develop a detailed analysis of their morphosyntax here, but see DSG (2013: ch. 16) for extensive description, as well as Chapter 10 for general discussion of the relationship between gender and declension class.

Plants and inanimate nouns are either masculine or feminine in Romanian. Masculine or feminine gender is assigned arbitrarily to these nouns; there are very few correlations between meaning and gender,[159] or between the phonological shape of the noun and gender (setting aside generalizations based on the final vocalic morphemes).

(39)   **Inanimate gender in Romanian**
        a. genunchi   'knee (m.)'   c. ureche   'ear (f.)'
        b. pom   'tree (m.)'   d. grădină 'garden (f.)'
                                    (DSG 2013: 6, Farkas and Zec 1995: 90)

Romanian also has some fixed-gender nouns, i.e. animate nouns that are have a single arbitrary gender like plants and inanimates.

(40)   **Romanian fixed-gender nouns**
        a. sugar   'toddler (m.)'   d. persoană 'person (f.)'
        b. decan   'dean (m.)'   e. călăuză 'guide (f.)'
        c. viezure 'badger (m.)'   f. balenă   'whale (f.)' (DSG 2013: 7–8, P. Ganga, p.c.)

For example, *persoană* 'person' triggers feminine agreement even when it refers to a man.[160]

So far, the Romanian gender system closely resembles the Spanish gender system, even insofar as the word for 'person' is a feminine fixed-gender noun in both languages. However, they diverge in that Romanian has a set of "neuter" nouns which take masculine agreement in the singular, but feminine agreement in the plural. Compare the agreement triggered by the feminine noun in (41) and the masculine noun in (42) to the neuter noun in (43).

(41)   a. o   femeie   b. două   femei   **Feminine**
           a.FS   woman   two.FPL   woman.FPL
           'a woman'   'two women'   (Maurice 2001: 231)

(42)   a. un   bărbat   b. doi   bărbați   **Masculine**
           a.MS   man   two.MPL   man.MPL
           'a man'   'two men'   (Maurice 2001: 231)

---

[159] Bateman and Polinsky (2010: 69) observe that all trees are masculine, and that all abstract nouns are feminine.

[160] There is one key exception. If *persoană* 'person' is the head of a coordinated DP, it triggers agreement like a masculine noun would, e.g. it triggers masculine agreement when conjoined with a feminine noun (Farkas and Zec 1995: 95). Additionally, *persoană* 'person' when it refers to a man is referenced by a masculine pronoun, but I do not consider pronominal reference to be agreement. See Ch. 4.

(43) a. un   glas   b. două   glas-uri   **Neuter**
         a.MS voice   two.FPL voice-PL
       'a voice'   'two voices'   (Maurice 2001: 231)

The neuter nouns in Romanian are difficult to characterize exhaustively (Kihm 2007). The vast majority are inanimate, but a few are (capable of being) animate (e.g. *model* 'model,' *personaj* 'character,' *animal* 'animal'; DSG 2013: 8). They also do not have a consistent morphophonological profile separate from the other genders; they are often pluralized with the suffix -*uri* ((43)b) but -*uri* also pluralizes certain feminine nouns and some neuter nouns are pluralized via -*e* (DSG 2013: 836).

Even the label "neuter" for these nouns is somewhat controversial, since these nouns do not behave like "neuter nouns" in languages like Mangarayi, Wari', and Lavukaleve (see Chapter 7). Instead of a separate set of agreement morphology for nouns in this class, in Romanian, the masculine agreement is reused in the singular and the feminine agreement in the plural. Whether or not these nouns should be considered a separate gender, and how to analyze them in general, has thus been the focus of a substantial amount of linguistic research in Romanian (for comprehensive literature reviews, see Corbett 1991, Bateman and Polinsky 2010, Croitor and Giurgea 2009, and Giurgea 2014). I continue to refer to these nouns as "neuter," because (as will become clear in the next section) I believe these nouns are directly analogous to neuter nouns in German, Russian, and Lavukaleve in terms of their gender features on *n*.

I proceed to lay out the prevailing analysis of Romanian neuters and show how it ports over easily into a Distributed Morphology, *n* approach to gender. I assume for now that number features are on Num in Romanian, as suggested in DSG (2013: 11) and assumed in much of the Romanian DP literature (see e.g. Cornilescu 1995, Dobrovie-Sorin et al. 2006). I return to the question of whether number is on *n* in Romanian, as it is in Somali, in Section 8.3.3.

8.3.2 *The analysis of Romanian gender*

The main analysis of Romanian gender posits that neuter nouns are not specified for gender (see e.g. Farkas 1990, Chitoran 1992, Farkas and Zec 1995, Croitor and Giurgea 2009 (in part), DSG 2013, Giurgea 2014). In this approach, neuter nouns have no gender features, and trigger default gender agreement. Default gender agreement is claimed to be singular in the masculine and feminine in the plural. This is the approach with the most support in the Romanian literature, and I proceed to develop a Distributed Morphology/*n* analysis of Romanian gender in this vein.[161]

---

[161] Within the Romanian gender literature, there is another approach to the analysis of neuter nouns. This approach posits that Romanian has a third, fully specified neuter gender, e.g. with a feature [NEUTER] that is on all neuter nouns. Then, the realization of the neuter feature is completely syncretic with masculine gender in the singular, and with feminine gender in the plural. This is perhaps the most "traditional" view of Romanian gender; for example, it is upheld by the grammar of the Romanian

The analysis of Romanian gender that I will develop has four key components: (i) neuter nouns have no gender features, (ii) there are only two Vocabulary Items for each gender agreement target, (iii) masculine is the default gender agreement with singular nouns, and (iv) feminine is the default gender agreement for plural nouns. I deal with the formalization/mechanization of each in turn.

Formalizing the lack of gender features of neuter nouns requires an account of gender features in Romanian in general. In terms of the approach to gender outlined in this book, the fact that neuter nouns lack gender features will be a fact about the gender features on *n* licensed with a subset of Romanian roots.[162] Given the facts laid out in Section 8.3.1, I submit that Romanian has the same set of *n*s as Lavukaleve, listed in (44).

(44)   **Types of *n* (Romanian)**
      a. *n*   *i* [+FEM]
      b. *n*   *i* [−FEM]
      c. *n*
      d. *n*   *u* [−FEM]
      e. *n*   *u* [+FEM]

(44)ab are needed for roots licensed only as female or only as male, like √FRATE 'brother' and √SOR 'sister.' They are also needed for same-root nominals formed via roots like √PRIETEN 'friend.' (44)e is necessary to form feminine inanimate nouns and feminine fixed-gender nouns, i.e. nouns with uninterpretable feminine gender, like *grădină* 'garden.' That leaves unaccounted for the masculine inanimate and fixed-gender nouns, and the neuter nouns.

If Romanian had a Spanish-style gender system, then we would only need (44)c plain *n* to license these nouns. As I have shown for a variety of gender systems earlier in the book, it is easy to ensure that inanimate and fixed-gender nouns licensed under plain *n* receive the same gender (masculine) as male-referring animates through underspecification in the Vocabulary Items for agreement targets. However, in Romanian, inanimates and fixed-gender nouns that trigger masculine agreeing forms in the singular are not a unified class. Some of them continue to trigger masculine agreeing forms in the plural, but the others (the neuters) trigger feminine agreeing forms. Thus, I assume that the two sets are licensed under different *n*s: neuter nouns like *glas* 'voice' are formed via plain *n* ((44)c), whereas so-called

Academy of Language (*GALR* 2005; see also Lumsden 1992). However, I do not pursue this analysis because my approach to neuter nouns across languages assumes that they have no gender features, as we saw in Ch. 7 for neuter nouns in Mangarayi, Wari', and Lavukaleve.

[162] Farkas 1990 assumes that Romanian nouns either have [+F] (feminine), [−F] (masculine), or no features for gender. Farkas and Zec (1995) have a variant of this: they assume that neuter nouns have a zero value for [F], i.e. they are [0F]. Croitor and Giurgea (2009) and Giurgea (2014) do not formalize their assumption that neuter nouns lack gender features.

"traditional" masculines like *pom* 'tree' are formed under a *n* with an uninterpretable masculine feature ((44)d).

The question that naturally arises, then, is how the neuter nouns and the traditional masculine nouns both trigger masculine agreement in the singular—they do not trigger the same agreement in Lavukaleve. Thus enters the second component of the analysis: Romanian has only two Vocabulary Items per gender agreement target.

In general, roots that are licensed under plain *n* will have the default gender of the language: since they have no gender features, their agreeing forms can only be morphologically realized with whatever Vocabulary Item has no gender features. However, the difference between Lavukaleve and Romanian is that Lavukaleve has three Vocabulary Items for each agreement target—a masculine one, a feminine one, and a neuter one where the "neuter" Vocabulary Item lacks gender features altogether. Romanian has only two Vocabulary Items for each agreement target—a feminine and a masculine/neuter (for the singular) where the masculine/neuter one lacks gender features.

Romanian is thus like Spanish in terms of its inventory of Vocabulary Items (only two), but like Lavukaleve in terms of its inventory of *n*s. This is a way of cashing out Farkas and Zec's (1995: 92) insight that Romanian has a "three-way contrast in the gender system, neutralized to a binary contrast in the actual shapes of agreeing forms."

This results in masculine being the default gender in the singular in Romanian. To take a specific example, recall the masculine/feminine/neuter singular paradigm from Section 8.3.1, repeated in (45)–(47).

(45) o   femeie
      a.FS woman
      'a woman'   (Maurice 2001: 231)

(46) un   bărbat
      a.MS man
      'a man'   (Maurice 2001: 231)

(47) un   glas
      a.MS voice
      'a voice'   (Maurice 2001: 231)

Given this data and the analysis outlined above, the Vocabulary Items for the indefinite determiner are as in (48).

(48) a. $[\text{D}],[-\text{DEF}],[+\text{FEM}] \leftrightarrow$ o
      b. $[\text{D}],[-\text{DEF}] \leftrightarrow$ un

(48) a will be inserted whenever the noun that the indefinite determiner agrees with is feminine (i.e. female-referring, a feminine inanimate, or a feminine fixed-gender

noun). (48)b will be inserted for all other nouns—both those formed by n[−FEM] (male-referring, masculine inanimate, masculine fixed-gender) and those formed by n (neuter nouns).[163] I will henceforth gloss exponents that are equivalent to (48)b as M/N for masculine/neuter.

There is independent evidence that masculine/neuter is the default gender for singulars. It is the gender used for agreement in weather predicates ((49)), agreement with sentential subjects ((50)), and for singular animates of unknown natural gender ((51)).

(49) E   noros   afară
      is   cloudy.M/NS   outside
      'It is cloudy outside.'   (Farkas 1990: 543)

(50) [A-ţi   iubi   duşmanii]   e   imposibil
      to-you.DAT love.INF   enemies.DEF   is   impossible.M/NS
      'To love one's enemies is impossible.'   (Croitor and Giurgea 2009: (6))

(51) Vorbeşte   cu   cineva   priceput
      talk.IMP.2S   to   somebody   skillful.M/NS
      'Talk to someone skillful.'   (DSG 2013: 6)

These facts are predicted assuming that adjectival agreement Vocabulary Items are structured like (48) in the singular: one exponent which has a [+FEM] feature, and another exponent that lacks gender features altogether. The exponent that lacks gender features must be inserted when an agreement controller has no gender features, whether because it is non-nominal (like weather predicates and sentential subjects) or because it has unspecified natural gender.[164]

---

[163] Farkas (1990) and Farkas and Zec (1995) use a lexical rule to encode the singular masculine default, whereas Croitor and Giurgea (2008) and Giurgea (2014) appeal to the underspecification of Vocabulary Items similar to the current analysis.

[164] There is a major exception to the generalization that all non-gender-specified, singular agreement targets are realized as masculine: singular demonstrative pronouns are feminine when they refer to an entity of unclear gender (e.g. 'what is this?') or when they refer to a non-nominal entity like a clause ('Peter is home. That is fantastic!'). It cannot be that 'feminine' is simply the default for singular demonstratives, since demonstrative pronouns that refer to singular neuters are masculine (see Farkas 1990: 540, (5)). I tentatively follow Giurgea (2014) in assuming that demonstrative pronouns in these cases are numberless (cf. Picallo 2002, 2007 on "neuter" pronouns in Spanish). The following Vocabulary Items would then generate the facts (I use the direct case, short form, proximal determiner for concreteness; forms from DSG 2013: 855):

    (i)   a. [D],[DEM],[PROX], [−PL], [+F] ↔ asta
          b. [D],[DEM], [PROX],[−PL] ↔ ăsta
          c. [D],[DEM],[PROX],[+PL],[−F] ↔ ăştia
          d. [D],[DEM], [PROX],[+PL] ↔ astea
          e. [D],[PROX],[DEM] ↔ asta

A masculine singular demonstrative is realized by (i)b and a feminine singular demonstrative by (i)a; this ensures that neuter singular demonstratives have masculine forms. (i)cd ensure that plural demonstratives have a feminine default, so that neuter plural demonstratives are feminine (see Farkas 1990: 540, (6)).

The final plank of the analysis is that feminine is the default gender in the plural. This will ensure that neuter nouns have feminine gender in the plural, whereas traditional masculine nouns do not. Recall the plural agreement data from Section 8.3.1.

(52) două   femei
      two.FPL   woman.FPL
      'two women'   (Maurice 2001: 231)

(53) doi   bărbaţi
      two.MPL   man.MPL
      'two men'   (Maurice 2001: 231)

(54) două   glas-uri
      two.FPL   voice-PL
      'two voices'   (Maurice 2001: 231)

The Vocabulary Items in (55) will generate the right forms. [TWO] represents whatever features 'two' expones in terms of its content (not its inflection).[165] I treat *doi/două* as separate Vocabulary Items for simplicity, but it is possible that they could be decomposed into [*do*-Agr] where Agr is agreement on some functional head that is part of the numeral.

(55) a. [TWO], [−FEM] ↔ doi
      b. [TWO] ↔ două

(55)a will be inserted whenever the noun that 'two' agrees with is male-referring, a masculine inanimate (i.e. an inanimate formed via *n*[−FEM]), or a fixed-gender masculine. (55)b will be inserted in all other cases—a female-referring noun, a feminine inanimate, a feminine fixed-gender noun, or, most crucially, a neuter noun that lacks gender features altogether.

By necessity, the indefinite determiner 'a' agrees only with singular nouns, whereas the numeral 'two' agrees only with plural nouns. To see how the analysis works for an

---

A numberless demonstrative, though, can only be realized by (i)e, since that is the only Vocabulary Item that lacks number features.

This analysis renders it coincidental that the feminine singular form of the demonstrative is homophonous with the numberless form, but previous analyses have also had to appeal to some kind of idiosyncratic rule that associates these demonstratives with a form that is also used for feminine gender (cf. Farkas 1990: 543, (15) where demonstratives with unspecified gender are given feminine gender via a lexical rule). Moreover, there is no deep or necessary association between feminine form and numberlessness in Romanian: the numberless form of the Romanian object clitic is in fact null, and not homophonous with the feminine object clitic (Giurgea 2014: 58).

[165] The analysis at this point is broadly similar to Croitor and Giurgea (2009) (in part) and Giurgea (2014), although I include many more details about the Vocabulary Items.

element that agrees with both singular and plural nouns, consider the paradigm for the adjective *bun* 'good' in (56).

(56)   'good'
MASC/N.SG   FEM.SG   MASC.PL   FEM/N.PL
bun-Ø   bun-ă   bun-i   bun-e   (DSG 2013: 852)

The adjective has a different final vocalic ending depending on the gender and number of the noun it modifies. The agreement on the adjective is realized by the Vocabulary Items in (57). I intend to be extremely neutral about what category that agreement is on, so I represent it as [C] for category.

(57)   a. [c], [+FEM] ↔ ă
       b. [c] ↔ Ø
       c. [c], [−FEM], [+PL] ↔ -e
       d. [c], [+PL] ↔ -i

In the singular, either (57)a or (57)b must be inserted, since (57)cd both have features that would not match those of the terminal node. Thus, (57)a is inserted for all feminine singular nouns, and (57)b for all masculine and neuter singular nouns, just like the indefinite determiner in (48). For the plural, the neuter nouns are realized with the same exponent as the feminine nouns, which is the exponent that lacks gender features altogether, i.e. (57)d. (57)c is inserted only for male-referring nouns and "traditional" masculine nouns.[166]

There are a couple of pieces of additional evidence that feminine is the default plural in Romanian. The first comes from gender agreement with coordinated subjects, also referred to as "resolution" (see e.g. Corbett 1991: ch. 9, Wechsler and Zlatić 2003, Hock 2009). I have set aside resolution data so far for most of the book (with the exception of Chapter 7) since it often seems to access the gender of discourse referents and their gender can be different from the gender features on *n*. Resolution is also subject to other effects that muddy its effectiveness for determining default gender like Closest Conjunct Agreement, or even avoiding such structures altogether (see Corbett 1991, Hock 2009). I will not use data on resolution for animate-referring subjects because of the effect of discourse referent biological sex (e.g. in Romanian, fixed-gender nouns behave under coordination as if they had the gender of their discourse referents; Farkas and Zec 1995, Sadler 2006). However, the discourse referent problem does not apply to inanimate subjects, whose discourse referents do not have a biological sex that could conflict with the gender feature on *n*. Also, it seems that closest-conjunct agreement only plays a limited, non-systematic role in resolution in Romanian (Mallinson 1984, Croitor and Giurgea 2009). I thus consider resolution with inanimate coordinated subjects as useful information about the default gender in Romanian, and proceed to present the facts.

---

[166] If PF receives the feature bundle [C],[+FEM],[+PL], then (57)d is inserted because plural is higher than gender on a feature hierarchy (see e.g. Noyer 1997: lxxv). See fn. 150.

Agreement with coordinated subjects is always plural in Romanian, and if the two coordinated DPs have the same gender, then that gender is used for agreement (Farkas and Zec 1995, Sadler 2006). Two traditional masculine inanimate DPs are coordinated in (58) and two feminine inanimate DPs in (59).

(58)   **Masculine + masculine = masculine**

Nucul	și	prunul	sînt	uscați
walnut.M.DEF	and	PLUM.M.DEF	are	dry.MPL

'The walnut tree and the plum tree are dry.'   (Farkas and Zec 1995: 96)

(59)   **Feminine + feminine = feminine/neuter**

Podeaua	și	ușa	sînt	albe.
floor.F.DEF	and	door.F.DEF	are	white.F/NPL

'The floor and the door are white.'   (Farkas and Zec 1995: 96)

For two neuters, since the resulting agreement is plural on the verb or predicate adjective, the agreement surfaces as feminine/neuter since feminine/neuter is the exponent used for agreement with plural neuters.

(60)   **Neuter + neuter = feminine/neuter**

Scaunul	și	dulapul	sînt	albe.
chair.N.DEF	and	cupboard.N.DEF	are	white.F/NPL

'The chair and the cupboard are white.'   (Farkas and Zec 1995: 96)

The same generalization ensures that agreement will be feminine/neuter for the combination of a neuter and feminine noun, since they both trigger the insertion of the same, feminine/neuter exponent.

(61)   **Feminine + neuter = feminine/neuter**

Podeaua	și	scaunul	sînt	albe.
floor.F.DEF	and	chair.N.DEF	are	white.F/NPL

'The floor and the chair are white.'   (Farkas and Zec 1995: 96)

The key cases will be when the gender features of the coordinated DPs conflict: this occurs when one is traditional masculine and one neuter ((62)) and when one is traditional masculine and one is feminine ((63)). In both cases, the resulting agreement is feminine/neuter.

(62)   **Masculine + neuter = feminine/neuter**

Peretele	și	scaunul	sînt	albe.
wall.M.DEF	and	chair.N.DEF	are	white.F/NPL

'The wall and the chair are white.'   (Farkas and Zec 1995: 96)[167]

---

[167] A minority of speakers are capable of having masculine plural agreement in this context if the masculine DP is closer to the verb. See Mallinson (1984), Croitor and Giurgea (2009).

(63) **Feminine + masculine = feminine/neuter**

Podeaua	și	plafonul	sînt	albe
floor.F.DEF	and	ceiling.M.DEF	are	white.F/NPL

'The floor and the ceiling are white.'   (Farkas and Zec 1995: 96)

Along with Farkas and Zec (1995), I conclude that this supports the position of feminine/neuter as the default gender in the plural. In the case of a conflict between the gender features of two coordinated DPs, the language falls back on the default gender for plural nouns, i.e. feminine/neuter.[168]

Mixed-gender or unclear-gender groups also can trigger feminine plural agreement.

(64) Ce-s   alea?
      What-are those.F/NPL
      'What are those things?'   (Giurgea 2008: 109)

(65) Toate   astea   mi   se   par   incredibile.
      all.F/NPL these.F/NPL me.DAT REFL seem.3PL incredible.F/NPL
      'I find all these things/all that incredible.'   (Giurgea 2008: 109)

(66) d-ale   carnaval-ul-ui
      of-POSS.ART.F/NPL carnival-DEF-M.SG.GEN
      'of those belonging to the carnival'   (Farkas and Zec 1995: 100)

This supports the idea that feminine/neuter is generally the default gender for agreement in the plural in Romanian.

However, in Farkas (1990) and DSG (2013) (as well as to some extent in Farkas and Zec 1995, depending on how the distribution of the feature [FO] is formalized), feminine is the default gender in the plural for neuter nouns only. This is enforced in Farkas (1990) by having the rule that adds feminine as the default gender in the plural be a feature-filling rule, i.e. it cannot "overwrite" the lexically specified gender of feminine or traditional masculine nouns. This approach is supported by the fact that mixed-gender groups of animates trigger masculine agreement.

(67) respect   profesorii
      respect.1S teachers.MPL
      'I respect teachers (males and females).'   (DSG 2013: 6)

(68) [seeing an unclear group of people in the distance]
      ăstia   sînt   înalți
      these.MPL are   tall.MPL
      'These (people) are tall.'   (D. Farkas, p.c.)

---

[168] There is one noteworthy open question here: what agreement is triggered when two neuter animate DPs are coordinated? As far as I know, there are no published data that address this question.

However, if masculine is the default gender for agreement for all non-neuter nouns, the resolution facts for inanimates, and the mixed-group facts in (64)–(66), are left unexplained. The overall pattern seems to be that feminine/neuter is the default for plurals most of the time, with masculine used as the default for animate plurals with unclear gender. This is very similar to the three-gender-language default data from Section 7.6, where I observed that there is a resistance to using neuter agreement for sex-differentiable controllers (e.g. humans in Romanian). The fact that feminine/neuter default agreement is licit for non-sex-differentiable controllers, but that masculine default agreement is used for (at least) humans, is in fact typical for a language with the n inventory like (40).

In this section I have shown that the standard analysis of Romanian gender is straightforwardly portable into an approach where gender features are on n. Romanian has the set of ns in (40), where neuter nouns crucially lack gender features on n (following Chapter 7). There are only two Vocabulary Items per number for each gender agreement target, and the features of the VIs are configured such that masculine is the default for gender agreement in the singular and feminine is the default in the plural. This generates the facts successfully, and captures the fact that Romanian behaves in many ways like the three-gender language Lavukaleve (has the same inventory of ns, has the same unexpected non-neuter defaults), but in other ways like the two-gender language Spanish (only two exponents for realizing gender contrasts in a given agreement target).

Interestingly, having a different default for singular nouns and plural nouns is predicted to occur, given the broad claims of the book so far. Nothing prevents different defaults for different types of agreement targets (e.g. singular vs. plural targets), although I assume some kind of extralinguistic pressure ensures uniformity across targets in the majority of cases (perhaps related to learnability). Additionally, I speculated at the end of Chapter 6 that it would be difficult to acquire a two-gender language with an inventory like (40) unless the roots licensed under plain n behaved differently in two different contexts: Romanian provides an example of such a language. The roots licensed under plain n trigger masculine agreement in the singular, and feminine agreement in the plural.

However, it remains to be seen whether any alternative analyses can approach the facts better, especially one where gender features are on Num. I present and argue against some of these alternative analyses in the next section.

8.3.3 Alternative analyses

In this section, I focus first on analyses that place gender features *only* on Num in Romanian: Ritter (1993), Giurgea (2008), and Croitor and Giurgea (2009) (in part). I discuss how this type of analysis fares less well compared to the n analysis of neuter gender developed in Section 8.3.2, partially drawing on arguments from Giurgea

(2014). I then briefly argue against the lexicalist, two-gender approach to Romanian advanced in Bateman and Polinsky (2010). I conclude by returning to Somali, and exploring whether plurality is on *n* in Romanian.

Ritter (1993) was the first to suggest that Num is the location of gender features in Romanian. The Num-based approach allows for a simple, two-gender analysis of Romanian gender. Num can be [+/–FEMININE], and [+/–PLURAL]. It will be [–FEMININE] for masculine nouns across numbers, and [+FEMININE] for feminine nouns across numbers. However, for a singular neuter noun Num will be [–FEMININE,–PLURAL] and for a plural neuter noun, Num will be [+FEMININE, +PLURAL]. The analysis is deliberately preliminary, so Ritter does not specify how these correlations between Nums and nouns are enforced. However, the idea that gender is on Num is taken up and developed in more detail in Giurgea (2008) and Croitor and Giurgea (2009), with a typological twist.

Giurgea (2008) and Croitor and Giurgea (2009) aim to formalize Corbett's (1991) typological approach to Romanian, and rely on Ritter's proposal to do so. Corbett differentiates "target gender," the gender shown by agreement targets, from "controller gender," which is essentially the agreement class of a noun. In Corbett's view, Romanian has two target genders (masculine and feminine) and three controller genders, labeled with Roman numerals I, II, III in Figure 8.1, where I is masculine sing/masc plural, II is feminine sing/feminine plural, and III is masculine sing/feminine plural. I corresponds to traditionally masculine nouns, II to feminine nouns, and III to neuters.

Giurgea (2008) and Croitor and Giurgea (2009) assume that each noun is lexically specified for its agreement class, and that gender features are on Num. Then, Num selects for particular agreement classes, as laid out in (69).

(69)   **Selectional restrictions for Num**
      a. Num [–PL][–FEM] selects for Class I and Class III
      b. Num [–PL][+FEM] selects for Class II
      c. Num [+PL][–FEM] selects for Class I
      d. Num [+PL][+FEM] selects for Class II and Class III
           (slightly modified for clarity from Croitor and Giurgea 2009: (13))

This results in neuter nouns (= Class III) having masculine gender in the singular but feminine gender in the plural.

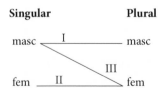

Singular   **Plural**

masc ——— I ——— masc

III

fem ——— II ——— fem

FIGURE 8.1 Controller genders in Romanian (modified from Corbett 1991: 152)

However, there are many reasons not to pursue this kind of analysis. First of all, it provides no explanation for why there is not a feminine singular/masculine plural controller gender. This would be a class of nouns that is singular in the feminine (selected by singular feminine Num) and masculine in the plural (selected by plural masculine Num), i.e. the opposite of the pattern displayed by Class III/neuter nouns. Nothing in the formalization of selectional restrictions would prevent this combination from occurring. Moreover, in Somali, where gender features are actually on the head that carries plurality, we saw in Section 8.2.1 that both masculine–feminine and feminine–masculine switches from singular to plural were attested. There is no deep property of language that prevents nouns from being feminine in the plural and masculine in the singular.

The analysis in Section 8.3.2 that relies on default gender offers an explanation for this gap. Recall that neuter nouns must be masculine in the singular and feminine in the plural because they lack gender features, and the default gender is masculine in the singular and feminine in the plural. While it is possible for the default gender to be configured the opposite way using underspecification of Vocabulary Items (masculine in the plural and feminine in the singular), there is no easy way of stating this over individual nouns/roots in Distributed Morphology. Default genders can vary by agreement target because default-ness is encoded via the underspecification of the VIs that realize agreement targets. However, defaults cannot easily vary by noun or root, since the features on n do not wholly determine the default gender for an agreement target. This predicts that, while singular agreement targets and plural agreement targets may have different defaults in Romanian, all nouns will be subject to the same default gender in the same context. Since the default is masculine in the singular and feminine in the plural, there can never be a noun that is feminine in the singular and masculine in the plural.

Moreover, a Num-based analysis faces a serious empirical challenge from the resolution data, as Croitor and Giurgea (2009) acknowledge (this problem causes Giurgea 2014 to argue against a Num-based analysis). The problem is that the Num-based analysis predicts that masculine (Class I) and neuter nouns (Class III) will behave identically when coordinated. Both masculine/Class I and neuter/Class III nouns are selected by a Num that is [−FEMININE, −PLURAL], and thus they have the same gender (masculine). Nouns that have the same gender trigger agreement forms with that gender in resolution contexts. Recall that two coordinated Class I/masculine nouns do in fact trigger masculine gender on the predicate adjective ((70)), as predicted, but two coordinated Class III/neuter nouns triggers feminine gender ((71)).

(70)   **Masculine + masculine = masculine**

Nucul	și	prunul	sînt	uscați
walnut.M.DEF	and	plum.M.DEF	are	dry.MPL

'The walnut tree and the plum tree are dry.'   (Farkas and Zec 1995: 96)

(71)   **Neuter + neuter = feminine/neuter**

Scaunul	şi	dulapul	sînt	albe
chair.N.DEF	and	cupboard.N.DEF	are	white.F/NPL

'The chair and the cupboard are white.'   (Farkas and Zec 1995: 96)

Moreover, coordinating a Class I/masculine noun with a Class III/neuter noun results in feminine gender again.

(72)   **Masculine + neuter = feminine/neuter**

Peretele	şi	scaunul	sînt	albe.
wall.M.DEF	and	chair.N.DEF	are	white.F/NPL

'The wall and the chair are white.'   (Farkas and Zec 1995: 96)

This is unexpected from the perspective of a Num-based analysis; Class I and Class III nouns have the same, masculine gender and should always trigger masculine agreement when coordinated with a noun of the same class or with each other.[169] However, this is predicted by the analysis in Section 8.3.2—there is gender mismatch in (71) and (72), which causes the default feminine plural gender to be inserted.

A final indication that a Num-based analysis is not on the right track concerns the characterization of Class III/neuter nouns. Recall that almost all of these nouns are inanimate, and that very few are human-referring animates. Under the analysis in Section 8.3.2, neuter nouns are licensed under plain n, i.e. a n that has no gender features. It is therefore unsurprising that the majority of the roots licensed in this class are inanimate since animate nouns, especially human-referring nouns, are more often licensed under ns that have interpretable gender features. The default gender analysis thus goes some way towards explaining why the neuter class is mostly inanimate. However, in the Num-based analysis, it is completely arbitrary which nouns are in which agreement class. There is no connection between the semantics of the noun and its agreement class, and thus there is no way to explain why Class III consists mostly of inanimates.

Given the fact that the Num-based analysis cannot prevent the generation of feminine singular/masculine plural nouns, that it makes a false prediction about resolution, and that it cannot explain the characteristics of neuter nouns, I conclude that it is a less viable analysis for Romanian than the n-based analysis developed in Section 8.3.2. It is also telling that no linguist currently espouses this analysis for Romanian; Ritter (1993) makes a plausible suggestion but does not develop it further, whereas Giurgea (2014) argues against Giurgea (2008) and Croitor and Giurgea (2009) (and in favor of the default gender analysis).

I round out this section by briefly considering two other analyses of Romanian: the lexicalist approach of Bateman and Polinsky (2010), and an approach that tries to equate Romanian with Somali.

---

[169] See Giurgea (2014) for some argumentation against putting a high plural Num that has the right gender features on top of the coordination phrase.

Bateman and Polinsky (B&P) (2010) develop a detailed, careful analysis of Romanian nominal morphology that pivots on nominal form determining nominal agreement class. They propose that there are four agreement classes in Romanian, two for singular nouns and two for plural nouns. Class membership is determined mostly by the morphophonological characteristics of a particular noun. The analysis sorts masculine and neuter nouns into the same class (Class B) in the singular, and feminine nouns into the other class in the singular (Class A). It also sorts masculine nouns into one class in the plural (Class C), and feminine and neuter nouns into the other class (Class D).

Agreement markers are divided into two sets (Set I and Set II), and rules connect Classes B and C with Set I and Classes A and D and Set II. The analysis works in that neuter nouns (Class B, Class D) have the same set of agreements as masculine nouns in the singular (Set II) and feminine nouns in the plural (Set I). The classification system is pre-syntactic, in that nouns are assigned to a class via a lexical rule on the basis of which endings they are combined with in the lexicon, and B&P do not discuss the syntactic position of gender or number features.

I have deliberately avoided any explicit discussion of nominal morphophonology in the analysis so far. Any in-depth Romanian analysis that takes up these facts seriously in the future must address the relationship between the gender/number of nouns and their vocalic ending, and I trust that an analysis like the one in Section 8.3.2 will be capable of being wedded to some plausible analysis of Romanian nominal inflection. However, setting aside this future challenge, it is clear that B&P's particular approach to the relationship between gender and number has some of the same drawbacks as the Num-based analysis.

Specifically, the B&P analysis treats singular masculine nouns and singular neuter nouns as having the same class (Class B) and thus the same set of agreements (Set II). It then predicts that neuter (Class B) nouns would trigger Set II (masculine) agreement when coordinated (as B&P 2010: 64–5 acknowledge), which is contrary to fact (see (71)). It also predicts that a neuter DP (Class B) coordinated with a masculine DP (Class B) would trigger Set II (masculine) agreement, again contrary to fact (see (72)).

The B&P analysis also does not explain why the subset of nouns which are Class B in the singular and Class D in the plural are almost all inanimate. This set of nouns has no formal status in the analysis and thus cannot be characterized uniquely. In the analysis in Section 8.3.2, these nouns are expected to be mostly inanimate since they must lack gender features.

Finally, there is no explanation of why the nouns sorted into Sets A and D (the feminine nouns) are mostly the same across singular and plural, and why the nouns sorted into Sets B and C (the "traditional" masculine nouns) are as well. B&P (2010: 76) acknowledge this, noting that the analysis "does not currently attempt to formalize any correspondences between singular and plural classes." In the analysis in Section 8.3.2, the gender features on *n* for these nouns do not change from singular to plural, so feminine nouns are expected to take the same kind of agreement in the plural, and traditional masculine nouns are as well (they have their own *n* : *n u*[−FEM]).

I conclude that the B&P analysis of Romanian nominal morphology is not as fruitful a direction to pursue as the default gender analysis in Section 8.3.2. However, it must be left for future work how to bridge the gap between the analysis in Section 8.3.2 and the thorough, morphophonological generalizations about Romanian nominal inflection highighted by B&P.

I close this section with one last alternative analysis: the Romanian-as-Somali approach. What if the plural strategies in Romanian were *n*s and carried gender features themselves? Focusing on DSG (2013)'s "major types" of plural strategies, there are four plural strategies in Romanian, each of which is associated with gender.

(73)   **Romanian plural strategies**
   a. Masculine -*i*
      bărbat ~ bărbați   'man'
   b. Feminine/neuter -*i*
      bunică ~ bunici   'grandmother'
   c. Feminine/neuter -*e*
      fată ~ fete   'girl'
   d. Feminine/neuter -*uri*
      tren ~ trenuri   'train'

I follow B&P in assuming there are two different plural -*i*s, one associated with feminine gender (their Class D) and one with masculine gender (their Class C). The basic idea would be that (73)a is the only plural *n* packaged with a [−FEM] feature, and would thus be the only plural strategy available for male-referring and traditional masculine inanimate nouns (cf. B&P 2010: 57). Singular noun endings can be similarly analyzed, with two different singular -*e*s, one associated with feminine gender and one with masculine gender.

(74)   **Romanian singular strategies**
   a. Masculine/neuter -Ø/-*u* (phonologically conditioned allomorphy)
      bărbat 'man'
   b. Masculine/neuter -*e*
      iepure 'rabbit'
   c. Feminine -*e*
      carte 'book'
   d. Feminine -*ă*
      fată 'girl'

Neuter nouns are then those whose roots are licensed under (74)ab in the singular and (73)bcd in the plural.

However, this type of two-gender analysis runs into the same problems again: the feminine agreement for coordinated neuter nouns (and a coordinated masculine and neuter noun) is unexpected. There is also no reason why the neuter nouns are inanimate. Moreover, the evidence for a *n* approach to Romanian plurality in the first place is mixed—although there is a fair amount of non-determinism (see DSG 2013: 839, B&P 2010: 73–4), there are no double plurals to the best of my knowledge. Also, it is even more problematic that the analysis provides no explanation for why there are no feminine-singular/masculine-plural nouns, as there are in Somali. Overall, then, I do not believe a *n* analysis for Romanian is worth taking up.

In this section, I have reviewed and presented arguments against several alternative analyses: gender on Num, the B&P lexicalist approach, and plurality on *n*. Each approach relied on there being two genders only in Romanian, which incorrectly conflates the behavior of masculines and neuters in resolution, and neither approach could explain certain key generalizations about the neuters.

8.3.4 Interim conclusion

In this case study of Romanian, I have shown that even though gender seems to be conditioned by number, there is no reason to have gender features located anywhere but *n*. The standard analysis of the Romanian gender system can be easily adapted from its lexicalist beginnings to a Distributed Morphology analysis that includes all the assumptions about gender that have been developed thus far in this book. It also confirms the no-gender-features approach to neuter nouns in three-gender languages that was proposed in Chapter 7, and fares better at explaining the facts than alternative approaches to Romanian gender, some of which do not have gender on *n*.[170]

8.4 Conclusion

Before properly concluding, I would like to quickly review some corroborating evidence that gender features and number features are on different projections. First, a variety of psycholinguistic studies have demonstrated that gender and number have different effects, in terms of processing (see e.g. Antón-Méndez et al. 2002, Carminati 2005, Fuchs et al. to appear), ERP effects (see e.g. Barber and Carreiras 2005), and accuracy in second-language acquisition tasks (see e.g. White et al. 2004). Granted, almost all of these studies used Spanish, where it is not controversial that number and gender are in separate locations, and mapping these

---

[170] Giurgea (2014) argues that gender features are on Num for Albanian, which has a superficially similar system to Romanian. However, Albanian is different from Romanian in that it has both (i) nouns that switch genders from masculine to feminine in the singular, and (ii) a "neuter" gender (i.e. a third set of agreement targets for a subset of nouns). Albanian thus could be described as a four-gender language, and I leave it for future research.

results into a particular theory of gender and number is not necessarily straightforward. However, the fact that gender and number behave distinctly across a range of psycholinguistic methodologies/approaches bodes well for a theory where they are features on separate projections.

Another research area in which fundamental differences between gender and number have been observed is nominal ellipsis. It has been well established that mismatches in number between the antecedent and the elided nominal are grammatical (see e.g. Merchant 2014: appendix). However, mismatches in gender vary in grammaticality depending on the nominal—e.g. some same-root nominals resist mismatches, whereas others allow it (see e.g. Bobaljik and Zocca 2011, and the extensive references within Merchant 2014). Of course, as with the psycholinguistic research, there are no guarantees that an empirical result can be plugged smoothly into a particular theory. It is also an important task for future research conducted within the approach to gender outlined in this book to interpret the results about different types of same-root nominals. Nevertheless, the differential behavior of gender and number under ellipsis points towards a theory where they are separate, and thus provides some preliminary support for the conclusion of this chapter from another empirical domain.

I have taken a close look in this chapter at the gender and number systems of two genetically and areally distant languages: Somali and Romanian. Although they are far from each other, they both contain nouns that seem to change genders when pluralized, and thus both initially seemed to be best analyzed by locating gender features on Num. However, I argued that Somali has plural *n*s which bring gender features of their own that override the gender features of the *n*P they combine with. I also argued that the Romanian nouns that seem to change genders are in fact underspecified for gender, and it is the default gender that changes in Romanian from singular to plural. Having the default gender change depending on the Vocabulary Items of the agreement target (whether they contain plural features or not) is in fact independently predicted to occur, given the reliance of the analysis on the Vocabulary Item configuration of particular agreement targets to ensure defaults. I conclude that it is highly unlikely that gender features are on Num, and thus the central thesis of the monograph is upheld: gender features are on *n*.

9

Gender and nominalizations

9.1 Introduction

In Chapter 3, I presented a variety of evidence from Amharic that gender is on *n*, including evidence from the interaction of gender and number. In Chapter 8, I explored the interaction of gender and number further, arguing that even cases where a noun seems to change gender in the plural do not require that gender features be on Num. In this chapter and Chapter 10, I explore the other evidence presented in favor of a *n* approach to gender in Chapter 3, focusing mostly on nominalizations, i.e. derived nouns (this chapter and Chapter 10), with a brief excursion into declension class (Chapter 10).

In Section 9.2, I first demonstrate how gender on *n* predicts that nominalizations will at least be capable of being gendered. I provide data from a range of languages, both ones previously encountered in the book and ones not mentioned before, that demonstrates this prediction is borne out. In Section 9.3 I widen the scope of the analysis in three ways. First, I consider "nominalizations" that have been argued to lack *n*P, and show how they have default gender as predicted. Next, I look closely at French deadjectival nominalization, which is realized using a variety of suffixes that all have the same gender; following Beard (1990), I show how this supports a Distributed Morphology approach to nominalizations and gender. Finally, I return to languages with animacy-based gender systems and show how the *n*s I proposed in Chapter 6 for Algonquian languages can also be used to nominalize. Section 9.4 identifies two potential problems for the analysis: putative cases of a nominalizer and a gender feature being exponed separately, and cases where a single nominalizer seems to have multiple genders. I argue that both of these potential problems pose no difficulties for the analysis upon closer investigation. I conclude in Section 9.5.

9.2 Nominalizations are gendered: data

9.2.1 Theoretical background

Within the Distributed Morphology literature, derived nouns are formed by a *n* selecting for a phrase that is not headed by a root (Marantz 2001, Alexiadou 2001 et

The Morphosyntax of Gender. First Edition. Ruth Kramer.
© Ruth Kramer 2015. Published 2015 by Oxford University Press.

seq., Arad 2003, Borer 2005, and many others). In the simplest cases, *n* selects for a *v*P
to form a deverbal noun ((1)), an *a*P to form a deadjectival noun ((2)) and another *n*P
to form a denominal noun ((3)).

(1)   **n + vP = deverbal noun**

(2)   **n + aP = deadjectival noun**

(3)   **n + nP = denominal noun**

In more complex cases, *n* may attach to a larger projection (e.g. VoiceP or AspectP to
make a deverbal noun; see Alexiadou 2010b for an overview). Following Comrie and
Thompson (2007), I refer to all derived nouns as nominalizations. I refer to nominalizations as phrase-derived (where phrase = any phrase not headed by a root) and
non-derived nouns as root-derived.

   If *n* has a gender feature when it combines with roots, there is no *a priori* reason
that it could not carry a gender feature when it combines with phrases. This
prediction is borne out: adding a particular nominalizer to a phrase often causes
the resulting nominalization to have a particular gender (I strengthen this claim in
Chapter 10, arguing that a nominalizer *always* causes the derived noun to have a
particular gender).

   That nominalizations have gender due to *n* carrying gender features has already
been proposed in two separate strands of literature: a strand that argues for gender
features on *n* (Kihm 2005, Ferrari(-Bridgers) 2005, 2008, Kramer 2009), and a strand
that focuses on nominalizations (see e.g. Markova 2010, Markovskaya 2012, Soare
2014).[171] Building on this literature, I present in the following sections some examples

---

[171]   See also Alexiadou (2011a) and Armoskaite (2014). In these approaches, nominalizations are formed
via a gendered *n* but the gender feature is either not inserted (Alexiadou 2011a) or not valued (Armoskaite
2014) until after the syntax, seemingly too late for syntactic agreement relations to be established.

of gendered nominalizations. I begin by showing that all the common types of nominalization can be gendered, and then demonstrate that each *n* that I have proposed in this book can be used to nominalize phrases.

First, though, a caveat is necessary. In some cases, it is ambiguous whether *n* is attaching to a phrase or to a root (see Arad 2003). To ensure accuracy, I will include only nominalizations (i) for which a good case can be made that they are phrase-derived or (ii) for which an argument has been made in previous literature that they are phrase-derived.

9.2.2 *Various types of nominalizations are gendered*

Taking (1)–(3) as a starting point, there are attested cases of deverbal, deadjectival, and denominal nominalizations with gender. I discuss each in turn, starting with deverbal and deadjectival nominalizations. Comrie and Thompson (2007) identify seven different types of deverbal nominalizations; I focus here on the types that are common to deverbal and deadjectival nominalizations: action/state nominalization (e.g. deverbal: *creation*, deadjectival: *quietness*), and agentive nominalization (e.g. deverbal: *singer*, deadjectival: 'one who is tall').

"Action/state deverbal nominalization" is essentially a cover term for the many different types of deverbal nominalizations that nominalize the event or state denoted by the verb, rather than nominalizing it as one of its arguments (e.g. agent, instrument). There is a substantial literature on the syntactic and semantic properties of deverbal action/state nominalizations, starting with the transformational analysis of Lees (1960) and including the influential analysis in Chomsky (1970). I will focus here on their morphological properties; see Alexiadou et al. (2007), Alexiadou (2010a, 2010b) for a detailed review of the syntax/semantics literature on these nominalizations.

Romanian furnishes a particularly clear example of a gendered action/state nominalization. The nominalization traditionally called the infinitive is formed from a verbal phrase[172] (not a root; Iordăchioaia and Soare 2008) and it is always feminine (see e.g. Iordăchioaia and Soare 2008, Alexiadou et al. 2010).

(4) **Romanian action/state deverbal nominalization: infinitive**

    o   bună   spăla-re   a   rufelor   e   recomandat-ă   pentru țesătură
    a.FS good.FS wash-INF of clothes is recommended-FS for   fabric
    'A good clothes-washing is recommended for fabric.'   (Soare 2014)

---

[172] I use the term "verbal phrase" because some authors do not adopt lexical decomposition and instead form nominalizations from VPs.

In (4), the infinitive *spalare* 'washing, to wash' triggers feminine agreement on the indefinite determiner, the adjective, and the passive participle.

Agentive deverbal nominalizations are generally assumed to be phrase-derived, i.e. formed by adding a *n* to a verbal phrase (see e.g. Marantz 2001, Schäfer 2008, Baker and Vinokurova 2009). In the dialect of Somali described in Lecarme (2002), agentive nominalizations are clearly gendered.

(5)   **Somali agentive deverbal nominalizations**
   a. ababuul-é   b. abaabu-shó
      organize-NMLZ.M   organize-NMLZ.F
      'male organizer'   'female organizer'   (Lecarme 2002: 120)

In (5), the suffix *-é* is used for masculine agentive nominalizations, and the suffix *-tó* (realized as *shó* in (5)) for feminine agentive nominalizations.

Turning now to deadjectival nominalizations, the action/state deadjectival nominalizer *-ité* in French does not attach to a root (Roy 2010), and it causes the resulting noun to be feminine.

(6)   **French action/state deadjectival nominalizations**
   a. la national-ité   'the.FS national-ity'
   b. la banal-ité   'the.FS banal-ity'

I return to French deadjectival nominalization in Section 9.3.2. An example of agentive deadjectival nominalizations comes from Luganda (Niger-Congo (Bantoid); Uganda). A deadjectival nominalization denoting a human is formed by adding a Class 1 prefix *mu-/mw-* to an adjective (Bantu noun classes meet the definition for genders; see Chapter 4).

(7)   **Luganda agentive deadjectival nominalizations**
   a. genge 'leprous'   d. mu-genge 'leper'
   b. lungi 'beautiful'   e. mu-lungi 'beautiful person'
   c. gezi 'clever'   f. mu-gezi 'clever person'
                     (Ferrari 2005: 56, Ferrari-Bridgers 2008: 246)

So far, both action/state nominalizations and agentive nominalizations can be gendered, regardless of whether they are deverbal or deadjectival.

Another key type of deadjectival nominalization is gentilic nouns, i.e. nouns denoting people from a certain location. In languages with biological sex-based gender systems, gentilic nouns denoting men are generally masculine and gentilic nouns denoting women are generally feminine. I presented an example of deadjectival gendered gentilic nouns in Chapter 3 for Amharic where this holds true, and it is repeated in (8).

(8) **Amharic gentilic deadjectival nominalization**

a. ityop'p'iy-awi	b. ityop'p'iy-awi-Ø	c. ityop'p'iy-aw-it
Ethiopia-ADJ	Ethiopia-ADJ-NMLZ.M	Ethiopia-ADJ-NMLZ.F
'Ethiopian (adjective)'	'Ethiopian man'	'Ethiopian woman'[173]

The suffix -*awi* is productive adjectivalizer, so this is a nominalization built on an *a*P (not a root). The adjective 'Ethiopian' ((8)a) is combined either with a null nominalizer that has masculine gender and leads to a male interpretation ((8)b) or with an overt nominalizer -*it* that has feminine gender and leads to a female interpretation ((8)c).[174]

Comrie and Thompson (2007) describe two kinds of denominal nominalizations: abstract nominals (*child-hood*) and expressive morphology like diminutives (*pig-let*). Both types of nominalizations can be gendered, and German provides an example of each. In German, the suffix -*schaft* attaches to *n*Ps and creates a "collective or state" (Durrell 2011: 479).

(9) **German abstract denominal nominalization**
a. die Bürger-schaft   'the.FS citizens (collectively)'
b. die Freund-schaft   'the.FS friend-ship'
c. die Studenten-schaft   'the.FS student body'

The resulting noun is always feminine, as shown by the feminine agreement on the definite article.

German also has a diminutive suffix -*chen*.

(10) **German diminutive denominal suffixation**

a. die Karte	'the.FS card'	b. das Kärt-chen	'the.NS card-DIMIN'
c. die Stadt	'the.FS town'	d. das Städt-chen	'the.NS town-DIMIN'
e. die Flasche	'the.FS bottle'	f. das Fläsch-chen	'the.NS bottle-DIMIN'

(data from Wiltschko and Steriopolo 2007, Durrell 2011)

Nouns that are diminutivized with -*chen* are all neuter, as evidenced by the neuter agreement on the definite article. Following Wiltschko (2006), Wiltschko and Steriopolo (2007), and Steriopolo (2008), I assume that German diminutives are denominal nouns formed via a diminutive *n* attaching to a *n*P, so this is another instance of a gendered nominalization (although not all diminutives have their "own" gender; see Section 10.3). In general, denominal nominalizations involve "stacked"

---

[173] The final vowel in -*awi* is deleted when the -*it* suffix is added in order to avoid hiatus. See Leslau (1995: 35–6).

[174] Gentilic nouns can also be denominal, e.g. formed from the country name itself, e.g. Russian denominal nouns with -*ec* are masculine, e.g. *šotland-ec* 'Scottish man' (Corbett 1991: 34). However, in such cases, it can be difficult to determine if the nominalizer is attaching to a root or to a *n*P.

*n*Ps, and thus raise the question of which gender feature ends up being the agreeing gender of the nominal. I explore this question in Chapter 10.

Overall, all of the well-attested types of nominalizations can be gendered, which lends support to the idea that *n* has gender features.

9.2.3 *All of the gender-relevant* ns *can nominalize*

In addition to asking what types of nominalizations can be gendered, it is fruitful to ask what types of *n*s can be used to nominalize phrases. I submit that all the *n*s proposed so far in this book ((11)) are attested as nominalizers.[175]

(11)   **Types of *n* (total)**
     a. *n* *i* [+FEM]
     b. *n* *i* [−FEM]
     c. *n*
     d. *n* *u* [−FEM]
     e. *n* *u* [+FEM]

I shall review each in turn.

We have already seen examples of nominalizations licensed under (11)abe. The *n*s with interpretable masculine and feminine features ((11)ab) are used in agentive nominals in Somali like (5) and gentilic nominals in Amharic like (8)bc. The derivation of (8)b is in (13), and the derivation of (8)c is in (12).[176]

(12)

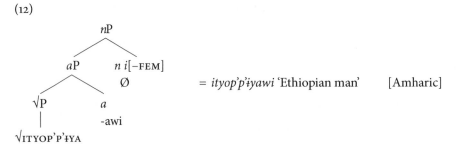

= *ityop'p'iyawi* 'Ethiopian man'   [Amharic]

---

[175] I do not expect that a given language must use each of its *n*s as a nominalizer; I am investigating only whether each *n* that I have proposed will be attested in some language as a nominalizer. I also assume that a language is not limited to using only the *n*s it contains for root-licensing as nominalizers. Nothing prevents a language from containing another flavor of *n* that only selects for phrases, never roots. For example, in Ch. 2, I described some dialects of Amharic where feminine gender is only used for diminutive nouns, never feminine inanimate nouns. This dialect thus contains *n* *u*[+FEM] but it selects only for *n*P, never a root.

[176] I assume that the adjective *ityop'p'iy-awi* 'Ethiopian' is root-derived, but it could also be denominal (i.e. derived from the *n*P *ityop'p'iya* 'Ethiopia'). It does not matter to the argument here which option is correct.

(13)

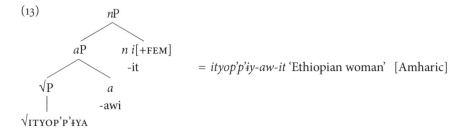

= *ityop'p'iy-aw-it* 'Ethiopian woman' [Amharic]

The *n* with an uninterpretable feminine feature ((11)e) is used to make French deadjectival nouns like those in (6). The structure of (6)a is in (14); I assume head movement or a post-syntactic movement operation (Embick and Noyer 2001) unites the root and *-ité* into one Morphological Word.

(14)

= *banalité* 'banality'   [French]

Nominalizations licensed under the plain *n* ((11)c) or the uninterpretable masculine *n* ((11)d) are also attested. In Lavukaleve, nouns with the action/state deverbal nominalizer *-e/-i* are always neuter (the quality of the suffix is determined by vowel harmony).

(15)   **Lavukaleve action/state deverbal nominalization**
    a. lo 'finish'   d. lo-e 'end.N'
    b. honia 'know'   e. honia-e 'knowledge.N'
    c. iru 'sleep (verb)'   f. iru-i 'sleep.N'   (Terrill 2003: 348)

It is plausible that this nominalization is derived from a verbal phrase because it can contain verbal morphology (e.g. object agreement prefixes; see Terrill 2003: 352, (633)). Neuter gender in Lavukaleve is triggered by plain *n* (see Chapter 7), so the structure of (15)b is as in (16).

(16)

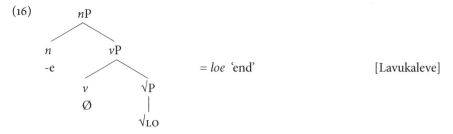

= *loe* 'end'   [Lavukaleve]

One example of a nominalization licensed under the uninterpretable masculine *n* is found in Serbian-Croatian (Slavic; Serbia, Croatia). Serbian-Croatian has a gender system similar to Lavukaleve: three genders (masculine, feminine and neuter), and inanimates are found in all three genders (see e.g. Hammond 2005: 111 on Serbian). It thus contains the uninterpretable masculine *n* like Lavukaleve (see Chapter 7). In Serbian-Croatian, the uninterpretable masculine *n* is used to form diminutives, even of female-denoting nouns like *devojka* 'girl.' In (17)a, non-diminutive 'girl' triggers feminine gender agreement on the demonstrative and adjective, whereas in (17)b, diminutive 'girl' triggers masculine agreement.

(17) a ova   pametna   devojka   **Non-diminutive**   **Serbian-Croatian**
         this.FS   smart.FS   girl

      b. ovaj   pametni   devojčurak   **Diminutive**
         this.MS   smart.MS   girl.DIM

(Wechsler and Zlatić 2003: 64)

Recall that I assume that diminutives are denominal nouns formed via a diminutive *n* attaching to a *n*P (although see Chapter 10 for a refinement of this analysis). Evidence for this is that the natural gender of 'girl' is still present in the interpretation of (17)b, i.e. the *n i*[+FEM] that licenses the root which forms 'girl' must be part of its structure. Under this approach, the structure of (17)b is in (18) (I do not specify Vocabulary Items for the root or the *n*s to avoid making commitments about Serbian-Croatian morphology).

(18)

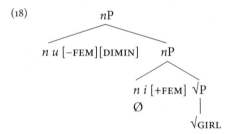

Overall, I have shown that, as predicted, nominalizing *n*s also have gender features. Many different types of nominalizations are gendered (see Chapter 10 for the strengthening of this prediction to: all nominalizations are gendered), and all the *n*s that I have proposed are attested as nominalizers. Besides the *n* analysis being compatible with this data, though, it also makes several predictions about nominalizations that I show are borne out in the next section.

9.3 Nominalizations are gendered: predictions

In this section, I explore some consequences of the idea that nominalizing *n*s have gender features. First, some derived nouns have been argued to lack *n* entirely, and the analysis predicts that any such nouns will trigger default gender agreement (similar to the non-nominal controllers discussed in Chapter 7). Building on work by Iordăchioaia and Soare (2008), I show how this prediction is borne out in Romanian. Second, a non-lexical approach to gender predicts that a single, gendered *n* that subcategorizes for a particular type of phrase could be realized with a variety of Vocabulary Items. Following Beard (1990), I show how this state of affairs holds in deadjectival nominalization in French. Finally, the analysis also predicts that *n*s in animacy-based gender systems could be used for nominalization, and I present data from Algonquian languages that confirms this prediction.

9.3.1 *Derived nouns without* n

It has long been recognized that deverbal nouns vary in terms of how many nominal properties they have—some behave like typical nominals (e.g. modified by adjectives), whereas others are more verbal (e.g. modified by adverbs), whereas others seem to be hardly nominal at all (e.g. they consist merely of a determiner followed by a clause). Determining what projections various derived nouns contain, and how this correlates with their nominal/verbal properties, is a vast and robust area of research (see e.g. Alexiadou et al. 2007, Alexiadou 2010a, 2010b, Alexiadou and Rathert 2010, Kornfilt and Whitman 2011, Paul 2014, and references therein).

Here, I focus on a recent strand of work on this topic by Alexiadou, Iordăchioaia, Soare, and Schäfer (see e.g. Iordăchioaia and Soare 2008, Alexiadou 2010b, Alexiadou et al. 2010, Alexiadou et al. 2011, Iordăchioaia 2013, Soare 2014). These authors have identified several derived nouns in a variety of languages that primarily have verbal properties, and they have analyzed these derived nouns as lacking *n*Ps. If *n*s have gender features, then these nominalizations accordingly lack gender features. Any agreement target that agrees with a DP that lacks gender features must have the default gender, and thus we arrive at the prediction: a nominalization that lacks a *n*P will always trigger default gender agreement.

Building on the results from Chapter 8, I center the discussion here on Romanian deverbal nominalizations, which have been thoroughly documented and analyzed in e.g. Cornilescu (2001), Iordăchioaia and Soare (2008), Alexiadou (2010b), Alexiadou et al. (2010), Alexiadou et al. (2011), Iordăchioaia (2013), Dobrovie-Sorin and Giurgea (DSG) (2013), and Soare (2014). I demonstrate that the Romanian deverbal nominalization which lacks a *n*P triggers default gender agreement, as predicted, and I close with some thoughts on the cross-linguistic robustness of the prediction.

Romanian has two primary deverbal action/state nominalizations: the infinitive and the supine (see DSG 2013: 665–6 for other deverbal nominalizations). The infinitive is formed via the suffix *-re*, and the supine is formed most often via the suffix *-t* (more precisely, via a set of suffixes used for (passive) participles; DSG (2013: 664–5)).

(19)   **Romanian infinitive**
    a. cânta-re   'sing/singing'
    b. coborâ-re   'descend/descent'
    c. vede-re   'see/seeing'   (DSG 2013: 664)

(20)   **Romanian supine**
    a. cânta-t   'sing/singing'
    b. sosi-t   'arrive/arriving'
    c. ocăr-ât   'insult/insulting'   (DSG 2013: 665)

In a series of papers (Iordăchioaia and Soare 2008, Alexiadou 2010b, Alexiadou et al. 2010, Alexiadou et al. 2011, Alexiadou 2011b, Iordăchioaia 2013), it has been argued that the Romanian infinitive has internal nominal structure, whereas the supine has no *n*P. One main piece of evidence for this is that the infinitive is modified by adjectives (e.g. *bună* 'good' in (21)a), whereas the supine is modified by adverbs (e.g. *bine* 'well' in (21)b; see e.g. Iordăchioaia and Soare 2008).

(21)   a. o   spălare   bună   a   rufelor   **Romanian infinitive**
        a.FS   wash.INF   good.FS   of   laundry.GEN
        'a good washing of laundry'

     b. spălatul   bine/*bun   al   rufelor   **Romanian supine**
        wash.SUP.DEF   well/*good   of   laundry.GEN
        'the washing of laundry well'   (Iordăchioaia 2013: 3)

Assuming that a *n*P is required to support adjectival modification (Iordăchioaia 2013), this is evidence that the infinitive contains a *n*P and the supine lacks a *n*P. The structure for the supine originally proposed in Iordăchioaia and Soare (2008), and taken up in the later literature, is given in (22).[177]

(22)   **Romanian Supine**

A D is present because the supine form is compatible with definite determiners (see (21)b), and the AspP is assumed to be present because the supine can combine with the adverb *constantly* (argued by Cinque 1999 to require an AspP).[178]

---

[177]   I change the bottom projection from a VP to a *v*P to remain compatible with the lexical decomposition approach assumed here. It is important to be clear, though, that the *v* head of *v*P is only a verbalizer in this case and not a Voice projection.
[178]   Iordăchioaia and Soare (2008) suggest that the supine suffix is either located within the *v*P or is a realization of Asp.

Given this structure, it is predicted that the supine must trigger default gender agreement. It has no gender features to be agreed with, so any element that has obligatory gender agreement and agrees with a supine will be forced to be exponed with the Vocabulary Item that lacks gender features, i.e. the default. In Chapter 8, I argued that the default gender in Romanian is masculine/neuter in the singular, and feminine/neuter in the plural. Supine nominalizations cannot be pluralized (DSG 2013: 708), but in the singular, they clearly trigger masculine/neuter gender on a predicate adjective.[179]

(23) mâncat-ul   la orice oră   e nesănătos   **Romanian supine triggers Masc Agr**
      eat.SUP-DEF at any   hour is unhealthy.M/N
      'Eating at any time is unhealthy.'   (DSG 2013: 694)

The infinitive, in contrast, contains a nP, and thus is not required to trigger default gender agreement. In fact, infinitives are always feminine in Romanian, as shown by the feminine forms of the indefinite determiner and the adjective in (21)a. I conclude that the prediction of the analysis is borne out in Romanian: the deverbal nominalization that lacks nP necessarily trigger the default gender.

More work must be done to confirm this prediction, and the facts can be somewhat tricky since these nominalizations also lack NumP and therefore often trigger the insertion of numberless forms (which can be different than the default gender form; see Chapter 7). However, one final promising indication comes from clausal/CP "nominalizations." Clausal nominalizations consist of a determiner followed by a finite CP, and are found in e.g. Polish and Greek (see e.g. Borsley and Kornfilt 2000, Kornfilt and Whitman 2011).

(24) Dhen   amfisvito   [to   oti   efighe].   **Greek CP nominalization**
      NEG   dispute-1S   DEF.N.ACC   that   left.3S
      'I do not dispute that he left.'   (Kornfilt and Whitman 2011: 1299)

In (24), the determiner *to* is followed by a CP headed by *oti* 'that' which contains a finite verb *efighe* 'he/she left.' Crucially, the determiner here is neuter. Greek has a three-gender system that seems roughly similar to Lavukaleve (e.g. inanimates in all three genders; see e.g. Holton et al. 1997: Part II, Ch. 2). If that is correct, then neuter is used for default gender agreement, and neuter is the form that the article takes in this clearly nP-less nominalization. I conclude that the prediction that nominalizations lacking nP must trigger default gender agreement is generally borne out.

---

[179] Iordăchioaia and Soare (2008) observe that the supine can be pluralized when it is a simple event nominal (i.e. a deverbal nominalization lacking argument structure). In that case, it takes the standard neuter plural suffix *uri* (i.e. it seems to have default gender), but I hesitate to build on this fact, since it is unclear whether a n is present.

9.3.2 *One gender, many exponents*

The fact that nominalizations lacking *n*P have default gender in Romanian is compatible with a *n* approach to gender, but it does not constitute definitive evidence for a *n* approach. A lexicalist approach to gender features, where gender is located on the traditional "big N" head, would make the same prediction because in all the cases so far where nominalizations lack *n*P, they could be plausibly analyzed as lacking NP (e.g. the Romanian supine in (22)). However, gendered nominalizations do provide an opportunity to tease apart lexical and non-lexical approaches to gender, in a way first recognized by Beard (1990). In this section, I present Beard's argumentation from the perspective of a *n* locus for gender, and show how the facts support a non-lexical approach.

Beard (1990) primarily argues for the Separationist Hypothesis, which was later included as one of the fundamental assumptions of Distributed Morphology. The Separationist Hypothesis separates the rules/operations that form words (e.g. "add a past tense feature") from morphophonological exponents (e.g. *-ed, -t, -Ø*). This hypothesis was encoded in DM as Late Insertion: the feature bundles which syntactic operations manipulate are abstract and do not have phonological content. Phonological content is inserted later in the derivation at PF via Vocabulary Insertion. Morphophonological exponents are thus formally distinct from the syntactic features that they expone. In contrast, a standard lexicalist approach assumes that morphophonological exponents are lexical items manipulated by the syntax and carry the features that they express.

With this background, consider the data on French deadjectival nominalizations in (25) (partially repeated from (6)).

(25)   **French deadjectival nominalizations**
      a. la banal-ité   'the.FS banal-ity'
      b. la faibl-esse   'the.FS weak-ness'
      c. la moit-eur   'the.FS damp-ness'
      d. la drôl-erie   'the.FS funni-ness'

It is reasonable to assume that all of the nominalization suffixes (*-ité, -esse, -eur, -erie, -isme*) are realizations of a *n* that takes an *a*P complement, as shown above in (14) for *-ité* (repeated as (26)). Alexiadou and Martin (2012) argue that *-ité, -erie*, and *-isme* select specifically for *a*P (not a root) and Roy (2010) shows how the presence of *a*P (her AP) is crucial in order to capture certain semantic restrictions on the distribution of the suffixes.[180]

---

[180] I depart from Roy's (2010) analysis, though, because she assumes that the suffixes themselves are realizations of a Pred(icate) head. Note also that Alexiadou and Martin (2012) maintain that the suffixes *-ité, -esse, -eur, -erie*, and *-isme* all have different semantic effects, which could be interpreted as indicating that the suffixes are all different *n*s. If they were different *n*s, though, it would remain unexplained why they

(26)

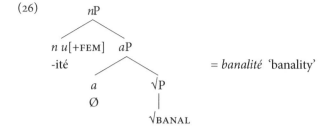

= *banalité* 'banality'

The crucial fact is that all the suffixes trigger the same type of gender agreement: feminine. Despite the various morphophonological exponents, deadjectival nominalization in French always results in a feminine noun.

This fact is relatively straightforward to capture in Distributed Morphology. I assume that French has a gender system roughly similar to Spanish and Somali: two genders (masculine and feminine), many feminine inanimates (e.g. *la table* 'the.F table'), several feminine fixed-gender nouns (e.g. *la sentinelle* 'the sentinel (male or female)'), and masculine default gender (see e.g. Schafroth 2003, Atkinson 2012). Therefore, as for other languages with these characteristics, I assume that French contains a n u[+FEM] that forms part of the feminine inanimates and feminine fixed-gender nouns. This n u[+FEM] then happens to be the only n in the language that selects for *a*Ps. The different exponents come about when the n u[+FEM] is realized as different Vocabulary Items depending on context, as shown in (27). In other words, the exponents are all contextual allomorphs of n u[+FEM].

(27)   a. n u[+FEM]↔ ité / $\begin{bmatrix} X \\ \\ Y \end{bmatrix}$

b. n u[+FEM]↔ esse / $\begin{bmatrix} A \\ \\ B \end{bmatrix}$

c. n u[+FEM]↔ erie / $\begin{bmatrix} C \\ \\ X \end{bmatrix}$

all have feminine gender. It may be that the effects that Alexiadou and Martin (2012) identify are not explained by differing features on n (and to be clear, Alexiadou and Martin (2012) do not take a stance on how to formalize the effects). One point in favor of this is that the effects are not categorical, as they would be if a certain semantic feature were attached to n or not. The effects hold most of the time, but there are often many exceptions (see e.g. Alexiadou and Martin 2012: 11 on the individual-level reading of -*isme*), and coercion is possible (Alexiadou and Martin 2012: 12 on the coercion of the individual-level reading for -*erie*). I leave for future work more focused on the semantics of nominalizations the question of how to encode these effects in the grammar.

Specifying exactly what contextual features trigger the insertion of what suffix would require a more in-depth study of French than there is space to pursue here. However, there are several plausible possibilities. It could be that particular combinations of *a* and root trigger the insertion of particular Vocabulary Items (although the locality conditions on the allomorphy would be complex; see e.g. Embick 2010, Svenonius 2012, Merchant to appear). Another possibility is that particular *a*s with specific features trigger the insertion of particular VIs. As is typical for derivational morphology, some *a*Ps are compatible with more than one VI, e.g. *importun-ité, importunisme* 'unwelcome-ness' (Alexiadou and Martin 2012: 8). This means that some contexts (e.g. certain combinations of *a* and root) will be part of the conditioning context for Vocabulary Insertion for more than one Vocabulary Item. Regardless of how the context is ultimately characterized, though, it is straightforward for one syntactic terminal node with one gender feature to be responsible for all deadjectival nominalization. Regardless of which allomorph is chosen, the [+FEM] feature on the *n* in the syntax ensures that the nominalized adjective will have feminine gender.

This configuration of facts, though, is difficult for a standard lexicalist approach. Each suffix would have different lexical entries, as shown in (28).

(28)   *-ité*   *-esse*   *-eur*   *-erie*   *-isme*
       [N]   [N]   [N]   [N]   [N]
       [+F]   [+F]   [+F]   [+F]   [+F]
       [ADJ_]   [ADJ_]   [ADJ_]   [ADJ_]   [ADJ_]   (based on Beard 1990: 162, (7))

However, it would be a coincidence for each of these deadjectival nominalizers to have feminine gender as part of their lexical entries. Essentially, if the lexical entries for the exponents have gender features, there is no clear way to connect the rule for deadjectival nominalization with feminine gender. Moreover, it is not clear in this approach why there are e.g. no masculine deadjectival nominalizations. Nothing prevents a lexical entry like those in (28) where the gender feature is [−F] or not present at all.

This pattern of facts is not limited to French. Beard (1990) demonstrates how all deadjectival nominalizations in German, Italian, and Russian are feminine—despite being realized by a variety of suffixes in each language. While the similarity in deadjectival nominalization across these western Indo-European languages undoubtedly has a diachronic explanation, the basic situation of a gendered nominalization being realized by multiple exponents is seemingly a stable pattern.[181] The Somali plural system, analyzed in Chapter 8, furnishes another example: there are several cases of a plural *n* that has a consistent gender being realized by different exponents depending on context (the identity of the root, in this case).

---

[181] It remains open whether all the suffixes that Beard includes are root-derived or phrase-derived.

The opposite pattern of facts would support lexicalism, i.e. one type of nominalization (e.g. action/state deverbal, abstract nominal) that is realized by different exponents, where each exponent has a different gender.[182] Beard (1990) discusses one putative example of this phenomenon: locative denominal nominalizations in Serbian-Croatian.

(29) **Serbian-Croatian locative denominal nominalizations**
    a. knjiga 'book'   d. knjiž-nica 'library-LOC.F'
    b. raž 'rye'   e. raž-iste 'rye field-LOC.N'
    c. guska 'goose'   f. gus-injak 'goose pen-LOC.M'   (Beard 1990: 164)

In (29), the same kind of nominalization is associated with three different suffixes that each trigger different genders. DM would require there to be three *n*s in the syntax with three different gender features that suspiciously all select for *n*Ps and all have the same semantic interpretation ('location related to the *n*P').[183]

However, Beard (1990) presents evidence that suggests that each of the suffixes in (29) corresponds to a different *n*. The feminine -*nica* is the "*in* locative" interpreted as 'enclosed place of *n*P,' like 'library' in (29)d. In contrast, the neuter -*iste* is the "*on* locative" interpreted as 'open place of *n*P,' like 'rye field' in (29)e. As for (29)f, the masculine suffix is used for any '*in* locative' that is derived from an animate noun, as shown in (30).

(30) **Serbian-Croatian masculine locative denominal nominalizations: animate nouns**
    a. svinja 'hog'   d. svinj-ac 'pig sty.M'
    b. zec 'rabbit'   e. zeč-injak 'rabbit warren.M'
    c. žaba 'frog'   f. žab-njak 'frog pond.M'   (Beard 1990: 166)

Therefore, the [–FEM] "*in* locative" *n* has different selectional properties from the other '*in* locative' *n* [+FEM]. Overall, each locative *n* is different in terms of its semantics (or its selectional properties, in the case of the masculine "*in* locative"), and it is plausible that each has its own gender features and each is realized by a different Vocabulary Item.[184]

In sum, as Beard (1990) originally noticed, a DM approach to gender predicts that one *n* terminal node in the syntax (e.g. the deadjectival nominalizer) can be realized as many different exponents depending on context, but can always have the same gender. This

---

[182] See Sect. 4 for discussion of one exponent being associated with different genders.

[183] It is unclear whether Serbian-Croatian locative nominalization is a root-based or *n*P-based nominalization. In so far as it seems to specify a location for a previously formed *n*P, it seems to be *n*P-attached. However, the resulting noun is not necessarily in a semantically transparent relationship with the base *n*P, and it is unclear whether these nominalizations are morphophonologically regular. Regardless, the point still goes through: it is problematic for a *n* approach to gender to have multiple suffixes with multiple genders having the same structural/semantic properties whether they are root-attached or *n*P-attached.

[184] For similar argumentation (although not presented in terms of gender or DM), see Fábregas (2010a) on Spanish deverbal nominalizations. Fábregas argues that seemingly synonymous Spanish deverbal nominalizers each are associated with structurally and/or semantically distinct verbal phrases.

phenomenon is widespread in western Indo-European deadjectival nominalization (and see Beard 1990 for further examples, e.g. the Serbian-Croatian "*in* locative" can actually be realized by several different exponents, all with feminine gender). In contrast, a lexicalist approach that ties gender features to particular exponents struggles to explain the uniformity in gender features, but plurality of exponents. Thus, this pattern of nominalization data provides further evidence for a *n* approach to gender features.

9.3.3 *Nominalizations in an animacy gender system*

Almost all the data in this chapter so far has been from languages with gender systems based on biological sex features. However, in this book I have also examined languages with gender systems based on animacy. In particular, I proposed that Algonquian languages have the *n*s in (31): a *n* with an interpretable animate feature (forming nouns with animate gender that are animate semantically), a plain *n* that is interpreted as inanimate (forming nouns with inanimate gender that are inanimate semantically), and a *n* with an uninterpretable animacy feature (forming nouns with animate gender that are inanimate semantically).[185]

(31)   *n*s in Algonquian
    a. *n i* [ANIMATE]
    b. *n*
    c. *n u* [ANIMATE]

I show each of these *n*s can be used for nominalization in Algonquian in this section.[186]

Since (31)a is the only *n* with an interpretable animate feature, any nominalization that forms a semantically animate noun must be formed via (31)a. Menomini (Central Algonquian) has an agentive deverbal nominalization that forms a semantically animate noun, shown in (32).

(32)   **Menomini agentive deverbal nominalizations**
    a. anohkii 'work (verbal stem)'   c. anohkii-w 'workman'
    b. moohkotaaqsi 'whittle (verbal stem)' d. moohkotaaqso-w 'carpenter'
                                             (Bloomfield 1962: 242)

Bloomfield (1962) describes agentive nouns as formed from a -*w* suffix attaching to intransitive verbs, so I assume that the -*w* is a *n* that attaches to a verbal phrase (although it is worth noting that the -*w* is homophonous with 3rd person singular

---

[185] I set aside Lealao Chinantec (Ch. 5) since there is no mention of nominalization in Rupp (1989). Rupp (2009) has an example of a "nominalizer" prefix attached to the verb 'speak' forming the noun 'word,' but no further information is given.

[186] There has been a recent flurry of research on Algonquian nominalizations (see e.g. Johansson 2011, 2012, 2013, Wiltschko 2014, Bliss 2014, Mathieu 2014, Ritter 2014). There is not space to address this literature in full here, but see fn. 187 for discussion of some of these sources in the context of participial nominalizations.

subject agreement, so this analysis remains to be confirmed; it could be that the *n* is phonologically null). The *n* that attaches to the *v*P must be (31)a in order to interpret 'carpenter' and 'workman' as semantically animate, and thus nominalizations with (31)a are attested.[187,188]

There are also attested nominalizations that create only inanimate nouns, i.e. that are formed by adding (31)b to a phrase. One of these is the Ojibwe (Central Algonquian) deverbal action/state/instrumental nominalization realized by the suffix *-win* (Bloomfield 1957: 68, Valentine 2001: 506–7).

(33)   **Ojibwe deverbal action/state/instrumental nominalization**
    a. apabi 'sit' → apab-win 'chair'
    b. ataaso 'store' → ataaso-win 'cupboard'
    c. nibaa 'sleep (v.)' → nibaa-win 'sleep (n.)'   (Mathieu 2014: 7, 13)

Mathieu (2014) analyzes *-win* as a *n* that attaches to a *v*P. The structure of (33)b under this analysis is given in (34).

(34)

          (Mathieu 2014: 14)

[187] Although to the best of my knowledge there is no analytical work on these nominalizations in Menomini, similar nominalizations in Ojibwe and Blackfoot (Johansson 2011, 2012, 2013, Wiltschko 2014, Bliss 2014, Mathieu 2014) are highly controversial. These nominalizations (sometimes called "participles") do not behave like typical nouns, so a fundamental question has been whether they are truly nominalizations (Bliss 2014, Wiltschko 2014) or clauses (Johansson 2011, 2012, 2013, Mathieu 2014). Additionally, although all the nominalization analyses have a nominal feature or head being attached to a clause in some way, there is no clear consensus across the approaches. For now, I assume the nominalization approach is correct for Menomini and that, however the attachment of *n* is formalized, it carries an animate feature like (31)a.

[188] It is widely known that inanimates can "shift" gender to animate as a mark of high status, especially in narratives (see e.g. Black-Rogers 1982, Goddard 2002, Valentine 2001: 118; see also Goddard 2002: 211 for an animate noun shifting to inanimate). However, as Mathieu (2012) notes, it must be kept in mind that there is considerable variation across Algonquian languages in the extent to which shifting happens (see e.g. Goddard 2002, Johansson 2008). I suggest that gender shift in narratives is not nominalization, but instead occurs when a root that is normally licensed under an inanimate *n* is licensed under an animate *n*. There are several reasons to think this is the case. First, semantically, it seems contradictory, if not impossible, to generate an interpretation where a root combines with a *n* interpreted as inanimate, and then the resulting *n*P combines with a *n* interpreted as animate. Secondly, the behavior of shifted nouns in Cree (Goddard 2002, Johansson 2008) is reminiscent of hybrid nouns (Corbett 1991: ch. 8), which are not nominalized. Finally, roots which are capable of being licensed under more than one *n* are common in many Algonquian languages (Goddard 2002: 214), e.g. Fox *aseni* 'stone' is inanimate and *asenya* 'stone used in sweat lodge' is animate. Since these narrative gender shifts are most likely not nominalizations, I set them aside.

Thus, the *n* in (31)b is also used to nominalize in Algonquian.

Finally, even the *n* with an uninterpretable animate feature can nominalize, resulting in a nominalization that triggers animate agreement but may denote an inanimate entity. However, to see how this nominalization works, more background is required. Consider the nominal pairs in (35) from Fox (Central Algonquian); recall from Chapter 6 that Fox marks animacy/number via nominal suffixes, -*i* for inanimate singular and -*a* for animate singular.

(35)   **Fox collectives and singulatives**
a. zhooniyaah-i   'silver, money-INANIM'   zhooniyaah-a   'a coin, a bill-ANIM'
b. miichipeh-i   'game-INANIM'   miichipeh-a   'a game animal-ANIM'
c. owiiyaas-i   'meat, flesh-INANIM'   owiiyaas-a   'a piece of meat-ANIM'
d. owiinenw-i   'fat (generic)-INANIM'   owiinenw-a   'a piece of fat-ANIM'
e. anakehkw-i   'bark-INANIM'   anakehkw-a   'a piece of bark-ANIM'
f. mazhkochiis-a 'beans, a bean-ANIM'   mazhkochiiseeh-a 'a small amount of beans,
(Goddard 2002: 213)[189]   a single bean-ANIM'

The nouns in the left-hand column are collectives or mass nouns, whereas those in the right-hand column have a simple unit reading ((35)abf) or a unit of measure reading ((35)cde). Mathieu (2012) analyzes the nouns in the right-hand column (as well as similar nouns in Ojibwe) as singulatives, derived from the collective or mass nouns on the left.[190] Singulative morphology creates an individual from a collective/mass noun, and it is attested in Breton, various dialects of Arabic, and a range of other languages (see Mathieu 2012 for a cross-linguistic overview). The singulatives can be pluralized, e.g. *zhooniyaaha-ki* 'coin/bill-ANIM' 'coins, bills, money' (Mathieu 2012: 664).

For present purposes, the most important facts about the singulatives are that they are denominal nominalizations (nouns derived from collective/mass nouns) and all have uninterpretable animate gender. It is clear that they have uninterpretable animate gender because they all have an animate suffix, despite the fact that almost all of them denote inanimate entities. I propose therefore that the singulative is derived by adding a *n* with semantic features corresponding to a singulative reading and an uninterpretable animate gender feature to a collective/mass *n*P. I show this schematically in (36) to avoid making morphological commitments about Ojibwe roots.[191]

---

[189] Although the data is from Goddard (2002), the transcription follows Mathieu (2012).

[190] Mathieu (2012) does not treat (35)g, perhaps because the distinction between the collective reading and the singulative reading is not as sharp. Nevertheless, I include it here to show that singulatives are not necessarily associated with "gender shift," i.e. an animate collective can be turned into a singulative and the resulting noun is (still) animate. Cf. putative gender polarity in Somali in Ch. 8.

[191] One key question that (36) raises is why the lower *n* is not morphologically realized (this question is also relevant to Mathieu (2012), although the analysis there is different). If the singulative *zhooniyaha* 'a coin, a bill' is derived from an inanimate collective like *zhooniyaahi* 'money,' why is the -*i* suffix that indicates gender not retained? The answer, I believe, lies in the fact that the Fox suffixes -*a* and -*i* are

(36)

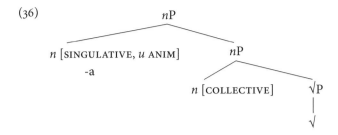

Consequently, the Algonquian language Fox has nominalizations that are formed via the *n* with an uninterpretable animate feature.

However, Mathieu (2012) proposes that the singulative is not formed via a denominal nominalization, but by adding a divider head (DIV) to a *n*P (see Borer 2005 on DIV). This analysis is shown in (37) for *zhooniyaha* 'a coin, a bill.'

(37)

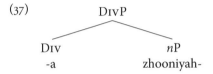

The DIV head is the source of the singulative reading, and Mathieu (2012) also has it encode a gender shift. Nevertheless, it is worth noting that gender shift is not obligatory in the singulative in Fox (see (35)g); I submit that the generalization that singulatives are always animate is encoded by the head that has singulative features also having an uninterpretable animate feature.

The key question is, though: what is the head that has the singulative reading? Several facts point towards it being a flavor of *n* (cf. Acquaviva 2008 on Breton for additional argumentation along these lines). The singulative nouns in a particular language often all have the same gender. They are all animate in Fox and Ojibwe, they are all feminine in Breton (Acquaviva 2008: 243), and they are all feminine in Iraqi Arabic (Erwin 1963: 166). They often cause the gender of a nominal to change, but gender shift is not required (see (35)g for Fox, Erwin 1963: 174 for Iraqi Arabic). Singulative nouns are generally considered to be part of a language's number system, and they are included in Corbett's (2000) typological survey of number. Finally, singulatives can be choosy about which collective nouns they attach to (e.g. they do not attach all collective nouns in Classical Arabic; Greenberg 1972: 20).

sensitive to both gender and number features. Recall that Fox has a four-way paradigm for nominal suffixes: singular animate (*-a*), singular inanimate (*-i*), plural animate (*-aki*), and plural inanimate (*-ani*). It may be that these suffixes are not realizations of *n*, but gender/number portmanteau morphemes that result from e.g. Fusion of *n* with Num. The topmost *n* is closest to Num, and thus locality might dictate that Num must be sensitive to or fuse with only the topmost *n*. This would result in only one gender/number marker for nouns like (36), which would reflect the gender of the topmost *n*, i.e. animate gender.

In all these respects, the singulative bears a strong resemblance to the Somali plural (Chapter 8). Each plural *n* in Somali is associated with a particular gender, and that gender ends up being the gender of the nominal as a whole. The Somali plural often (but not always) "shifts" the gender of the *n*P base it attaches to but not always. The Somali plurals are of course part of the number system. I also showed that the Somali plurals have selectional restrictions, i.e. some plurals only attach to certain nouns. This is highly reminiscent of how singulatives only attach to certain types of collectives. The Somali plurals are best analyzed as formed via a *n* attaching to a *n*P (see Chapter 8 for argumentation), so I submit that the singulatives have the same structure: a *n* attaching to a *n*P, as in (36).[192]

One final indication that singulatives are formed via *n* is that, in many languages, a singulative reading for a noun can also be formed by diminutivization (Mathieu 2012). For example, in Ojibwe, forming the diminutive of a mass noun results in a simple unit reading, as shown in (36).

(38)   **Ojibwe diminutives/singulatives**

a.	mtig	'wood/forest'	f.	mtigoons	'stick'
b.	mkwam	'ice'	g.	mkwamiins	'icicle'
c.	zhoonya	'money'	h.	zhoonyaans	'coin'
d.	ziisbaakwad	'sugar'	i.	ziisbaakdoons	'candy'
e.	mshkiki	'medicine'	j.	mshkikiins	'pill'	(Mathieu 2012: 675)

Insofar as diminutives are formed via *n* (see above as well as Chapter 10), this is further evidence that it is a *n* that carries singulative features generally. In cases like (38), the singulative feature is also packaged with a diminutive feature on *n*. In cases like (35), it is packaged with a gender feature. If *n* is not involved, it must simply be stipulated that DIV can affect gender and also be realized as a diminutive. However, if singulatives are formed via *n*, then their ability to be expressed via diminutives or via gender is unsurprising.

Overall, then, there is evidence from Algonquian languages for all the proposed animacy *n*s also being used to nominalize, just like all the proposed biological gender *n*s. I also argued that singulative nouns are formed via *n* attaching to a collective noun, and are therefore naturally associated with a particular gender and with diminutivization.

9.3.4 *Interim summary*

In this section, I have explored the predictions of the idea that the nominalizing *n* has gender. I showed that the Romanian nominalization which lacks *n* triggers default gender agreement, as predicted since it lacks gender features. I also showed how a *n*

---

[192] One minor drawback of this approach is that it forces there to be two heads in the syntactic structure with dividing properties: DIV for regular plurals (assuming Borer 2005) and a *n* [SINGULATIVE].

approach to gender predicts that a nominalization can have a single gender but multiple exponents, and showed how this is attested in French deadjectival nominalization and how it is problematic for a lexicalist approach to gender. Finally, I turned to Algonquian languages, with animacy-based gender systems, and demonstrated how each type of *n* that I proposed for Algonquian languages in Chapter 6 is capable of nominalizing. Overall, then, the predictions of a *n* approach to gender and nominalizations are borne out. In the next section, I discuss a few potential problems for the analysis before concluding.

9.4 Two problems (and their solutions)

Here, I identify and address two potential problems for a gendered *n* approach to nominalizations. The first problem concerns nominalizations where the nominalizer and the gender feature are (putatively) exponed as separate Vocabulary Items. If *n* both nominalizes and has gender features, it is *a priori* unexpected to expone this single morphosyntactic head as multiple Vocabulary Items. The second problem concerns the same nominalizer having multiple genders; under a DM approach, this would mean there would be multiple homophonous, synonymous *n*s in the syntax that differ only in their gender features (the inverse of the problem for lexicalism discussed in Section 9.3.2). In this section, I show how both of these problems shrink under closer scrutiny, and I conclude that a gendered *n* approach to nominalizations is viable.

9.4.1 *Gender features exponed separately?*

Certain languages contain nominalizations that seem to be morphologically decomposable into one Vocabulary Item that expresses nominalization, and another VI that expones gender. Examples from Spanish, German, and Amharic are given in (39)–(41).

(39) **Spanish abstract denominal nominalization (glossing to be changed)**
      el   alcohol-**ism**-o
      the.MS   alcohol-NMLZ-M
      'the alcoholism'   (Lang 1990: 135)

(40) **Amharic gentilic nominalization (glossing to be changed)**
      a. ityop'p'iy-awi   b. ityop'p'iy-**awi-t**
         Ethiopia-NMLZ   Ethiopia-NMLZ-F
         'Ethiopian man'   'Ethiopian woman'

(41) **German agentive deverbal nominalization**
      a. Lehr-er   b. Lehr-**er-in**
         teach-NMLZ   teach-NMLZ-FEM
         'male teacher'   'female teacher'

The idea is that the suffixes *-o, -t,* and *-in* express gender separately from the nominalizing suffixes *-ism, -awi,* and *-er.* All things being equal, this is unexpected for a gendered *n* approach to nominalization. In an ideal world, the nominalizing feature and the gender feature would always be on the same head.

However, I submit that there are alternative explanations for each of the cases. First, the morphological analysis inherent in the glossing in (39) and (40) is incorrect. I show below that, in Spanish, the "masculine" suffix is not a masculine suffix, and in Amharic, the "nominalizer" suffix is not a nominalizer. For the German data, there is evidence that both *-er* and *-in* are nominalizers, and that *-in* is a feminine suffix. Therefore, I argue that in German there are two stacked *ns*: one is *-er,* and one is *-in.*

Consider again the Spanish data in (39). The abstract denominal suffix *-ismo* seems to be decomposable into a nominalizer *-ism* and a "masculine" suffix *-o.* However, the "masculine" is in quotes because, as shown in Chapter 6, there is widespread consensus that Spanish *-o* is a theme vowel/declension class marker, not a gender marker (see e.g. Harris 1991 and many others). Gender is related to declension class in Spanish, but they are not the same phenomenon, and they are not realized by the same exponents. In Chapter 10, I develop a DM analysis of Spanish declension class that formalizes the relationship between gender, declension class, and theme vowel (gender influences the choice of declension class), but keeps them on separate nodes (*n* and Theme). Overall, then the accurate gloss of (39) is in (42), where *-o* is a theme vowel.

(42)   **Spanish abstract denominal nominalization (correct glossing)**
        el   alcohol-**ism-o**
        the.MS   alcohol-NMLZ-TV
        'the alcoholism'   (Lang 1990: 135)

In general, it will be necessary for a given language to determine whether a "separate" gender morpheme is truly an exponent of gender or whether it is a theme vowel/declension class marker.

Turning now to the Amharic data in (40), the suffix *-awi* is glossed as a nominalizer. However, there is evidence that it is instead an adjectivalizing head *a* (as was assumed in Chapter 3 and above, where this data is also discussed). The suffix *-awi* is productively used in Amharic to convert nouns to adjectives (Leslau 1995: 240, Fulass 1966: 114–15, Hartmann 1980: 243–4).

(43)   a. lìbb   lìbb-awi
           'heart'   'intelligent, sincere'

        b. mìdr   mìdr-awi
           'earth'   'earthly'

    c. mänfäs   mänfäs-awi
      'spirit'   'spiritual'

    d. ïlät   ïlät-awi
      'day'   'daily'

    e. hawarya   hawary-awi
      'apostle'   'apostolic'   (Leslau 1995: 240)

In fact, words like *ityop'p'ïyawi* 'Ethiopian' and *amerikawi* 'American' are not only nominals, but also adjectives denoting the property of being from or of a region (these words also do double duty in English: *I met an Ethiopian, I met an Ethiopian woman*).

(44)   afrik-awi-t-wa   agär   Burkina Faso
       Africa-awi-FEM-DEF.F country Burkina Faso
       'the African country Burkina Faso'   (Walta mes22a5)

(45)   ityop'p'ïy-awi-w   atlet   Täsfaye Jifar
       Ethiopia-awi-DEF.M athlete Tesfaye Jifar
       'the Ethiopian athlete Tesfaye Jifar'   (Walta tah23a8)

(46)   and ertr-awi   mïhur
       an Eritrea-awi   scholar
       'an Eritrean scholar'   (Walta mes22a3)

Therefore, I propose that *-awi* is always the realization of an *a* that selects an *n*P complement. In (40)b, the suffix *-it* is thus both a nominalizer and the home of the gender feature (there is a null suffix that nominalizes and has a [−FEM] feature in (40)a).

(47)   = *ityop'p'ïyawit* 'Ethiopian (woman)'

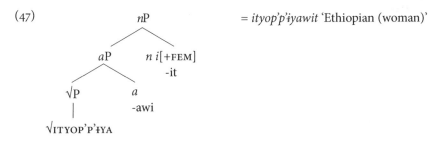

Therefore, the Amharic data behaves as predicted: a *n* both nominalizes and has the gender features.

    The German data in (41) is more of a challenge. There is no indication that declension class is relevant (to the best of my knowledge), and it is clear that the nominalizer *-er* is truly a nominalizer. I propose that in German there are two stacked *n*s, a lower *n* that is exponed as *-er*, and a higher *n* that nominalizes again the resulting nominal—turning it into a noun that has interpretable gender features. The higher *n* is exponed as *-in* when feminine, and null when masculine. The structure of (41)ab under this analysis is in (48) and (49), assuming that German agentive nominalization is formed by a *n* being added to a *v*P (or some other verbal projection; see Schäfer 2008).

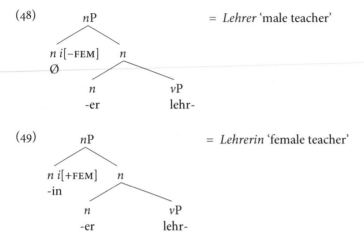

(48)   *n*P   = *Lehrer* 'male teacher'

    n i[−FEM] *n*
    Ø

      n   *v*P
     -er   lehr-

(49)   *n*P   = *Lehrerin* 'female teacher'

    n i[+FEM] *n*
    -in

      n   *v*P
     -er   lehr-

Support for this approach comes from the fact that the female suffix *-in* and the male suffix *-Ø* are used to indicate female and male gender respectively with root-derived nouns (on *-in* in particular; see the list in e.g. Plank 2012).

(50)   **German female *-in* and male *-Ø* nominalize roots**
    a. der Löwe 'the.MS lion'   b. die Löw-in 'the.FS lion-ess'
    c. der Fuchs 'the.MS fox'   d. die Füchs-in 'the.FS female fox'
    e. der Arzt 'the.MS doctor'   f. die Ärzt-in 'the.FS female doctor'   (Durrell 2011)

When (50)ace are interpreted as referring to male entities, they must contain a *n* [−FEM]. However, there is no phonological indication of it in these nouns—it must be null. In (50)bdf, the *-in* suffix conveys female natural gender. In German, therefore, the pre-syntactic lexicon contains the feature bundles *n i*[+FEM], usually realized as *-in* and *n i*[−FEM] usually realized as *-Ø*. I submit that the two *n*s are productively used to create female-denoting and male-denoting nominalizations of roots ((50)) and of *n*Ps ((48) and (49)).

Moreover, the suffix *-er* is used in German to form instruments, which lack natural gender and are always masculine (it is unclear whether these are root-derived or *v*P-derived).

(51)   **German masculine *-er* forms an inanimate noun**
    a. bohren 'to drill'   b. der Bohr-er 'the.MS drill'
    c. empfangen 'to receive'   d. der Empfäng-er 'the.MS receiver'
    e. Staub saugen 'to suck up dust' f. der Staubsaug-er 'the.MS vacuum cleaner'

                                        (Durrell 2011)

Thus, there is independent evidence for each stacked *n* in (48) and (49): *-er* is generally used to nominalize (a root or a phrase) and forms a masculine noun with uninterpretable gender, a null suffix indicates male gender, and *-in* is used to form a female-denoting noun.

I suggest that stacking is enforced in German because the agentive suffix *-er* always has an uninterpretable masculine feature, as it does when it is used as the instrumental suffix in (51). If we assume that *ns* cannot contain multiple gender features, then the grammar will be forced to add another *n* in order to convey the natural gender of a human agent. Indeed, the *ns* added are exactly what would be expected: the all-purpose male *n* which is null, and the all-purpose female *n* which is *-in*.

Overall, then, I have argued that all of these putative cases of decomposition have plausible alternative explanations. The Spanish "masculine" suffix is in fact a declension class marker, the Amharic "nominalizing" suffix is in fact an adjectivalizing suffix, and the German data contains two *ns*—one which has the agentive reading and has an obligatory uninterpretable masculine feature, and another which adds a natural gender feature (see Chapter 10 on how the resulting nominalization is predicted to have the gender of the highest *n*). Naturally, it remains to be seen whether all cases of apparent decomposition can be reanalyzed in one of these ways. However, it looks promising that such cases will prove not to be seriously challenging to a *n* approach to gender.

9.4.2 *Same nominalization, different genders?*

In Section 9.3.2, we saw a single type of nominalization (French deadjectival nominalization) that always has the same gender (feminine) regardless of how it is exponed (*-esse, -ité*, etc.). Following Beard (1990), I argued that this configuration of facts supports a DM approach to gender and nominalizations. In this section, I consider some cases of a single type of nominalization that has two different genders, which initially raises questions for the idea that nominalizations are always associated with one particular gender. Such cases would require two *ns* in the pre-syntactic lexicon, one for each gender associated with the nominalization, and this may seem suspicious since the *ns* are otherwise synonymous and homophonous. However, I submit that in such cases, the two different genders are associated with different properties of the nominalization, providing evidence that each gender in fact corresponds to a different *n* in the syntax. I present support for this analysis below from Russian deverbal nominalization and from human-denoting nominalizations in Amharic and Spanish. Although it is not possible to survey all such cases, the fact that several clear-cut instances are amenable to this analysis bodes well for a DM approach.

In Russian, the suffix *-k* is found in deverbal eventive nominalizations with feminine gender ((52)a) and with masculine gender ((52)b). I retain the glossing from Markovskaya (2012), but I assume *-a* and *-o* are declension class markers.

(52) **Russian deverbal activity(= eventive) nominalizations**
  a. žar-k-a   grib-ov
      fry-NMLZ-F   mushroom-PL.GEN
      'an act of frying mushrooms'

  b. pin-o-k   (*golov-y)
      kick-o-NMLZ.M   head-GEN
      'a kick'

(Markovskaya 2012)

Markovskaya (2012) observes that this is the same kind of nominalization in both (52) a and (52)b (eventive deverbal), and analyzes both as a *n* attaching to a verbal projection. Therefore, under the approach I have sketched, there would be two synonymous *n*s in the pre-syntactic lexicon: one with an uninterpretable feminine feature, and one with an uninterpretable masculine feature (assuming Russian has a gender system similar to German, Lavukaleve, etc.). They would both be realized as -*k* at Vocabulary Insertion.

However, Markovskaya discovered a correlation between the gender of the nominalization and the argument structure of the verb that it nominalizes. Verbs with internal arguments are nominalized with feminine gender (like 'fry' in (52)a), whereas unergatives are nominalized with masculine gender (like 'kick' in (52)b). If argument structure differences are captured via different features on functional projections (e.g. on *v*—see e.g. Folli and Harley 2005 et seq.), the feminine *n* and the masculine *n* select for different verbal projections. Thus, they are different *n*s in the syntax since they have different selectional features, and it is no longer problematic that they have different gender features as well.

Nominalizations that form human-denoting nouns sometimes use one exponent for both male and female. However, the male-denoting nouns trigger masculine gender, whereas the female-denoting nouns trigger feminine gender. For example, in the Amharic data in (53), the nominalizer is -*ä̈ñña* (the -*t* is epenthetic), and (as shown by determiner agreement) the resulting noun is masculine when it denotes a male and feminine when the noun denotes a female.

(53) **Amharic agentive deverbal nominalizations**
  a. särra-täñña-w   b. yä-bet   särra-täñña-wa
      work-NMLZ-DEF.M   of-house work-NMLZ-DEF.F
      'the male worker' (Fulass 1966: 88)   'the female house worker (= maid)'[193]

---

[193] Addis Admass News, http://www.addisadmassnews.com/index.php?option=com_k2&view=item& id=12789:%E1%8B%A8%E1%89%A4%E1%89%B5-%E1%88%B0%E1%88%AB%E1%89%B0%E1%8A%9B% E1%8B%8B-%E1%8A%A84%E1%8A%9B-%E1%8D%8E%E1%89%85-%E1%8B%88%E1%8B%B0%E1%89% 80%E1%89%BD%E1%8D%A4%E1%8A%A0%E1%88%B0%E1%88%AA%E1%8B%8B-%E1%89%B3%E1% 88%B5%E1%88%A8%E1%89%BD&Itemid=180

In Spanish, the nominalizer is *-ista*, and again the determiner is masculine or feminine depending on whether the noun is male-denoting or female-denoting.

(54) **Spanish denominal nominalization**

    a. el   art-ista   b. la   art-ista

      the.MS art-NMLZ   the.FS art-NMLZ

      'the male artist'   'the female artist'   (Butt and Benjamin 2011: 3)

In these cases, even though only one exponent is used, it is not a case of synonymous *n*s. The *n*s in question differ in their interpretable gender features: one has an interpretable male feature, whereas the other has an interpretable female feature. Thus, there are two *n*s in the presyntactic lexicon, as shown in (55). I use the feature [AGT] to stand for the agentive meaning of these nominalizations.

(55)   a. *n*   b. *n*

      i [−FEM]   *i* [+FEM]

      [AGT]   [AGT]

These two *n*s are realized by the same Vocabulary Item (*-äñña* in Amharic, *-ista* in Spanish) and that VI is underspecified for gender features. This is shown for Amharic in (56).

(56) *n*, [AGT] ↔ *-äñña*

Regardless of which *n* from (55) is chosen, the VI in (56) will be inserted.[194]

It is arbitrary whether a gender contrast across *n*s is maintained in Vocabulary Items, or collapsed via underspecification. This is particularly clear in Amharic, where the gentilic deadjectival nominalization (in (57), repeated from (8)) has similar underlying *n*s to (55) but two Vocabulary Items.

(57) **Amharic gentilic deadjectival nominalization**

    a. ityop'p'ɨy-awi-Ø   b. ityop'p'ɨy-aw-it

      Ethiopia-ADJ-NMLZ.M   Ethiopian-ADJ-NMLZ.F

      'Ethiopian man'   'Ethiopian woman'

(57)a and (57)b are formed via different *n*s—both with gentilic meaning, but one with an interpretable male feature and one with an interpretable female feature.

---

[194] I assume that no other VIs have an [AGT] feature and a *n* category feature. The VI in (56) might tie the competition for insertion at (55)b since there is a VI that would match the *n* and [+FEM] features and most likely does not have any other features: the suffix *-it*. However, I assume that in such cases a hierarchy of features is invoked (see e.g. Harley 1994, Noyer 1997: lxxv, Harley and Noyer 1999). The individual features of the VIs are inspected with reference to an independently motivated feature hierarchy, and the VI that uniquely has the feature highest on the hierarchy (or which has the fewest nodes in the hierarchy) "wins" and is inserted. In all the feature hierarchy approaches, gender features are ranked very low, and thus the VI exponing the agentive feature wins the competition.

They are realized by two distinct VIs (null for male, *-it* for female), i.e. the VIs are not underspecified for gender.

Overall, then, all the putative cases of two synonymous *n*s having different genders have turned out to be cases of two *n*s with different features—different either in terms of selection or in terms of natural gender. It is plausible that all such cases will be capable of being differentiated along these lines, thus rendering them less problematic for a DM approach to gender and nominalizations. This remains to be confirmed, especially for certain Algonquian nominalizations (see e.g. Wiltschko 2012), but the signs are promising for the DM approach.

9.5 Conclusion

Overall in this chapter, we have seen that the *n* that nominalizes phrases carries gender features just like the *n* that combines with roots to form non-derived nouns. I showed how three predictions made by this approach are borne out (Section 9.3), and how two putative counterexamples have viable alternative explanations (Section 9.4). The findings here therefore provide broad support for an analysis where gender features are always on *n*.

10

The highest gender wins and the interaction of gender and declension class

10.1 Introduction

This chapter has two goals, both related to exploring the implications of having gender features located specifically on n. First, in Section 10.2, I investigate nominals that contain multiple, stacked ns, i.e. multiple gender features. I show how the highest n determines the agreeing gender of the nominal, and develop an explanation of this fact based on independently-motivated assumptions about morphosyntactic cyclicity. One of the most common scenarios in which a nominal has two gender features is when it is diminutivized, yet some diminutive nouns retain the gender of their base noun (e.g. in Spanish). In Section 10.3, I show how this apparent counterexample to the "highest gender wins" generalization receives a straightforward explanation given current approaches to diminutive morphosyntax.

The second goal of the chapter is to briefly consider declension class, which is often inserted post-syntactically at/near n in the Distributed Morphology literature. In Section 10.4, I demonstrate that declension class/pattern is not isomorphic with gender, but that gender can affect the choice of declension class—as predicted if it is adjoined to n and gender is on n. I develop a case study of declension class in Spanish that articulates the relationship between gender and declension class in this approach. Section 10.5 concludes.

10.2 May the highest gender win: gender and multiple ns

The fact that gender features are on n, and that nominalizations are formed via n, allows for the generation of structures like (1).

The Morphosyntax of Gender. First Edition. Ruth Kramer.
© Ruth Kramer 2015. Published 2015 by Oxford University Press.

(1)

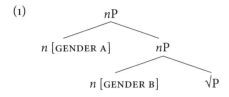

(1) is a denominal derived noun. The base noun has Gender B, whereas the nominalizing *n* has Gender A. Is Gender B or Gender A the agreeing gender of the nominal, i.e. the gender shown by elements that agree with (1)?

In this section, I provide an answer to this question, and then propose an explanation for the answer. As may be expected from the data considered in Chapter 9, Gender A is always the agreeing gender, i.e. the gender of the highest *n* is the gender that is agreed with (cf. Kramer 2009, Steriopolo and Wiltschko 2010, de Belder 2011b, Ott 2011), and I show this in Section 10.2.1. In Section 10.2.2, I consider two analyses of this effect, one based on the properties of agreement relations (de Belder 2011a), and one based on cyclicity. I show how data from Somali and Amharic indicate that the cyclicity analysis is correct. I conclude with some consideration of alternative explanations, and the implications of this result for morphosyntactic theory.

10.2.1 *The highest gender wins: data*

In principle, either Gender A or Gender B could "win" and be the gender used for agreement purposes with (1). In practice, Gender A is always the winner, to the best of my knowledge. In this section, I first review relevant cases of (1) that have already been analyzed within this book—from Somali, German, Serbian-Croatian, and Fox. Then, I present fresh data from the language that informed the first several chapters of this book—Amharic—and show how it provides additional support from the highest gender winning. I wrap up by considering the possible gender features and possible morphophonological realization of the stacked *n*s, drawing on further data from German and other languages.

In all the cases of (1) that have come up so far, the highest gender has been the agreeing gender of the nominal. The relevant data include plural formation in Somali (Chapter 8) and denominal noun formation in Serbian-Croatian, German, and Fox (Chapter 9). In Chapter 8, I argued that Somali plurality is expressed via one of a set of *n*s where the *n*s can differ in gender features and/or selectional features. The plural *n*s are exponed via a variety of different pluralization strategies (i.e. Vocabulary Items). Recall that the plural, feminine *n* is exponed as the *o*-plural in the context of certain roots. One such root is *ínan* 'boy, son' and (2) shows the structure of *inammó* 'sons' (RED stands for reduplicant).

(2)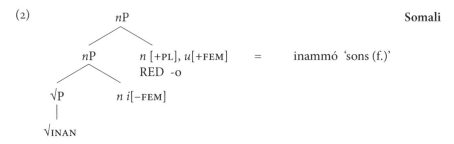

As in (1), there is one *n*P stacked on top of another. The lower *n*P has the masculine gender feature [–FEM], which is why the nominal is interpreted as male-referring. However, the upper *n*P has the feminine gender feature, and the gender of the resulting nominal is feminine, i.e. the gender of the upper *n* (Gender A in (1)).

In Chapter 9, I presented a very similar case from Serbian-Croatian.

(3) a. ova   pametna   devojka   **Serbian-Croatian**
        this.FS smart.FS   girl

     b. ovaj   pametni   devojčurak
        this.MS smart.MS   girl.DIM   (Wechsler and Zlatić 2003: 64)

In (3)b, the diminutive nominal *devojčurak* 'girl' triggers masculine agreement on the demonstrative and adjective, despite being interpreted as female. Accordingly, I proposed the structure in (4) where a diminutive *n* with uninterpretable masculine gender combines with the [+FEM] female-denoting *n*P.

(4)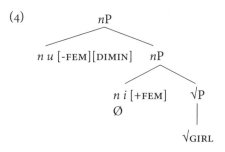

The highest gender is the agreeing gender, although the gender on the lower *n* is still present because it is interpreted. It is common that the gender feature on a diminutive morpheme determines the gender of the nominal, across all types of gender (e.g. feminine: Amharic, neuter: German and Yiddish, masculine: Serbian-Croatian). All these cases are probably a diminutive *n* with a gender feature combining with a *n*P. However, not all diminutives behave this way—for example, in Spanish, the diminutive does not change the gender of the noun. I sketch out an explanation for this difference in behavior in Section 10.3.

In Section 9.2.2, there was an example of abstract denominal nominalization from German via the suffix -*schaft*. Some of the data are repeated in (5).

(5) **German abstract denominal nominalization**
　　a. die Studenten-schaft　'the.FS student body'
　　b. die Freund-schaft　'the.FS friend-ship'　　　　　　(Durrell 2014: 479)
　　c. die Lehrer-schaft　'the.FS faculty'

The noun *Lehrer* 'teacher' is formed by a *n* being added to a *v*P (or some other verbal projection; see Schäfer 2008 and Chapter 9, Section 9.4.1). This *n* is phonologically overt, i.e. the suffix -*er*. Therefore, the suffix -*schaft*, itself a *n*, stacks on top of -*er*, thus creating another instantiation of (1). This is shown in (6).

(6)　　　　　　　　　　　　　　　　　　　　　　　　　　　　　**German**

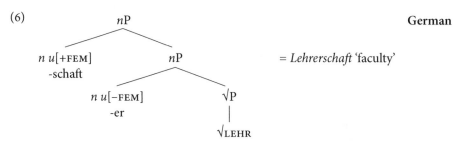

　　　　　　　　　　　　　　　　　　　　　= *Lehrerschaft* 'faculty'

As per Chapter 9, Section 9.4.1, I assume that *Lehrer* is formed via an uninterpretable masculine *n*. However, the resulting nominal with -*schaft* is feminine, as shown by the agreement on the definite determiner in (5)c. Therefore, it is the gender on the highest *n* that is the agreeing gender. In fact, this effect is even more widespread: in German, it is widely recognized that the gender of the nominalizing suffix always is the agreeing gender (Köpcke 1982, Wiltschko 2012, and references therein).

　　Also in Chapter 9, I argued that singulatives in Fox are denominal nouns with stacked *n*'s. The schematic structure is in (7).

(7)　　　　　　　　　　　　　　　　　　　　　　　　　　　**Fox Singulative**

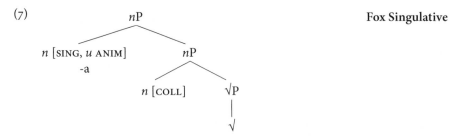

The gender of the singulative *n* is animate (uninterpretable) whereas the lower *n* collective for this root is inanimate (i.e. has no gender features). The gender that wins out is the higher gender, i.e. the resulting singulative is treated as animate, as shown by the animate singular suffix *-a*. It is worth asking what the gender would be if the situation were reversed, i.e. if a *n* with no gender features were higher than a *n* with gender features. I return to this important question in Section 10.2.2.

So far, then, all the instances of a structure like (1) that have been discovered while pursuing other questions have the highest gender being the resulting gender of the nominal. Chapters 2 and 3 focused on the gender system of Amharic, but do not contain any phenomena that would have a structure like (1). However, recall that Amharic has a productive diminutive indicated only by feminine gender. A masculine inanimate noun like *bet* 'house' ((8)) receives a diminutive interpretation ((9)) when it is used with feminine agreeing forms (e.g. the definite marker, verbal agreement; see e.g. Leslau 1995: 167–9).

(8) a. bet-u   Non-diminutive   **Amharic**
         house-DEF.M
         'the house'

     b. bet-wa   t-amïr-all-ätʃtʃ   Diminutive
         house-DEF.F   3FS-be.cute-AUX-3FS
         'The (adorable little) house is cute'

I analyzed the diminutive as a *n* with uninterpretable feminine gender added to a *n*P, so that the diminutive of *bet* would have the structure in (9).

(9)   *n*P   **Amharic**

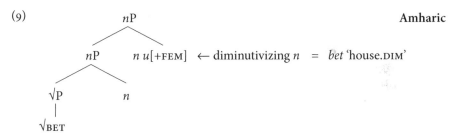

                  *n*P   *n* u[+FEM]   ← diminutivizing *n*   =   *bet* 'house.DIM'

          √P   *n*

          |
         √BET

Since *bet* is a masculine inanimate noun, it is analyzed as licensed under plain *n*. However, what if a root that is licensed under a *n* with gender features is diminutivized in Amharic?

Perhaps unsurprisingly at this point, the resulting nominal is feminine. This is shown in (10)b for the noun *bäre* 'ox,' licensed under *n* [–FEM]. The demonstrative is feminine even though *bäre* denotes a male animal (oxen are all male in Ethiopia) and triggers masculine agreement when not diminutivized ((10)a).

(10) a. yïh   bäre   Non-diminutive   **Amharic**
          this.M   ox
          'this ox'

b. yɨtʃtʃ   bäre   Diminutive
    this.F   ox
    'this (cute) ox' (Cohen 1970: 77)

The structure for *bäre* in (10)b is given in (11).

(11)   *n*P   **Amharic**

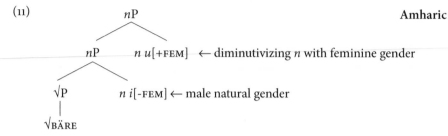

Thus, once again, the gender feature of the highest *n* is the gender of the resulting nominal.

The highest *n* determines the gender in more languages than just those treated in this book. Scatton (1984) observes that nominalizing morphemes in Bulgarian "carry their own inherent grammatical gender which supplants the gender of the base" (p. 247). De Belder (2011a: 262–4) demonstrates that nouns with multiple nominalizing suffixes in Dutch have the gender of the outermost, i.e. the highest *n*. Armoskaite (2014: 182) shows that Lithuanian nouns with multiple suffixes, where each suffix has its own gender, have the agreeing gender of the outermost suffix. Finally, Markovskaya (2012) characterizes Russian gender in nominalizations as regulated by the nominalizing affix involved, where each affix is associated with a specific gender. Overall, then, it is at the very least extremely common across several language families for the gender of the topmost *n* to be the agreeing gender. I know of no counterexamples to this claim (except for affective morphology like diminutives; see Section 10.3), and I therefore take the empirical hypothesis to be tentatively confirmed.

(12) **Highest Gender Hypothesis (first pass)**
      The gender of the highest *n* is the agreeing gender of the nominal.

Principles/hypotheses similar to (12) have been proposed previously in Kramer (2009), Steriopolo and Wiltschko (2010), de Belder (2011a), and Ott (2011). Kramer (2009) and Steriopolo and Wiltschko (2010) develop a generalization like (12) because they assume gender features can be in multiple locations in the DP for non-derived nouns (Kramer: root and *n*, Steriopolo and Wiltschko: root, *n* and D). I argue against these approaches to the location of gender features in Chapter 3, but retain their fundamental insight about the primacy of the highest gender feature. De Belder (2011a) proposes that (12) holds because of the nature of agreement relations, whereas Ott (2011) explains it in terms of percolation of the features of the highest head; I investigate both of these explanations in the following section.

Two final comments are necessary beforehand. First, in all of the data above, the lower *n* has natural gender and the higher *n* has uninterpretable arbitrary gender. However, neither condition is necessary for the highest gender to be the agreeing gender. Armoskaite (2014) analyzes Lithuanian denominal locative nouns as derived from deadjectival nouns; the deadjectival noun has a nominalizing suffix -*um* and masculine gender ((13)a), and the denominal locative noun is formed by changing the gender to feminine ((13)b).

(13)   **Lithuanian locative denominal nominalization**

    a. aišk-um-as   b. aišk-um-a

       clear-NMLZ-MS.NOM   clear-NMLZ-FS.NOM

       'clarity'   'a clear place'   (Armoskaite 2014: 174)

Armoskaite (2014) analyzes the structure of (13)b as having a lower masculine *n* realized as -*um* (that nominalizes *a*Ps), and a higher feminine *n* that is phonologically null (and nominalizes *n*Ps). Thus, Lithuanian presents an example where the lower *n* does not have natural gender.

German furnishes an example of a higher *n* having interpretable natural gender: female-denoting agentive deverbal nouns.

(14)   **German female agentive deverbal nominalization**

      a. die Lehr-er-in   'the.FS teach-er-FEM' = 'the female teacher'

      b. die Fahr-er-in   'the.FS drive-r-FEM' = 'the female driver'

      c. die Gärtn-er-in   'the.FS garden-er-FEM' = 'the female gardener'

      d. die Bettl-er-in   'the.FS begg-ar-FEM' = 'the female beggar'

            (Wiltschko 2012, Durrell 2011, Scholze-Stubenrecht and Sykes 1999)

Assuming that agentive deverbal nominalizations are word-derived (see e.g. Schäfer 2008 on German), then (14) has a sequence of two *n*s: lower masculine -*er* that creates an agentive nominalization (see Chapter 9), and higher -*in* that adds female natural gender. Therefore, this is a case of stacked *n*Ps where the highest *n* has interpretable, natural gender features and determines the gender of the whole nominal (the nouns in (14) trigger feminine agreement on the determiner).

The second issue to be discussed before moving on concerns the morphological realization of the stacked *n*s. In the majority of the data in this section, either (i) the higher *n* is overtly realized (e.g. Somali plurals; see (30)) or (ii) neither *n* is morphologically realized (e.g. Amharic diminutives, see (11)). However, again, these are not necessary conditions. In German denominal nominalization with -*schaft*, and deverbal nominalizations with -*er-in*, both *n*s were overtly morphologically realized; see (6) and (14). Both *n*s can also be realized morphologically in certain nominalizations in Lithuanian (Armoskaite 2014: 182) and Dutch (de Belder 2011a: 264). Finally, only the lower *n* is realized in Armoskaite's (2014) analysis of locative denominal nominalizations, shown in (13). Therefore, all possible combinations of null and overt stacked *n*s are attested.

10.2.2 A cyclicity explanation for the highest gender hypothesis

The investigation of gender features on nominalizing *n*s has led us to the hypothesis in (12): the gender of the highest *n* is the agreeing gender of the nominal.
However, many questions are still open. For example, recall that plain *n* nominalizes verbs in Lavukaleve (see Chapter 9), but plain *n* has no gender features, so it
is unclear how (12) applies to it. Most pressingly, (12) cries out for an explanation.
What grammatical mechanisms are such that the highest *n* is the one that is agreed
with?

   In this section, I investigate two possible explanations for (12); the deciding
argument between them is intimately connected to nominalizations with plain *n*.
Both explanations are based on the properties of agreement relations, i.e. determining which *n* can serve as the agreement controller. However, one analysis
focuses on hierarchical relations, whereas the other is based on cyclicity. They
make very similar predictions, except when it comes to nominalizations with plain
n. I show how Amharic and Somali plain *n* nominalizations (as well as plain *n*
nominalizations from German and Serbian-Croatian) confirm the predictions of a
cyclicity approach, and end with some discussion of the ramifications of the
findings.

   The schematic tree with which this section started is repeated in (15).

(15)

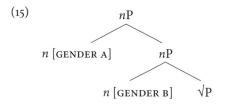

I argued that Gender A is always the agreeing gender in the nominal, and called this
the Highest Gender Hypothesis, repeated in (16).

(16)   **Highest Gender Hypothesis (first pass)**
       The gender of the highest *n* is the agreeing gender of the nominal.

One plausible explanation for the Highest Gender Hypothesis centers on the independently motivated locality properties of agreement relations, across different
formalizations of agreement. For example, in classic Minimalism (Chomsky 2000,
2001), the syntactic Agree relation holds between a probe and a goal: the probe
searches downwards into its c-command domain for a goal with an appropriate
feature, and enters into an Agree relation with the first, i.e. highest, goal that it
encounters. In a post-syntactic agreement approach like Bobaljik (2008), the highest
accessible agreement controller in a particular domain (e.g. the DP domain; de Belder
2011a) is the one that is agreed with. It is controversial whether DP-internal agreement is best analyzed via the same mechanisms as predicate agreement, but even in

approaches that use e.g. percolation for DP-internal agreement, it is the highest feature that must be percolated (see e.g. Ott 2011, Norris 2014: 135).

This area of significant consensus across theories of agreement offers an immediate explanation for the Highest Gender Hypothesis: the highest *n* is the one which is agreed with because agreement (or percolation) is sensitive to hierarchical structure and agreement relations are stated over higher controllers. De Belder (2011a) takes this approach in her discussion of gender and nominalizations. She adopts a post-syntactic approach to agreement, and shows how the highest gender-bearing head in Dutch is predicted to (and in fact does) serve as the agreement controller under this formalization of agreement. Ott (2011: 36) adopts a percolation perspective, explaining the neuter gender on German diminutives by stating that the diminutive hosting head is higher than the nominalizing head, and that the gender feature of the diminutive head percolates.

Even though a hierarchical structure explanation at first seems plausible, there is another way to explain the Highest Gender Hypothesis that centers on cyclicity. When taken together, three well-established assumptions about cyclicity predict that the highest *n* is the one whose gender is agreed with. The first of these assumptions is that *n* is a phase head, i.e. a head of a cyclic domain (see e.g. Marantz 2001: 6, Embick 2010: 51, Marvin 2002, 2013). The second is that phase heads trigger spell-out of any cyclic domains below them (or possibly their entire complement; see different formalizations of this effect in Chomsky 2001, Embick 2010, Marvin 2002, 2013). The last assumption is that previously spelled-out material is not accessible to later syntactic operations, also known as the Phase Impenetrability Condition (Chomsky 2001; see Marvin 2002, 2013 for implementation below the word level, Kramer 2010 for implementation at PF). These assumptions are summarized in (17).

(17)   **Three assumptions about cyclicity**
      a. *n* is a phase head, i.e. head of a cyclic domain.
      b. Phase heads trigger the spell-out of any cyclic domains that they c-command.
      c. Phase Impenetrability Condition.

Taking a look at (15) in the light of (17), it is clear that the *n*P with Gender A will trigger the spell-out of its complement, the lower *n*P, since that lower *n*P is a cyclic domain. The lower *n*P will then be inaccessible to later syntactic operations like the establishment of the Agree relation or feature percolation. This predicts that only the higher *n*P can be agreed with, since the lower *n*P will have been sent to PF before any agreement targets have even been merged. Even in a post-syntactic approach to agreement, a cyclicity analysis stands to explain the Highest Gender Hypothesis. In Kramer (2010), I argued that the Phase Impenetrability Condition holds at PF, i.e. that morphosyntactic material that has arrived at PF previously as a chunk, and been through PF operations, cannot subsequently be accessed by later PF operations, like agreement.

As the reader can confirm, a hierarchical structure analysis and a cyclicity analysis make almost the exact same set of predictions. However, there is one case in which they differ, shown schematically in (18) (for a head-final language). It is the case when a *n*P with a gender feature (feminine in this case) is nominalized by a plain *n*.

(18)

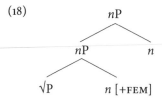

In a hierarchical structure analysis, any higher agreement target or probe has access to the lower, feminine *n*. This is because the plain *n* lacks gender features and thus is not a suitable goal (minimalist Agree relation) or controller (PF agreement) for a target/probe that is looking to agree in gender. In a percolation approach, it simply has no gender features to percolate. Thus, the hierarchical structure analysis predicts that the agreement relation will be established with the lower *n* and a nominal with the structure in (18) will have feminine agreeing gender.[195]

Under the cyclicity analysis, it is irrelevant that the higher *n* lacks gender features. The agreement relation or percolation mechanism will never have access to the lower *n* since it will have already been spelled out, so all gender agreement has to work with is the highest *n* no matter what features it has. Setting aside the details in order to keep from going too far afield, I assume that a situation similar to Preminger's (2011, 2014) failed agreement occurs, where the agreement operation must be triggered but fails because the potential probe lacks the relevant features. The probe then must be realized with the "default" gender at PF, since any other Vocabulary Item would have gender features with a specified value, i.e. the probe is exponed via the VI that lacks gender features (see Chapter 3 for a brief discussion of this issue in Amharic).

The cyclicity analysis predicts that a nominal with the structure in (18) will have the default gender. The predictions of both analyses are summed up in (19).

(19)   **Predictions for the gender of (18)**
    a. Hierarchical structure analysis: feminine
    b. Cyclicity analysis: default

---

[195] Ott (2011: 36) articulates this prediction and uses it to explain why, in some languages, diminutives determine the gender of the nominal whereas in others they do not. In languages where diminutives do not affect gender, the diminutive head lacks gender features and agreeing elements see only the gender features below. Since the hierarchical structure approach turns out not to be viable, I explain this difference in the gendered behavior of diminutives in a different way; see S. 10.3.

The task that remains now is to find instances of (18) and see what gender they are.

I focus first on instances of (18) in Amharic and Somali, where the default gender is masculine (see Chapter 2 for Amharic gender and Chapter 8 on Somali gender). Starting with Amharic, a structure like (18) is generated when a feminine nominal combines with the nominalizing suffix *-innät* '-hood.' The suffix *-innät* is a highly productive, abstract nominalizer (Fulass 1966: 79–83, Leslau 1995: 234–6). It attaches to *n*Ps as well as other categories; some examples of *-innät* as a denominal nominalizer are given in (20).

(20)   **Abstract denominal nominalization in Amharic with** *-innät*

a. bet   'house'   d. bet-innät   'the fact of being a house, house-hood'
b. wättaddär   'soldier'   e. wättaddär-innät   'soldiering, soldier-hood'
c. lik'   'scholar'   f. lik'-innät   'being a scholar, scholarship'

                                                     (Fulass 1966: 79–81)

It is relatively clear that the suffix *-innät* selects for an *x*P and not a root. All the words that *-innät* attaches to retain their morphophonology, including their pattern/template (encoded by their own particular *n/v/a*, following Arad 2005). Moreover, the derived word always has a regular meaning, i.e. *-innät* does not trigger any idiosyncratic interpretations of the root.

Recall that languages like Amharic have only four *n*s: male *n*, female *n*, plain *n*, and uninterpretable feminine *n*. It is clear that *-innät* is not the realization of a male or female *n*, since it forms abstract nouns. Additionally, when it attaches to a non-nominal category like an *a*P, the resulting nominal is masculine. In (21), the deadjectival noun *dägg-innät* 'kind-ness' triggers masculine agreement on the copular verb.

(21)   dägg-innät   hulgize   t'iru   **näw**
        kind-NMLZ   always   good   be.3MS
        'Kindness is always good.'   (Fulass 1966: 80)

Therefore, *-innät* is not the realization of the uninterpretable feminine *n* either. It must be the realization of a plain *n*.

With this in mind, we can then add *-innät* to a noun formed by a root and *n* [+FEM] , to ensure a [+FEM] feature on the lower *n* like in (18). The results are given in (22).

(22)   a. innat-innät   b. mist-innät   c. lam-innät
           mother-NMLZ   wife-NMLZ   COW-NMLZ
           'motherhood'   'the state of being a wife'   'the state of being a cow'

The *n*Ps *innat* 'mother,' *mist* 'wife,' and *lam* 'cow' are all licensed under the female *n*. Thus, the structure of (22)a is as in (23), a replica of (18).

(23)

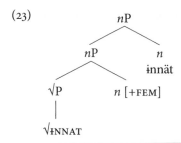

The last step is what gender agreement the nouns in (23) trigger. They trigger masculine agreement, as shown in (24)–(26).

(24)   ɨnnat-ɨnnät   käbbad   **näw**
         mother-NMLZ   difficult   **be.3MS**
         'Motherhood is difficult.'

(25)   mist-ɨnnät   käbbad   **näw**
         wife-NMLZ   difficult   **be.3MS**
         'Being a wife is difficult.'

(26)   lam-ɨnnät   käbbad   **näw**
         cow-NMLZ   difficult   **be.3MS**
         'Being a cow is difficult.'

Thus, the predictions of the cyclicity analysis (see (19)) are borne out: a *n*P with the structure in (18) has masculine, i.e. default, agreement in Amharic.

Somali provides another example of the structure in (18) triggering default, masculine agreement. Recall that Somali has a range of pluralization strategies that correspond in a complicated way to a smaller set of *n*s. The table that connects up pluralization strategies to *n*s is repeated from Chapter 8.

TABLE 10.1. **Analysis of the Somali plural**

Syntactic head	Selects for	Vocabulary Items/plural strategies
n_I [+PL], [+FEM]	M	• Broken-plural (root-specific) • Prosodic-plural (root-specific) • *o*-plural:feminine (root-specific)
n_{II} [+PL], [+FEM]	Ø	*aan*-plural (root-specific)
n_{III} [+PL], [+FEM]	*n* realized as *é*	*yaal*-plural
n_I [+PL]	M	Reduplication-plural (root-specific)
n_{II} [+PL]	Ø	*o*-plural:masculine: • Root-specific for masculine nouns • Remainder of feminine nouns not specified in *aan*-plural context
n_{III} [+PL]	*n* realized as *ó*	*oyin*-plural

The most crucial part of Table 10.1 for present purposes is the plural *n*s that lack gender features, i.e. the last three rows of the table. These are all plain *n*s that select for a *n*P, partially replicating (18). In particular, the n_{II}[+PL] has no gender features, yet it combines with feminine nouns to make an *o*-plural:masculine. An example of this type of pluralization is given in (27).

(27) **o-plural:masculine, from feminine noun (Somali)**
    a. náág-ta   'the woman (f.)'
    b. naag-ó   'women (m.)'
    c. naag-á-ha 'the women (m.)'   (Green et al. 2014a)

The structure of *naagó* 'women' is given in (28).

(28)   **Somali**

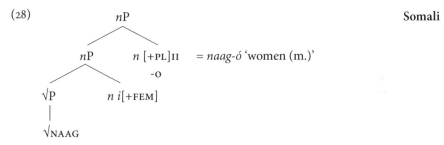

This is another instantiation of (18), with a plain *n* nominalizing a *n*P whose head has a [+FEM] feature. Like Amharic, the resulting noun is masculine, as shown by the masculine agreement on the determiner in (27)c.

Moreover, structures like (18) triggering default gender are not limited to languages spoken in the Horn of Africa. Some Germanic and Slavic languages have neuter denominal diminutives, as shown in (29) for German and (30) for Serbian-Croatian.

(29) **German denominal diminutives**
    a. die Karte   'the.FS card'   d. das Kärt-chen 'the.NS card-DIMIN'
    b. die Stadt   'the.FS town'   e. das Städt-chen 'the.NS town-DIMIN'
    c. die Flasche 'the.FS bottle'   f. das Fläsch-chen 'the.NS bottle-DIMIN'
                                    (Wiltschko and Steriopolo 2007, Durrell 2011)

(30) **Serbian-Croatian neuter diminutives**
    a. ova   pametna devojka
        this.FS   smart.FS   girl

    b. ovo   pametno devojče
        this.N   smart.NS   girl.DIM   (Wechsler and Zlatić 2003: 64)

The German nouns in (29) in the left-hand column are feminine inanimates, licensed under the uninterpretable feminine *n*. The diminutive suffix *-chen* is added to these nouns in the right-hand column, and the resulting nominal is neuter. Recall that plain *n* corresponds to neuter in three-gender languages structured like German. Therefore, the structure of (29)e is as in (31).

(31)

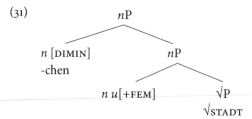

This is another instantiation of (18), and the resulting noun has neuter gender, thus confirming the cyclicity analysis. The Serbian-Croatian neuter diminutive makes the same point, albeit with a lower female *n*; still, the higher neuter diminutive *n* determines the agreeing gender of the resulting nominal.

Overall, then, the cyclicity analysis is supported, to the detriment of the hierarchical structure analysis.[196] I conclude with a re-statement of the Highest Gender Hypothesis that takes into account data with plain *n*s.

(32) **Highest Gender Hypothesis (final version)**
   a. Take the highest *n* (call it *n*-Alpha) in a DP which contains multiple *n*s.
   b. The gender agreement triggered by the *n*P headed by *n*-Alpha is the gender agreement triggered by the *n*P that would be formed by combining *n*-Alpha with a root and no further *n*s.

10.2.3 Conclusion and implications

I finish this section with a few observations on the implications of the cyclicity analysis. First of all, this result buttresses all of the assumptions about cyclicity on which it is built: the phase head status of categorizing heads, that phase heads trigger spell-out of lower cyclic domains, and the Phase Impenetrability Condition. Moreover, it provides specific support for all of these assumptions holding within words (as per Marantz 2001, Marvin 2002, 2013) and support for the theory of Distributed Morphology, within which many of the phases-within-words analyses have been couched.

An unexpected benefit of this result is that it prevents an otherwise unfortunate consequence of having gender features be on *n*. In Chapter 9 and this section, I have focused on nominalizations—nouns being formed from other categories. However,

---

[196] Two other relevant scenarios which there is not space to pursue here would decide between the analyses: a noun with inanimate gender derived from an animate noun in Algonquian, and a noun with feminine default gender derived from a male-denoting noun in Maa.

*n*Ps can themselves be the basis for forming verbs and adjectives, as shown schematically in (33) and (34).

(33)   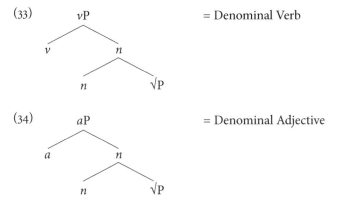   = Denominal Verb

The *n*s in (33) and (34) could potentially have gender features, but to the best of my knowledge, these features never affect the resulting verb or adjective (Stump 1993: 1–2). For example, denominal adjectives agree in gender with the noun they modify, not with the *n*P that they are formed from. Similarly, denominal verbs agree in gender with their arguments, not with the *n*P they are formed from. The cyclicity analysis offers an explanation for this. Once another categorizing head is added, the gender on *n* is no longer accessible for agreement relations. It is predicted to have no effect on gender agreement with the verbs or adjectives.

Finally, the cyclicity analysis leads to a much stronger (and therefore more interesting) prediction than was assumed in Chapter 9: denominal nominalizations **must** be gendered, not just that they *can* be gendered. There will never be a denominal nominalization that is formed solely by retaining the gender of the lower *n*P, because the gender of the lower *n*P is never accessible for agreement. I leave the confirmation of this prediction to future research on cross-linguistic nominalization.[197]

10.3 A diminutive digression

In this chapter, we have seen how diminutives in Amharic ((10)), German ((29)), and Serbian-Croatian ((30)) support (32) in that the gender of the diminutive *n* is the agreeing gender. Other languages where diminutives determine the agreeing gender

---

[197] Another interesting prediction that this analysis raises is that any agreement target that is merged between the two *n*s will show agreement with the lower gender feature. It is not immediately apparent what phrases would be merged in the middle of a derived nominal, but I leave this prediction open for confirmation/refutation.

include Dutch (Dressler and Barbaresi 1994: 104), Russian (in part; Wiltschko and Steriopolo 2007, Steriopolo 2008), Yiddish (Lowenstamm 2008), the Wollega dialect of Oromo (Clamons 1993), many (if not all) Bantu languages (Maho 1999: 88–9), and Santali (Austro-Asiatic (Munda); India; Nieuwenhuis 1985: 60).

However, not all diminutives behave this way; some languages contain diminutives that do not affect the agreeing gender of the nominal at all. For example, Spanish diminutives have the same gender as the base noun, i.e. they "preserve" or "retain" the gender of the nP from which the diminutive is formed (see e.g. Jaeggli 1980: 152, Eguren 2001: 75, Marrero et al. 2007: 156). In (35) a feminine noun remains feminine when diminutivized, and a masculine noun remains masculine.

(35)   Base noun   Diminutive
        a. la madre 'the.FS mother'   e. la madre-cita 'the.FS mother-DIM'
        b. la piedra 'the.FS stone'   f. la piedre-cita 'the.FS stone-DIM'
        c. el padre 'the.MS father'   g. el padre-cito 'the.MS father-DIM'
        d. el armario 'the.MS wardrobe'   h. el armar-ito 'the.MS wardrobe-DIM'

Other languages that preserve gender in diminutives include Judeo-Spanish (Bradley and Smith 2011: 249), Brazilian Portuguese (Bachrach and Wagner 2007: 4), Breton (Nieuwenhuis 1985: 305), and Czech (Fábregas 2010b: 22) (see also Stump 1993, who considers this to be a hallmark of evaluative/expressive morphology in general). This type of diminutive at first seems to be a counterexample to (32). Spanish diminutives would be denominal nouns whose gender is determined by the gender of the lower nP.

However, much recent research on diminutives (and on expressive/evaluative morphology generally) has built on this empirical difference to argue that diminutives are not all formed in the same way. Some diminutives are analyzed as n heads that take a nP complement, and these diminutives are predicted to affect gender (following (32)). However, other diminutives are analyzed as Dim(inutive) heads adjoined to some projection in the nominal phrase, and thus are not ns at all. Adjoined diminutives, therefore, are not predicted to affect gender, like the Spanish diminutives in (35). In this section, I review the recent literature on diminutives, and show how it allows for (32) to be upheld.[198]

---

[198] The discussion centers on diminutives for the sake of clarity, with a brief foray into Russian expressive suffixes in describing Steriopolo (2008). However, similar claims have been made about other types of expressive/evaluative morphology like augmentatives (see e.g. Stump 1993, Fortin 2011 for overviews of the key issues surrounding this type of morphology generally). There seems to be interesting cross-linguistic and intra-linguistic variation in the behavior of different kinds of expressive/evaluative morphology with respect to gender. For example, in Spanish (for at least some speakers), augmentatives do change the gender of the underlying noun (e.g. *el mujerón* 'the woman.AUG'). There is unfortunately not space to map out this variation here.

I start by focusing on results from Wiltschko (2006), Wiltschko and Steriopolo (2007), and Steriopolo (2008), since they show the contrast between *n* diminutives and adjoined diminutives most clearly. In these works, Wiltschko and Steriopolo use data primarily from German, Halkomelem, and Russian. In order to explain the similarity between diminutives and classifiers in German, Wiltschko (2006) proposes that diminutives are light nouns (*n*s) that take "full nouns" (=*n*Ps) as their complements. In Wiltschko and Steriopolo (2007), this analysis is taken up again, but in the context of cross-linguistic variation in the properties of diminutives. German diminutives are contrasted to Halkomelem diminutives; the two types of diminutives differ along several dimensions. German diminutives always have neuter gender ((29), repeated as (36)), and change mass nouns to count nouns ((37); cf. Ojibwe singulatives in Chapter 9).

(36) **German diminutives are neuter**
    a. die Karte 'the.FS card'   d. das Kärt-chen 'the.NS card-DIMIN'
    b. die Stadt 'the.FS town'   e. das Städt-chen 'the.NS town-DIMIN'
    c. die Flasche 'the.FS bottle'   f. das Fläsch-chen 'the.NS bottle-DIMIN'
                    (data from Wiltschko and Steriopolo 2007, Durrell 2011)

(37) **German diminutives change mass nouns to count nouns**
    a. viel   Brot   b. viele   Bröt-chen
       Q   bread   Q.PL   bread-DIM
       'much bread'   'many rolls'   (Wiltschko and Steriopolo 2007)

In contrast, Halkomelem diminutives do not affect the properties of the base at all. Moreover, they can attach to nouns, adjectives or verbs without changing the category of the base ((38)).

(38) **Halkomelem diminutives**
    a. N → N
       q'á:mi   – q'á-q'emi
       girl   DIM-girl
       'girl'   'small girl'

    b. V → V
       lhí:m   – lhi-lhi:m
       picking   DIM-picking
       'picking'   'picking a little bit'

    c. A → A
       p'eq'   – p'í-p'eq'
       white   DIM-white
       'white'   'a little white, whitish'   (Wiltschko and Steriopolo 2007)

These differences lead Wiltschko and Steriopolo to propose that German diminutives and Halkomelem diminutives have different structures. Specifically, they propose that the German diminutive is formed via a *n* selecting for a nominal complement (following Wiltschko 2006), whereas the Halkomelem diminutive is formed via a DIM head adjoining to a root. These structures are shown in (39).

(39)   **German Diminutive**   **Halkomelem Diminutive**

From the perspective of a *n* approach to gender, the German diminutive affects gender because it is a *n*, and the fact that the Halkomelem diminutive is not a *n* explains why it does not affect the properties of the base (it is not a categorizing head at all). Moreover, the fact that the Halkomelem diminutive attaches to a root allows for a *v, n,* or *a* to be merged above it, resulting in diminutive nouns, verbs, or adjectives.

Building on Bachrach and Wagner (2007), Steriopolo (2008) proposes three diagnostics for determining whether a particular expressive suffix is a head (like German) or an adjunct (like Halkomelem). Those diagnostics are given in (40).

(40)   **Diagnostics for head/adjunct status of expressive suffixes** (Steriopolo 2008: 64)
        Diagnostic I: Do expressive suffixes change syntactic category?
        Diagnostic II: Do expressive suffixes change grammatical gender?
        Diagnostic III: Do expressive suffixes change inflectional class?

If the answer to any diagnostic is yes, then it is evidence for head status. Steriopolo (2008) uses these diagnostics to argue that certain Russian expressive suffixes are heads, while others are adjuncts. For example, the expressive suffix *-in* always forms a noun with feminine gender ((41)), whereas diminutive suffixes do not ((42)).

(41)   **Russian expressive suffix *-in* enforces feminine gender**
        a. ovrág   b. ovráž-in-a
           ditch.NOM.S (MASC)   ditch-EXPR-NOM.S (FEM)
           'ditch'   'ditch (vulg)'

        c. jám-a   d. jám'-in-a
           pit-NOM.S (FEM)   pit-EXPR-NOM.SG (FEM)
           'pit'   'pit (vulg)'

        e. bolót-o   f. bolót'-in-a
           swamp-NOM.S (NEUT)   swamp-EXPR-NOM.S (FEM)
           'swamp'   'swamp (vulg)'   (Steriopolo 2008: 84)

(42)   **Russian diminutive suffixes do not affect gender**

    a. l'és   b. l'es-ók

       forest.NOM.S (MASC)   forest-DIM-NOM.S (MASC)

       'forest'   'forest (dim)'

    c. róšč'-a   d. róšč'-ic-a

       grove-NOM.S (FEM)   grove-DIM-NOM.S (FEM)

       'grove'   'grove (dim)'

    e. bolót-o   f. bolót'-c-e

       swamp-NOM.S   swamp-DIM-NOM.S

       (NEUT)   (NEUT)

       'swamp'   'swamp (dim)'   (Steriopolo 2008: 91–2)

Steriopolo ultimately argues that suffixes like (41) in Russian are *n*s that select for a *n*P or a root, whereas those in (42) are Expr(essive) heads that adjoin to *n*. However, regardless of where/how selection/adjunction happens, the correlation with gender is clear: a suffix that is a *n* affects gender, whereas a suffix that is not has no effect.

Further work has supported the fundamental structural difference between *n* diminutives which affect gender and all other diminutives which do not. Brazilian Portuguese diminutives do not affect gender, and Bachrach and Wagner (2007) analyze them as DIM heads adjoined to *n* or Num. We saw in (35) that Spanish diminutives do not affect gender, and Eguren (2001) analyzes them as DimP adjoined to NP. Fábregas (2010b) compares diminutives in Spanish and Czech (non-gender-affecting) to diminutives in German (gender-affecting). He analyzes Spanish and Czech diminutives as specifiers of ClassP, and German diminutives as heads of ClassP. If we understand ClassP as *n*P (not implausible; see Section 10.4 on declension class), then this is essentially the same result: the *n* diminutive affects gender, the specifier diminutive (which has category Affix for Fábregas) does not.

It is telling that different authors working from various perspectives, and using data from many different languages, have converged on the same bifurcated analysis of diminutives. Under this analysis, (32) is supported in that all diminutives that are *n*s affect gender, whereas those which are not do not affect gender. This trend also provides further support for a *n* approach to gender in general. However, this approach is not the only analysis of diminutives available. I will comment on a few alternatives before wrapping up this section.

Within the Germanic literature, de Belder (2011b) and Ott (2011) both treat diminutives as heads of projections relating to countability—SizeP for de Belder and UnitP for Ott. Their primary reason for doing so is because diminutives in Dutch and German turn mass nouns into count nouns (see e.g. (37) for German). This is problematic for a *n* approach to gender: Dutch and German diminutives affect gender, yet they would not be *n* heads. However, Fortin (2011: ch. 4) argues that the "countifying" effect of diminutives (which is relatively common cross-linguistic-ally) is due to a semantic presupposition: that the referent of the base that the diminutive attaches to is bounded. This semantic approach (if correct) would obviate the need for the diminutive to realize a Size or Unit head.

De Belder, Faust, and Lampitelli (to appear; henceforth dBFL) elucidate another type of empirical contrast across diminutives: whether they behave like a low affix, i.e. close to the root, or higher, up above the category-defining head. Marantz (2001), Arad (2003), and others have shown that low affixes trigger non-compositional meanings, whereas high affixes trigger regular, compositional meanings. dBFL apply this to diminutives, demonstrating that even in the same language a diminutive can have a non-compositional meaning or a compositional meaning (e.g. Italian compositional *nas-ino* 'nose-DIM' 'small nose' vs. non-compositional *pan-ino* 'bread-DIM' 'sandwich'). They conclude that there are two syntactic positions available to diminutives. They analyze non-compositional diminutives as a LexP added between the root and the categorizing head, and compositional diminutives as a SizeP above *n*.

The empirical contrasts between non-compositional and compositional diminutives give us important information about where diminutives attach in a nominal spine, and dBFL's conclusion that there are at least two positions for diminutives is well-supported. However, it is less clear why the diminutives must be heads, and why those heads must be Lex and Size. It is relatively easy to integrate dBFL's observations with the approach taken here: lower, non-compositional diminutives would be either *n* heads that select for a root or DIM heads adjoined to the root (depending on whether they affect gender), whereas higher, compositional diminutives would be either *n* heads that select for *n*P or DIM heads adjoined to *n* or a higher projection.[199] Whether or not a diminutive affects gender, then, cross-cuts its classification as high or low. dBFL provide empirical evidence: Dutch diminutives are compositional and change gender, whereas some Italian diminutives are compositional and do not change gender.

Overall, I conclude that (32) is upheld in that diminutives that do not affect gender are not *n*s. Of course, it remains to be seen whether this approach can be confirmed across a broader swath of data, and there is also at least one major open question: it has been coincidental that all the diminutives that have been proposed to be adjoined thus far have been analyzed as DIM heads, whereas those that have been analyzed as

---

[199] dBFL see no purpose in distinguishing between head and adjunct diminutives, and consider all the diminutives they propose to be modifiers. However, it is unclear in what sense they use the term "modifiers," since the diminutives they propose are all heads. They comment that if the only evidence for head/adjunct status is gender change, it is unclear how a root-adjoined diminutive (like that in Halkomelem) is an adjunct, since it adjoins to a root which does not have gender. This is a fair point, but root-adjoined diminutives are not the only type that Wiltschko and Steriopolo (2007) identify. Wiltschko and Steriopolo (2007) and Steriopolo (2008) propose that Russian has *n*P-adjoined diminutives—these do not affect gender and it is possible that they could, since they are adjoined to a *n*P.

heads are *n*s. Could there be an adjoined *n* diminutive that affects gender, or head DIMs that do not? However this strand of questioning is ultimately resolved, it is promising that the recent major trend in diminutive literature allows for (32) to be maintained; I take this as evidence that (32) is on the right track.

10.4 Declension class and gender

In Chapter 3, I explored how nominal vocalic patterns in Semitic languages are inserted at PF as a type of *n* (following Arad 2005). This predicts that vocalic pattern can be sensitive to gender since gender is on *n*, and I showed how this is borne out for Amharic nouns. As the final step in my investigation of the interaction of *n*-based phenomena and gender, I turn to a similar phenomenon that interacts with *n*: nominal declension class.

I adopt the definition of declension class shown in (43), adapted from Aronoff (1994).

(43)   A declension class is a set of roots whose members each share the same set of inflectional realizations.

I use the term "declension class" throughout for consistency, but the same phenomenon is also referred as "inflection(al) class" or "conjugation class." Standard examples of languages with nominal declension class include Latin (Maidhoff 2009), Greek (Alexiadou and Müller 2008), and Russian (Corbett 1991).

I first review the arguments that declension class and gender are distinct phenomena, which were originally presented in Chapter 4. I then discuss how Distributed Morphology approaches to declension class generally assume that a declension class node is inserted post-syntactically at/near *n*, just like the nominal pattern for Amharic. This predicts that gender can (although it need not) influence declension class, and I show how this is borne out in a case study of Spanish declension class.

10.4.1 Background

In Chapter 4, I introduced the definition of gender repeated in (44).

(44)   Gender is ...
      (i) the sorting of nouns into two or more classes;
      (ii) depending on biological sex and/or animacy (at least for some nouns);
      (iii) as reflected by agreement patterns on other elements (e.g. adjectives, determiners, verbs, auxiliaries, etc.).

According to this definition, declension classes are not genders since they do not trigger agreement. For example, Latin *anima* 'soul' is Declension Class 1 whereas *lēx* 'law' is Declension Class 3, but both nouns trigger the same agreement (feminine; see

Maidhoff 2009: 17ff.). Moreover, gender often cross-cuts declension class (Comrie 1999). In Latin, the first declension tends to have feminine nouns and the second tends to have masculine nouns, but the third declension contains nouns of all genders (feminine, masculine and neuter). Finally, there is not a one-to-one relationship between declension classes and genders; as Comrie (1999) observes, there are five nominal declensions in Latin and three genders. Due to these fundamental differences, there is a wide consensus that gender and declension class/nominal pattern are distinct phenomena (see e.g. Roca 1989, Harris 1991, 1996, Halle 1992, Aronoff 1994, Comrie 1999, Thornton 2001, Wechsler and Zlatić 2003, Alexiadou 2004).

As for the analysis of declension class, it is generally agreed that declension class features do not play a role during the syntactic derivation (see e.g. Harris 1991, 1996, Aronoff 1994, Oltra-Massuet 1999, Alexiadou 2004, Oltra-Massuet and Arregi 2005, Embick and Halle 2005, Alexiadou and Müller 2008).[200] From a minimalist syntactic perspective, declension class features are not semantically interpretable, and they do not participate in or facilitate any syntactic relations (e.g. agreement, selection). Therefore, there is no reason for them to be present during the syntactic derivation (see e.g. Alexiadou and Müller 2008 for detailed argumentation), and economy considerations dictate that they are therefore not present at all.

Within Distributed Morphology, the fact that declension class features are not syntactic is captured by having declension class be a dissociated node, i.e. a node that is inserted post-syntactically at PF (see e.g. Embick 1997 on dissociated nodes; see Oltra-Massuet 1999, Oltra-Massuet and Arregi 2005, Embick and Halle 2005, Halle and Matushansky 2006, Lahne 2006, Embick and Noyer 2007, Embick 2010 on nominal and verbal declension class in DM). The key part of this analysis for present purposes is that the dissociated node for declension class is most often assumed to be inserted adjoined to the category-defining head, i.e. *n* for nouns (see all sources cited within previous parentheses, as well as Kihm 2005, Steriopolo 2008, Alexiadou 2011a, 2011b).[201] Because gender features are therefore local to the node that expones declension class, this approach predicts that gender could (but need not) condition declension class, in the same way that nominal pattern can (but need not) be affected by gender in Amharic. To confirm this prediction, and to illustrate the mechanics of a

---

[200] The major alternative analysis here is Bernstein (1993a, 1993b), where it is proposed that declension class projects in the syntax as a Word Marker Phrase (see also Josefsson 2001 for an alternative perspective on the interpretation of declension classes). Bernstein (1993a, 1993b) argues that the Word Marker syntactic head licenses certain types of nominal ellipsis in Romance languages. However, see Harris (1996), Alexiadou (2004), and Alexiadou and Müller (2008) for counterarguments and different approaches to nominal ellipsis.

[201] An alternatives is to insert the dissociated node at Num(ber) (Bachrach and Wagner 2007). In this case, it is most likely still close enough to *n* to be conditioned by gender; however, this approach requires careful attention to cyclicity to ensure that the features on the *n* head are still accessible.

DM approach to declension class, I present a brief case study of Spanish declension class in Section 10.4.2.[202]

10.4.2 Spanish declension class: a case study

Spanish is an apt choice for a case study of declension class for several reasons. First of all, its declension class system has been the object of generative morphological and syntactic research for over twenty years, providing a rich literature of observations and analysis to draw from (see e.g. Harris 1991, 1992, 1996, Bernstein 1993a, 1993b, Aronoff 1994, Halle and Marantz 1994, Alexiadou 2004, Oltra-Massuet and Arregi 2005, Bermúdez-Otero 2006, 2007, 2013; see also Oltra-Massuet 1999 on Catalan). Secondly, much of that literature has adopted a Distributed Morphology approach to declension class. Finally, the analysis of the Spanish gender system in Chapter 6 provides a solid starting point for the discussion.

To be clear, I will assume throughout this section that a DM approach to declension class is correct, primarily because it makes the clearest predictions for the interaction of declension class and gender in a *n* approach to gender. However, a DM approach has not been without controversy, and I direct the interested reader to Bermúdez-Otero (2006, 2007, 2013) for another perspective on the Spanish facts.

In the remainder of this section, I first lay out the data and show how gender and declension class are interrelated (albeit distinct) in Spanish. I also demonstrate that gender affects declension class, as predicted by a *n* approach to gender. I then sketch an analysis of declension class assignment and theme vowel realization in Spanish, clarifying the relationship between gender on *n* and post-syntactic declension class features.

It is broadly recognized that Spanish has three main nominal declension classes, and each is expressed with a different theme vowel (see e.g. Roca 1989, Harris 1991, 1992, 1996, Halle and Marantz 1994, Aronoff 1994, Alexiadou 2004). The three main classes (I, II, III) and their theme vowels (*-o, -a, -e/Ø*) are illustrated in Table 10.2.

The theme vowel for Declension Class III has two phonologically conditioned allomorphs: the null allomorph appears after roots ending in segments that are phonotactically licit in domain-final position (e.g. [θ] for *lápiz* 'pencil'), and the *-e* allomorph appears in all other cases.[203]

---

[202] Another approach to declension class is developed in Müller (2004) and Alexiadou and Müller (2008). They assume that there is a pre-syntactic morphology level in which a declension class feature enters into an Agree relation with a goal inflectional marker in order to create fusional inflection. I do not explore it fully here, since it is not consonant with the fundamental DM assumption of no pre-syntactic generative morphology.

[203] For the sake of simplicity, I omit Class III nouns that take the *-e* allomorph despite ending in a phonotactically licit consonant (e.g. *cruc-e* 'crossing') as well as certain complications involving proper names. For more details, see Harris (1991, 1992), Bermúdez-Otero (2013), and references cited therein. See also fn. 208 on athematic nouns.

TABLE 10.2. **Spanish declension classes**

Declension class	Theme vowel	Noun	Gloss	Gender
I	-o	a. lí-o	'muddle'	Masculine
		b. man-o	'hand'	Feminine
II	-a	c. dí-a	'day'	Masculine
		d. pas-a	'raisin'	Feminine
III	-e/Ø	e. padr-e	'father'	Masculine
		f. madr-e	'mother'	Feminine
		g. lápiz-Ø	'pencil'	Masculine
		h. luz-Ø	'light'	Feminine

(based on Bermúdez-Otero 2013: 10, (4))

Importantly, gender cross-cuts declension class in Spanish. As Table 10.2 shows, both masculine and feminine nouns are found in Classes I, II, and III (as well as with both allomorphs of the theme vowel of Class III). Spanish therefore provides further evidence that gender and declension class are separate and distinct phenomena.[204]

However, one gender is often more common than another in a given declension class. Almost all of the nouns in Class I are masculine. The feminine Class I noun in Table 10.2(c), *mano* 'hand,' is the most frequently attested member of a short list of invariably feminine nouns in Class I, joined by a few same-root nouns (e.g. *testigo* 'witness') and truncations (e.g. *moto* 'motorcycle') (see Harris 1991: 37, Bermúdez-Otero 2013: 17–18). The majority of the nouns in Class II are feminine, although the masculine exceptions like *día* 'day' are much more numerous than the feminine exceptions in Class I. Harris (1991) estimates there are 600 masculine nouns in Class II, e.g. *problema* 'problem,' *cometa* 'comet,' *colega* 'colleague' (masculine when referring to a male colleague). Masculine and feminine nouns are equally attested in Class III.

Overall, then, there are some generalizations that connect gender and declension class in Spanish: Class I nouns are almost always masculine and Class II nouns are usually feminine. Thus, Spanish is an example of a language where declension class and gender are related, as a *n* approach to gender and declension class predicts. Although these generalizations both have exceptions, and Class III is not related to gender at all, this is not evidence against a *n* approach to gender. A *n* approach to gender guarantees that gender features are local enough to the declension class

---

[204] Spanish provides additional evidence that gender and declension class are distinct in that adjectives agree in gender, not in declension class (see e.g. Alexiadou 2004: 33). Adjectives describing *mano* 'hand' and *madre* 'mother' display the same gender agreement markers (feminine), despite the fact that the nouns have different declension classes.

node such that they *can* affect declension class, not that they *must* affect declension class. I now sketch out a possible analysis of Spanish declension class from a DM perspective that captures these facts, and which is integrated with a *n* approach to gender.

There are two minimal components of a DM approach to nominal declension class, as discussed in e.g. Oltra-Massuet (1999), Oltra-Massuet and Arregi (2005), Embick and Halle (2005), Embick and Noyer (2007), and Embick (2010). The first component is that a Theme head is inserted post-syntactically as a dissociated node, adjoined to *n*; this ensures that declension class is purely a morphological phenomenon. A schematic example of Theme node insertion for a feminine noun is shown in (45).

(45)   **Syntax**   **PF: Theme Node Insertion**

The second component is that the Theme node is morphophonologically realized as the theme vowel via Vocabulary Insertion.

The question remains of how to include the declension class features themselves in the picture; at first it may seem that they are unnecessary. The grammar would be simpler if the Theme head could simply be realized as the theme vowel in the context of the appropriate root, with no declension classes mediating the relationship between them.

However, this approach is unsuccessful because declension class is not just specified per individual root in Spanish. Typically, Class I is analyzed as the least marked class in general (e.g. it is used with "neuter" determiners and pronouns; see Chapter 6), and Class II is considered the least marked class for feminine nouns since it contains the majority of the feminine nouns (see e.g. Harris 1991, 1992). This means that if there were no declension class features, the theme vowel Vocabulary Items *-o* and *-a* would have disjunctive conditions on insertion. For example, the Vocabulary Item/theme vowel *-o* would be inserted *either* in the context of certain roots (e.g. √MAN 'hand'; see Table 10.2) *or* in the context of any nominal whose root is not on a conditioning list. The first condition captures the fact that *-o* is idiosyncratically specified to appear with certain roots like √MAN, but the second condition captures the fact that it is also the elsewhere theme vowel. These disjunctive conditions on insertion are notationally equivalent to there being two homophonous theme vowels *-o* with different conditions on insertion—a clearly undesirable situation. I conclude that Vocabulary Insertion cannot do all the work of matching nominals with theme vowels; declension class features must be referenced.

The question then is how to integrate the declension class features. Many DM approaches (e.g. Oltra-Massuet 1999, Embick and Halle 2005) have assumed that declension class is a feature on roots. At PF, after the Theme node has been inserted, the declension class feature is copied from the root to the Theme vowel and then determines the realization of the Theme vowel node. This is shown in (46)a–c for a feminine, Class III noun, e.g. *madre* 'mother.'

(46)   **Syntax**   **PF: Theme Node Insertion**

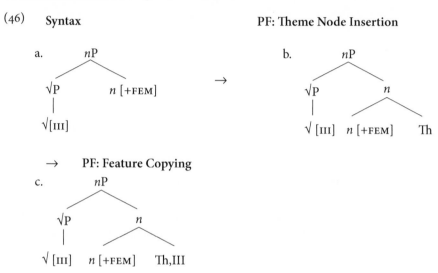

However, this would mean that a declension class feature is present (on the root) in the syntax, which is objectionable, since it plays no role at all syntactically.[205] Moreover, it may be that putting the declension class feature on the root is not a firm commitment within this approach. Embick (2010: 196) considers as equivalent three different analyses of declension class: (i) feature copying of a declension class feature onto the Theme node ((5)), (ii) Vocabulary Insertion at a theme node conditioned by the declension class feature of the root, or (iii) simply having the Theme node acquire a declension class feature in the context of a root.

---

[205] If it is assumed instead that the declension class feature is inserted on the root at PF, then the PF operations involved become rather complicated: declension class is inserted as a dissociated feature on the root, the Theme node is inserted as a dissociated node adjoined to *n*, and then the declension class feature is copied to the Theme node.

For Spanish, I follow Embick's final suggestion that the dissociated Theme node carries the declension class feature. This keeps declension class features off roots, and suffices to capture the complex interplay between defaultness and listedness in the Spanish declension class system. Specifically, I assume that a dissociated Theme node is inserted according to the rules in (47), which are ordered as per the Pāṇinian Principle like other morphological rules.[206]

(47) **Theme node insertion rules for Spanish**

    a i. Insert [THEME, III] in the context of √MADR, √PADR, √LÁPIZ, √LUZ...

       ii. Insert [THEME, II] in the context of √DÍ...

      iii. Insert [THEME, I] in the context of √MAN...

    b. Insert [THEME, II] in the context of n[+FEM]

    c. Insert [THEME] elsewhere.

The first set of insertion rules ((47)a) inserts Theme nodes with particular declension class features in the context of certain roots. This captures all the "listed" information about which roots go with which declension class, including all roots in Class III, Class II roots that are masculine, and Class I roots that are feminine. The second insertion rule is slightly less specific, so it applies later: it inserts a Class II theme node at all nominals with a [+FEM] feature (without a theme node yet inserted). Finally, all other contexts receive a plain Theme node.[207,208]

    The Vocabulary Items that realize the Theme node are then very simple, although one additional item will be added below (cf. the analysis of Spanish declension class in Halle and Marantz 1994, Harris 1996).[209]

(48) **Vocabulary Insertion for Theme node in Spanish (first pass)**

    a. [THEME, III] ↔ -e/Ø[210]

    b. [THEME, II] ↔ -a

    c. [THEME] ↔ -o

---

[206] I leave these roles in prose because there is no standard way to formalize the rules guiding the insertion of dissociated nodes.

[207] An equivalent analysis (as far as I can tell) would insert [THEME, I] at this step.

[208] Spanish also has athematic nouns, often loanwords, e.g. *tribu* 'tribe' and *clip* 'paperclip.' I assume that Theme node insertion is blocked for these nominals, with the result that a theme vowel can never be inserted.

[209] Many DM approaches to declension class have focused on decomposing declension class features in order to capture syncretisms across declension classes (see e.g. Oltra-Massuet 1999, Müller 2004, 2005). I leave open whether Spanish declension class can and should be decomposed in this way.

[210] I set aside here the question of how to capture the phonologically conditioned allomorphy.

(47) combined with (48) predict the basic facts of Spanish class correctly, and specify the relationship between gender and declension class. Class III nouns (*padre, madre*) have no relationship between gender and declension class: they are derived via inserting a Class III theme node in the context of a particular root regardless of gender, and realizing the theme vowel as *-e/Ø*. This is shown for the feminine Class III noun *madre* in (49).

(49)   **Derivation of a Class III noun: *madre* 'mother'**

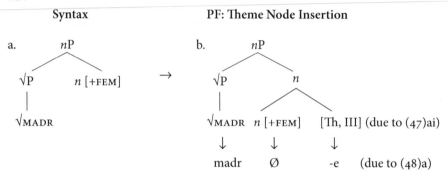

Class II nouns are derived in one of two ways. The first is by inserting a Class II theme node in the context of a particular root (e.g. √DÍ), ignoring gender features. The second is by inserting a Class II theme node in the context of a [+FEM] feature for a root that is not on any conditioning list in (6); this is the key instance of a gender feature conditioning declension class in Spanish. This is shown in (50) for the feminine Class II noun *pasa* 'raisin.'

(50)   **Derivation of a Class II noun: *pasa* 'raisin'**

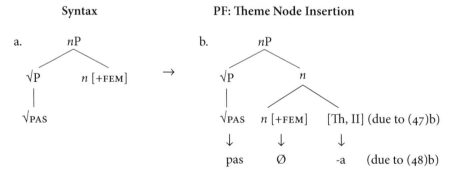

Class I nouns (e.g. *mano*) are derived via inserting a Class I theme node in the context of a particular root, and are realized with the elsewhere theme vowel *-o* because the other matching Vocabulary Items clash in terms of the declension class feature. This is shown in (51) for *mano* 'hand.'

(51)   **Derivation of a Class I noun:** *mano* 'hand'

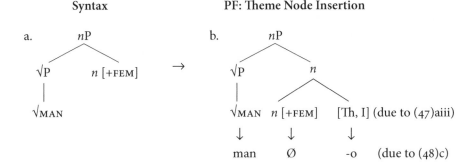

Finally, the remaining nouns that receive an *-o* theme vowel simply receive a plain Theme node at PF, and are realized with the elsewhere theme vowel *-o*. This set of nouns are all masculine, but not because there is an explicit connection between masculine gender features and Class I; they are all masculine because any feminine nouns will have received Class II when the more specific rule (47)b applies. A sample derivation with *lío* 'muddle' is given in (52).

(52)   **Derivation of** *lío* 'muddle'

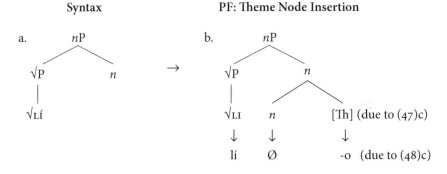

Overall, gender plays a minor but significant role in conditioning which theme vowel is inserted at *n* in Spanish, and this is highly plausible since the gender feature is on *n* as well. Although the locality conditions on dissociated node insertion are under-investigated (see e.g. McFadden 2004, Baker and Kramer 2014), it is expected that the features on the node adjacent to the insertion site will be able to condition what node is inserted. Thus, the Spanish declension system behaves as predicted by a *n* approach to gender. However, I want to stress that the analysis here is one among many possibilities, and I constructed it primarily to illustrate as clearly as possible how gender and declension class interplay in a particular language. Hopefully, future research will discover evidence firmly in favor of one particular approach to declension class in DM.

As a final note, it is worth discussing briefly how this analysis extends to nominalizations and diminutives. In Spanish nominalizations, the theme vowel occurs after all suffixes except the plural suffix, and the identity of the theme vowel is determined by the rightmost suffix before the plural suffix (with a crucial exception below; see Harris 1991, 1992, 1996, Oltra-Massuet and Arregi 2005, Bermúdez-Otero 2013, and many others). For example, in (53)a, the root √HERMAN triggers insertion of a plain theme node which is realized as -*o*. However, in (53)b, the suffix -*dad* triggers insertion of [THEME, III], realized as a null theme vowel, and it is ungrammatical for the theme vowel -*o* associated with the root to be retained ((53)c).[211]

(53) a. herman-o   b. herman-dad-Ø   c. *herman-o-dad-Ø
         brother-TV   brother-hood-TV   brother-TV-hood-TV
         'brother'   'brotherhood'
         (Harris 1996: 104)

Oltra-Massuet and Arregi (2005) provide an explanation for this effect. Following Oltra-Massuet (1999), they assume that theme vowel nodes are inserted at each functional head (including categorizing heads; this goes some way towards explaining theme vowels on verbs and adverbs). However, the theme node is realized overtly only if it is left-adjacent to the number head Num.[212] The necessary Vocabulary Items in this approach are in (54).

(54) **Vocabulary Insertion for Theme node in Spanish (complete)**
      a. [THEME, III] ↔ -e/Ø / ___ Num
      b. [THEME, II] ↔ -a / ___ Num
      c. [THEME] ↔ -o / ___ Num
      d. [THEME] ↔ Ø

This can be characterized as an allomorphic explanation: theme vowels have a null allomorph if they are anywhere but adjacent to Num. As for the Theme vowel being sensitive to the nature of the outermost suffix, I assume that the insertion of Theme vowel nodes can be conditioned not just by root identity, but by the identity of a nominalizing suffix that it adjoins to, such that e.g. the *n* that is realized as -*dad* is a member of the conditioning list for inserting [THEME, III]. This is a broad claim, and there is no space to substantiate it fully here. But even though it remains to be confirmed, the DM approach to declension class at a minimum clearly points towards a way to encode the generalizations connecting nominalizers (which are *n*s) and Theme vowels (inserted at *n*).

---

[211] This discussion assumes that *hermandad* 'brotherhood' is derived from a *n*P, and not from a root.
[212] This presentation is an elaboration of an idea suggested by Oltra-Massuet and Arregi (2005) in a footnote. It is explained more fully (and then argued against) in Bermúdez-Otero (2013).

A reader might also wonder how this approach to declension class relates to the claim from Section 10.3 that Spanish diminutives are adjuncts. The interaction of diminutives and declension class is highly complex in Spanish, and the morpho-phonology and morphosyntax of Spanish diminutives has spurred almost a cottage industry of literature (see e.g. Jaeggli 1980, Colina 2003, Smith 2011, Bermúdez-Otero 2013, and the many references therein). One of the most complex parts of the problem is what theme vowel/Vocabulary Item is inserted on/at the diminutive morpheme. It is clear that only *-o* and *-a* are attested, but every other generalization seems to have exceptions. Some nouns retain their theme vowel (*madrecita* 'mother. DIM), whereas some nouns do not (*costumbre* ~ *costumbrita* 'habit.DIM'). Sometimes the diminutive theme vowel is the same as the root would have (*problema* ~ *problemita* 'problem.DIM'), whereas other times it is not (*mano* ~ *manita* 'hand.DIM' in some dialects). Intricate allomorphy involving the diminutive morpheme itself (*-it/-cit*) may also play a role. It is impossible to do justice to the complexity of the literature or the facts in the space available, so I leave this as an open area for future research, especially within Distributed Morphology approaches to declension class.

10.4.3 Summary, and directions of correlations

In this section I constructed a mini-analysis of Spanish declension class—both demonstrating how declension class and gender are connected in a DM approach and confirming the predictions of a *n* approach to gender. Spanish is also not the only language for which gender (at least partially) correlates with declension class as predicted. This also occurs in e.g. Latin (see Section 10.4.1), Italian (Thornton 2001), Latvian (Halle 1992), German and Swedish (Kürschner and Nübling 2008), Greek (Alexiadou and Müller 2008: 120), Icelandic (Müller 2005), Slovene (Börjesson 2005), and Vedic (Stump 2001). Aronoff (1994: 63) observes that "inflectional classes are almost always partially determined by gender," as expected if they are located morphosyntactically adjacent to the node with the gender feature.

However, a key question that comes up for any language where declension class correlates with gender is the direction of the correlation. In Section 10.4.2, following previous work on Spanish, I analyzed gender as partially determining declension class, in that *n* [+FEM] conditions the insertion of a dissociated Theme node with Class II. However, it has been argued that, in some languages (for some nouns), declension class determines gender (see e.g. Corbett 1991, Aronoff 1994 on Russian, Nesset 2003 on Ukrainian, Enger 2004 on Norwegian). For example, Russian has three declension classes (following Aronoff 1994), and feminine nouns are mostly in Class 2. However, Class 3 (a small class) is also comprised of only feminine nouns. Aronoff (1994: 73–4) thus posits a rule that assigns feminine nouns to class 2 by default, and a rule that assigns a noun in class 3 (which is lexically listed under his assumptions) to the feminine gender.

If such an analysis is correct, it seems troubling for a post-syntactic approach to declension class. If declension class is inserted post-syntactically, there is no way it can determine gender features, since they are present during the syntax, i.e. at an earlier stage of the derivation. However, there are (at least) two ways around this problem. First, it may be that declension class features are on roots, and form part of the licensing conditions that match up roots and *n*s. That would allow either for declension class to determine gender (via a root-*n* licensing condition) or for gender to determine declension class (post-syntactically via insertion of a Theme vowel node at *n*). However, this comes with the trade-off that the declension class features are present in the syntax.

Secondly, it is not crystal clear that declension class does in fact determine gender features. Beard (1995b) argues that declension class does not determine gender in Russian, since (for example) there is a set of nouns which are Class 3 and have neuter gender. The question of whether declension class determines gender or gender determines declension class has been the topic of several studies, often with authors reaching compromise positions (see e.g. Aronoff 1994, Doleschal 2001 on Russian, Enger 2004 on Norwegian, Thornton 2001 on Italian vs. Russian, Kürschner and Nübling 2008 on Germanic languages). Clearly, more research is needed to settle this question within individual languages, and to explore the consequences of root declension class features as opposed to post-syntactically inserted declension class features. Such research must be left to another book, though, and I close only by reiterating that the tight relationship between gender and declension class, whichever way the correlation goes, is exactly as expected in a *n* approach to gender.

10.5 Conclusion

This chapter concludes the exploration of the ramifications of gender on *n* for nominalizations and declension class. I focused on nominalizations in Chapter 9, and showed how nominalizations are often gendered across languages, as predicted. In this chapter, I presented an analysis of gender assignment in nominalizations that contain multiple *n*s, arguing that the highest *n* determines the gender ((32)) for cyclicity-motivated reasons. I also showed how recent literature on diminutives also supports (32) in Section 10.3. Finally, Section 10.4 took on declension class, which is on/near *n* in DM approaches, showing that gender affects declension class as expected if it is on *n*.

11

Conclusion

This conclusion contains three parts. The first section focuses on drawing together the results and claims across chapters—revisiting the questions raised in Chapter 1 about gender morphosyntax and identifying how they have been answered. The second section identifies areas of future research, including phonologically motivated gender assignment and gender systems that contain more than three genders. The third section provides some final thoughts on the results of the book.

11.1 Putting it all together

In Chapter 1, I posed a series of questions about the morphosyntax of gender, and provided a chapter-by-chapter summary of the results of the book. In this conclusion, I return to the series of questions about the morphosyntax of gender. The questions are repeated in (1).

(1) **Question A:** Where is gender located in the hierarchical structure?
     Question B: What is the relationship between natural gender and arbitrary gender?
     Question C: How is gender assignment accomplished morphosyntactically?

I observed in Chapter 1 (and confirmed in Chapter 2) that the previous morphosyntactic literature has not converged upon answers to these questions. Here, I review the answers to these questions argued for in this book, knitting together the results across chapters to characterize the contribution of the book as a whole. I close this section by laying out how the book supports Distributed Morphology as a framework.

11.1.1 Question A: Gender on n

From the perspective of this book, the answer to Question A is clear: gender is located on the nominalizing head *n*, not on the category-neutral root or on the Num(ber) head.[213]

---

[213] Gender is also not the head of its own projection: Gen(der)P. In Ch. 2, I argued that the original empirical motivation for GenP (Picallo 1991) is not compelling. I also observed that GenP would be a

The Morphosyntax of Gender. First Edition. Ruth Kramer.
© Ruth Kramer 2015. Published 2015 by Oxford University Press.

In Chapter 2, I argued that gender is not located only on the category-neutral root, because such an analysis would require two homophonous, synonymous roots for every nominal that can have either masculine or feminine gender (e.g. *hakim* 'doctor' in Amharic). Moreover, gender is a syntactically active feature, since it participates in agreement relations, and it is specific to nouns. If a category-neutral root had a gender feature, it would have a category-specific feature that is syntactically relevant, undercutting the assumption that roots are category-neutral and violating the restrictions on root features proposed by Borer (2005), Embick and Noyer (2007), and Acquaviva (2009). I concluded that gender is not located on roots.

The evidence against gender being on Num is contained in two chapters: Chapters 2 and 8. In Chapter 2, I argued against gender being on Num in Amharic, showing how the facts in Ritter (1993) that support gender being on Num for Romance languages are not found in Amharic. In Chapter 8, I mounted a large-scale analysis of Somali and Romanian gender switch, i.e. when a noun has one gender in the singular and another in the plural. *A priori*, gender switch offers some of the strongest evidence for gender features being on Num. However, I argued that gender is not in Num in either of these languages. Somali contains evidence that all number features are on *n*, and gender switch is therefore expected since gender is also on *n*. The standard, non-Num-based analysis of the Romanian gender system can be easily adapted into a Distributed Morphology analysis that incorporates all the assumptions about gender developed in the book, and that is more successful than a gender-on-Num approach. Overall, then, I have argued that there is no compelling evidence that gender features are on Num.

The book also contains empirical evidence in favor of gender being located on *n*. In Chapter 3, I amassed a range of evidence from Amharic for gender-on-*n*, including the interaction of irregular plurals and gender, the distribution of gendered plurals, and the existence of gendered nominal patterns. I also showed how nominalizations are gendered in Amharic, and I returned to nominalizations in Chapters 9 and 10. In Chapter 9, I examined nominalization from a cross-linguistic perspective, demonstrating that nominalizations are often gendered and that each type of *n* proposed in the book is attested as a nominalizer. I confirmed several predictions that follow from gender being on the nominalizing head, including the prediction that one kind of nominalization can always have the same gender, even it is realized as different Vocabulary Items (e.g. French deadjectival nouns are always feminine, regardless of the nominalizing suffix used). In Chapter 10 I turned to another phenomenon located on *n*: declension class. I argued that the tight correlation between gender and declension class across languages falls out if gender is also located on *n*.

---

projection that (in some contexts) contained only uninterpretable features, *pace* Chomsky (1995). See also Ritter (1993) for further arguments against GenP.

In sum, I have argued that gender is not located on the category-neutral root, nor is it located on Num. I have also provided cross-linguistic evidence from the interaction of gender with number, the role of gender in nominalizations, and the relationship between gender and declension class/nominal pattern that gender is located syntactically on *n*.

11.1.2 *Question B: The relationship between natural and arbitrary gender*

In the book, natural and arbitrary gender are different in one respect, and the same in another respect. They are different in their interpretability, i.e. whether they impact LF. Natural gender is interpretable at LF, whereas arbitrary gender is uninterpretable and is ignored by LF. They are the same in their fundamentals, though: both are represented via the feature [+/−FEM]. Therefore, PF treats them as the same for the purposes of Vocabulary Insertion. This is why the same Vocabulary Item is inserted for e.g. both interpretable [+FEM] contexts (e.g. *innat* 'mother' in Amharic) and uninterpretable [+FEM] contexts (e.g. *s'ähay* 'sun' in Amharic), resulting in both nouns having "feminine gender."[214]

Clarifying the relationship between natural gender and arbitrary gender led me to develop essentially a theory of the gender features on *n*. Focusing on languages with biological sex, the basic contrast is three-way: [+FEM], [−FEM], and lacking gender features altogether. In Chapter 5, I showed how this basic inventory of *n*s generates the gender systems of Dieri and Zayse/Zargulla. In Chapters 3 and 6, I explored languages that augment this basic inventory with a single uninterpretable [+/−FEM] feature, including Maa (uninterpretable [−FEM]), Amharic, and Spanish (uninterpretable [+FEM]). In Chapter 7, I introduced three-gender languages, showing how they can have the basic three-*n* inventory (Mangarayi), the one uninterpretable [+/−FEM] inventory (Wari'), and two uninterpretable features (both [+FEM] and [−FEM]) (Lavukaleve). A summary of *n* inventories and languages is set out in Table 11.1. (Interestingly, Romanian (Chapter 8) is a language that has the same *n* inventory as Lavukaleve, but only two Vocabulary Items for realizing gender. Nouns that contain plain *n* always receive the default gender, which is masculine in the singular and feminine in the plural.)

Insofar as all the possible combinations of gender features are attested (with the assumption that all languages need at least the basic three to make the female/male/unsexed distinction), this supports the theory of gender features following from this book's approach to natural and arbitrary gender.

I have not contrasted this theory of gender features with other possible approaches to gender features (e.g. using MASC as the identity of the feature, or privativity for

---

[214] In Ch. 6, I argued that animacy is similar. The [ANIMATE] feature is either interpretable or uninterpretable, but always triggers the insertion of the same Vocabulary Item on an agreement target at PF.

TABLE 11.1. Possible inventories of gender-relevant *n*s

	Two-gender language	Three-gender language
n	● Dieri	● Mangarayi
n i[+FEM]	● Zayse and Zargulla	
n i[−FEM]		
n	● Amharic	● Arakul' dialect of Lak
n i[+FEM]	● Spanish	
n i[−FEM]		
n u[+FEM]		
n	● Maa	● Wari'
n i[+FEM]		
n i[−FEM]		
n u[−FEM]		
n	● Romanian (see Ch. 8)	● Lavukaleve
n i[+FEM]		
n i[−FEM]		
n u[−FEM]		
n u[+FEM]		

biological sex features). Moreover, strictly speaking, this theory of gender features is separable from the answer to Question A: *n* could still be the locus of gender, but the features expressing gender could be arrayed differently. However, this theory is certainly compatible with gender on *n*, and I take the fact that its cross-linguistic predictions are borne out as strong initial evidence in its favor. I hope future research will explore the impact of this theory on the theory of (phi) features in general, as explored e.g. in Adger (2010), Adger and Svenonius (2011), and Harbour (2011, 2013). Harbour (2011, 2013) in particular argues in favor of three way +/−/absent contrasts for all phi features, and the proposals here about biological-sex-based gender systems offer further support for such an approach.

11.1.3 *Question C: Gender assignment*

The term "gender assignment" is somewhat vague, even though it permeates the literature on gender. In one sense, it refers to the assignment of gender to a noun by a rule, e.g. a lexical rule that assigns feminine gender to all nouns with a female feature in the lexicon. In another sense, it refers to the distribution of gender across the nouns of a language, whether the assignment is by rule or by fiat, e.g. *s'ähay* 'sun' is assigned feminine gender in Amharic, even though there is no semantic, morphological, or phonological reason why. I deal with each sense in turn.

Corbett (1991 et seq.) is the ur-source on gender assignment rules. His approach can be characterized as dividing gender assignment rules into three types: semantic, morphological, and phonological. Semantic assignment rules for biological gender systems typically include the type of rule mentioned above that assigns feminine gender to all nouns with a female feature and another rule that assigns masculine gender to all nouns with a male feature. This type of gender "assignment" is accomplished in this book because all nouns that are interpreted as female-referring must contain an interpretable [+FEM] feature, and the [+FEM] feature will trigger the insertion of Vocabulary Items described as feminine on agreement targets at PF. The same goes for the [–FEM] feature. A similar process is at play for animacy: all animate nouns receive animate gender in e.g. Lealao Chinantec because they contain an [ANIMATE] feature that results in the insertion of Vocabulary Items identified as animate on agreement targets at PF.

Morphological gender assignment rules include rules that assign a gender because of the presence of a particular nominalizing affix, and because of the presence of a particular declension class. I argued in Chapters 9 and 10 that the highest nominalizing affix determines the gender of the resulting noun due to certain independently-proposed assumptions about cyclicity, which has the same effect as a rule that assigns gender due to the presence of an affix (and see Chapter 9 for reasons to prefer a non-rule-based analysis). In Chapter 10, I showed that it is not technically easy in DM to have gender be determined from declension class, but it is possible, and perfectly compatible with gender being on *n*. The only case not covered, then, is phonological assignment rules. I return to these in Section 11.2.

"Gender assignment" in the sense of "how all nouns are given gender in a certain language" is done via a two-part process in this book. First, a root is licensed with a particular *n*. Then, the feature content of that *n* determines how targets agree with the nominal. However, the relationship between *n* and the agreement target is not necessarily one-to-one. A given pair of roots can be licensed under different *n*s and have the same type of gender agreement, because the Vocabulary Item inserted at the agreement target may be underspecified.[215] Interestingly, two roots that are licensed under the same *n* must have the same gender, and (I believe) this prediction is borne out.

Overall, I am not arguing for or against any particular analysis of gender in this section—the arguments in favor of gender on *n* and the theory of gender features have

---

[215] Recall that masculine nouns that are male-referring and masculine nouns that are inanimate in two-gender languages like Amharic and Spanish trigger the same kind of agreement, despite being licensed under different *n*s (male referring: *n i* [–FEM], inanimate: *n*). This opens the possibility that they may act differently syntactically (e.g. selected for by different heads) or morphologically (e.g. trigger the insertion of different declension classes). I leave it as an open question whether these differences are attested. If the facts turn out that male-referring nominals and masculine inanimate nominals are treated identically by a large number and variety of grammatical operations, it may be that (in the language in question or generally) masculine inanimates are licensed by *u* [–FEM]. I do not think this would substantially alter the predictions of the analysis for this type of two-gender language.

already been made. However, I hope to have made it clear how a traditional "gender assignment" approach maps onto the analysis of gender developed in this book.

11.1.4 Evidence for Distributed Morphology

Insofar as the approach to gender in this book is successful, it provides support for Distributed Morphology as a framework. It relies crucially on DM assumptions about lexical decomposition, the syntax–morphology interface, and Vocabulary Insertion. In Chapter 10, the explanation for the Highest Gender Hypothesis centered on DM assumptions about cyclicity. Gender may seem like a very "lexicalist" phenomenon in that many of the facts are "listed" or idiosyncratic. However, not only is DM capable of being used for a complex gender analysis, but I have argued against lexicalist approaches in Chapters 2, 8, and 9, demonstrating that they fare less well than DM on a variety of empirical fronts. One of the larger impacts of this book, then, is providing evidence in favor of Distributed Morphology as a theory of the grammar.

11.2 Areas of future research

In this section, I identify four gender-related questions that the book leaves open. The first is the proper analysis of gender systems where gender is assigned phonologically. The second is how to approach gender systems with more than three genders. I then speculate on how the results here may be influenced by social factors relating to gender, and close with a discussion of languages that lack gender entirely.

11.2.1 Phonologically determined gender assignment

I mentioned in Section 11.1 that some languages have been claimed to assign gender phonologically, i.e. the gender of a noun is determined by its phonology (see e.g. Corbett 1991: 51–62). In DM, phonological features are not inserted until after the syntax—too late to affect gender. So, any DM approach to gender requires a different approach, namely, that the phonological correlate of a particular gender is a realization of a gender feature which was already present in the syntax. In the particular DM approach to gender advanced in this book, a phonological indicator of gender will be a realization of n.

  This is at least plausible for some straightforward cases. Consider again the 'basic' three-n inventory: n i [+FEM] female, n i [−FEM] male, and n that lacks gender features. Each of these ns is exponed by a different Vocabulary Item in Anfillo (Omotic, Ethiopia; the facts here are from Amha 2012). Most nouns referring to males end in -o (e.g. *bakk-o* 'rooster'), which I hypothesize is the realization of n i [−FEM]. Most nouns referring to females end in -*em* (e.g. *bakk-em* 'hen'), likely the realization of n i [+FEM]. It is predicted that nouns which do not specify which natural gender they belong to would end in a different suffix, since their roots would be licensed under *n*. This is borne out: nouns that can refer to males or females end in *-i* (e.g. *igicc-i* 'goat').

However, some notoriously complex gender systems have been analyzed as phonologically determined gender systems (e.g. Aronoff 1994's treatment of Arapesh and Yimas). In order to support a DM approach to gender, such cases would have to be shown to be amenable to an approach where the phonology is determined by the gender. Moreover, there are often sub-generalizations within a language whereby certain nouns that all have the same gender have (or lack) a certain piece of phonology, but not all nouns with that gender do (see e.g. Aronoff 1994 on Latin, Terrill 2003 on Lavukaleve). These sub-generalizations could be analyzed as contextual allomorphy of a particular *n*, conditioned by a root, but it remains to be seen whether this is plausible. A major next step for a DM approach to gender would be a careful investigation of these questions.

11.2.2 *Languages with more than three genders*

Another major area of future research centers on languages with more than three genders (henceforth >3G languages). In Chapter 1, I explained that I would not be covering >3G languages for a few reasons: limited space, two-/three-gender languages provide enough gender puzzles, and the majority of languages with gender systems have two or three genders. Another reason for the omission of >3G languages from this book can be added to this list now that the analysis has been presented: it is impossible to generate a >3G language from the *n* inventories in Table 11.1, an additional type of gendered *n* must be present to do so, and developing a plausible analysis of the resulting gender system is a complex undertaking.

To see this clearly, consider the largest inventory of gendered *n*s, used for Romanian and Lavukaleve in the last row of Table 11.1. These languages have five gendered *n*s: interpretable [+FEM], uninterpretable [+FEM], interpretable [−FEM], uninterpretable [−FEM], and *n* lacking gender features. Assuming that PF does not care about interpretability, this set of *n*s yields a maximum of three different Vocabulary Items for an agreement target: a [+FEM] VI, a [−FEM] VI, and a VI lacking gender features. In order to have a fourth VI for agreement targets, i.e. a fourth gender as defined in Chapter 4, there must be an additional *n* that has a different type of gender feature. It is easiest to see how this would work with an example, and one of the best-known sets of >3G languages is the Bantu language family.

Bantu languages have multiple "noun classes" (= genders) marked by a prefix or prefixes on the noun (see overviews in Maho 1999, Demuth 2000, Katamba 2003). The class of a particular noun affects how other elements agree with the noun, and the system is partially based on human-ness, so these noun classes qualify as genders according to the definition in Chapter 4. Traditionally, the singular and plural of the same noun are considered separate classes, since they are marked by different

TABLE 11.2. **Noun classes in Sesotho**

	Class	Singular	Class	Plural
'person'	1	mo-tho	2	ba-tho
'aunt'	1a	rakhádi	2a	bo-rakhádi
'dress'	3	mo-sé	4	me-sé
'day/sun'	5	le-tsatsí	6	ma-tsatsí
'tree'	7	se-fate	8	di-fate
'dog'	9	n-tjá	10	din-tjá
'health'	14	bo-phelo		
'to cook'	15	ho-phéha		

(Demuth 2000: 273)

prefixes, and the number of noun classes from this perspective ranges from five to around twenty (Maho 1999). Table 11.2 shows the noun classes of Sesotho (Bantu; Lesotho, South Africa).

I will assume that the singular and plural of the same noun have the same noun class, and the realization of the noun class varies depending on number. Following Bantuist convention, I will refer to such classes as "Class Singular/Plural," e.g. "Class 1/2."

The Bantu noun class system is rooted in semantics, like all other gender systems, but it is not rooted in biological sex. It is rooted in human-ness: Class 1(a)/2(a) only contains human nouns in almost all Bantu languages (e.g. *mo-tho* 'person' in Sesotho). There are also a few less robust semantic generalizations within/across Bantu languages (Maho 1999); e.g. animals tend to be class 9/10 (e.g. *n-tjá* 'dog' in Sesotho), inanimate objects tend to be class 7/8 (e.g. *se-fate* 'tree' in Sesotho). Otherwise, however, there is a "ragbag" of meanings associated with particular classes (Katamba 2003: 114, *pace* Contini-Morava 1997).

I assume any feature(s) relevant to noun class is on *n* (cf. Ferrari 2005), so roots in class 1(a)/2(a) are licensed under *n* [HUMAN].[216] However, since there is more than one non-human noun class, it cannot be that a single [−HUMAN] feature (or *n* lacking gender features) suffices to derive the rest of the system. Instead, other features must come into play.

Ferrari (2005) and Carstens (2010, 2011) propose that noun classes have identity features, which are uninterpretable. This is shown in (2).

(2)   *n*

      u [9/10]

---

[216] General evidence in favor of gender being on *n* in Bantu languages is that, in many Bantu languages, diminutives and/or augmentatives are expressed via a change in noun class. See Chapters 9 and 10.

These identity features are required to generate noun classes that cannot be characterized semantically, and (I believe) will be required for any >3G language that has a fourth/fifth/etc. gender which is not characterizable by an interpretable feature.

As for the noun classes that seem to have interpretable features (e.g. animals in Class 9/10), there are several analytical options. They could be encoded as interpretable features on *n*s in certain classes, e.g. *u* [9/10], *i* [ANIMAL] (this is the option adopted by Ferrari 2005 from a *n* perspective, Carstens 2010, 2011 from a lexical perspective). Another option would be for all the nouns in the same semantically motivated class to have the same feature, e.g. [ANIMAL]. The feature would be interpretable for some nouns, but uninterpretable for others. Radically, it may be that these sub-generalizations are not even part of the generative grammar, because only human-ness plays a significant role in loanword noun class assignment and in the acquisition of noun class (Demuth 2000). Distinguishing these analyses empirically, and exploring their conceptual consequences, is an interesting but complex task, especially because some of the semantic generalizations for Bantu noun classes hinge on properties that are less palatable to represent as features, e.g. liquids (Maho 1999: 77–8; see Corbett 1991: 30–32 on what kinds of interpretable features are available to gender systems generally).

In sum, >3G languages are significantly different from two- to three-gender languages in that they most likely require some kind of uninterpretable gender/ noun class identity feature. Moreover, it is unclear how to integrate semantic generalizations (if they exist) into this kind of system. I therefore leave >3G languages to future research, with the hope that the proposals and predictions here will serve as a useful jumping-off point.

11.2.3 The role of social factors

There are potentially fruitful connections between this book and the sociolinguistic literature on "the representation of women and men in language," as Hellinger and Bußmann (2001: 2) phrase it. This vein of literature explores questions about how femaleness and maleness are encoded across languages, regardless of whether a language has gender as defined in Chapter 4. This research tradition and the present book are both concerned with gender defaults, especially from a cross-linguistic perspective. In particular, there are a few areas where social factors may explain why masculine defaults have a wider distribution than the analysis would predict, in a variety of contexts.

First of all, in a two-gender system, the analysis developed in this book predicts that either masculine or feminine will be the default gender; I showed examples of languages with feminine defaults in Chapters 5 (Zayse and Zargulla) and Chapter 6 (Maa). In other words, there is nothing inherent in the grammar that forces a masculine default, and feminine defaults are attested. Impressionistically, however, it seems that languages with masculine defaults are more common, which the analysis here does not explain. It remains to be confirmed whether this empirical claim is correct, but if so, it may be that social factors are the reason why masculine is the default in more languages.

In a three-gender language, the analysis developed in this book predicts that neuter is the default gender, which is mostly borne out as shown in Chapter 7. However, many three-gender languages use a non-neuter gender for sex-differentiable nouns, as discussed in the last section of Chapter 7. In the languages that I examined (Mangarayi, Wari', Lavukaleve, Russian, Icelandic, Tamil), masculine was possible as the non-neuter default in almost every language. Feminine was used as the non-neuter default in only one language (Wari') and in only one context (mixed-gender groups). Again, social factors may explain the dominance of the masculine default for sex-differentiable nouns.

Finally, some of the languages discussed throughout this book contain nominals that undergo root allomorphy for gender where the root allomorph used for males is the one used in non-gender-specified contexts. Examples are in (3).[217]

(3) a. säw   'man, person'   set   'woman'   (Amharic, Chapter 2)
     b. padre 'father, parent' madre 'mother' (Spanish, Chapter 6)

Nothing in the analysis prevents the feminine allomorph being used for the non-gender-specified context (e.g. *set* 'person,' *madre* 'parent'). However, again, social pressure towards males being the default human may explain why the feminine form is never used in the cases seen here.

Of course, how to integrate social factors into this analysis remains to be seen, and this discussion leaves many questions open (e.g. how/why certain nouns end up having feminine defaults within a particular languages). However, the explicitness of the gender analysis here allows us to begin hypothesizing precisely where the analysis stops and social factors begin. Hopefully, further work will be able to continue and to confirm/refute the hypotheses.

11.2.4 *Languages that lack gender*

A final area of open questions concerns languages that lack gender according to the definition in Chapter 4, i.e. languages that lack gender agreement. Such languages are quite common (56 per cent of the languages surveyed in Corbett 2011a), and well-known examples include Estonian, Turkish, Thai and Indonesian. I will refer to them as "non-gender languages."

---

[217] Additionally, many languages reuse the root for 'man' as the root for 'person,' even when it is (seemingly) unrelated to the word 'woman,' e.g. Lavukaleve *ali* 'man, person,' *homela* 'woman' (Terrill 2003).

There are a few potential approaches to non-gender languages given the proposals of this book. First, it may be that these languages lack gender features altogether, i.e. the *n*s of these languages never carry [+/−FEM] or [ANIMATE]. However, this may render the interpretation of certain roots different than the interpretation of roots in languages with gender. If the claims in Chapter 3 are taken very seriously that √ɨNNAT 'mother' in Amharic is interpreted as female only because it is licensed in the context of *n*[+FEM], then it must be the case that roots in non-gender languages are different from those in gender languages. This is because non-gender languages do in fact contain words that convey information about natural gender, like 'mother;' if non-gender languages lack *n* [+FEM], then the natural gender information can only come from the root.

Another possibility is that non-gender languages do in fact contain *n*s with gender features, and 'mother' is interpreted the same way as in languages with gender systems. However, in non-gender languages, gender features are for some reason ignored by the agreement system. If agreement is accomplished via the Agree relation, one way to make this more precise would be to say that such languages lack gender probes (see e.g. Béjar 2008 on how phi features probe separately). Alternatively, it may be that syntactic gender agreement works as normal, but gender features are not part of the Vocabulary Items that realize gender targets, and thus they are basically ignored by the morphophonological system.

One way to distinguish between a "roots are different" and an "agreement is different" analysis would be to look for evidence of gendered *n*s elsewhere in the language, e.g. as nominalizers. If a non-gender language contains such *n*s, even though they do not participate in agreement relations, then an "agreement is different" analysis is supported. Estonian provides such evidence: it contains a non-productive suffix *-nna* that is used to convey female natural gender, as in (4)

(4) a. sõber   b. sõbra-nna
        friend   friend.GEN-FEM
        'friend, male friend'   'female friend'[218]

Under the approach here, *-nna* is the realization of a *n i*[+FEM], so Estonian contains a gendered *n*. This is tentative evidence, then, that non-gender languages have different agreement systems and in fact contain gender features. Granted, the remarks here are very speculative, and are meant to stimulate further thinking rather than to provide answers. To the best of my knowledge, there is very little work on how non-gender languages differ from gender languages, and the proposals here provide a place to start addressing this puzzle.

---

[218] The genitive form of a noun is sometimes used as the stem for suffixation in Estonian.

11.3 Meta-conclusion

The goal of this book was the development of a large-scale cross-linguistic theory of the morphosyntax of gender. Such a theory has emerged: gender is located on *n*, gender features are interpretable or uninterpretable, gender features make a fundamental three-way contrast for biological sex (+/–/absent) (or two-way contrast for animacy: present/absent). This theory was supported by data from the gender systems of Amharic, Dieri, Zayse and Zargulla, Lealao Chinantec, Spanish, Maa, Algonquian languages, Mangarayi, Wari', Lavukaleve, Somali, and Romanian, not including the many languages mentioned in the chapters on nominalization and declension class. Many open areas of research remain (see Section 11.2), but the proposals here will hopefully serve as a useful touchstone for future research on the intricate and fascinating morphosyntax of gender.

References

Acquaviva, Paolo (2008). *Lexical Plurals*. Oxford: Oxford University Press.

Acquaviva, Paolo (2009). Roots and lexicality in Distributed Morphology. *York Essex Morphology Meeting* 2: 1–21.

Adger, David (2010). A minimalist theory of feature structure. In A. Kibort and Greville Corbett (eds), *Features: Perspectives on a Key Notion in Linguistics*. Oxford: Oxford University Press, 185–218.

Adger, David, and Daniel Harbour (2007). Syntax and syncretisms of the Person Case Constraint. *Syntax* 10: 2–37.

Adger, David, and Peter Svenonius (2011). Features in minimalist syntax. In Cedric Boeckx (ed.), *The Handbook of Linguistic Minimalism*. Oxford: Blackwell, 27–51.

Aikhenvald, Alexandra (2000). *Classifiers: A Typology of Noun Classification Devices*. Oxford: Oxford University Press.

Aikhenvald, Alexandra (2001). Wari': the Pacaas Novos Language of western Brazil [review]. *Anthropological Linguistics* 43: 223–6.

Aksenov, A. T. (1984). K probleme èkstralingvističeskoj motivacii grammatičeskoj kategorii roda. *Voprosy jazykoznanija* 1: 14–25.

Alexiadou, Artemis (2001). *Functional Structure in Nominals: Nominalization and Ergativity*. Amsterdam: Benjamins.

Alexiadou, Artemis (2004). Inflection class, gender and DP-internal structure. In Gereon Müller, Lutz Gunkel, and Gisela Zifonun (eds), *Explorations in Nominal Inflection*. Berlin: Mouton, 21–50.

Alexiadou, Artemis (2010a). Nominalizations: a probe into the architecture of grammar. Part 1: The nominalization puzzle. *Language and Linguistics Compass* 4: 496–511.

Alexiadou, Artemis (2010b). Nominalizations: a probe into the architecture of grammar. Part 2: The aspectual properties of nominalizations, and the lexicon vs. syntax debate. *Language and Linguistics Compass* 4: 512–23.

Alexiadou, Artemis (2011a). Adjectival nominalizations: qualities and properties. Paper presented at the Workshop on the Syntax and Semantics of Nounhood and Adjectivehood, Barcelona.

Alexiadou, Artemis (2011b). Aspectual properties of nominalization structures. In George Tsoulas, Glyn Hicks, and Alexandra Galani (eds), *Morphology and its Interfaces*. Amsterdam: Benjamins, 195–220.

Alexiadou, Artemis, Liliane Haegeman, and Melita Stavrou (2007). *Noun Phrase in the Generative Perspective*. New York: Mouton.

Alexiadou, Artemis, Gianina Iordăchioaia, and Elena Soare (2010). Number/aspect interactions in the syntax of nominalizations: a distributed approach. *Journal of Linguistics* 46: 537–74.

Alexiadou, Artemis, Gianina Iordăchioaia, and Florian Schäfer (2011). Scaling the variation in Romance and Germanic nominalizations. In Petra Sleeman and Harry Perridon (eds), *The Noun Phrase in Romance and Germanic*. Amsterdam: Benjamins, 25–40.

Alexiadou, Artemis, and Fabienne Martin (2012). Competing affixes as aspectual morphemes: the case of deadjectival nominalization. In Angela Ralli et al. (eds), *Proceedings of the 8th Mediterranean Morphology Meeting*, 8–22: Available at: <http://www.uni-stuttgart.de/linguistik/sfb732/files/mmm8_proceedingsteil1.pdf>.

Alexiadou, Artemis, and Gereon Müller (2008). Class features as probes. In Asaf Bachrach and Andrew Nevins (eds), *Inflectional Identity*. Oxford: Oxford University Press, 101–55.

Alexiadou, Artemis, and Monika Rathert (eds) (2010). *The Syntax of Nominalizations across Languages and Frameworks*. Berlin: Mouton.

Allan, Edward J. (1976). Dizi. In M. Lionel Bender (ed.), *The Non-Semitic Languages of Ethiopia*. East Lansing: Michigan State University, 377–92.

Alpher, Barry (1987). Feminine as the unmarked grammatical gender: buffalo girls are no fools. *Australian Journal of Linguistics* 7: 169–87.

Amberber, Mengistu (1996). Transitive alternations, event-types and light verbs. Doctoral dissertation, McGill University.

Amha, Azeb (2007). Are -a- and -o- in the indicative verb paradigms of Zargulla nominalizers? In Amha Azeb, Sava Graziano, and Mous Maarten (eds), *Omotic and Cushitic Languages Studies: Papers from the Fourth Cushitic Omotic Conference*. Cologne: Köppe, 1–22:

Amha, Azeb (2008). Gender distinction and affirmative copula clauses in Zargulla. In John D. Bengtson (ed.), *In Hot Pursuit of Language in Prehistory*. Amsterdam: Benjamins, 39–48.

Amha, Azeb (2009). The morpho-syntax of negation in Zargulla. In W. Leo Wetzels (ed.), *The Linguistics of Endangered Languages: Contributions to Morphology and Morpho-Syntax*. Utrecht: LOT, 199–220.

Amha, Azeb (2010). From gender identification to assertion: on the use of -tte and -tta in Zargulla, an endangered Omotic languages. *Journal of West African Languages* 37: 57–73.

Amha, Azeb (2012). Omotic. In Zygmunt Frajzyngier and Erin Shay (eds), *The Afroasiatic Languages*. Cambridge: Cambridge University Press, 423–504.

Anagnostopoulou, Elena (2003). *The Syntax of Ditransitives: Evidence from Clitics*. Berlin: Mouton de Gruyter.

Anand, Pranav (2006). De de se. Doctoral dissertation, MIT.

Andrzejewski, Bogumil W. (1964). *The Declensions of Somali Nouns*. London: School of Oriental and African Studies.

Antón-Méndez, Inés, Janet L. Nicol, and Merrill F. Garrett (2002). The relation between gender and number agreement processing. *Syntax* 5: 1–25.

Appleyard, David (1995). *Colloquial Amharic: A Complete Language Course*. New York: Routledge.

Arad, Maya (2003). Locality constraints on the interpretations of roots. *Natural Language and Linguistic Theory* 21: 737–78.

Arad, Maya (2005). *Roots and Patterns: Hebrew Morpho-syntax*. Dordrecht: Springer.

Arden, A. H. (1942). *A Progressive Grammar of Common Tamil*, 5th edn. Madras: Christian Literature Society for India.

Armoskaite, Solveiga (2011). The destiny of roots in Blackfoot and Lithuanian. Doctoral dissertation, University of British Columbia.

Armoskaite, Solveiga (2014). Derivation by gender in Lithuanian. In Ileana Paul (ed.), *Cross-linguistic Investigations of Nominalizations*. Amsterdam: Benjamins, 169–87.

Armoskaite, Solveiga, and Martina Wiltschko (2012). There are many ways to be gendered. In Paula Caxaj (ed.), *The Proceedings of the 2012 Annual Conference of the Canadian Linguistic Association*. Available at: <http://homes.chass.utoronto.ca/~cla-acl/actes2012/actes2012:%20html>.

Aronoff, Mark (1994). *Morphology by Itself: Stems and Inflectional Classes*. Cambridge, Mass.: MIT Press.

Asher, R. E. (1982). *Tamil*. Amsterdam: North-Holland.

Asudeh, Ash, and Christopher Potts (2004). Honorific marking: interpreted and interpretable. MS, University of Canterbury/University of Massachusetts, Amherst.

Atkinson, Emily A. (2012). Gender features on *n* & the root: an account of gender in French. Paper presented at the 42nd Linguistic Symposium on Romance Languages (LSRL), Southern Utah University, Cedar City.

Audring, Jenny (2009). Gender assignment and gender agreement: evidence from pronominal gender languages. *Morphology* 18: 93–116.

Austin, Peter K. (1981a). *A Grammar of Diyari, South Australia*. Cambridge: Cambridge University Press.

Austin, Peter K. (1981b). Switch-reference in Australia. *Language* 57: 309–34.

Austin, Peter K. (1982). The deictic system of Diyari. In Jürgen Weissenborn and Wolfgang Klein (eds), *Here and There: Cross-Linguistic Studies on Deixis and Determination*. Amsterdam: Benjamins, 273–84.

Austin, Peter K. (2011). *A Grammar of Diyari, South Australia*, 2nd edn. Available at: <http://soas.academia.edu/PeterAustin>.

Bach, Emmon (1970). Is Amharic an SOV language? *Journal of Ethiopian Studies* 7: 9–20.

Bachrach, Asaf, and Michael Wagner (2007). Syntactically driven cyclicity vs. output–output correspondence: the case of adjunction in diminutive morphology. MS, MIT and Cornell University. Available at: <http://ling.auf.net/lingbuzz/000383>.

Baker, Mark C. (2012). On the relationship of object agreement and accusative case: evidence from Amharic. *Linguistic Inquiry* 43: 255–74.

Baker, Mark C., and Ruth Kramer (2014). Rethinking Amharic prepositions as case markers inserted at PF. *Lingua* 145: 141–72.

Baker, Mark C., and Nadya Vinokurova (2009). On agent nominalizations and why they are not like event nominalizations. *Language* 85: 517–56.

Bani, Ephraim (1987). Garka i ipika: masculine and feminine grammatical gender in Kala Lagaw Ya'. *Australian Journal of Linguistics* 7: 189–201.

Barber, Horacio, and Manuel Carreiras (2005). Grammatical gender and number agreement in Spanish: an ERP comparison. *Journal of Cognitive Neuroscience* 17: 137–53.

Bateman, Nicoleta, and Maria Polinsky (2010). Romanian as a two-gender language. In Donna Gerdts, John Moore, and Maria Polinsky (eds), *Festschrift for David Perlmutter*. Cambridge, Mass.: MIT Press, 41–77.

Beachy, Marvin (2005). An overview of Central Dizin phonology and morphology. Master's thesis, University of Texas at Arlington.

Beard, Robert (1990). The empty morpheme entailment. In Wolfgang U. Dressler et al. (eds), *Contemporary Morphology*. Berlin: Mouton, 159–70.

Beard, Robert (1995a). *Lexeme-Morpheme Based Morphology*. Lewsisburg, Penn.: Bucknell University.

Beard, Robert (1995b). The gender-animacy hypothesis. *Journal of Slavic Lingustics* 3: 59–96.

Beermann, Dorothee, and Binyam Ephrem (2007). The definite article and possessive marking in Amharic. In *Texas Linguistic Society 9* (ed. F. Hoyt et al.), 21–33.

Béjar, Susana (2008). Conditions on phi-agree. In Daniel Harbour, David Adger, and Susana Béjar (eds), *Phi Theory*. Oxford: Oxford University Press, 130–54.

Béjar, Susana, and Milan Rezac (2009). Cyclic Agree. *Linguistic Inquiry* 40: 35–73.

Bender, M. L., J. D. Bowen, R. L. Cooper, and C. A. Ferguson (1976). *Language in Ethiopia*. Oxford: Oxford University Press.

Bentley, Mayrene (1999). Animacy: a principle of grammatical organization. *CLS* 35: 291–309.

Bermúdez-Otero, Ricardo (2006). Morphological structure and phonological domains in Spanish denominal derivation. In Fernando Martínez-Gil and Sonia Colina (eds), *Optimality-Theoretic Studies in Spanish Phonology*. Amsterdam: Benjamins, 278–311.

Bermúdez-Otero, Ricardo (2007). Spanish pseudoplurals: phonological cues in the acquisition of a syntax–morphology mismatch. In Matthew Baerman et al. (eds), *Deponency and Morphological Mismatches (Proceedings of the British Academy 145)*. Oxford: Oxford University Press, 231–69.

Bermúdez-Otero, Ricardo (2013). The Spanish lexicon stores stems with theme vowels, not roots with inflectional class features. *Probus* 25: 3–103.

Bernstein, Judy (1991). DPs in Walloon: evidence for paramateric variation in nominal head movement. *Probus* 3: 101–26.

Bernstein, Judy (1993a). Topics in the syntax of nominal structure across Romance and Germanic languages. Doctoral dissertation, City University of New York.

Bernstein, Judy (1993b). The syntactic role of word markers in null nominal constructions. *Probus* 5: 5–38.

Bhattacharya, Sudhibhushan (1957). *Ollari: A Dravidian Speech*. Calcutta: Government of India Press.

Birchall, Joshua (2008). Determining gender markedness in Wari'. In Joye Kiester and Verónica Muñoz-Ledo (eds), *Proceedings from the 11th Workshop on American Indian Languages*. Santa Barbara Papers in Linguistics 19, 15–24. Available at: <http://www.linguistics.ucsb.edu/research/santa-barbara-papers>.

Birchall, Joshua (to appear). The multi-verb benefactive construction in Wari' and Oro Win. In F. Queixalós, A. C. Bruno, and S. Telles (eds), *Valency Increase in Amazonian Languages*.

Black-Rogers, Mary B. (1982). Algonquian gender revisited: animate nouns and Ojibwa 'power'—an impasse? *Papers in Linguistics* 15: 59–76.

Blake, Barry J. (1979). Pitta-Pitta. In R. M. W. Dixon and Barry Blake (eds), *Handbook of Australian Langauges*, vol. 1. Amsterdam: Benjamins, 182–242.

Blake, Barry J. (2001). The noun phrase in Australian languages. In Jane Helen Simpson et al. (eds), *Forty Years On: Ken Hale and Australian Languages*. Canberra: Pacific Linguistics, Research School of Pacific and Asian Studies, Australian National University, 415–25.

Bliss, Heather (2014). Assigning references in clausal nominalizations. In Ileana Paul (ed.), *Cross-Linguistic Investigations of Nominalization Patterns*. Amsterdam: Benjamins, 85–117.

Bloomfield, Leonard (1933). *Language*. Chicago: University of Chicago Press.

Bloomfield, Leonard (1957). *Eastern Ojibwa: Grammatical Sketch, Texts and Word List.* Ann Arbor: University of Michigan Press.

Bloomfield, Leonard (1962). *The Menomini Langauge.* New Haven, Conn.: Yale University Press.

Bobaljik, Jonathan David (2008). Where's phi? Agreement as a post-syntactic operation. In David Adger, Susana Béjar, and Daniel Harbour (eds), *Phi-Theory: Phi Features across Interfaces and Modules.* Oxford: Oxford University Press, 295–328.

Bobaljik, Jonathan David, and Cynthia Zocca (2011). Gender markedness: the anatomy of a counter-example. *Morphology* 21: 141–66.

Borer, Hagit (2005). *Structuring Sense*, vol. 1: *In Name Only.* Oxford: Oxford University Press.

Borer, Hagit (2009). Very late insertion. Paper presented at 'Root Bound', USC, Los Angeles.

Borer, Hagit (2010). Root bound. Talk given at the University of Maryland, College Park.

Börjesson, Kristin (2006). Argument encoding in Slovene: a Distributed Morphology analysis of Slovene noun declension. *Linguistische Arbeits Berichte* 84: 115–30.

Borsley, Robert D., and Jaklin Kornfilt (2000). Mixed extended projections. In Robert D. Borsley (ed.), *The Nature and Function of Syntactic Categories.* New York: Academic Press, 101–31.

Bouchard, Denis (1984). *On the Content of Empty Categories.* Dordrecht: Foris.

Bowern, Claire (2001). Karnic classification revisited. In Jane Helen Simpson et al. (eds), *Forty Years On: Ken Hale and Australian Languages.* Canberra: Pacific Linguistics, Research School of Pacific and Asian Studies, Australian National University, 245–61.

Bradley, Travis G., and Jason Smith (2011). The phonology–morphology interface in Judeo-Spanish diminutive formation: a lexical ordering and subcategorization approach. *Studies in Hispanic and Lusophone Linguistics* 4: 247–300.

Brown, Jason, Karsten Koch, and Martina Wiltschko (2004). The person hierarchy: primitive or epiphenomenal? Evidence from Halkomelem Salish. In Keir Moulton and Matthew Wolf (eds), *Proceedings of NELS 34.* Amherst, Mass.: GLSA, 147–62.

Bruening, Benjamin (2001). Syntax at the edge: cross-clausal phenomena and the syntax of Passamaquoddy. Doctoral dissertation, MIT.

Butler, Lindsay K. (2012). The DP-adjoined plural in Yucatec Maya and the syntax of plural marking. MS, University of Rochester.

Butt, John, and Carmen Benjamin (2011). *A New Reference Grammar of Modern Spanish.* Oxford: Oxford University Press.

Carminati, Maria Nella (2005). Processing reflexes of the Feature Hierarchy (Person > Number > Gender) and implications for linguistic theory. *Lingua* 115: 259–85.

Carstens, Vicki (2000). Concord in Minimalist Theory. *Linguistic Inquiry* 31: 319–55.

Carstens, Vicki (2010). Implications of grammatical gender for the theory of uninterpretable features. In Michael Putnam (ed.), *Exploring Crash-Proof Grammars.* Amsterdam: Benjamins, 31–57.

Carstens, Vicki (2011). Hyperactivity and hyperagreement in Bantu. *Lingua* 121: 721–41.

Chitoran, Ioana (1992). The Romanian gender system in the framework of markedness theory. *Revue roumaine de linguistique* 37: 177–90.

Chitoran, Ioana (1996). Prominence vs. rhythm: the predictability of stress in Romanian. In Karen Zagona (ed.), *Grammatical Theory and Romance Langauges.* Amsterdam: Benjamins, 47–58.

Chitoran, Ioana (2002). *The Phonology of Romanian: A Constraint-Based Approach*. Berlin: Mouton de Gruyter.

Chomsky, Noam (1970). Remarks on nominalization. In R. A. Jacobs and P. S. Rosenbaum (eds), *Readings in English Transformational Grammar*. Waltham, Mass.: Ginn, 184–221.

Chomsky, Noam (1981). *Lectures on Government and Binding*. Dordrecht: Foris.

Chomsky, Noam (1995). *The Minimalist Program*. Cambridge: MIT Press.

Chomsky, Noam (2000). Minimalist inquiries: the framework. In Roger Martin, David Michaels, and Juan Uriagereka (eds), *Step by Step: Essays on Minimalist Syntax in Honor of Howard Lasnik*. Cambridge, Mass.: MIT Press, 89–155.

Chomsky, Noam (2001). Derivation by phase. In Michael Kenstowicz (ed.), *Ken Hale: A Life in Language*. Cambridge, Mass.: MIT Press, 1–52.

Chomsky, Noam (2004). Beyond explanatory adequacy. In Adriana Belletti (ed.), *Structures and Beyond*. New York: Oxford University Press, 104–31.

Cinque, Guglielmo (1999). *Adverbs and Functional Heads: A Crosslinguistic Perspective*. Oxford: Oxford University Press.

Clamons, Cynthia (1993). Gender assignment in Oromo. In Mushira Eid and Gregory Iverson (eds), *Principles and Prediction: The Analysis of Natural Language*. Amsterdam: Benjamins, 269–84.

Cohen, Marcel (1970). *Traité de langue amharique*, 2nd edn. Paris: Institut d'Ethnologie.

Colina, Sonia (2003). Diminutives in Spanish: a morpho-phonological account. *Southwest Journal of Linguistics* 22(2): 45–88.

Comrie, Bernard (1981). *Language Universals and Linguistic Typology*. Chicago: University of Chicago Press.

Comrie, Bernard (1999). Grammatical gender systems: a linguist's assessment. *Journal of Psycholinguistic Research* 28: 457–66.

Comrie, Bernard, and Sandra A. Thompson (2007). Lexical nominalization. In Timothy Shopen (ed.), *Language Typology and Syntactic Description*, vol. 3, 2nd edn. Cambridge: Cambridge University Press, 334–81.

Contini-Morava, Ellen (1997). Noun classification in Swahili: a cognitive-semantic analysis using a computer database. In Robert K. Herbert (ed.), *African Linguistics at the Crossroads: Papers from Kwaluseni 1994*. Cologne: Köppe, 599–628.

Corbett, Greville (1980). Neutral agreement. *Quinquereme* 3: 164–70.

Corbett, Greville (1991). *Gender*. Cambridge: Cambridge University Press.

Corbett, Greville (2000). *Number*. Cambridge: Cambridge University Press.

Corbett, Greville (2006a). *Agreement*. Cambridge: Cambridge University Press.

Corbett, Groville (2006b). Gender, grammatical. In Keith Brown, (ed.), *Encyclopedia of Language and Linguistics*. Amsterdam: Elsevier, 749–56.

Corbett, Greville (2007). Canonical typology, suppletion, and possible words. *Language* 83: 8–42.

Corbett, Greville G. (2011a). Number of genders. In Matthew S. Dryer and Martin Haspelmath (eds), *The World Atlas of Language Structures Online*. Munich: Max Planck Digital Library, ch. 30. Available at: <http://wals.info/chapter/30>.

Corbett, Greville G. (2011b). Sex-based and non-sex-based gender assignment. In Matthew S. Dryer and Martin Haspelmath (eds), *The World Atlas of Language Structures Online*. Munich: Max Planck Digital Library, ch. 31: Available at: <http://wals.info/chapter/31>.

Corbett, Greville G. (2011c). Systems of gender assignment. In Matthew S. Dryer and Martin Haspelmath (eds), *The World Atlas of Language Structures Online*. Munich: Max Planck Digital Library, ch. 32: Available at: <http://wals.info/chapter/32>.

Corbett, Greville G., and Norman M. Fraser (2000a). Default genders. In Barbara Unterbeck (ed.), *Gender in Grammar and Cognition*, part 1: *Approaches to Gender*. Berlin: Mouton de Gruyter, 55–98.

Corbett, Greville G., and Norman M. Fraser (2000b). Gender assignment: a typology and model. In Gunter Senft (ed.), *Systems of Nominal Classification*. Cambridge: Cambridge University Press, 293–325.

Cornilescu, Alexandra (1995). Rumanian genitive construtions. In Giuliana Giusti and Guglilemo Cinque (eds), *Advances in Roumanian Linguistics*. Amsterdam: Benjamins, 1–54.

Cornilescu, Alexandra (2001). Romanian nominalizations: case and aspectual structure. *Journal of Linguistics* 37: 467–501.

Croitor, Blanca, and Ion Giurgea (2009). On the so-called Romanian "neuter." *Bucharest Working Papers in Linguistics* 11(2): 21–39.

Curzan, Anne (2003). *Gender Shifts in the History of English*. Cambridge: Cambridge University Press.

Dahl, Östen (2000). Animacy and the notion of semantic gender. In Barbara Unterbeck (ed.), *Gender in Grammar and Cognition*, part 1: *Approaches to Gender*. Berlin: Mouton de Gruyter, 99–116.

Dahlstrom, Amy (1995). Motivation vs. predictability in Algonquian gender. In David H. Pentland (ed.), *Papers of the 26th Algonquian Conference* (Winnipeg: University of Manitoba), 52–66.

Darnell, Regna, and Anthony L. Vanek (1976). The semantic basis of the animate/inanimate distinction in Cree. *Papers in Linguistics* 9: 159–80.

Dawe-Sheppard, Audrey, and John Hewson (1990). Person and gender hierarchies in Micmac. *Journal of the Atlantic Provinces Linguistic Association* 12: 1–12.

de Belder, Marijke (2011a). Roots and affixes: eliminating lexical categories from the syntax. Doctoral dissertation, Universiteit Utrecht.

de Belder, Marijke (2011b). A morphosyntactic decomposition of countability in Germanic. *Journal of Comparative Germanic Linguistics* 14: 173–202.

de Belder, Marijke, Noam Faust, and Nicola Lampitelli (to appear). On an inflectional and a derivational diminutive. In Artemis Alexiadou et al. (eds), *The Syntax of Roots and the Roots of Syntax*. Oxford: Oxford University Press.

Demeke, Girma A. (2001). N-final relative clauses: the Amharic case. *Studia Linguistica* 55: 191–215.

Demeke, Girma A. (2003). The clausal syntax of Ethio-Semitic. Doctoral dissertation, University of Tromsø.

Demeke, Girma A. (2013). Grammatical changes in Semitic: a diachronic grammar of Amharic. MS, Institute of Semitic Studies, Princeton, NJ.

Demeke, Girma A., and Mesfin Getachew (2006). Manual annotation of Amharic news items with part-of-speech tags and its challenges. *Ethiopian Languages Research Center Working Papers* 2: 1–16.

Demuth, Katherine (2000). Bantu noun class systems: loanword and acquisition evidence of semantic productivity. In Gunter Senft (ed.), *Systems of Nominal Classification*. Cambridge: Cambridge University Press, 270–92.

den Dikken, Marcel (2007). Amharic relatives and possessives: definiteness, agreement and the linker. *Linguistic Inquiry* 38: 302–20.

Denny, J. P., and C. A. Creider (1986). The semantics of noun classes in Proto-Bantu. In Colette G. Craig (ed.), *Noun Classes and Categorization*. Amsterdam: Benjamins, 217–39.

Déprez, Viviane (2005). Morphological number, semantic number and bare nouns. *Lingua* 115: 857–83.

di Domenico, Elisa (1997). *Per una teoria del genere grammaticale*. Padua: Unipress.

Dixon, R. M. W. (2002). *Australian Languages: Their Nature and Development*. Cambridge: Cambridge University Press.

Dobrovie-Sorin, Carmen, Tonia Bleam, and M. Teresa Espinal (2006). Bare nouns, number and types of incorporation. In Svetlana Vogeleer and Liliane Tasmowski (eds), *Non-definiteness and Plurality*. Amsterdam: Benjamins, 51–79.

Dobrovie-Sorin, Carmen, and Ion Giurgea (eds) (2013). *A Reference Grammar of Romanian*, vol. 1: *The Noun Phrase*. Amsterdam: Benjamins.

Doleschal, Ursula (2001). Gender assignment revisisted. In Barbara Unterbeck and Matti Rissanen (eds), *Gender in Grammar and Cognition*. Berlin: Mouton, 117–65.

Doleschal, Ursula, and Sonja Schmid (2001). Doing gender in Russian: structure and perspective. In Hadumod Bussmann and Marlis Hellinger (eds), *Gender across Languages: the Linguistic Representation of Women and Men*, vol. 1. Amsterdam: Benjamins, 253–82.

Dowty, David, and Pauline Jacobson (1989). Agreement as a semantic phenomenon. In *Proceedings of ESCOL* 5: 95–108.

Dresher, B. Elan (2003). Contrasts and asymmetries in inventories. In Anna Maria di Sciullo (ed.), *Asymmetry in Grammar*, vol. 2. Amsterdam: Benjamins, 239–58.

Dressler, Wolfgang U., and Lavinia Merlini Barbaresi (1994). *Morphopragmatics: Diminutives and Intensifiers in Italian, German, and Other Languages*. Berlin: Mouton.

Dryer, Matthew S., and the WALS author team (2011). Language page for Hungarian. In Matthew S. Dryer and Martin Haspelmath (eds), *The World Atlas of Language Structures Online*. Munich: Max Planck Digital Library. Available at: <http://wals.info/languoid/lect/wals_code_hun> Accessed on 20 Aug. 2013.

Duek, Karen (2014). Bare singulars and gender agreement in Brazilian Portuguese. *Proceedings of CLS 48*. Chicago: CLS, 205–19.

Durrell, Martin (2011). *Hammer's German Grammar and Usage*, 5th edn. London: Hodder Education.

Eguren, Luis (2001). Evaluative suffixation in Spanish and the syntax of derivational processes. In Julia Herschensohn et al. (eds), *Features and Interfaces in Romance*. Amsterdam: Benjamins, 71–84.

Eilam, Aviad (2009). The absence of intervention effects in Amharic: evidence for a non-structural approach. MS, University of Pennsylvania.

Embick, David (2000). Features, syntax and categories in the Latin perfect. *Linguistic Inquiry* 31: 185–230.

Embick, David (2003). Linearization and local dislocation: derivational mechanics and interactions. *Linguistic Analysis* 33: 303–36.

Embick, David (2010). *Localism versus Globalism in Morphology and Phonology*. Cambridge, Mass.: MIT Press.

Embick, David, and Morris Halle (2005). On the status of stems in morphological theory. In Twan Geerts, Ivo von Ginneken, and Haike Jacobs (eds), *Romance Languages and Linguistic Theory 2003*. Amsterdam: Benjamins, 37–62.

Embick, David, and Alec Marantz (2008). Architecture and blocking. *Linguistic Inquiry* 39: 1–53.

Embick, David, and Rolf Noyer (2001). Movement operations after syntax. *Linguistic Inquiry* 32: 555–95.

Embick, David, and Rolf Noyer (2007). Distributed morphology and the syntax/morphology interface. In Gillian Ramchand and Charles Reiss (eds), *The Oxford Handbook of Linguistic Interfaces*. Oxford: Oxford University Press, 289–324.

Enger, Hans-Olav (2004). On the relation between gender and declension: a diachronic perspective from Norwegian. *Studies in Language* 28: 51–82.

Epstein, Samuel, Hisatsugu Kitahara, and T. Daniel Seely (2010). Uninterpretable features: what are they, and what do they do? In M. Putnam (ed.), *Exploring Crash-Proof Grammars*. Amsterdam: Benjamins, 125–42.

Erwin, Wallace (1963). *A Short Reference Grammar of Iraqi Arabic*. Washington, DC: Georgetown University Press.

Evans, Nicholas, Dunstan Brown, and Greville G. Corbett (2002). The semantics of gender in Mayali: partially parallel systems and formal implementation. *Language* 78: 111–55.

Everett, Daniel L. (1998). Wari' morphology. In Andrew Spencer and Arnold M. Zwicky (eds), *Handbook of Morphology*. Oxford: Blackwell, 690–706.

Everett, Daniel L. (2005). Periphrastic pronouns in Wari'. *International Journal of American Linguistics* 71: 303–26.

Everett, Daniel L. (2009). Wari' intentional state constructions. In Robert D. van Valin Jr (ed.), *Investigations of the Syntax–Semantics–Pragmatics Interface*. Amsterdam: Benjamins, 381–412.

Everett, Daniel L., and Kern, Barbara (1997). *Wari: the Pacaas Novos Language of Western Brazil*. London: Routledge.

Fabb, Nigel (1988). English suffixation is constrained only by selectional restrictions. *Natural Language and Linguistic Theory* 6: 527–39.

Fábregas, Antonio (2010a). A syntactic account of affix rivalry in Spanish nominalizations. In Artemis Alexiadou and Monika Rathert (eds), *The Syntax of Nominalizations across Languages and Frameworks*. Berlin: Mouton, 67–91.

Fábregas, Antonio (2010b). Revisiting the phonological properties of morphological constituents: the case of diminutives. MS, University of Tromsø. Available at: <http://ling.auf.net/lingbuzz/001122>

Farkas, Donka (1990). Two cases of underspecification in morphology. *Linguistic Inquiry* 22: 27–62.

Farkas, Donka, and Draga Zec (1995). Agreement and pronominal reference. In Guglielmo Cinque and Giuliana Giusti (eds), *Advances in Roumanian Linguistics*. Amsterdam: Benjamins, 83–102.

Fathi, Radwa, and Jean Lowenstamm (2014). Allomorphy? (or What gender does do?). Paper presented at 'Allomorphy: Its Logic and Limitations,' Jerusalem.

Faust, Noam (2013). Decomposing the feminine suffixes of Modern Hebrew: a morphosyntactic analysis. MS, Hebrew University of Jerusalem.

Feldman, Harry (1986). *A Grammar of Awtuw*. Canberra: Department of Linguistics, Research School of Pacific Studies, Australian National University.

Ferrari, Franca (2005). A syntactic analysis of the nominal systems of Italian and Luganda: how nouns can be formed in the syntax. Doctoral dissertation, New York University.

Ferrari-Bridgers, Franca (2008). A unified syntactic analysis of Italian and Luganda nouns. In Cécile de Cat and Katherine Demuth (eds), *The Bantu–Romance Connection*. Amsterdam: Benjamins, 239–58.

Fodor, Istvan (1959). The origin of grammatical gender I. *Lingua* 8: 186–214.

Fortin, Antonio (2011). The morphology and semantics of expressive affixes. Doctoral dissertation, Oxford University.

Franceschina, Florencia (2005). *Fossilized Second-Language Grammars: The Acquisition of Grammatical Gender*. Amsterdam: Benjamins.

Fraser, Norman M., and Greville G. Corbett (1995). Gender, animacy, and declension class assignment: a unified account for Russian. *Yearbook of Morphology 1994*: 123–50.

Fraser, Norman M., and Greville G. Corbett (1997). Defaults in Arapesh. *Lingua* 103: 25–57.

Freeman, Dena (2006). Who are the Gamo? And who are the D'ache? In Siegbert Uhlig (ed.), *Proceedings of the Fifteenth International Conference of Ethiopian Studies*. Wiesbaden: Harrassowitz, 85–91.

Friedman, Victor A. (1996). Gender, class, and age in the Daghestanian highlands: towards a unified account of the morphology of agreement in Lak. In Howard I. Aronson (ed.), *Linguistic Studies in the Non-Slavic Languages of the Commonwealth of Independent States and the Baltic Republics*. Chicago: Chicago Linguistic Society, 187–99.

Fuchs, Zuzanna, Maria Polinsky, and Gregory Scontras (to appear). The differential representation of number and gender in Spanish. *Linguistic Review*.

Fulass, Hailu (1966). Derived nominal patterns in Amharic. Doctoral dissertation, UCLA.

Fulass, Hailu (1972). On Amharic relative clauses. *Bulletin of the School of Oriental and African Studies* 35: 487–513.

GALR (2005). *Gramatica Limbii Române*. Bucharest: Editura Academiei Române.

Gardiner, Sir Alan (1957). *Egyptian Grammar*, 3rd edn. Oxford: Griffith Institute.

Gazdar, Gerald, Ewan Klein, Geoffrey Pullum, and Ivan Sag (1985). *Generalized Phrase Structure Grammar*. Oxford: Blackwell.

Ghaniabadi, Saeed (2012). Plural marking beyond count nouns. In Diane Massam (ed.), *Count and Mass across Languages*. Oxford: Oxford University Press, 112–28.

Ghomeshi, Jila (2003). Plural marking, indefiniteness, and the noun phrase. *Studia Linguistica* 57: 4–74.

Gil, David (2011). Numeral classifiers. In Matthew S. Dryer and Martin Haspelmath (eds), *The World Atlas of Language Structures Online*. Munich: Max Planck Digital Library. Available at: <http://wals.info/feature/55A>.

Giurgea, Ion (2008). Gender on definite pronouns. *Bucharest Working Papers in Linguistics* 10 (1): 97–121.

Giurgea, Ion (2014). Possible syntactic implementations of the controller vs. target gender distinction: the view from ambigenerics. *Language Sciences* 43: 47–61.

Goddard, Cliff (1982). Case systems and case marking in Australian languages: a new interpretation. *Australian Journal of Linguistics* 2: 167–96.

Goddard, Ives (2002). Grammatical gender in Algonquian. In H. C. Wolfart (ed.), *Proceedings of 33rd Algonquian Conference*. Winnipeg: University of Manitoba Press, 195–231.

Green, Christopher, and Michelle E. Morrison (2014). "One tone per word" is not enough: revisiting diagnostics of Somali wordhood. Paper presented at the 45th Annual Conference on African Linguistics, Lawrence, Kan.

Green, Christopher R., Michelle E. Morrison, Evan Jones, Nikki B. Adams, and Erin Smith Crabb (2014a). *A Grammar of Common Somali*, part 1: Technical Report 2.1, DO50. College Park: University of Maryland, Center for Advanced Study of Language.

Green, Christopher, Michelle E. Morrison, Nikki B. Adams, Erin Smith Crabb, Evan Jones, and Valerie Novak 2014b. Reference and pedagogical resources for 'Standard' Somali. *Electronic Journal of Africana Bibliography* 15. Available at: <http://ir.uiowa.edu/ejab/vol15/iss1/1>.

Greenberg, Joseph H. (1954). Concerning inferences from linguistic to nonlinguistic data. In Harry Hoijer (ed.), *Language in Culture*. Chicago: University of Chicago Press, 3–19.

Greenberg, Joseph H. (1972). Numeral classifiers and substantival number: problems in the genesis of a linguistic type. *Working Papers on Language Universals* 9: 2–39.

Greenberg, Joseph H. (1978). How does a language acquire gender markers? In Joseph H. Greenberg (ed.), *Universals of Human Language*, vol. 3: *Word Structure*. Stanford, Calif.: Stanford University Press, 47–82.

Greenberg, Joseph (1987). *Language in the Americas*. Stanford, Calif.: Stanford University Press.

Grönberg, Anna Gunnarsdotter (2002). Masculine generics in current Icelandic. In Marlis Hellinger and Hadumod Bußmann (eds), *Gender Across Languages: The Linguistic Representation of Women and Men*, vol. 2: Amsterdam: Benjamins, 163–85.

Güldemann, Tom (2000). Noun categorization in non-Khoe lineages of Khoisan. *Afrikanistische Arbeitspapiere* 53: 5–33.

Halefom, Girma (1994). The syntax of functional categories: a study of Amharic. Doctoral dissertation, University of Quebec at Montreal.

Halle, Morris (1990). An approach to morphology. In *NELS* 20. University of Massachusetts, Amherst: GLSA, 150–84.

Halle, Morris (1992). The Latvian declension. In Geert Booij and Jaap van Marl (eds), *Yearbook of Morphology* 1991. Dordrecht: Springer, 33–47.

Halle, Morris (1997). Distributed morphology: impoverishment and fission. In Benjamin Bruening et al. (eds), *MIT Working Papers in Linguistics 30: Papers at the Interface*. Cambridge, Mass.: MITWPL, 425–49.

Halle, Morris, and Alec Marantz (1993). Distributed morphology and the pieces of inflection. In Ken Hale and Samuel Jay Keyser (eds), *The View from Building 20*. Cambridge, Mass.: MIT Press, 111–76.

Halle, Morris, and Alec Marantz (1994). Some key features of Distributed Morphology. *MIT Working Papers in Linguistics* 21: 275–88.

Halle, Morris, and Ora Matushansky (2006). The morphophonology of Russian adjectival inflection. *Linguistic Inquiry* 37: 351–404.

Hallowell, A. Irving (1960). Ojibwa ontology, behavior, and world view. In Stanley Diamond (ed.), *Culture in History: Essays in honor of Paul Radin*. New York: Columbia University Press, 19–52.

Hamann, Jakob (2010). On the syntax and morphology of double agreement in Lavukaleve. In Sebastian Bank, Doreen Georgi, and Jochen Trommer (eds), *2 in Agreement*. Leipzig: Universität Leipzig, 197–225.

Hammond, Lila (2005). *Serbian: An Essential Grammar*. London: Routledge.

Harbour, Daniel (2007). *Morphosemantic Number: From Kiowa Noun Classes to UG Number Features*. Dordrecht: Springer.

Harbour, Daniel (2011). Valence and atomic number. *Linguistic Inquiry* 42: 561–94.

Harbour, Daniel (2013). "Not plus isn't not there": bivalence in person, number and gender. In Ora Matushansky and Alec Marantz (eds), *Distributed Morphology Today*. Cambridge, Mass.: MIT Press, 135–50.

Harley, Heidi (1994). Hug a tree: deriving the morphosyntactic feature hierarchy. *MIT Working Papers in Linguistics 21*. Cambridge, MA: MITWPL, 289–320.

Harley, Heidi (2009). Compounding in Distributed Morphology. In Rochelle Lieber and Pavol Stekauer (eds), *The Oxford Handbook of Compounds*. Oxford: Oxford University Press, 129–44.

Harley, Heidi (2014). On the identity of roots. *Theoretical Linguistics* 40. 225–76.

Harley, Heidi, and Rolf Noyer (1998). Licensing in the non-lexicalist lexicon: nominalizations, vocabulary items, and the encyclopaedia. *MIT Working Papers in Linguistics* 32: 119–37.

Harley, Heidi, and Rolf Noyer (1999). Distributed morphology (state-of-the-article). *Glot International* 4. 3–9.

Harley, Heidi, and Rolf Noyer (2000). Formal versus encyclopedic properties of vocabulary: evidence from nominalisations. In Bert Peeters (ed.), *The Lexicon–Encyclopedia Interface*. New York: Elsevier, 349–74.

Harley, Heidi, and Elizabeth Ritter (2002). Person and number in pronouns: a feature-geometric analysis. *Language* 78: 482–526.

Harris, James (1991). The exponence of gender in Spanish. *Linguistic Inquiry* 22: 27–62.

Harris, James (1992). The form classes of Spanish substantives. In Geert Booij and Jaap van Marl (eds), *Yearbook of Morphology 1991*. Dordrecht: Springer, 65–88.

Harris, James (1996). The syntax and morphology of class marker suppression in Spanish. In Karen Zagona (ed.), *Grammatical Theory and Romance Languages*. Amsterdam: Benjamins, 99–122.

Hartmann, Josef (1980). *Amharische Grammatik*. Wiesbaden: Steiner.

Hasselbach, Rebecca (2007). External plural markers in Semitic: a new assessment. In Cynthia L. Miller (ed.), *Studies in Semitic and Afroasiatic Linguistics Presented to Gene B. Gragg*. Chicago: Oriental Institute, 123–38.

Hayward, Richard J. (1989). The notion of "default gender": a key to interpreting the evolution of certain verb paradigms in East Ometo, and its implications for Omotic. *Afrika and Übersee* 72: 17–32.

Hayward, Richard J. (1990). Notes on the Zayse language. In Richard Hayward (ed.), *Omotic Language Studies*. London: SOAS, 210–355.

Hayward, Richard J. (2000). Afroasiatic. In Bernd Heine and Derek Nurse (eds), *African Languages: An Introduction*. Cambridge: Cambridge University Press, 74–98.

Heath, Jeffrey (1990). Verbal inflection and macro-subgroupings of Australian languages: the search for conjugation markers in non-Pama-Nyungan. In Philip Baldi (ed.), *Linguistic Change and Reconstruction Methodology*. New York: Mouton, 403–18.

Heim, Irene, and Angelika Kratzer (1998). *Semantics in Generative Grammar.* Oxford: Blackwell.

Hellenthal, Anneke (2010). *A Grammar of Sheko.* Utrecht: LOT.

Hellinger, Marlis, and Hadumod Bußmann (eds) (2001). *Gender Across Languages: The Linguistic Representation of Women and Men.* 3 vols. Amsterdam: Benjamins.

Henderson, Brent (2003). Case as tense and universal head-initial structure: relative clauses in English and Amharic. Paper presented at the Michigan Linguistic Society Meeting.

Hetzron, Robert (1970). Toward an Amharic case-grammar. *Studies in African Linguistics* 1: 301–54.

Hewitt, B. George (1979). *Abkhaz.* Amsterdam: North-Holland.

Hock, Hans Heinrich (2009). Default, animacy, avoidance: diachronic and synchronic agreement variations with mixed-gender antecedents. In Sarah Rose et al. (eds), *Gramatical Change in Indo-European Languages.* Amsterdam: Benjamins, 29–42.

Hockett, C. F. (1958). *A Course in Modern Linguistics.* New York: Macmillan.

Hollis, Alfred (1905). *The Masai: Their Language and Folklore.* Westport, Conn.: Negro Universities Press.

Holton, David, Peter Mackridge, and Irene Philippaki-Warburton (1997). *Greek: A Comprehensive Grammar of the Modern Language.* London: Routledge.

Huehnergard, John, and Aaron D. Rubin (2011). Phylas and waves: models of classification of the Semitic languages. In Stefan Weninger (ed.), *The Semitic Languages: an International Handbook.* Berlin: Mouton, 259–78.

Iordăchioaia, Gianina (2013). *The determiner restriction in Romance and Germanic nominalizations.* Paper presented at the 43rd Linguistic Symposium on Romance Languages (LSRL), City University of New York.

Iordăchioaia, Gianina, and Elena Soare (2008). Two kinds of event plurals: evidence from Romanian nominalizations. In Olivier Bonami and Patricia Cabredo Hofherr (eds), *Empirical Issues in Syntax and Semantics 7.* Paris: CSSP, 193–217. Available at: <http://www.cssp.cnrs.fr/eiss7/>.

Iscrulescu, Cristian (2003). Morphological faithfulness and phonological markeness: the case of Romanian nominals. *USC Working Papers in Linguistics* 1: 13–27.

Jaeggli, Osvaldo (1980). Spanish diminutives. In F. H. Nuessel (ed.), *Contemporary Studies in Romance Languages.* Bloomington: Indiana University Linguistics Club, 142–55.

Johansson, Sara (2008). The status of nominal gender in Algonquian: evidence from psych verbs. In Susie Jones (ed.), *Proceedings of the 2008 Annual Conference of the Canadian Linguistic Association.* Available online at: <http://homes.chass.utoronto.ca/~cla-acl/actes2008/actes2008.html>.

Johansson, Sara (2011). Towards a typology of Algonquian relative clauses. *University of British Columbia Working Papers in Linguistics* 31 (*Proceedings of WSCLA 16*), 92–104. Available at: <http://lingserver.arts.ubc.ca/linguistics/wscla/16>

Johansson, Sara (2012). Relative clauses, or clause-sized nominalizations? A consideration of Blackfoot. *Working Papers of the Linguistic Circle of the University of Victoria* 21: 1–15. Available online at: <http://journals.uvic.ca/index.php/WPLC/article/view/7818>.

Johansson, Sara (2013). A participle account of Blackfoot relative clauses. *Canadian Journal of Linguistics* 58: 217–38.

Josefsson, Gunlog (2001). The meaning of lexical classes. *Nordic Journal of Linguistics* 24. 218–31.

Josefsson, Gunlog (2006). Semantic and grammatical genders in Swedish. *Lingua* 116: 1346–68.

Jones, Wendell, and Paula Jones (1991). *Barasano Syntax*. Dallas: Summer Institute of Linguistics and the University of Texas at Arlington.

Kane, Thomas Leiper (1990). *Amharic–English Dictionary*. Wiesbaden: Harrassowitz.

Kapeliuk, Olga (1989). Some common traits in the evolution of neo-Syriac and neo-Ethiopian. *Jerusalem Studies in Arabic and Islam* 12: 294–320.

Kapeliuk, Olga (1994). *Syntax of the Noun in Amharic*. Wiesbaden: Harrassowitz.

Katamba, Francis X. (2003). Bantu nominal morphology. In Derek Nurse and Gérard Phillipson (eds), *The Bantu Languages*. London: Routledge, 103–20.

Kayne, Richard S. (2005). On parameters and on principles of pronunciation. In Hans Broekhuis et al. (eds), *Organizing Grammar: Linguistic Studies in honor of Henk van Riemsdijk*. Berlin: Mouton, 289–99.

Kelly, Justin (2013). The syntax–semantics interface in Distributed Morphology. Doctoral dissertation, Georgetown University.

Kern, Jonathan (1996). Participant reference in Wari': a VOS language of the Amazonian lowland. Master's thesis, University of Texas, Arlington.

Khaidakov, S. M. (1966). The dialect divisions of Lak. *Studia Caucasica* 2: 9–18.

Kihm, Alain (2005). Noun class, gender and the lexicon–syntax–morphology interfaces: a comparative study of Niger-Congo and Romance languages. In Guglielmo Cinque and Richard S. Kayne (eds), *The Oxford Handbook of Comparative Syntax*. Oxford: Oxford University Press, 459–512.

Kihm, Alain (2007). Romanian nominal inflection: a realizational approach. *Revue roumaine de linguistique* 52(3): 255–302.

Kilarski, Marcin (2007). Algonquian and Indo-European gender in a historiographic perspective. *Historiographia Linguistica* 34: 333–49.

Klein, Philip W. (1989). Spanish "gender" vowels and lexical representation. *Hispanic Linguistics* 3: 147–62.

Koopman, Hilda (2003). Inside the "noun" in Maasai. In Anoop Mahajan (ed.), *Syntax at Sunset 3: Head Movement and Syntactic Theory*. UCLA Working Papers in Linguistics 10: 77–115.

Köpcke, Klaus-Michael (1982). *Untersuchungen zum Genussystem der deutschen Gegenwartssparche*. Tübinger: Niemeyer.

Kornfilt, Jaklin, and John Whitman (2011). Afterword: nominalizations in syntactic theory. *Lingua* 121: 1297–1313.

Kramer, Ruth (2009). Definite markers, phi-features, and agreement: a morphosyntactic investigation of the Amharic DP. Doctoral dissertation, UC Santa Cruz.

Kramer, Ruth (2010). The Amharic definite marker and the syntax–morphology interface. *Syntax* 13: 196–240.

Kramer, Ruth (2012). A split analysis of plurality: evidence from Amharic. In Nathan Arnett and Ryan Bennett (eds), *The Proceedings of WCCFL 30*. Somerville, Mass.: Cascadilla Press, 226–36.

Kramer, Ruth (2014a). Clitic doubling or object agreement: the view from Amharic. *Natural Language and Linguistic Theory* 32: 593–634.

Kramer, Ruth (2014b). Gender in Amharic: a morphosyntactic approach to natural and grammatical gender. *Language Sciences* 43: 102–15.

Kramer, Ruth (to appear). A split analysis of plurality: evidence from Amharic. *Linguistic Inquiry.*

Kramer, Ruth, and Aviad Eilam (2012). Verb-medial word orders in Amharic. *Journal of Afroasiatic Languages* 5: 75–104.

Kürschner, Sebastian, and Damaris Nübling (2008). The interaction of gender and declension in Germanic languages. *Folia Linguistica* 45: 355–88.

Ladefoged, Peter, and Daniel L. Everett (1996). The status of phonetic rarities. *Language* 72: 794–800.

Lahne, Antje (2006). When features are not deleted: contextual allomorphy in Sanskrit noun declension. *Linguistiche Arbeits Berichte* 84: 143–60.

Lakoff, George (1987). *Women, Fire and Dangerous Things: What Categories Reveal about the Mind.* Chicago: University of Chicago Press.

Lambdin, Thomas O. (1978). *Introduction to Classical Ethiopic (Ge'ez).* Ann Arbor, Mich.: Scholars Press.

Lampitelli, Nicola (2010). Nounness, gender, class and syntactic structure in Italian nouns. In Reineke Bok-Bennema, Brigitte Kampers-Manhe, and Bart Hollebrandse (eds), *Romance Languages and Linguistic Theory 2008.* Amsterdam: Benjamins, 195–214.

Lampitelli, Nicola (2013). The decomposition of Somali nouns. *Brill's Annual of Afroasiatic Languages and Linguistics* 5: 117–58.

Lampitelli, Nicola (2014). Allomorphic alternations are epiphenomenal: evidence from Somali and Italian. Paper presented at workshop on "Allomorphy: Its Logic and Limitations," Jerusalem.

Lang, M. F. (1990). *Spanish Word Formation: Productive Derivational Morphology in the Modern Lexis.* New York: Routledge.

Lecarme, Jacqueline (2002). Gender "polarity": theoretical aspects of Somali nominal morphology. In Paul Boucher and Marc Plénat (eds), *Many Morphologies.* Somerville, Mass.: Cascadilla Press, 109–41.

Lees, Robert (1960). *The Grammar of English Nominalizations.* The Hague: Mouton.

Legate, Julie Anne (2002). Phases in "Beyond Explanatory Adequacy." MS, MIT.

Lehmann, Christian (2002). Thoughts on grammaticalization, 2nd edn. *Arbeitspapiere des Seminars für Sprachwissenschaft der Universität Erfurt* 9.

Leslau, Wolf (1969). *Hebrew Cognates in Amharic.* Wiesbaden: Harrassowitz.

Leslau, Wolf (1976). *Concise Amharic Dictionary.* Berkeley: University of California Press.

Leslau, Wolf (1995). *Reference Grammar of Amharic.* Wiesbaden: Harrassowitz.

Lewis, M. Paul, Gary F. Simons, and Charles D. Fennig (eds) (2013). *Ethnologue: Languages of the World,* 17th edn. Dallas, Tex.: SIL International. Available at: <http://www.ethnologue.com>.

Lloret, Maria-Rosa, and Joaquim Viaplana (1997). On the morphological category of gender in Catalan and Spanish. In Wolfgang U. Dressler et al. (eds), *Advances in Morphology.* Berlin: Mouton, 171–88.

Lockwood, Hunter T., and Monica Macaulay (2012). Prominence hierarchies. *Language and Linguistics Compass* 6/7: 431–46.

Lowenstamm, Jean (2008). On little n, √, and types of nouns. In Jutta Hartmann, Veronika Hegedűs, and Henk van Riemsdijk (eds), *Sounds of Silence: Empty Elements in Syntax and Phonology.* Amsterdam: Elsevier, 105–44.

Lowenstamm, Jean (2012). Feminine and gender, or why the feminine profile of French nouns has nothing to do with gender. In Eugeniusz Cyran, Henryk Kardela, and Bogdan Szymanek (eds), *Linguistic Inspirations: Edmund Gussmann in memoriam*. Lublin: Wydawnictwo Katolicki Uniwersytet Lubelski, 371–406.

Lowenstamm, Jean (2014). Derivational affixes as roots, no exponence (phasal spellout meets English stress shift). In Artemis Alexiadou, Hagit Borer, and Florian Schäfer (eds), *The Syntax of Roots and the Roots of Syntax*. Oxford: Oxford University Press.

Lumsden, John S. (1992). Underspecification in grammatical and natural gender. *Linguistic Inquiry* 23: 469–86.

MacEachern, Margaret R., Barbara Kern, and Peter Ladefoged (1997). Wari' phonetic structures. *Journal of Amazonian Languages* 1: 3–28.

Maho, Jouni (1999). *A Comparative Study of Bantu Noun Classes*. Gothenburg: Acta Universitatis Gothoburgensis.

Maidhoff, Rafaela (ed.) (2009). *Latin Grammar*. Hauppauge, NY: Barrons.

Malchukov, Andrej (2008). Animacy and asymmetries in differential case marking. *Lingua* 118: 203–21.

Mallinson, Graham (1984). Problems, pseudo-problems and hard evidence: another look at the Romanian neuter. *Folia Linguistica* 18: 439–51.

Manahlot, Demissie (1977). Nominal clauses in Amharic. Doctoral dissertation, Georgetown University.

Marantz, Alec (1995). "Cat" as a phrasal idiom: consequences of late insertion in Distributed Morphology. MS, MIT.

Marantz, Alec (1997). No escape from syntax. *University of Pennsylvania Working Papers in Linguistics* 4: 201–25.

Marantz, Alec (2001). Words. MS, Massachusetts Institute of Technology.

Marantz, Alec (2007). Phases in words. In S. H. Choe et al. (eds), *Phases in the Theory of Grammar*. Seoul: Dong In, 191–222.

Markey, T. L. (1985). On suppletion. *Diachronica* 2(1): 51–66.

Markova, Angelina (2010). The syntax of deverbal nominals in Bulgarian. In Artemis Alexiadou and Monika Rathert (eds), *The Syntax of Nominalizations across Languages and Frameworks*. Berlin: Mouton, 93–128.

Markovskaya, Evgenia (2012). Derivational account of gender in deverbal nominals in Russian. In Markéta Ziková and Mojmír Docekal (eds), *Slavic Languages in Formal Grammar: Proceedings of FDSL 8.5*. Frankfurt am Main: Lang, 135–48.

Marrero, Victoria, Carmen Aguirre, and M. J. Albalá (2007). The acquisition of diminutives in Spanish: a useful device. In Ineta Savickienė and Wolfgang U. Dressler (eds), *The Acquisition of Diminutives: A Cross-Linguistic Perspective*. Amsterdam: Benjamins, 155–82.

Marvin, Tatjana (2002). Topics in the stress and syntax of words. Doctoral dissertation, MIT.

Marvin, Tatjana (2013). Is word structure relevant for stress assignment? In Ora Matushansky and Alec Marantz (eds), *Distributed Morphology Today*. Cambridge, Mass.: MIT Press, 79–94.

Matasović, Ranko (2004). *Gender in Indo-European*. Heidelberg: Winter.

Mathieu, Éric (2012). Flavors of division. *Linguistic Inquiry* 43: 650–79.

Mathieu, Éric (2014). Nominalizations in Ojibwe. In Ileana Paul (ed.), *Cross-Linguistic Investigations of Nominalization Patterns*. Amsterdam: Benjamins, 3–23.

Matushansky, Ora (2013). Gender confusion. In Lisa Lai-Shen Cheng and Norbert Corver (eds), *Diagnosing Syntax*. Oxford: Oxford University Press, 271–94.

Maurice, Florence (2001). Deconstructing gender: the case of Romanian. In Marlis Hellinger and Hadumod Bußmann (eds), *Gender across Languages: The Linguistic Representation of Women and Men*. Amsterdam: Benjamins, 229–52.

McFadden, Thomas (2004). The position of morphological case in the derivation: a study on the syntax/morphology interface. Doctoral dissertation, University of Pennsylvania.

Meira, Sérgio, and Angela Terrill (2005). Contrasting contrastive demonstratives in Tiriyo and Lavukaleve. *Linguistics* 43: 1131–52.

Mel'čuk, Igor A. (1976). On suppletion. *Linguistics* 170: 45–90.

Merchant, Jason (2014). Gender mismatches under nominal ellipsis. *Lingua* 151A: 9–32.

Merchant, Jason (to appear). How much context is enough? Two cases of span-conditioned stem allomorphy. *Linguistic Inquiry*.

Merlan, Francesca (1981). Some functional relations among subordination, mood, aspect and focus in Australian languages. *Australian Journal of Linguistics* 1: 175–210.

Merlan, Francesca (1982). *Mangarayi*. Amsterdam: North-Holland.

Merlan, Francesca (2003). The genetic position of Mangarayi: evidence from nominal prefixation. In Nicholas Evans (ed.), *The Non-Pama-Nyungan Languages of Northern Australia*. Canberra: Pacific Linguistics, Research School of Pacific and Asian Studies, Australian National University, 353–67.

Mithun, Marianne (2001). *The Languages of Native North America*. Cambridge: Cambridge University Press.

Morin, Regina (2010). Terminal letters, phonemes, and morphemes in Spanish gender assignment. *Linguistics* 48: 143–69.

Mullen, Dana (1986). Issues in the morphology and phonology of Amharic: the lexical generation of pronominal clitics. Doctoral dissertation, University of Ottawa.

Müller, Gereon (2004). A Distributed Morphology approach to syncretism in Russian noun inflection. In Olga Arnaudova et al. (eds), *Proceedings of Formal Approaches to Slavic Linguistics 12*. Ann Arbor: Michigan Slavic Publications, 353–74.

Müller, Gereon (2005). Syncretism and iconicity in Icelandic noun delcensions: a Distributed Morphology approach. In Geert Booij and Jaap van Marle (eds), *Yearbook of Morphology 2004*, 229–71.

Murray, Ben, and Peter K. Austin (1981). Afghans and aborigines: Diyari texts. *Aboriginal History* 5. 71–80.

Nesset, Tore (2003). Gender assignment in Ukrainian: language-specific rules and universal principles. *Polyjarnyj Vestnik* 6: 71–85.

Newell, Heidi C. (2005). A consideration of feminine default gender. Master's thesis, University of Cincinnati.

Newman, Paul (2000). *The Hausa Language*. New Haven, Conn.: Yale University Press.

Nichols, Johanna (1992). *Linguistic Diversity in Space and Time*. Chicago: University of Chicago Press.

Nieuwenhuis, Paul (1985). Diminutives. Doctoral dissertation, University of Edinburgh.

Nikunlassi, Ahti (2000). On gender assignment in Russian. In Barbara Unterbeck et al. (eds), *Gender in Grammar and Cognition*. Berlin: Mouton, 771–92.

Norris, Mark (2014). A theory of nominal concord. Doctoral dissertation, University of California, Santa Cruz.

Noyer, Rolf (1997). *Features, Positions, and Affixes in Autonomous Morphological Structure.* New York: Garland.

Nuger, Justin (2010). Architecture of the Palauan verbal complex. Doctoral dissertation, University of California, Santa Cruz.

Oltra-Massuet, Maria Isabel (1999). On the notion of theme vowel: a new approach to Catalan verbal morphology. Master's thesis, MIT.

Oltra-Massuet, Isabel, and Karlos Arregi (2005). Stress-by-structure in Spanish. *Linguistic Inquiry* 36: 43–84.

Orwin, Martin (1995). *Colloquial Somali.* London: Routledge.

Osthoff, H. (1899). *Vom Suppletivwesen der indogermanischen Sprachen.* Heidelberg: Kommissions-verlag von Alfred Wolff.

Ott, Dennis (2011). Diminutive-formation in German: spelling out the classifier analysis. *Journal of Comparative Germanic Linguistics* 14: 1–46.

Ouhalla, Jamal (2000). Possession in sentences and noun phrases. In Jacqueline Lecarme, Jean Lowestamm, and Ur Shlonsky (eds), *Research in Afroasiatic Grammar.* Philadelphia: Benjamins, 221–42.

Ouhalla, Jamal (2004). Semitic relatives. *Linguistic Inquiry* 35: 288–300.

Oxford English Dictionary (2014). "sool, v.". OED Online, March 2014. Oxford University Press. <http://www.oed.com.proxy.library.georgetown.edu/view/Entry/184681?redirectedFrom=sool&>. Acccessed 6 May 2014.

Pak, Marjorie (2008). The postsyntactic derivation and its phonological reflexes. Doctoral dissertation, Universty of Pennsylvania, Philadelphia.

Paul, Ileana (ed.) (2014). *Cross-Linguistic Investigations of Nominalization Patterns.* Amsterdam: Benjamins.

Payne, Doris (1998). Maasai gender in typological perspective. *Studies in African Linguistics* 27: 159–75.

Percus, Orin (2011). Gender features and interpretation: a case study. *Morphology* 21: 167–96.

Pesetsky, David, and Esther Torrego (2007). The syntax of valuation and the interpretability of features. In Simin Karimi, Vida Samiian, and Wendy K. Wilkins (eds), *Phrasal and Clausal Architecture.* Amsterdam: Benjamins, 262–94.

Pfau, Roland (2000). Features and categories in language perception. Doctoral dissertation, Goethe Universität.

Pfau, Roland (2009). *Grammar as Processor: A Distributed Morphology Account of Spontaneous Speech Errors.* Amsterdam: Benjamins.

Picallo, M. Carme (1991). Nominals and nominalization in Catalan. *Probus* 3: 279–316.

Picallo, M. Carme (2002). Abstract agreement and clausal arguments. *Syntax* 5: 116–47.

Picallo, M. Carme (2006). Some notes on grammatical gender and l-pronouns. In Klaus von Heusinger, Georg A. Kaiser, and Elisabeth Stark (eds), *Proceedings of the Workshop "Specificity and the Evolution/Emergence of Nominal Determination Systems in Romance."* Konstanz Arbeitspapier 119, 107–22: Available at: <http://www.ub.uni-konstanz.de/kops/volltexte/2006/1718/>.

Picallo, M. Carme (2007). On gender and number. MS, Universitat Autònoma de Barcelona.

Picallo, M. Carme (2008). Gender and number in Romance. *Lingue e linguaggio* 7: 47–66.

Plank, Frans (2012). Why*-ling-in? The pertinacity of a wrong gender. *Morphology* 22: 277–92.

Platzer, Hans (2005). The development of natural gender in English, or: sex by accident. In Nikolaus Ritt and Herbert Schendl (eds), *Rethinking Middle English*. Frankfurt am Main: Lang, 244–62.

Prado, Marcial (1982). El género en español y la teoría de la marcadez. *Hispania* 65: 258–66.

Preminger, Omer (2009). Breaking agreements: distinguishing agreement and clitic doubling by their failures. *Linguistic Inquiry* 40: 619–66.

Preminger, Omer (2011). Agreement as a fallible operation. Doctoral dissertation, MIT.

Preminger, Omer (2014). *Agreement and its Failures*. Cambridge, Mass.: MIT Press.

Quinn, Conor McDonough (2004). A preliminary survey of animacy categories in Penobscot. MS, Harvard University.

Quinn, Conor McDonough (2006). Referential-access dependency in Penobscot. Doctoral dissertation, Harvard University.

Ralli, Angela (2002). The role of morphology in gender determination: evidence from Modern Greek. *Linguistics* 40: 519–51.

Richards, Marc (2008). Defective agree, case alternations and the prominence of person. In Marc Richards and Andrej L. Malchukov (eds), *Scales*. Leipzig: Institut für Linguistik, 137–61.

Rice, Curt (2006). Optimizing gender. *Lingua* 116: 1394–1417.

Riente, Lara (2003). Ladies first: the pivotal role of gender in the Italian nominal inflection system. *McGill Working Papers in Linguistics* 17(2): 1–54.

Ritter, Elizabeth (1993). Where's gender? *Linguistic Inquiry* 24: 795–803.

Ritter, Elizabeth (2013). Featuring animacy. Paper presented at "Features in Morphology, Phonology, Syntax and Semantics—What are They?," Center for the Advanced Study of Language, Tromsø.

Ritter, Elizabeth (2014). Nominalizing inner aspect: evidence from Blackfoot. In Ileana Paul (ed.), *Cross-Linguistic Patterns of Nominalization*. Amsterdam: Benjamins, 25–50.

Ritter, Elizabeth, and Sara Rosen (2010). Animacy in Blackfoot: implications for event structure and clause structure. In Malka Rappaport Hovav, Edit Doron, and Ivy Sichel (eds), *Syntax, Lexical Semantics, and Event Structure*. Oxford: Oxford University Press, 124–52.

Roberts, Ian (2011). FOFC in DP: Universal 20 and the nature of demonstratives. Available at: <http://ling.auf.net/lingbuzz/001502>.

Roca, I. M. (1989). The organisation of grammatical gender. *Transactions of the Philological Society* 87: 1–32.

Roca, I. M. (2000). On the meaning of gender. *Hispanic Research Journal* 1: 113–28.

Roca, I. M. (2005). La gramática y la biología en el género del español, Part 1. *Revista española de lingüística* 35: 17–44.

Rounds, Carol (2001). *Hungarian: An Essential Grammar*. London: Routledge.

Roy, Isabelle (2010). Deadjectival nominalizations and the structure of the adjective. In Artemis Alexiadou and Monika Rathert (eds), *The Syntax of Nominalizations across Languages and Frameworks*. Berlin: Mouton, 129–58.

Rubin, Aaron D. (2008). The subgrouping of the Semitic languages. *Language and Linguistics Compass* 2: 79–102.

Rubin, Aaron D. (2010). *A Brief Introduction to the Semitic Languages*. Piscataway, NJ: Gorgias Press.

Rupp, James E. (1989). *Lealao Chinantec Syntax*. University of Texas at Arlington: SIL.

Rupp, James E. (1990). The Lealao Chinantec syllable. In William R. Merryfield and Calvin R. Resnch (eds), *Syllables, Tones and Verb Paradigms*. Dallas: SIL, 63–73.

Rupp, James E. (2009). Animacy in two Chinantec varieties. Available at: <http://www.sil.org/mexico/workpapers/WP007i-ChinantecAnimacy-cle-chz.pdf>.

Sadler, Louisa (2006). Gender resolution in Romanian. In Miriam Butt, Mary Dalrymple, and Tracy Holloway King (eds), *Intelligent Linguistic Architectures*. Stanford, Calif.: CSLI, 301–21.

Saeed, John (1993). *Somali Reference Grammar*, 2nd revised edn. Kensington, Md.: Dunwoody Press.

Saeed, John (1999). *Somali*. Amsterdam: Benjamins.

Sands, Kristina (1995). Nominal classification in Australia. *Anthropological Linguistics* 37: 247–346.

Sauerland, Uli (2004). A comprehensive semantics for agreement. MS, ZAS, Berlin.

Sauerland, Uli (2008). On the semantic markedness of phi-features. In Daniel Harbour, David Adger, and Susana Béjar (eds), *Phi Theory*. Oxford: Oxford University Press, 57–82.

Scatton, Ernest A. (1984). *A Reference Grammar of Modern Bulgarian*. Columbus, Oh.: Slavica.

Schäfer, Florian (2008). Event denoting -er nominalizations in German. *Working Papers of the SFB 732 Incremental Specification in Context* 1: 173–87.

Schafroth, Elmar (2003). Gender in French: structural properties, incongruences and asymmetries. In Marlis Hellinger and Hadumod Bußmann (eds), *Gender Across Languages: The Linguistic Representation of Women and Men*, vol. 3. Amsterdam: Benjamins, 87–118.

Schlenker, Philippe (1999). Propositional attitudes and indexicality: a cross-categorial approach. Doctoral dissertation, MIT.

Schlenker, Philippe (2003a). A plea for monsters. *Linguistics and Philosophy* 26: 29–120.

Schlenker, Philippe (2003b). Indexicality, logophoricity and plural pronouns. In J. Lecarme (ed.), *Research in Afroasiatic Grammar II*. Amsterdam: Benjamins, 409–28.

Scholze-Stubenrecht, W., and J. B. Sykes (eds) (1999). *The Oxford–Duden German Dictionary*. Oxford: Oxford University Press.

Sedighi, Anousha (2005). Subject–predicate agreement restrictions in Persian. Doctoral dissertation, University of Ottawa.

Sessarego, Sandro, and Javier Gutiérrez Rexach (2011). A minimalist approach to gender agreement in the Afro-Bolivian DP: variation and the specification of interpretable features. *Folia Linguistica* 45: 465–88.

Seyoum, Mulugeta (2008). *A Grammar of Dime*. LOT: Utrecht.

Sharpe, Margaret (2008). Alawa and its neighbors. In Claire Bowern, Bethwyn Evans, and Luisa Miceli (eds), *Morphology and Language History*. Amsterdam: Benjamins, 59–70.

Shirtz, Shahar, and Doris Payne (2012). Gendered prefixes in Maa. Paper presented at the 45th Annual Meeting of the Societas Linguistica Europeaea, Stockholm.

Shirtz, Shahar, and Doris Payne (2013). The problem of 'head' in Maa (Maasai) nominal phrases. In Olanike Ola Orie and Karen W. Sanders (eds), *Selected Proceedings of the 43rd Annual Conference on African Linguistics*. Somerville, Mass.: Cascadilla Press, 207–21.

Siddiqi, Daniel (2009). *Syntax within the Word: Economy, Allomorphy and Argument Selection in Distributed Morphology*. Amsterdam: Benjamins.

Smith, Jason (2011). Subcategorization and Optimality Theory: the case of Spanish diminutives. Doctoral dissertation, University of California, Davis.

Soare, Elena (2014). Nominalizing with or without *n*. Talk presented at Université Paris Diderot.

Sommer, Gabriele, and Rainer Vossen (1993). Dialects, sociolects or simply lects? The Maa language in time perspective. In Thomas Spear and Richard Waller (eds), *Being Maasai: Ethnicity and Identity in East Africa*. Athens: Ohio University Press, 25–37.

Steriopolo, Olga (2008). Form and function of expressive morphology: a case study of Russian. Doctoral dissertation, University of British Columbia.

Steriopolo, Olga, and Martina Wiltschko (2010). Distributed GENDER hypothesis. In G. Zybatow et al. (eds), *Formal Studies in Slavic Linguistics: Proceedings of the Formal Description of Slavic Languages 7.5*. New York: Lang, 155–72.

Straus, Anne Tery, and Robert Brightman (1982). The implacable raspberry. *Papers in Linguistics* 15: 97–137.

Stump, Gregory T. (1993). How peculiar is evaluative morphology? *Journal of Linguistics* 29: 1–38.

Stump, Gregory T. (2001). Default inheritance hierarchies and the evolution of inflection classes. In Laurel J. Brinton (ed.), *Historical Linguistics 1999*. Amsterdam: Benjamins, 293–307.

Svenonius, Peter (2012). Spanning. MS, CASTL, University of Tromsø.

Taraldsen, K. Tarald (2010). The nanosyntax of Nguni class prefixes and concords. *Lingua* 120: 1522–48.

Terrill, Angela (2001). Activation levels in Lavukaleve demonstratives: oia versus foia. *Linguistic Typology* 5: 67–90.

Terrill, Angela (2002a). Why make books for people who don't read? A perspective on documentation of an endangered language from Solomon Islands. *International Journal of the Sociology of Language* 155–6: 205–19.

Terrill, Angela (2002b). Systems of nominal classification in East Papuan languages. *Oceanic Linguistics* 41: 63–88.

Terrill, Angela (2003). *A Grammar of Lavukaleve*. Berlin: Mouton.

Terrill, Angela (2004). Coordination in Lavukaleve. In Martin Haspelmath (ed.), *Coordinating Constructions*. Amsterdam: Benjamins, 427–43.

Terrill, Angela (2006). Body part terms in Lavukaleve, a Papuan language of the Solomon Islands. *Language Sciences* 28: 304–22.

Terrill, Angela (2010). Complex predicates and complex clauses in Lavukaleve. In John Bowden et al. (eds), *A Journey through Austronesian and Papuan linguistic and Cultural Space: Papers in Honour of Andrew K. Pawley*. Canberra: Australia National University, 499–512.

Terrill, Angela (2011). Languages in contact: an exploration of stability and change in the Solomon Islands. *Oceanic Linguistics* 50: 312–37.

Terrill, Angela, and Niclas Burenhult (2008). Orientation as a strategy of spatial reference. *Studies in Language* 32: 93–136.

Thornton, Anna M. (2001). Some reflections on gender and inflectional class assignment in Italian. In Chris Schaner-Wolles, John Rennison, and Friedrich Neubarth (eds), *Naturally!*

Linguistic studies in honor of Wolfgang Ulrich Dressler presented on the occasion of his 60th birthday. Turin: Rosenberg & Sellier, 479–87.

Toebosch, Annemarie (2003). Gender-animacy and the morpho-syntax of clitics in Dutch. Doctoral dissertation, University of Michigan.

Toebosch, Annemarie (2011). Plautdietsch gender: between Dutch and German. In Michael T. Putnam, *Studies on German-Language Islands.* Amsterdam: Benjamins, 67–110.

Tremblay, Mireille, and Ouadia Kabbaj (1990). The internal structure of PPs in Amharic. In John Hutchison and Victor Manfredi (eds), *Current Approaches to African Linguistics* 7: 167–78.

Tropper, Josef (2002). *Altäthiopisch: Grammatik des Ge'ez mit Übungstexten und Glossar.* Münster: Ugarit.

Tucker, A. N., and M. A. Bryan (1966). *Linguistic Analyses of the Non-Bantu Languages of North-Eastern Africa.* Oxford: Oxford University Press.

Tucker, Archibald, and John Mpaayei (1955). *A Maasai Grammar, with Vocabulary.* Leiden: African Institute.

Turner, Ingrid (2006). Intonation and information structure in Wari'. Master's thesis, University of Manchester.

Unterbeck, Barbara, and Matti Rissanen (2000). Preface. In Barbara Unterbeck et al. (eds), *Gender in Grammar and Cognition.* Berlin: Mouton, ix–xiv.

Valentine, Randy (2001). *Nishnaabemwin Reference Grammar.* Toronto: University of Toronto Press.

van Riemsdijk, Henk (1990). Functional prepositions. In Harm Pinkster and Inge Genée (eds), *Unity in Diversity: Papers Presented to Simon C. Dik on his 50th Birthday.* Dordrecht: Foris, 229–41.

Velupillai, Viveka (2012). *An Introduction to Linguistic Typology.* Amsterdam: Benjamins.

Veselinova, Ljuba N. (2006). *Suppletion in Verb Paradigms.* Amsterdam: Benjamins.

Wakasa, Motomichi (2008). A descriptive study of the modern Wolaytta language. Doctoral dissertation, University of Tokyo.

Wechsler, Stephen, and Larisa Zlatić (2003). *The Many Faces of Agreement.* Stanford, Calif.: CSLI.

Weldeyesus, Weldu M. (2004). Case marking systems in two Ethiopian Semitic languages. In Adam Hodges (ed.), *Colorado Research in Linguistics* 17. Available at: <http://www.colorado.edu/ling/CRIL/Volume17_Issue1/index.htm>.

White, Lydia, Elena Valenzuela, Martyna Kozlowska-Macgregor, and Yan-Kit Ingrid Leung (2004). Gender and number agreement in nonnative Spanish. *Applied Psycholinguistics* 25: 105–33.

Wiltschko, Martina (2006). Why should diminutives count? In H. Broekhuis et al. (eds), *Organizing Grammar: Linguistic Studies in Honor of Henk van Riemsdijk.* Berlin: de Gruyter, 669–79.

Wiltschko, Martina (2008a). Person-hierarchy effects without a person-hierarchy. In Gunnar Hrafn Hrafnbjargson, Susann Fischer, and Roberta d'Alessandro (eds), *Agreement Restrictions.* Amsterdam: Mouton, 281–313.

Wiltschko, Martina (2008b). The syntax of non-inflectional plural marking. *Natural Language and Linguistic Theory* 26: 639–94.

Wiltschko, Martina (2012). Decomposing the mass/count distinction: evidence from languages that lack it. In Diane Massam (ed.), *Count and Mass across Languages*. Oxford: Oxford University Press, 146–71.

Wiltschko, Martina (2014). Patterns of nominalization in Blackfoot. In Ileana Paul (ed.), *Cross-Linguistic Patterns of Nominalizationx* Amsterdam: Benjamins, 189–214.

Wiltschko, Martina, and Olga Steriopolo (2007). Parameters of variation in the syntax of diminutives. In Milica Radisic (ed.), *Proceedings of the 2007 Canadian Linguistics Association Annual Conference*. Toronto: University of Toronto, 1–12.

Wolf, Matthew (2008). Optimal interleaving: serial phonology–morphology interaction in a constraint-based model. Doctoral dissertation, University of Massachusetts, Amherst.

Yabe, Tomoyuki (2007). The morphosyntax of complex verbal expressions in the Horn of Africa. Doctoral dissertation, CUNY.

Yanovich, Igor (2012). What can Russian gender tell about the semantics of φ-features? Paper presented at "Formal Approaches to Slavic Linguistics 21," Bloomington, Ind.

Yimam, Baye (1988). Towards a definition of nominal specifiers in Amharic. In Taddese Bayene (ed.), *Proceedings of the Eighth International Conference of Ethiopian Studies*. Addis Ababa: Institute of Ethiopian Studies, 599–612.

Yimam, Baye (1994). Some aspects of Zargulla morphology. In Bahru Zewde, Richard Pankhurst, and Taddese Beyene (eds), *Proceedings of the 11th International Conference of Ethiopian Studies, Addis Ababa*. Addis Ababa: Institute of Ethiopian Studies, 419–28.

Yimam, Baye (1996). Definiteness in Amharic discourse. *Journal of African Languages and Linguistics* 17: 47–83.

Zabbal, Youri (2002). The semantics of number in the Arabic number phrase. Master's thesis, University of Alberta.

Zaborski, Andrzej (1992). Afro-Asiatic languages. In William Bright (ed.), *The International Encyclopedia of Linguistics*. Oxford: Oxford University Press, 36–7.

Zamparelli, Roberto (2008). On the interpretability of phi features. In Katherine Demuth and Cecile de Cat (eds), *The Bantu–Romance Connection*. Amsterdam: Benjamins, 167–99.

Zwicky, Arnold, and Geoffrey K. Pullum (1986). The principle of phonology-free syntax: introductory remarks. *Ohio State University Working Papers in Linguistics* 32: 63–91.

Index of languages and language families

Subject index

OXFORD STUDIES IN THEORETICAL LINGUISTICS

Made in the USA
Middletown, DE
10 March 2021